ליקוטי שיחות

TORAH

Like Fire & Water

ליקוטי שיחות

TORAH

Like Fire & Water

THE

LUBAVITCHER REBBE

ON RASHI AND RAMBAM

BEREISHIT/GENESIS

Translated / Arranged by R' DAVID STERNE

CHECKED BY:
Rabbi Moshe Ginsburg, R' Moshe Miller
and R' Zalman Shimon Springer

EDITED BY:
Ms. Uriela Sagiv

TYPESET AND BOOK DESIGN BY:
Ms. Eden Chachamtzedek

COVER DESIGN BY:
Aviad Bensimon

Torah like Fire and Water,
The Lubavitcher Rebbe on
Rashi and Rambam
(Bereishit/Genesis)

ISBN 978-1-7321079-7-7

POB 28186
Jerusalem, Israel
jerconn1@gmail.com

Printed in Israel

Approbation from

Rabbi Schneur Zalman Gafne שליט"א

Rav and Mashpia in Kfar Chabad and in Tzfat, Israel

It's well known the pisgam (epigram) of the Rebbe the Tzemach Tzedek (third of the Nisiei Chabad) that a printed Torah word is effective (and influential) for all the generations to come (till and including Yemos HaMoshiach and thereafter).

This holds for divrei Torah in any form. How much more so when speaking about the translation of major Torah sources, which due to language barriers would have remained beyond the reach of large sections of the world public.

We see this from the early periods of Jewish rabbinic historical literature. Had it not been for the great Torah figures who assumed the task of translating classical basic works such as the Rambam's Perush HaMishnayos and his "Moreh Nevuchim," Rabbi Yehuda HaLevi's "Kuzari" etc. etc., where would we have been today? The impact of these classics is living and everlasting. We see in our day and age a spreading growth of the translation of Jewish rabbinic classics in all fields of Torah into the main languages, thus opening for the "layman" a wide library of available texts to him on his level.

A very significant cheilek (part) in this great unfolding of translation is being undertaken by Rabbi David Sterne, shlito. His prime goal is to make available to the English speaking (massive) public classic Chabad Chasidic texts, which are somewhat esoteric or withdrawn even from a significant number of Chabad Chasidim themselves. His recent publication of his translation (and explanation of) the Baal HaTanya's Siddur with lengthy Chassidic discourses on the Siddur nusach, from the Baal HaTanya's son, (the Mitteler Rebbe), is a noticeable example of the above aim. Here, before us, we have the latest fruit of his work, the translation of volumes of sichos of the great luminary of our time, the Lubavitcher Rebbe, thus presenting to a thirsty public the "direct hit" messages of this gigantic leader.

Frequently, translations (even good ones) tend to be slightly verbose and missing the "zest" of the original. Rabbi Sterne's translations transcend this problem. His versions are flowing and "informal" in style, whilst adhering precisely and faithfully to the point of the original. I know Rabbi Sterne for many years and am witness to the meticulous effort and "yegio" kepeshuto, that he invests in his work.

Thus, I recommend highly both him and his work, be eizer HaShem.

Schneur Zalman Gafne

ב"ה

RABBI MENACHEM M. GLUCKOWSKY
CHABAD RECHOVOT
12 HAGANA ST. RECHOVOT ISRAEL
Tel: 08-9493176 **Fax**:08-9457620 **Cel**: 058-4130770

מנחם מענדל גלוכובסקי
רב קהילת חב"ד ברחובות
מען: רח' ההגנה 12/1 רחובות
משרד 08-9493176 פקס. 08-9457620 נייד 058-4130770

11 Tevet 5780 (January 8, 2020)

To my good friend

Rabbi David Sterne שליט"א

Every generation is unique. Every generation of Jews faces its own challenges and possesses special abilities. For that reason, the One above made sure that there is a leader in every generation who is able to "speak" to that generation and provides for its needs, both physical and spiritual. He is, so to speak, the *Cohen Gadol* or "High Priest," who provides the container of "pure oil" that inspires his generation with words of spirituality that "kindle" the spark of spirituality within each and every one of us. Such was the personality and the leadership of the Lubavitcher Rebbe, R' Menachem Mendel Schneerson in our generation. With his *sichot*, or Torah discourses, the Rebbe reached the minds and hearts of millions of Jews all over the world, and "lit up" their weekdays, Sabbath and festivals, with inspiration for the heart and provocative intellectual "food" for the mind.

In our generation however, we also face the limitation that many (if not most) Jews are not familiar with either Hebrew or Yiddish, and they are unable to access the Rebbe's Torah, that he produced for them, in its original language. Therefore, R' David Sterne has performed an important service by translating many of the Rebbe's *sichot* into English. Most of the *sichot* ("Torah discourses") that appear in this volume, appear for the very first time in English, so that the general public can read and study them. In that way, hopefully the "pure oil" of the "High Priest" of our generation will find its way into the hearts of minds of as many people (Jews and non-Jews) as possible, and "illuminate" them with the warmth and pure spirituality of the Torah.

These translations of the Rebbe's sichot are a continuation of work that R' Sterne has produced previously: A translation of the *Kuntres Ha'avoda* of the Rebbe Rashab (entitled "Love like Fire and Water"), a siddur with accompanied translations of excerpts from the Chassidut of the Rebbe Rashab on the subject of prayer and meditation (entitled "Meditation like Fire and Water"), and yet another siddur including summaries of Chassidut on prayer from the Rebbe Rashab and his father, the Rebbe Maharash ("Praying like Fire and Water"), all of them in English. I bless him to continue to produce more sophisticated and provocative work in English that will satisfy the needs of the English speaking world that otherwise has limited access to the "pure oil" of Torah inspiration of our generation.

With Blessings,

Mendel Gluckowsky

Rabbi Menachem Mendel Gluckowsky

מנחם מענדל גלוכובסקי
רב קהילת קודש חבד
רחובות

THE Shul
Jewish Community Center
CHABAD LUBAVITCH

ב"ה

Baruch Hashem

1 Shevat, 5780

The Lubavitcher Rebbe (R' Menachem Mendel Schneerson) was a very rare, true international leader, millennial scholar and world influencing personality who embodies the yearnings and needs (both physical and spiritual) of our generation. Unique since Maimonides, the Rebbe was able to meet the emotional, intellectual and spiritual needs of Jews and of all humanity everywhere on the globe. After the Holocaust and the resettling of the Holy Land of Israel, the Rebbe, with unsurpassed Divinely gifted powers, led the Chabad/Lubavitch Movement transforming it into what is today the most impactful Jewish Movement of global reach with thousands of *shluchim*, or emissaries, serving in Chabad embassies all over the world.

At the fulcrum of this impressive achievement is the Rebbe's Torah scholarship of the highest caliber. His beyond comparison erudition is reflected in his profound communications with many of the greatest sages of the twentieth century, including R' Chaim Ozer Grudzinsky, the Rogotchover Gaon (R' Yosef Rozen), R' Yoseph Ber Soloveitchik, R' Moshe Feinstein, and many others. His Torah knowledge was voluminous, and his prodigious memory legendary. The Rebbe excelled and produced original Torah literature in every facet of the Torah, including Halacha, *sod* (Kaballah), *drosh* (Rabbinic exegesis), *remez* (alpha-numerical allusions) and *pshat* (simple textual meaning). It was however through *pshat*, the most basic and "simple" of Torah facets, that the Rebbe communicated and taught the most profound insights and lessons of Torah, making them relevant to our personal daily lives.

In the post-Holocaust period when the Jewish world was sitting on the debris of a shattered past, it was necessary to find a path to reach ALL Jews, in all walks of life and in all situations, even those who were not sufficiently knowledgeable in Jewish thought. As a true "Rebbe," (Rosh Bnei Yisrael), the Rebbe chose the path of simplicity ("simple textual level") as the vehicle to express the most profound concepts of Torah and Jewishness. The Rebbe's penetrating original approach (within the dimension of *pshat*) in his hundreds of published works appeal to the searching minds and educated intellects that are characteristic of the Jewish community today.

Rabbi David Sterne whom I have the privilege of knowing for about 30 years, and serves as a voluntary emissary of the Rebbe in the old city of Jerusalem, has done a great service to translate and adapt a collection of the Rebbe's writings and make them accessible to the English speaking public. I have not read or evaluated all of R' Sterne's translations, but I have perused enough of the material to feel confident of the accuracy of his translations and their faithfulness to the original text and the authenticity of his work.

I am happy to recommend Rabbi Sterne's new set of translations of the Rebbe's sichos.

With Torah greetings and Blessings,

Sholom D. Lipskar

"An Institution of The Lubavitcher Rebbe, Menachem M. Schneerson (May his merit shield us)"

Serving The Communities of Bal Harbour · Bay Harbor Islands · Indian Creek · Surfside

9540 Collins Avenue, Surfside, Florida 33154 • Tel (305) 868-1411 • Fax (305) 861-2426 • www.TheShul.org

Approbation from

Rabbi Zalman Dubinsky שליט"א

Rosh Yeshivat Tiferet Bachurim, Morristown

BS"D

19 Kislev of the year 5780
the year of *pedus nafsheinu* —
"redemption of our soul."
הי' תהי' שנת פדות נפשינו

A soul awakening of massive proportions is sweeping through the Jewish world, embracing into its midst very observant Jews, and also some amongst the so called "ultra orthodox." A deeply rooted soul thirst, of revolutionary magnitude, is developing and expanding vigorously. Unfortunately though, this movement is sometimes ignored and often misunderstood. What kind of thirst is this? It is a deep desire to not only learn and connect, but also to live with the "inner dimensions" of the Torah, -the *NESHAMA* ("soul") of the Torah, which are found in the Holy teachings of Chassidus in general, and in Chabad Chassidus in particular.

As we rapidly approach the era of Moshiach, it has become increasingly clear, especially in recent times, that Chassidus generates tremendous inspiration and joy to a generation facing difficult spiritual challenges. Chassidus is the *solution* and *panacea* that alleviates the challenges and darkness of exile in general, and especially the additional double and quadruple layers of tangible darkness in the last period of *galus* ("exile").

This characteristic of Chassidus is most evident in the teachings of the Lubavitcher Rebbe. In the Sichos (scholarly discourses) of the Rebbe, we find the foundations and structure of Judaism explained and illuminated with amazing clarity, reflecting and revealing the hidden spiritual fire of the Torah. The concepts contained in the Rebbe's Sichos deeply resonate within us, touching, uncovering, and exposing the hidden spiritual fire within our divine soul. These Holy Sichos from the Rebbe grant us the remarkable opportunity not only to appreciate but also to "live with" the inner hidden lights contained within the Torah. Those who have merited to taste the Rebbe's Sichos Kodesh, develop a deep love of God, love of the Torah and love of fellow Jews, intellectually emotionally, and most importantly-with concrete results.

Another observable phenomenon is the amazing manner in which the Rebbe's holy Sichos succeed in inspiring thousands of the Rebbe's emissaries (*Shluchim*), who do their Holy work worldwide. These Sichos are so powerful and life-changing, that they inspire the hearts and ignite the souls of the *Shluchim*, propelling them to dedicate their lives to these three fundamental loves: Love of God, love of every Jew, and, love of the Torah.

This holy work of the *Shluchim* is a phenomenon that, according to all available evidence, has no parallel throughout the history of Judaism. When else has it been possible to observe such a movement, in which thousands of families willingly choose to uproot themselves from their "comfort zone" (whether physical or spiritual), from their land, their birthplace and extended family — not only for a year or 2, but for a lifetime- for no other purpose than to express real love and concern for a fellow Jew, love of Torah, and love of God? And yet, the *Shluchim* (Rebbe's emissaries) do so joyously and with a full heart!

The Rebbe's teachings have affected not only the *Shluchim*, but also many others who are involved in making a living most of their day. Despite their immersion in everyday work, their soul 'is on fire' to the extent that they actually live with awareness and knowledge that the entire universe and all of the business that they conduct, was created only for the purpose of providing a "dwelling place" for *Hashem* in the "lower worlds", and they therefore also utilize their influence to exercise love and concern for their fellow Jew, sharing the treasure of Torah and Mitsvos with others.

However, many of those who are thirsty to hear the "words of God," are not accustomed to the language and/or style in which the Rebbe's Sichos are written. It is therefore imperative that the holy Sichos be translated in a manner and style that enables more people to grasp and understand them. My friend, the esteemed Harov David שליט"א Sterne has merited to translate many of the Rebbe's Sichos in a style that is clear for everyone to understand. The great demand and necessity for this translation project cannot be overstated.

It is clear that no translation can be an authentic substitute for learning the holy Sichos in their original language and style. In their source and origin, the Sichos are the words and style of the Rebbe himself, containing the depth, breadth, and richness of his Torah. For that reason, there are big differences between various translations as well as big differences in styles of translation. Every translator can translate and explain only according to his own intellect and abilities, and of course, no translation is perfect. Nevertheless, there is much benefit and necessity to translate and publicize the translations to the greatest extent possible. When I perused excerpts of the translations made by my friend, Harav David שליט"א Sterne, I saw that they were written in precisely the clear style that is fitting and appropriate for a large segment of the public. Due to limitations of time, I was not able to peruse and check each and every translation in this volume, but since my colleague and friend, HaRov Moshe שליט"א Miller went over the translations and made several comments and corrections, I feel comfortable recommending this wonderful work of translations. Without a doubt, it will bring great benefit to many people.

I wish to extend my blessings to my friend, HaRav David שליט"א Sterne, who already merited to translate and publish several Seforim, to continue with his holy work in good health and happiness. Without a doubt, this too will hasten the speedy arrival of Moshiach.

R' Zalman Dubinsky

Contents

VAYISHLACH

VAYEISHEV

MIKEITZ

VAYIGASH

Vayechi

INTRODUCTION

MY EXPERIENCE WITH the Lubavitcher Rebbe's sichos began very early in my career, when an older yeshiva student taught me rudimentary Yiddish, in order to be able to struggle through the Rebbe's Likutei Sichos on my own. He told me that I only need to learn about two hundred Yiddish words in order to understand the sichos. What he did not tell me is that merely translating the words would not help me fathom the scholarly erudition and depth of the Rebbe's Torah.

However, I did go on to attend yeshiva in the *chatzer* ("courtyard") of the Rebbe, at 770 Eastern Parkway in Brooklyn, and attend public farbrengens ("get together's" of Chasidim) with the Rebbe, in which the Rebbe spoke before thousands of people, and delivered some of the sichos which I was later to translate, and it was there that I began to develop respect and awe of the Rebbe's original scholarship.

Later, I made "aliya" to Israel and began studying in the Tzemach Tzedek Collel of the old city of Yerushalayim, and it is there that I met R' Zalman Dubinsky שיח', who engaged me in discussion of the sichos, and who inspired me to not only learn but to delve deeply into the fascinating concepts that the Rebbe presented in his sichos. Finally, after several years of study in the Collel, I took over the position of director of the Chabad House of the old city. In that capacity, I met R' Shalom Ber Lipskar, who delivered spellbinding lectures to crowds of hundreds of young Jews in Miami, Florida, based on the ideas contained in Likutei Sichos. I didn't realize it at the time, but a progression of learning and integration was taking place, that placed the Rebbe's Likutei Sichos at the epicenter of my spiritual development.

Roughly in 1990, I left the "shelter" of the Tzemach Tzedek shul/ Collel and the Chabad House, to strike out on my own and form the old city based outreach center, "Jerusalem Connection." While traveling extensively to raise money and simultaneously arranging Shabbatonim and classes in Jerusalem, one of my mentors suggested that I send out weekly words of Torah in order to maintain connection with my students and supporters all over the world. For several years, I sent out translations from *Shem miShmuel*, a Chassidic commentary on the Torah that in some ways parallels concepts found in Chabad Chassidus. In 2005, after publishing a translation with commentary of *Kuntres Ha'avoda* (titled "Love like Fire and Water") of the Rebbe Rashab, I began to send out weekly translations of Likutei Sichos. It is not easy to find material that on one hand challenges the mind and intellect, and on the other hand has daily practical application based on Torah. The Rebbe's sichos certainly possess both qualities, but without translation, they were not and are not accessible to most English speaking Jews. So, it became a project to translate and send out these translations to students and supporters. At the time, I had no intention of publishing the translations in print. I merely sought a suitable vehicle to communicate and remain in contact with many Jews, and the sichos fit the purpose nicely. [1]

From 2009 through 2015, I served as the rabbi for the English speaking students (who were the majority of students) at Ulpan Etzion, a Jewish Agency absorption center, in Jerusalem. The students there are new *olim* ("immigrants") who receive a five month intensive course

---

1. It is interesting to note that the "audience" for Chassidic literature has grown and expanded, even as knowledge and understanding of basic Judaism has receded and in some instances, nearly disappeared. In order to approach and have contact with the Alter Rebbe (R' Shneur Zalman of Liadi, founder of the Chabad Chassidic movement roughly 1780–1812), one needed to demonstrate full knowledge of Talmud (Babli and Yerushalmi), code of Jewish law, Midrash and Kaballistic sources. Only scholars of vast erudition were allowed into contact with the Alter Rebbe to hear him deliver his Chassidic discourses. One hundred years later during the leadership of the Rebbe Rashab (R' Shalom DovBer, fifth Lubavitcher Rebbe, 1883–1920), the circles of knowledge expanded to include yeshiva students (*Tomchei Tmimim*), who while versant and involved with Talmud and code of Jewish law, etc, were not on the same level of scholarship demonstrated during the time of the Alter Rebbe. Yet another hundred years later during the leadership of the Rebbe, R' Menachem Mendel Schneerson, the circles have expanded to include all of the Jews in the world (and in some cases, non-Jews). It is not unreasonable to state that at this point, the entire world is the audience to which the Rebbe directed his *sichos*.

in Hebrew that theoretically prepares them for life in Israel. There are roughly 250 new immigrants as students every six months, so it is quite challenging to meet as many of them as possible and introduce them to principles of Torah and Judaism. Challenging, but not impossible. Once again, the Rebbe's sichos became the basis of communication between myself and many of the students, as I taught a weekly class on the Torah portion, based on Likutei Sichos.[2] This teaching stint enabled me to focus intently on the Rebbe's message and forced me to develop tools to deliver the message succinctly and accurately.

In recent years, it finally occurred to me, "why haven't the Rebbe's sichos been translated into English?" Many of the relatively simple (although deep) sichos of the Rebbe in volumes 1 thru 4 of Likutei Sichos had long been translated, but where were the translations of the more learned and scholarly sichos that are found in volumes 5 thru 39? Why had nobody translated and published the deep, erudite and original concepts that are the hallmark of the Lubavitcher Rebbe's scholarship? It was at that point that I realized that I could adapt my earlier translations, from the years 2005-2010 that I had sent out as email communication to friends and supporters (and also posted on my website, www.jerusalemconnection.org) for publication, and I began to work on the project.

One of the first people with whom I discussed translations was R' Zalman Chanin שיח' of *Va'ad lehafatzas hasichos*. R' Chanin and his

---

2. As events turned out (quite without any intention on my part), Ulpan Etzion is a good example of the population to which the Rebbe directed his sichos. Theoretically an "academic" ulpan, attendees must be between the ages of 22 and 36 and must possess an academic degree. Those are the requirements of new immigrants who want to live at/ attend classes at Ulpan Etzion. At least one third of the students were not halachically Jewish, mainly because of the large number of immigrants from the former Soviet Union, who were either not Jewish or could not prove their Jewishness. Nevertheless, those who attended my shiurim on the Rebbe's sichos came from all nations of the world, whether Russia or Ukraine, the US and Canada, Europe or South America. The students were predominantly Jewish, but among them were also non-Jews and people who were just "interested." In this manner we see that the Rebbe's sichos have application to Jews of every walk of life and level of education, as well as to non-Jews. This is today's "neophyte" who is curious and wants to learn Torah. He or she has a well-developed and educated mind, and also possesses critical thinking faculties. But they are likely to be entirely lacking in Torah knowledge. It is to such people (among others) that the original and stimulating concepts found in the Rebbe's sichos, appeal.

organization were responsible for the original production of the Rebbe's sichos, which was an ongoing project involving input from several scholars but of course mostly from the Rebbe himself, who not only presented the sichos publicly during farbrengens, but also committed them to writing. Among the many interesting items that R' Chanin heard directly from the Rebbe, and passed on to me, was a directive involving translations. First, a proper translation is not a word for word translation, but a document that accurately conveys the message in the language of the reader. Second, translations should be checked for accuracy by two people. Both should be knowledgeable, but one should be an *ifcha mistabranik*– the kind of scholar who always "looks for the opposite position." In other words, one of the "checkers" should be one who has a tendency to disagree and look at the topic from another perspective, if not from the opposite perspective. I tried to use the Rebbe's guidelines, as conveyed by R' Chanin, when choosing two *talmidei chachamim* to check the translations for accuracy. R' Moshe Ginsburg, R' Moshe Miller and R' Zalmen Springer checked the translations of Bereishis, and R' Moshe Miller and R' Zalmen Springer checked the translations for the second volume; Shemos. I thoroughly enjoyed working with them, and my own impression is that the best translations are the ones in which we disagreed the most and argued over, until reaching conclusions.

If there are any misunderstandings of the Rebbe's sichos or mistranslations, that is entirely my responsibility, because even after discussing matters with R' Moshe and R' Zalmen, it was up to me to decide what and how to write. The "buck" stops here: I made the final decisions. At the same time, we are open to corrections and suggestions. The current work need not be considered "complete" and unchangeable. Constructive suggestions are encouraged.

As the first volume (Bereishis) neared completion in January of 2018, I consulted with R' Mendel Laine of Kehos Publication Society, which publishes Likutei Sichos in Hebrew and Yiddish. I sent a few of the translations to R' Laine, who told me that Kehos "liked" the work, but that it would need to be checked by the team at Kehos before publishing, and due to other projects, that would not happen anytime soon. He did, however give permission to publish the translations. Around this time, I also approached R' Yonah Avtzon (ע"ה) who similarly replied that Sichos in English has other projects on its agenda and cannot undertake to publish these translations at this time.

Very recently (late January 2020), it was brought to my attention that Sichos in English did indeed just bring out a volume of translations of some of the Rebbe's sichos. Therefore, one might ask, why is it necessary for more than one writer to produce translations of the same or nearly the same work? The answer though, will become readily apparent to anyone who opens both volumes of translations. The work produced by Sichos in English strives to remain very faithful to the original text of the Rebbe's sichos, and is close to being a "literal" translation (with interpolations in English to aid the reader). The current volume of "Torah like Fire and Water" does not strive to be a literal translation. It strives, as R' Chanin said that the Rebbe demanded of any translation, to convey the meaning and content of the sichos, not necessarily in *otiot haRav* ("the words of the author"). On the other hand the current volume is not a collection of "adaptations" that are "far" from the words of the Rebbe and far from the order in which the Rebbe organized his sichos. The translations in this volume roughly follow the order of topics as they appear in each sicha, while striving to convey the message and content in the most communicative way possible in the English language. There is room for both types of translation — both a literal and a "flowing" translation - it is up to the reader to determine which he prefers. In passing, it should be noted that the translations appearing in this volume for the most part, were published (via email and via our website) long before the volumes produced recently by Sichos in English.

Finally, this is the place to acknowledge the help and assistance that was extended by various people: R' Moshe Ginsburg, R' Moshe Miller and R' Zalmen Springer who all checked the manuscript for accuracy, R' Zalman Chanin for his advice, R' Leibel Shapira for encouragement, R' Zalman Dubinsky for his early Collel encouragement, Ms. Uriela Sagiv who edited the Bereishis volume, Ms. Eden Chachamtzedek who so brilliantly designed and typeset the book, and others.

Rabbi David Sterne
January 30, 2020

ליקוטי שיחות

TORAH

Like Fire & Water

Israel Belongs to the Jews

Bereishit 1:1

It is in the very beginning of the Book of Genesis — in the portion of *Breishit* — that the Torah establishes the status of the Holy Land, the Land of Israel. And, it is here that Rashi, the great 11th century Torah commentator, deals with the subject of the Land's ownership.

He says, in his very first commentary (on Genesis 1:1), "... if the nations of the world will claim that you (the Jews) are robbers, since you conquered the Land of the seven (idol-worshipping) nations, you should tell them that the entire Land is God's. He created it and gave it to whom He saw fit. It was His will to give it to them, and it was His will to take it from them and give it to us."[1]

A few questions arise:

1. Why does Rashi imply that God initially gave Israel to the seven Canaanite nations? When the earth was originally divided among the nations of the world, the Land of Israel fell into the portion of Shem, the son of Noach from whom the Jews descended. The seven Canaanite nations descended from Ham, another son of Noach who was not granted any portion in the Land of Israel. So, it was really the Canaanites who first took Israel from the Jews, not the other way around![2]

Since when does the conquest of a land constitute robbery?

2. Since when does the conquest of a land constitute robbery? It may or may not be moral to conquer another land, but it doesn't fit into the category of robbery! This we know because

the nations of the world constantly conquered and re-conquered each other, and yet none of them was ever punished for robbery! This despite the fact that all nations are governed by the Seven Noachide Laws, which include an injunction against robbery. Clearly, conquest of any kind was not considered to be robbery, so why would the nations of the world make such an accusation against the Jews?

3. Moreover, why does Rashi preface his commentary with the statement, "It was not necessary to begin the Torah like this..."? He goes on to say that the Torah should have begun with the first commandment that God gave the Jews [at the Exodus] — the mitzvah of sanctifying the new month. Rashi then asks, "Why did God begin the Torah with the creation narrative?" It seems that Rashi wants to emphasize the importance of the commandments of the Torah over the narrative stories, since these mitzvoth teach us how to lead our lives.[3] However, there are also stories that appear in the Torah after the first commandment of sanctifying the new month; does Rashi mean to suggest that they also "have no place" in the Torah? And there are commandments mentioned in the Torah before *kiddush hachodesh* ("sanctification of the month") so why does Rashi fail to mention them?[4]
4. But, most of all, the story of creation is the cornerstone of our belief and, therefore, it would seem obvious that it needs to appear in the beginning of the Torah. That being the case, what is the basis of Rashi's question implying that the Torah should have begun with the first commandment [that the Jews received as a nation]?[5]

To answer these questions, we first must grasp the uniqueness of the Jewish people and their relationship to the mitzvoth.

On a spiritual level, the Jews "arose in the thought of God" to be "His people," and "His only offspring," even before creation. However, that was only in regard to potential. In practice, what has set the Jews apart from the other nations of the earth is their acceptance of the mitzvoth of the Torah. These mitzvoth were given at the time of the Exodus from Egypt — more specifically, at their encounter with God at Mt. Sinai. Of course, there are commandments that were given even before the Exodus — such as: be fruitful and multiply, undergo circumcision, avoid eating the sciatic nerve of an animal — but these applied to all the descendants of Noach, before some of them became the Jewish nation. The commandments took on the full power of mitzvoth (that connect God with the Jews and with the physical world) only after the giving of the Torah at Mt. Sinai. And, therefore, it was the mitzvoth that were given at that time that made us into a nation. It was then that we took on these commandments willingly, of our own volition, and that is what defines our unique status as the Jewish people.

The mitzvoth that we received before the giving of the Torah were not intended for the Jews per se, since we did not yet exist as a people. Back then, we were a close-knit collection of families among the descendants of Noach with our own unique history and genealogy — but we were not yet a nation. For that reason, Rashi implies in his commentary that although the story of creation is very important, it does not belong in the beginning of the Torah, which is a book of instructions to the Nation of Israel. The Torah was not given to the loose collection of families (among the descendants of Noach) that eventually became the Jewish people. It was given to the Jews who became a nation upon leaving Egypt — more specifically, at Mt. Sinai. So why does the Torah include the creation narrative? It should begin with the first commandment that was given to us as a people, right at Exodus — the mitzvah of sanctifying the new month!

Back then, we were a close-knit collection of families among the descendants of Noach with our own unique history and genealogy — but we were not yet a nation.

To this Rashi answers that the Torah begins with the story of the creation because the creation narrative and the stories following it also contain an important lesson for us as Jews, as the Nation of Israel. The beginning of the Torah may not include mitzvoth per se, but it includes the story of creation and the stories of our forefathers because they tell us how to answer a significant claim that arises from the non-Jews, as will be explained.

When we look at normal transfer of ownership by way of purchase or grant, we see that the article changing hands does not itself change in any essential way. It is the same article no matter who owns it, and it is only the right to use and control it which changes. The item itself expresses no preference or predilection for one party or another, and has no more connection to one party than to the other. The Land of Israel, however, is different. Before the arrival of the Jews, it was a piece of land as any other piece of real-estate. After the Jews conquered it however, it became a different land, connected in essence only to the Jewish people. No other people have had any more than a superficial connection with Israel, such that even during our long exile, even while we have been "far from our Land," (as we mentioned in the *Musaf* prayer and have mentioned for the last two thousand years), Israel has always been referred to as "our Land." This even young children become aware of when they read the Bible and see that God promised the Land of Israel to Abraham's descendants.

[The Tanach,[6] as the Bible is known — and especially the Five Books of Moses or the Torah — is first and foremost a gift from God to the Jewish people. But, it is also a reliable historical record. Many of the events narrated in it can and have been confirmed by history and archaeology. Not only that, but no other world literature comes close to having the influence and impact which the Bible has had upon the world. Therefore, when it tells us that God promised the Land of Israel to the descendants of Abraham, Isaac and Jacob, we have the earliest and most reliable record in any literature connecting any part of the earth with any specific people. (For example, would anyone contest the claim of the Greek people to the country of Greece? Yet, Greek mythology deals with a history beginning many generations after that of the Bible, and has not had nearly the impact of the Bible upon humanity). Moreover, although many people have lived in the Land of Israel, and many empires have controlled it, none have made it their land. Whether it was the Romans, the Ottomans, or the British, their geographical center of gravity was elsewhere, while they ruled over local inhabitants who were never capable of making Israel into their own land. Looking at the overall picture, then, we are led to the conclusion that the initial conquest of the Land by the Jews produced a change which rendered Israel incapable of truly belonging to any other nation. Whether one looks from a spiritual, historical, cultural, or legal perspective, no other nation of the world has as strong and essential a bond to its land as the Jewish nation has to the Land of Israel. This is a qualitatively

When it tells us that God promised the Land of Israel to the descendants of Abraham, Isaac and Jacob, we have the earliest and most reliable record in any literature connecting any part of the earth with any specific people.

different kind of bond, based on a change in the Land of Israel itself. This bond was established when the Jews, emerging from the desert after forty years, conquered the seven idol-worshipping nations and transformed the land they had inhabited into the Holy Land and the cradle of civilization].

But herein also lies the claim of the non-Jews: if the Jews had conquered Israel like any other piece of real-estate on the earth, then another people could also come along and re-conquer it, and it would be in their possession. But, being that the bond of the Jews to the Holy Land is essential and immutable, producing a change which renders Israel forever connected with the Jewish people alone so that no one can reconquer it, the nations of the world claim that this constitutes "robbery." Now that even the possibility of re-conquering and making the Land of Israel into their own like any other country no longer exists, the nations of the world claim foul play. Their complaint is not that we conquered it from the seven nations. That — at least at the time it happened and for many generations afterward — was an accepted practice. The problem is that our conquest was permanent, and this, they say, constitutes "robbery." Ever since then, the nations of the world do not have even the potential to conquer the Land of Israel.

Now that even the possibility of re-conquering and making the Land of Israel into their own like any other country no longer exists, the nations of the world claim foul play.

To their claim, Rashi says, we need to answer that our claim to the Land of Israel goes back way before we re-conquered it. In fact, the Jewish claim goes all the way back to creation. "He [God] created it and gave it to whom He saw fit." Since the Bible, an authoritative document from any point of view, tells us that God created the earth and promised the Land of Israel to the Jews, the nations of the world must know that the same God who created the universe, and who granted us the Land immutably and permanently, promised it to the Jews at the very beginning of creation, and reiterated this promise to the forefathers. Since He is the Creator and the author of the Bible, it was His prerogative to do so.[7]

Based on this premise, we can now answer all the questions that we asked about Rashi's commentary: Rashi did not mention our initial ownership of Israel (as "Semites," descendants of Shem) before the seven Canaanite nations took it from the Semites, because his commentary refers only to the ownership that concretized our essential bond to the Land. That essential bond, based upon the mitzvoth, occurred later, when we re-entered the Land forty years after receiving the Torah at Mt. Sinai. It was when we re-conquered the Land of Israel from the Canaanite nations that it became immutably Jewish in such a way that it could never be taken away by another nation. The claim of the non-Jews who accuse us of "robbery" is not based alone upon our conquest of the Land when the Canaanite nations occupied it. That was "fair and square." Their claim is that by our actions, we "changed" the very nature of the Land of Israel, so that it could never again be taken away from the Jews — and this constitutes "robbery." Our conquest changed the Land of Israel forever, permanently removing it from the grasp of any other nation on earth.

But, if so, one might ask, why was Israel ever in the hands of another people, as it was in the time that the seven Canaanite nations lived there? Why did God allow the Canaanites to take it and, moreover, why did Rashi even mention it in his commentary? If his point was to describe how Israel belongs immutably to the Jewish people, why mention that it once fell under the dominion of the Canaanites?

To this, Rashi answers, "It was His will to give it to them, and His will to take it from them and give it to us." That is, the same will that determined that Israel is essentially Jewish is the divine will that gave the Land temporarily to the non-Jews. God allowed the seven nations to temporarily conquer Israel only in order to eventually place it permanently back in Jewish hands.[8]

Why?

There is a principle of human nature that something does not truly belong to us until we have struggled and invested in it. When something is given and granted with no effort on the part of the recipients, the gift is not appreciated. Only when we have to work for it and earn it, is it truly appreciated. For that reason, God wanted the Jews to put out effort of their own in order to "acquire" the Land. From His point of view, the Land was already given to the Nation of Israel. Yet, He also wanted us to fight and conquer the Canaanite nations, wresting control of the Land from them so that we should feel that the Land belongs to us. This was what led to the essential change — when the Jews engaged in self-sacrifice, willing to give up their lives for the Land, this constituted the true conquering of Israel and its change of status. The defeat of the seven

Canaanite nations is what concretized the concept for the Jews and made the Land of Israel truly "ours," not only from a divine point of view but also from a human point of view.

Nevertheless, one might still ask, why did the Land of Israel have to come into Canaanite hands for such a long period of time?

Precisely for that reason, the Torah writes at length about the history of creation and about all that our forefathers underwent. The Torah relates how God told Abraham that the Jewish people will go into exile (and the Land will be in the possession of others) for 400 years, and only then will the Jews return and re-conquer it. In this manner, we know that the same land that was promised to the Jews from the beginning of creation is the land that will return to Jewish possession after the Exodus and after the giving of the mitzvoth at Mt. Sinai. The Semites, who later became the Jews, were never dispossessed. They merely went through trials and tribulations in Egyptian exile and then returned.

The Torah's creation narrative and the historical narrative of our people from the days of our forefathers trace the unbroken connection of the Jews to the Land of Israel, even though it was interrupted for 400 years by the presence of the seven Canaanite nations. This, Rashi tells us, is the very purpose of the creation narrative and the other stories in the Torah — so that we can answer those who make false claims, "The entire Land is God's; He created it and gave it to whom He saw fit [to the descendants of Shem]. It was His will to give it to them [to the seven Canaanite nations], and it was His will to take it from them and give it to us [to the Jews who returned and re-conquered the Land from the Canaanites]."

But still — following Rashi's long explanation that the creation narrative, instead of the mitzvah of sanctifying the new month, was included in the Torah so that we would have an answer to non-Jews who would challenge our connection to the Land of Israel — we might ask yet another question: Isn't the Torah given to us Jews mainly as a means of instruction and guidance? How is it possible that a major section of the Torah was given only for the purpose of giving us a rejoinder to the claims of non-Jews? Even if knowing what to answer is an important part of our education and awareness as Jews, shouldn't there also be an intrinsic message or teaching for us in this section of the Torah? The answer is "yes," there are lessons for the Jews in the beginning of the Torah, apart from how to respond to non-Jews.

1. On the simplest level, children beginning their Jewish education need to hear the stories of the Torah in order to set the stage for a more advanced understanding of the text. Children need to be aware of Jewish history and identity before they can even begin to approach the Torah as a "legal system." There is an order to learning the Torah — first children begin with the history and belief system that is inspired by the creation narrative and the actions of our forefathers. Only afterward can they approach the mitzvoth that tell them in detail how to live.

   The same is true of adults who approach Judaism later in life. They must first imbibe and integrate the stories of the Torah that give us Jews our identity and only afterward can they approach the Torah as a legal system that guides our life. First, the "animal soul" inside of us must buy into the Torah, and then the divine soul will compel us to learn Torah on a daily basis so that we are guided by its directives. Therefore, the order of the Torah is important; the creation narrative and stories of our forefathers set the stage for the legal system that comes later.[9]
2. On a much deeper level, the Gemara (*Niddah* 30b) tells us that the embryo, while in the womb of its mother, is taught the entire Torah. When the moment arrives for the embryo to be born, an angel comes and causes it to forget all the Torah that it learned. The obvious question is: Why teach the embryo while it is in the womb, only to have it forget the Torah later when it is born? The answer is that we must work on learning and integrating the Torah into our lives. It is not sufficient for the Torah to be merely "given" to us as a gift from Above, because then it would lack value in our eyes — it would not be "ours," since nothing truly becomes a part of us until we struggle for it. However, if we were to rely on our own abilities and talents alone, we would be also limited by them, as we are a soul limited by our physical body. Thus, we might never accept upon ourselves the process of learning the Torah. And, even if we did, we would be unaware of its unlimited light and holiness. Hindered by the limitations of our body, we would never discover the *ohr ein sof,* the infinite light of the Torah, on our own. Therefore, God first teaches the embryo the entire Torah, so that it becomes aware of the infinite light of the Torah. Then, even when the details are forgotten after the

embryo matures and the baby is born, nevertheless, an impression of the infinite light remains. When the small child begins to learn the creation narrative and the stories of the forefathers, it slowly regains the infinite light of the Torah.

It is that impression of infinite light that inspires us and empowers us to recover what we once possessed — the knowledge of the entire Torah, including the story of creation and the early history of the Jews. An impression of the infinite light of the Torah remains with us even after we are born, and that is what motivates us to throw ourselves into learning Torah with great effort and devotion, in order to re-discover the infinite light of which we were once aware.

Something similar occurred with regard to the Holy Land. From the beginning of creation, God intended the Land to come into our possession. Yet, for a time, He took it away from us and gave it to the seven Canaanite nations. The purpose of this "gift," followed by its retraction, was to enable us to recover what once belonged to us (and remained essentially ours) by fighting for it. In that manner, the Holy Land became ours in an immutable manner. Now, it cannot possibly belong anymore to any other nation, as was explained.

The One Above wanted us to strive for and struggle for the Land of Israel, so that it would be truly "ours" in a way that we would value much more than if He had merely granted it to us outright. Yet, if we had gained ownership of the Land by merely conquering it and taking it by force, we would have nothing to answer to the non-Jews who would claim that we "stole" it from them. If we had gained possession of the Land only after fighting for it and conquering it, the Land wouldn't belong to the Jews in the unchangeable manner as it does now.

Therefore, our right to the Land as a grant from God needed to be established at the very beginning of the Torah, during the creation narrative. The Land belongs to God and He gave it to us initially (as the descendants of Shem) and then took it away (giving it to the seven Canaanite nations) so that the we could fight for and re-conquer it later (upon returning with Joshua) so that now the Land of Israel belongs to the Jews forever.

(From Likutei Sichot of the Lubavitcher Rebbe, vol. 5, p. 1)

NOTES

1. With this comment, Rashi gives us a general introduction and explanation regarding all of the Torah portions of *Bereishit* (Genesis) and *Shemot* (Exodus) preceding the commandment of sanctifying the new moon (which does not occur until parshat *Bo* in Exodus). More than that — this initial comment from Rashi explains the Torah in general. And with his answer to the question that he raises, Rashi indicates that all of the stories and themes right up to the very end of the Torah, provide us with teachings that are applicable to the very end of time (such as "If the non-Jews claim...").

2. Some commentators on Rashi ask, "Canaan (son of Ham) was a servant of Shem, and 'all that a servant acquires is acquired by his master,' so why would the Jews (descendants of Shem) be considered 'robbers'? However, it's understood that Noach's curse, 'and Canaan will be their servant...' (Genesis 9:26) did not necessarily turn Canaan into a servant of Shem immediately and, therefore, we cannot say that the Land of Israel immediately became the property of the Semites (ancestors of the Jews)." See Rashi on Genesis 9:26–27, 13:7, 15:16, *Likutei Sichos* vol. 15, p. 204.

3. Some commentaries on Rashi suggest that this is Rashi's main motivation: Even though there is no such thing as a narrative or story that is included in the Torah without reason, perhaps Rashi meant to emphasize that the Torah is mainly for the purpose of commanding the mitzvoth (and therefore the Torah should begin with the first mitzvah). But if so, then 1) Rashi should have asked his question not only on the narratives preceding the first mitzvah, but also on the stories in the Torah following the first mitzvah; 2) if that were the case, then Rashi's answer, "in order to provide a response to the non-Jews..." is not sufficient, since "to know what to answer the non-Jews" is not one of the mitzvoth of the Torah, but an instruction regarding how to conduct ourselves.

4. One possible answer — to this question and the questions following it — is that Rashi's intention was to suggest that the Torah should have started with the first mitzvah (*Kiddush Hahodesh*) and the creation narrative and stories of the forefathers, etc. should have followed. However: 1) Straightforward analysis of Rashi's lengthy comment ("It was not necessary for the Torah to begin like this...") lends itself more to the conclusion that none of the verses that preceded the mitzvah of *Kiddush HaHodesh* needed to have been written at all. 2) If this were Rashi's question, then the answer that Rashi provides is not clear as, even if the creation narrative and stories of the forefathers were written after *Kiddush HaHodesh*, they would have provided the same answer to the non-Jews regarding possession of Israel (and therefore their placement in the Torah really does not matter). And if the verses had to be included in the Torah, there is no reason to ask, "Why did the Torah open with them?" because most matters in the Torah do proceed in a chronological fashion. Rashi's question then, was "Why was the creation narrative included in the Torah at all?" 3) Rashi on Psalms (111:6), writes that the Torah includes the creation narrative "so that the non-Jews would not be able to say to the Jews, 'you are robbers'" — from this we see clearly that without this reason, there was no reason at all to include the creation narrative in the Torah (according to Rashi).

5. Several commentaries on Rashi ask, "Even if the Torah began with the commandment to sanctify the new month, we would still know that God created the world, either because it is says so in the Ten Commandments: "In six days God created the heavens and the earth..." (Ramban) or because the miracles that we see with our own eyes make it clear to us (*Gur Aryeh* authored by the Maharal of Prague) or because creation of the world is an oral "tradition" handed down to us, even if it is not recorded in the written Torah (Bahai). However: 1) It is understood that creation is a fundamental principle of faith, and as such, it is appropriate for it to be written in the Torah in a detailed and forthright manner (as the Bahai himself says, "The One Above did not want this important principle to remain a "tradition," but that the Torah should bear witness to creation.") 2) Since various miracles are recorded in the Torah even though they do not especially create a basis of our faith, all the more so that this great principle of creation that is a pillar of our faith should be recorded in the Torah. 3) According to this approach, there is no reason to include the story of creation in the Torah "in order to answer the non-Jews" who challenge the Jews over possession of the Land of Israel. Since, in any case, we know that God created the universe, we would also know how to answer the non-Jews on this subject.

6. The following paragraph is not a translation, but rather an addition written by the translator, based on general history and Chabad philosophy.

7. According to this understanding, we can answer a question that arises in the Rambam (*Hilchot Trumot* 1:3) — "The lands that King David conquered outside of Canaan ... even though he was a king of Israel and he acted in accordance with the instructions of the highest rabbinical court of his day, were not considered part of *Eretz Yisael* in every respect ... since David conquered them before he conquered all of the land of Canaan ... if he had first conquered all of Canaan throughout its borders and then conquered the other lands, then all of them would have been considered part of Israel in every respect." At first glance, since the holiness of Israel expands to encompass other lands outside of Canaan when they are conquered for the sake of the Jewish people (and the act of a king conquering another land is considered to be on behalf of all Jewish people, see Rambam *Halacha* 2 there), why should it matter if King David conquered other lands before or after conquering all of the land of Canaan? The answer is that the sanctity of the Land of Israel is not dependent upon "conquering" alone, but mainly upon the fact that the One Above *gave* the Land of Israel to the Jews. Therefore, the lands that were conquered after David conquered Canaan, fell into the category of, "they shall be for you [the Jews]," and "to you I gave it..." (Deuteronomy 11:24, Joshua 1:3, and see Rashi there: "will be holy"), and "they are like the Land of Israel that Joshua conquered, in every respect" — *Rambam Hilchot Melachim* 5:6). This however, does not apply to the lands that King David conquered previous to conquering *Eretz Yisrael*, since that was "not according to Torah" (see *Sifri* on *Eikev* there). The Jews under King David did "acquire" those lands as a result of conquering them, but they were not included in the category of "given to us" by God [and therefore lacked the same level of sanctity].

8. The transfer of the Land of Israel from the possession of the seven Canaanite nations back into the hands of the Jews (descendants of Shem) is analogous to the transformation from "dark to light." Accordingly, we can understand why so many

portions of the Torah were written in order to enable us to explain to the "nations of the world" that our conquering of Israel was not "robbery." The ultimate will of the One Above is that all lands, including those of the non-Jews, should become transformed into *Eretz Yisrael* — the "Land of Israel." And, therefore, it is appropriate for the non-Jews to agree to this transformation. Regarding this matter, see Zohar section 2, 67:2 and 68:1, and where it is mentioned and explained in a Chasidic discourse of the Frierdiker Rebbe, the Rayatz in 5709 "Vayomer Moshe" — Ch. 6, wherein he explains that it was Yitro's agreement that led to giving of the Torah.

9. We might say that the two stages of descent of the Torah are analogous to the two stages in which God "gave it to them" (the Land of Israel). The stage during which the embryo is caused to "forget" the Torah that he learned while "above," and remembers only that which is relevant to his sojourn in the lower physical world, is analogous to the potential stake that the Jews had in the Land of Israel, when the land was in the possession of Shem. And the stage during which one learns Torah *she'lo lishmah* ("not for the sake of Torah") but later arriving to that level is comparable to the early stage during which the Canaanites conquered the Land from the descendants of Shem (and the Jews under Joshua later came and took the it back).

Beginning with a Beit

Bereishit 1:1

There are three reasons given why the Torah begins with a *beit* — the second letter of the Hebrew alphabet, as opposed to an *aleph*, which is the first letter — each of which is problematic:

1. The Jerusalem Talmud (*Hagiga* 2:1) states that since the word *arrur*, meaning "curse," begins with an *aleph*, it was preferable to begin the Torah with a *beit*, which is the first letter of the word *baruch*, meaning "blessed."

   The problem with this explanation is, as the Ibn Ezra points out, that there are many words beginning with a *beit* which do not carry a positive denotation, while there are many words beginning with an *aleph* that do.
2. The Midrash (*Hane'elam* on *Shir Hashirim*) states that just as the shape of the letter *beit* is closed from three sides and open from the fourth, so God created the world complete on three sides, leaving the fourth side — opening to the "north" — open. (The world was created in this manner so that if a deluded fellow came along and declared that he is God, we would be able to respond, "Okay, please go and close up the fourth side of the world that was left open.")

   The problem with this explanation is that the Torah was not created for the sake of the world, but rather the world was created in order to fulfill the Torah. When God created the universe, He "looked into the Torah and created the world." Therefore, it makes little sense to say that the Torah was written to conform to the world. Quite the opposite — since according to the Torah the first letter of the Hebrew alphabet is *aleph*, it should have been the first letter of the Torah as well.[1]

3. According to Kabbalah (see *Likutei Torah* of the *Ariza"l*), the Torah that we learn here in the physical world descends from the higher spiritual world of *Atzilut*. In order to allude to the fact that the Torah descended to us on a lower/secondary level, the Torah begins with a *beit*. The Torah exists primarily in the higher worlds, and secondarily in our lower world, and therefore it begins with a *beit*.

   The problem with this explanation is that the Torah which was given to us here in the lower world is the same Torah that exists in the higher worlds. And, therefore, in the higher worlds, the Torah also must begin with a *beit*.[2] That leaves us with this question: Why does the Torah in the higher world of *Atzilut* (and even higher) also begin with a *beit*, the second letter of the Hebrew alphabet?[3]

In addition to the above, there is a story from the Talmud (*Megila* 9a) about a group of seventy scribes who translated the Torah into Greek in the 3rd century BCE for King Ptolemy. God worked a miracle, and all seventy scribes translated the Torah in the exact same fashion. Among the changes they made in order to satisfy Ptolemy (as a non-Jew) was that they all identically translated the beginning of the Torah with the words, *Elokim barah breishit* — "God created in the beginning." This was a miraculous event, since none of the scribes were in contact with one another. Nevertheless, all of them began their translation with an *aleph*, since the first word in their translation is *Elokim*.

Obviously then, there is a sound basis for beginning the Torah with an *aleph*. On the other hand, why would all the good reasons for beginning the Torah with a *beit* not be applicable to King Ptolemy? Why was it necessary to begin his translation with an *aleph*, to the point that God worked a miracle to that effect?

In order to explain this, it will be helpful to understand the following: There are two elements in the relationship of a Jew to the Torah: 1) First, there is the relationship of the Jew to the Giver of the Torah — to God. 2) Second, there is the relationship of the Jew to the Torah itself, which we are commanded to learn and grasp intellectually. The latter of course is an intellectual activity, obligating us to study and internalize the Torah. But the first element — our relationship with the Giver of the Torah — transcends intellect. The connection with God is beyond our feelings and understanding.[4] Nevertheless, the first element is essential since, without the connection with the Giver of the Torah, we learn the Torah in a completely different manner. In a sense, without a connection to the Giver of the Torah, we actually separate the Torah from the One Above while learning it. The Torah becomes a like any academic subject, lacking the spirituality and Godliness that should be present. But, once we establish that connection, we learn the Torah in a much more intimate fashion, always feeling the importance and vitality that the Torah imparts to us, infusing our lives with Godliness and spirituality.

Based on this differentiation, we may derive a simple explanation for why the Torah, on all levels, begins with a *beit* and not an *aleph*. The letter *aleph* represents the connection — it symbolizes the relationship of the Jew to the Giver of the Torah, while the letter *beit* symbolizes the second element — the relationship of the Jew to the intellect of the Torah. And that is why the Torah on all levels (including in *Atzilut*) begins with a *beit*. On every level that the Torah exists, both elements — the connection to the One Above, and the connection to the Torah — are present. On every level, in order to approach the Torah, we first need to make a connection with the Giver of the Torah. That is the first step — the *aleph*. Thereafter, we are obliged to learn Torah on that level — and that is the second step, symbolized by the *beit*. Once the connection is there, we learn the Torah, and it becomes our main occupation. That is why the Torah on all levels begins with the letter *beit*.

All explanations of every word of the Torah are interconnected. In our case, the three explanations of why the Torah begins with a *beit* all stem from one general point. And that is that the *aleph* of Torah alludes to a state of clinging and cleaving to God, a spiritual process beyond intellect. And the *beit* alludes to learning and understanding the Torah. The three explanations mentioned at the outset express this concept in three different modalities: within the Torah itself, in the effect of the Torah upon man, and in the effect of the Torah upon the world.

1. The Kabbalistic explanation of the *Ari z'l* — that the Torah as it exists in our world is on a lower level than in the world of *Atzilut*, which is why it begins with a *beit* — alludes to the Torah

itself. When we learn Torah with full awareness of the Giver of the Torah, then the Torah reveals its true essence as a "garment/parable" expressing Godliness. But, when we learn Torah without any consciousness of the Giver of the Torah, then the Torah becomes, in a sense, separate from God. The impression of separation is alluded to by the *beit,* symbolizing the lower worlds of *Briah, Yetzirah* and *Asiyah*, which reflect distance and separation from God. But, when we learn Torah preceded by an awareness of God, we unite it with Him, as is the case in the world of *Atzilut*, in which "God is obvious, and creation is secondary."

2. The explanation of the Jerusalem Talmud — that the Torah in our world begins with *beit* because it is also the first letter of *baruch* ("blessed") as opposed to an *aleph* with is the first letter of *arrur* ("cursed") — corresponds to the relationship of Torah to the Jew. If we learn with full awareness of the Giver of the Torah, then we draw down a blessing into the world. But, when our learning is without awareness of the Giver of the Torah, we remain separate from God. We may achieve intellectual knowledge of His Torah, but we may fail to follow its precepts, or we may follow them but only coldly and robotically, without divine awareness. This state is alluded to by the *aleph* of *arrur.*
3. The explanation of the Midrash — that God created the Torah with a *beit* to remind us of the world that was created with the north side open — alludes to the relationship of Torah to the world. (Elsewhere, the Torah tells us that "negativity comes from the north side." The north side in Kabbalah represents the sphere of *gevurah*, or strictness and power. When combined with the sweetening effects of holiness and spirituality, *gevurah* has a positive impact on the world and on our lives. Without holy input though, *gevurah* may turn into negativity and cruelty.) When we learn Torah with full awareness of the Creator, we draw down the Godliness that "completes" the north side, which is the fourth side of the *beit.* When, however, we learn Torah without awareness of the Creator, the result is a world that remains in need of rectification — there is no one there to fix and fill in the fourth side.

And now, we may also understand the significance of the translation of the Torah into Greek, which all seventy scribes began with the letter *aleph*. King Ptolemy was a non-Jew, and as such his obligation to learn the Torah was not equivalent to the Jewish obligation. While a Jew must learn the entire Torah with awareness of and cleaving to the One Above, a non-Jew must learn only those sections that apply to his fulfillment of the Seven Noachide Laws. He is certainly not obligated to involve himself in the Torah in order to cleave to God and become imbued with awareness of the Giver of the Torah. Therefore, the non-Jewish relationship to Torah lacks the first element that is present in the Jewish relationship — awareness of and clinging to the One Above. The only obligation of a non-Jew is intellectual awareness. Since for the non-Jew, intellectual awareness of the Torah is all that is required from him, his reading begins with the *aleph* — the first letter of the Hebrew alphabet. While for the Jew, the *aleph* is associated with cleaving to God, for the non-Jew the *aleph* is associated with the knowledge that he seeks to attain — how to live in accordance with the Seven Noachide Laws. And that is why it was appropriate for the scribes to begin Ptolemy's translation with an *aleph*.

From Likutei Sichot of the Lubavitcher Rebbe,
vol. 15, pp. 1–6

NOTES

1. According to what is explained in the Alter Rebbe's *siddur* regarding the *kavanot* of blowing the *shofar* on Rosh Hashanah, the *aleph* is an intermediate letter, joining the breath of the heart (lungs) which is undifferentiated, with the other letters of the Hebrew alphabet (*Siddur*, p. 244, col. 3)

2. *Torah Ohr* of the Alter Rebbe (42b) tells us that the letters of the Torah are higher in their source than even than the Torah itself. Letters come from the level of *keser.*

3. As also mentioned in *Likutei Torah* of the *Ariz'l*, "the *aleph* is the first letter of *Atzilut*, and the *beit* is the first letter of *Bria*."

4. In *Likutei Torah* of the Alter Rebbe, *Parshat Vayikrah*, in the discourse *Velo Tashbis Melach* (Ch. 2 and onward), it states: "by connecting the wisdom (*chochma*) and intellect of the soul with the wisdom of the Torah, a unity and inter-inclusion takes place merging the essence of the soul that is above the intellect with the infinite light that is beyond *chochma* of *Atzilut*." But see there (Page 8 first column) that this "inter-inclusion" takes place only after reciting the *Kriat Shema* … with selfless devotion (to give up the soul at *echad*). Then, when one involves himself in Torah, the unity and inter-inclusion … [takes place].

Shedding Light on the Creation of Light

Bereishit 1:3

Anything as important as light, deserves a lot of attention. Perhaps that is the reason that light was created in the first place. In the creation narrative of the Torah, the very first thing to be created *ex nihilo* — "from nothing into something" — was light.[1]

But what exactly is light? Even scientists cannot make up their minds if light is made up of particles or waves, or both. And, in the Torah, we learn that there are many "shades" of light. This raises a number of questions:

Light serves only to illuminate everything else. Hence our first question: Why didn't the One Above create everything else, and only then create light in order to illuminate it all?

Light does not seem to have any intrinsic purpose of its own. Light serves only to illuminate everything else. Hence our first question: Why didn't the One Above create everything else, and only then create light in order to illuminate it all?

Second question: The Midrash and some commentators on the Torah tell us that, immediately after creating light, God "set it aside for future use by the righteous."[2] Why would God create light only to "set it aside" for later?

Third question: The Zohar makes a point of equating the Hebrew word for "light" (*ohr*) with a word for "secret" (*raz*) because the two words have the same numerical value (*gematria*) of 207. According to the Zohar, this means that the two words also share a similarity in content. Yet, at first glance, they seem to be diametrically opposed to one another: Light implies revelation and illumination, while a secret is, by definition, a concealment. What does the Zohar see as the common thread?

Clearly, light is not a simple topic. But perhaps we can begin to answer our questions by examining our own human processes down here in this world. The universe was created with "plans and blueprints," coming from Above to below and, therefore, by using our own experience below, we may be able to decipher the intention of the Divine Above. At the very least, we can try…

When we conceive of a project, the first thing we want to do is to define and clarify our objectives. First, we must know what the goal is, and then we can act. With any project, what initially guides our path is a grand idea whose bright illumination inspires us to get to work and translate inspiration into reality. And so it was during the six days of creation. Since God's intent in creating the universe was that it should become imbued with His light, He first created light.

However, reading the Torah verses that comprise the creation narrative, we find that every day of creation ended with God looking at His creation and declaring that it was "good." The sages tell us that "good" in this context means "light" — that God saw that His creation was good because it contained light. If so, light was not hidden or set aside; there was an element of light present in all six days of the creation process.

Indeed, light was drawn down every day of the six days of creation. Why, then, does the Midrash tell us that the initial light of creation was set aside for the future? How does this daily dose of illumination mesh with the initial light of creation that was "set aside for the future use of the righteous"?

In order to answer this, we shall return to our example of the one who undertakes a project. In the process of bringing that project to fruition, something occurs that is similar to the ray of light that was drawn down every day of the six days of creation.

1. First, as mentioned above, there is the initial light of inspiration that encompasses all of the details of the project, from inception to conclusion. Or, if you will, from the initial idea down to the project's final completion.

2. Then, there is the process of working toward the goal in order to achieve it. While working on the project, we are involved in all of its details, and we are aware of how each and every detail fits into and serves the ultimate purpose. We are absorbed in the "fine print" and the minute components of the process, concerned with actualizing them so that they mesh together. But, while absorbed in the details, we do not feel the light and inspiration of the initial idea, because when we get involved in the details of our project, we forget about it. As we bury ourselves in the details of making our dream come true, the dream itself fades into the background.

Looking back into the Torah, we discern the same two stages in the supernal goal of creation:

1. The essence of the Godly light and illumination, as revealed on the first day of creation when light was initially created, preceded all other creations and served as the goal and purpose of all creation. This is the light that was "set aside."
2. A ray and reflection of that light that was drawn into each and every individual aspect of creation continues to provide the spirituality that enables every created being to achieve its purpose, which is to express the level of Godliness that enlivens it.

What we see operating here are two different kinds of light. The light of the first day is the revealed light (*ohr*) that we need in order to inspire us to get to work on our task. But this light was hidden, although a ray of this light was drawn into creation every day of the remaining six days of creation.

Analogously, we need an initial light and illumination in order to get us started on our project. But if we focus on that bright illumination alone, we would never get down to the vital task of putting our project into effect, of making it happen. Instead, we need to shift our focus from the bright light to the details. Only by hiding the bright light can we discern the tiny details and nuances of our project that bring it to fruition. For that purpose, there is a second kind of light, but it comes down to us in a concealed manner...

The sages asked, "Where did God hide the original light of creation?" They answered, "In Torah and its mitzvoth."[3] The hidden light of Torah and its mitzvoth (corresponding to *raz*) is what quietly motivates us every day, even though we no longer feel the original inspiration and illumination. In practice, it is by learning Torah and fulfilling the 613 mitzvoth that we gradually recover the original light and illumination that we need to work on the tasks of our lives.[4]

This light comes down to us each day in a contracted and concealed manner, like a ray of light from its source. And that is why the Zohar equates *ohr* and *raz*. Even though one is revealed and the other is concealed, each in its own way serves to inspire and encourage us on the path until we are able to perceive and experience Godly illumination in full force. Both the initial illumination that was created and hidden and the ray of light that subsequently descended on each of the six days of creation aid us to actualize the details of our project.

Finally, when we have completed it, we have to recall our initial point of inspiration and our original mission statement in order to ensure that we have met our goal. Whatever the details of our project, it is not sufficient to bring light to bear on it on a daily basis; our goal has to be to turn the project itself into light. Ultimately, we want the project itself to reflect the original light of creation. This means that we want the original light, which enabled us to initiate our project, to descend and infuse the project itself. That was the whole point of the original light of the first day of creation and why light was created first of all.[5] It is both the initiation and the culmination of our task in this world. That is why the sages also said that the original light of the first day of creation was "set aside for the use of the righteous in the future." The "future" occurs after we have concluded all of our individual projects, and the world has reached a pinnacle of refinement that reflects Godly light. And then, the Godly light that was hidden within each and within every aspect of creation, finally illuminates.

And that's why light was created first, even though it only serves to illuminate everything else. Without the initial revelation of light, which is also the ultimate goal, we would lack direction. Now that we understand why the original illumination was hidden, and only a ray of that light can be drawn into the world every day, we can use it to illuminate our path to bring our personal projects to fruition.

Since "He in His goodness constantly re-creates the universe at every instant,"[6] it is up to us to utilize His light at every hour and every minute and every second of our lives to illuminate the world with Godliness.[7]

Adopted from Likutei Sichot of the Lubavitcher Rebbe, vol. 10, pp. 7–12

NOTES

1. *The very first utterance, Bereishit bara Elokim...*("In the beginning of creation, God created...") is also a creative utterance, but it is considered a "general" utterance, meaning that it included all of creation in one statement. And, therefore, the nature of creation from the first utterance was also "general." (See *Pirkei d'Rebi Eliezer*, end of Ch. 3, and *Zohar* sec. 1, 16:272). The first particular creation, mentioned in the second utterance, is light.

2. Although the Midrash (*Bereishit Rabba* Ch.11) indicates that the initial light was "in service" on the first *erev* Shabbat and on Shabbat, Tractate *Chagiga* (12A) indicates that the light was hidden before the "luminaries" (the sun and moon) were created on the fourth day of creation (according to the *Chidushei Agada* of the *Maharsha*). If so, then the statement, "Adam could see from one end of the universe to the other," does not refer to *Adam Harishon* (who was only created on the sixth day), but rather to the intensity of the illumination that enabled man to see from one end of the universe to the other. And the Zohar (Sec.2, 148B) indicates that the light was "in service" only on the first day of creation, and thereafter it "was hidden and no longer used."

3. *Midrash Ruth* in *the Zohar Chadash* 85A. See also *Zohar* Sec. 1, 264A, Sec 2, 149A

4. The "ray" of illumination is not as revealed as it was before it became involved in "action." But, in addition, once the ray became "invested" in action, it remained only a ray and reflection of what it was before it was invested in action. From this, it is understood that only a reflection of the light that shone on the first day (from *chesed* and not from *keser*) illuminated every individual utterance that followed.

5. Possibly, this is the underlying reasoning behind the difference of opinion in *Breishit Rabba*, Ch.3: R' Yehuda declared that light was created first, followed by the heavens and the earth, but R' Nehemiah declared that first the heavens and earth were created, and thereafter light was created. R' Nehemiah was of the opinion that heavens and earth are analogous to "darkness," because creation conceals Godliness. His opinion was that man must elevate darkness, which he does by mastering and controlling his impulses and actively choosing "light" over darkness. And, therefore, he declared that the heavens and earth were created first — prior to light and "outside of it" — as a separate category, prior to light. That is, according to R'Nehemia, "darkness" is not within the realm of creation whose purpose was already determined — to become transformed into "light." Rather, darkness was created in the beginning because there was no purpose of turning it into light, and therefore it had no ultimate purpose. However, R' Yehuda opined that "darkness" also has a purpose — to be transformed into "light," and therefore darkness (in the form of the "heavens and earth") was created after light. That perhaps is why R' Yehuda held that "light was created first," meaning that the goal of creation — "Let there be light" — includes also the presence of darkness, with the potential of transformation into light.

6. From *nusach hatefila* in *birchot kriat shema*. Also Talmud *Chagiga* 12B in modified form (without the words *b'tuvo* or *tamid*).

7. Because at every instance, the universe is "re-created" totally anew just as during the initial creation (See *Shaar Hayichud* in *Tanya*, in the beginning). See also *Likutei Torah* of the Alter Rebbe on *Shir haShirim* p. 4, col. 4, that the ongoing creation of the universe out of Hashem's "goodness" is equivalent to the *ohr* or "light" that was created on the first day. Moreover, since man is capable of declaring that something is "light," when it is really the opposite, the Torah tells us that the "real" light that we must pursue is that which the Torah tells us is light, and it is the light hidden in the Torah.

ESTABLISHING MAN'S DIET

Bereishit 1:29

Since the Torah is a guide to life, it shouldn't be surprising that it talks about eating. What is surprising is where it talks about it — right in the beginning of the Torah. In this week's portion — *Parshat Breishit* — we find that, after God created man and told him to have dominion over the animal kingdom (Genesis 1:28–29), He revealed that in one respect, man and animals are equal — they have the same diet (which was vegan).

The question is: Why here? Why in the beginning of the Torah, in the middle of the story of creation, does God choose to define our diet?

Rashi explains, "[God] made man equal to the animals in regard to food and did not permit Adam and his wife to kill any living creature and eat meat. Only plants and herbs were eaten by every creature." It seems then that the purpose of this Torah passge was to forbid Adam and Chavah to eat meat. As the *Maharal* of Prague (in *Gur Aryeh* on the Torah) also says, "Just as animals eat nothing but plants, so man may eat plants and herbs and nothing else."

But this argument is difficult to accept, since there are many animals that eat meat as well as plants. And although there is an opinion (Ramban on *Behukotai* 26:6) that, before the sin of Adam, there was no such thing as a carnivorous animal, it is unlikely that Rashi shared this opinion since he makes no mention of it. In any case, the goal of Rashi is to clarify the simple meaning of scripture. If so, what is the difficulty that Rashi found in this Torah passage, and how does his statement ("they were created equal in regard to food") resolve the difficulty?

Furthermore, there are some subtle irregularities in Rashi's statement that need explanation:

1. Why does Rashi write that God "did not permit Adam and his wife to kill any living creature and eat meat" as if filling in the narrative, rather than in the generally accepted halachic style: "meat was forbidden"?
2. Since, according to Rashi, Adam and Chavah were not permitted "to kill," we can deduce that they were permitted to eat from animals that passed away from natural causes. If so, where does it say so in the Torah?

It turns out that Rashi's difficulty with the verse is the very one that we identified: Why does the Torah deal with diet in the middle of the story of creation? That man was commanded to be fruitful and multiply is understood; God created man and wanted the species to continue, so He added (in the middle of the creation narrative) the command to do so. In fact, the commandment to dominate the earth, as well as to be fruitful and multiply, defines man and his role in creation. But, how does the reference to diet which follows immediately after fit into the creation narrative?

In answer, Rashi begins his explanation by connecting two Torah verses. The first verse (from Genesis 1:29) reads, "And God said, behold, I have given you all the herbs of the field that produce seed all over the land and every tree that produces fruit and seed for you to eat." The second verse (from Genesis 1:30) reads, "And all the animals of the land and all fowl of the heavens and all that swarms on the land, that has a living soul, all the vegetation and herbs to eat." Rashi connects the end of the first verse with the second: "I have given you all the herbs … for you to eat and [for] all the animals of the land … herbs to eat…" By joining them together, Rashi makes the point that man and the animals are equal regarding food. According to Rashi, that is the intent of this passage — not to list forbidden food, nor to designate what man and animals can and cannot eat, but to establish the equality of man and animal with regard to food. While it is true that the beginning of the passage indicates that man was forbidden to eat meat, the end of it draws out the similarity between man and animals — they both eat the same thing. (The similarity is somewhat one-sided, since even then there were animals that ate other animals, but in one respect their diet was the same — they both ate plants.)

What caused Rashi go out of his way to emphasize this similarity between man and animals? That has to do with the preceding verse. There (in Genesis 1:28), man was commanded to have dominion and rule over the animal kingdom. Since the Torah follows immediately thereafter with the commandments to eat vegetation, Rashi logically concluded that "dominion" does not include eating animals. The line of thought that began by establishing man's rule over the animal kingdom continued by establishing the diet of man — he was to eat vegetables alone. Despite the fact that man was created superior to the rest of creation, he was not allowed to kill and eat them. Since killing and eating animals would imply that man dominates even the life-force of the animal kingdom, the Torah set limits. When it comes to their source of vital energy, man does not have that power. In fact, man and the animal world are equal when it comes to food.

Man, just like the animals, is no more or less than a creation of God. That's why Rashi says, "Adam and Chavah were not permitted to kill any creature and eat it." He doesn't say, "they were *forbidden* to kill," but they "were not permitted." That's because Rashi's goal was not to explain what man can and cannot eat, but to define the meaning of the word, "dominion." Man was to have "dominion" and rule over the animal kingdom, but this did not include uprooting their life-force by killing them to eat them. Therefore, Rashi expresses himself by saying "they were not permitted..."

Now we can understand why Rashi said that Adam and Chavah could not kill, from which we can also deduce that if an animal died from natural causes, it was permissible to eat it. Rashi wanted to explain that "dominion" did not include killing because, if so, it meant that man would have domination over the source of vital energy of the animal. However, if the animal died of natural causes, there was nothing in eating it to suggest that man dominated and controlled the life-force of the animal kingdom, and therefore it was permitted.

And here is the place to learn something about our relation with God and His creation. We tend to think that when we are successful, it is "the strength and power of my own hands" that created all the success (as noted in Deuteronomy 8:17). We forget that it is the One Above who brings success. Man was created to have dominion over creation, but his success is dependent upon recognizing the source of his success, the Creator of the universe. When Rashi (in his commentary on Genesis

1:26) explained the word "dominion," he said it could be construed in two different ways. "If the person merits, he will dominate (*rodeh*). If not, he will descend (*yored*) spiritually and the animals will rule over him."

The Hebrew word for "merit" — *zacha* — is also pregnant with meaning. It comes from the word *zach*, meaning pure. If man purifies and refines himself, purging his ego and concluding that all of his success comes from Above, then he will dominate. But, if he fails to elevate and purify himself, then he will fall lower than the animal kingdom itself.

And very possibly that is why Rashi explained that dominion over the animal kingdom does not include killing animals for food. If within our dealings with the creation, we recognize our own limitations and approach nature and each other with respect, not seeking to uproot another creature's life-force, then we ourselves will garner respect. When we are reminded that we, like the animals, are only a creation of God, we understand that our dominion over the animal kingdom is a power granted to us by God. Because it is God who creates and rules over all creatures. However, if in our actions we are inconsiderate and leave no room for other's positions, we ourselves will end up on the bottom of the pile.

If within our dealings with the creation, we recognize our own limitations and approach nature and each other with respect, not seeking to uproot another creature's life-force, then we ourselves will garner respect.

From Likutei Sichot of the Lubavitcher Rebbe, vol. 20, pp. 7–12

Naming the Creation

Bereishit 2:19

Names make a difference. A name can't be touched or felt, but when someone calls us by our name, we turn. The job of naming the creation fell to Adam, the first human. He zeroed in on every creature and determined what it should be called. But we see in our Torah portion — *Parshat Breishit* — that he left out one important category of creatures (and of our diet): Fish.

While everything on land, such as the bovines, the canines, the felines, the ursines, etc., received a name, the denizens of the watery deep remained anonymous and unnamed. Two explanations are offered for this curious omission. The first one — by the Midrash — suggests that perhaps Adam really did identify and name the fish world, but the Torah didn't find it necessary to record it. The second — by the Radak — says that Adam only named the creatures that came to him, and the fish could not come since they would die if they left their natural habitat.

The two explanations correspond to the dual purpose of names: 1) There are those who say that names exist for the benefit of man. Since he is commanded to take care of creation, he needs to apply a name to every creature in order to use it. 2) Then, there are those who say that names exist for the benefit of the creations. Since a name brings out the essence and nature of each creature, it lends enhanced stature to each one.

If the significance of names lies in their usefulness to man, then fish did not receive a name because they are not so subject to man's dominion and stewardship as is the rest of creation since, as soon as they are removed from water, they die. (Even though the commandment for

Adam to rule the environment specifically mentions fish, nevertheless, it is clear that the commandment is more applicable to inhabitants of the land, such as oxen, chickens, etc. than of the sea). But, according to the opinion that names are for the benefit of creation, fish did receive a name, although it wasn't transmitted or mentioned by the Torah.[1]

It would seem that Rashi subscribed to the second opinion — that names are for the benefit of creation. On the verse (in Genesis 2:19), "And whatever man called each living creature this is its name," Rashi commented, "...every living creature that will be named by man will be so named forever." Why did Rashi add the word "forever"? He could have explained that the phrase, "this is its name" implies that Adam named every creature according to its nature and qualities, as the Chizkuni said, "he applied the name that was appropriate; his observation was in agreement with the opinion of the Creator."[2] But apparently Rashi felt that a name does more than describe the creature — it draws out and emphasizes the essential qualities of each, and that's why he added the word "forever." By stating the name of each creature, Adam drew out and emphasized its essential qualities, which then became its nature forever. Thus, it seems that Rashi's believed the purpose of a name is for the benefit of the creation, rather than of man.

Even without the support of Rashi's commentary, we might conclude that the Torah gives names to the creatures mainly for their own benefit and not only for the benefit of man. This is evident in the passage regarding name-giving which starts, "And God formed all the animals..." (Genesis 2:19). Why is this phrase necessary? Previously, the Torah related the creation of animals, so we already know that they were formed during the six days of creation. It must be that the conclusion of the verse — "and whatever man called each living creature this is its name" — is what carries significance here. Apparently, even the simple meaning of the text implies that by naming all the creatures, Adam added a new and final dimension to creation. Something about the name has an effect on the body of the creature, and that is why the verse begins, "And God formed..."

This also makes sense in context. Since the Torah section on names is within the story of the formation of Chavah, there must be an internal connection between them. The formation of Chavah was the culmination and finale of her creation and that of Adam. (In the beginning she existed as one entity with Adam, and only now was her creation completed, as was his.) Therefore, it would seem logical that by calling all the creatures by their names, Adam also brought about the final step in the creation saga.

We may conclude then that, according to all opinions, names exist for the benefit of creation, although this may be understood in two different ways, corresponding to two aspects of creation: 1) Every creature exists independently and the presence of God is not recognizable within creation. 2) The goal of man is to reveal Godliness within creation by demonstrating its dependence upon God.

Indeed, as soon as Adam was created on the sixth day, he demanded of all creatures to accept upon themselves God's reign and authority, when he proclaimed, "Come, bow, kneel and bless God who made us."[3] Consequently, there are two ways to look at the names that Adam applied to creation: 1) as a continuation and culmination of God's creation, which has an added effect upon the body of the creature, or 2) as part of the effort and goal of man to reveal Godliness in the creation.

The creation story in the beginning of Genesis (relating the six days of creation) includes only general categories and divisions. We don't find, for example, that the ten utterances of God which brought creation into being include the names of all the individual creations.[4] For example, we are only told that, on the third day, vegetation was created and that, on the fifth day, sea-dwellers were created and that, on the sixth, creeping creatures and wildlife were created. We are not told of any particular names given to any of the animals, such as oxen, donkeys, and the like. That was left up to Adam. It was the influence of his name-giving that caused every creature to become recognized for what it was, an independent entity in its own right.

This understanding of Adam's naming of the creatures corresponds to the first aspect noted above — the existence of every creature as an independent creation that does not reveal Godliness. The effect of Adam's calling every creature by its name was to bring it into stark relief as a distinct being, a detail of a general category that was formed during the six days of creation.

However, we can explain this process in a more profound manner by saying that the name-giving was part of the task assigned Adam — to make of creation a vessel and receptacle for Godliness. The name of each creature enlivens and vitalizes it, from nothing into something. By giving them names, Adam revealed the spiritual source of every creature, the vital energy which enlivens it. In so doing, he attached every creature to the One Above. He did this by calling each individual creature by its appropriate name in the holy tongue of Hebrew, thus revealing its hidden spiritual source.

Taking this explanation one step further, we know that the Godly energy that descends to enliven every creature, descends in a contracted and constricted form, in accordance with our physical world which hides and conceals Godliness. It is explained in the Tanya (*Sha'ar Hayichud vehaEmuna*, ch. 1), that even though the names of individual creations are not found among the words and letters of the ten initial utterances, the names of all creatures emerge via combinations, permutations and substitutions of the letters of the original ten utterances. But, by calling every creature by its rightful name, according to its spiritual root, Adam achieved something even greater — he actually connected it to its spiritual source prior to creation.

We are told that the world could have been created with one "high energy" utterance that contained all of the details of creation. However, God created the world with ten utterances in order to bring a lower level of creative light into the world that could later be detected by His creatures, affording them free choice whether or not to connect with Him. If He had created with one utterance, the Godly energy present in the world would have been so great that every creature would have been automatically subsumed within the infinite light of the Creator. It would not have been a matter of choice; it would have been automatic and spontaneous. By giving names to all creatures, Adam gave each one the ability to "reach beyond" its source in the ten utterances (including the combinations, permutations etc. of letters), and connect with its spiritual roots in the one utterance [above the ten utterances]. That is a far higher and revealed level of Godliness.

If He had created with one utterance, the Godly energy present in the world would have been so great that every creature would have been automatically subsumed within the infinite light of the Creator.

Now, we can understand the two opinions regarding Adam's naming of the creatures; 1) either Adam gave names to all creatures, including fish, or 2), Adam named only the creatures of the land. According to the explanation that calling the creatures by name was meant to finalize and perfect the process of creation, it was not necessary to call the fish by name. Fish already live within their source.[5] They and their life source are one — a fish out of water is detached from its source, and it dies. Fish are so much part of the water that, the moment they are removed, they are unable to survive. Since fish have no "need" to return to their spiritual source, they have no need for a name.[6] According to this opinion, only land creatures received names, since they were created with as separate, independent entities. It is only land creatures that need names, since their existence is independent of the environment. (Of course, animals need certain ecosystems in order to survive, but within their ecosystems they are capable of independent existence.)[7]

On the other hand, according to the opinion that by calling the names of the creatures, Adam attached them to their spiritual source in God, not only land animals but all creatures, including fish, need names. If the purpose of a name is to reveal the spiritual source of all creation, then it is necessary for every creation to have a name so that it can strive to connect with its divine source and become one with the Creator.

From Likutei Sichot of the Lubavitcher Rebbe, vol. 35, pp. 1–6

NOTES

1. The Rogachover Gaon (R' Yosef Rosen) in his work, *Tzaphnas Paneach*, points out two different ways of understanding the names that Adam gave to the creatures: Either the name is a *segula* that describes the nature of the creature, or it is a means for man to "acquire" (establish a connection with) the creature.

2. The *Chizkuni* (on verse 19) concludes, "And all which Adam called by its name ... [was] in order for him to know and remember their names when needed, for if God had called their names and taught them to man, he would not learn them quickly and therefore it would have been difficult for him get involved with them." Clearly the Chizkuni was of the opinion that the names of creatures were for the benefit of man.

3. Psalms 95:6 See Zohar Sect 1, 221B: Section 3, 107B, *Tikunei Zohar* 456 (90B), *Pirkei d'Rebi Eiezer* Ch 11, *Ohr HaTorah Va'era* end of Page 236.

4. According to the statement of the sages in *Pirkei Avot*, God "could have created the universe with one creative utterance," nevertheless, there would not have been any divisions or variations among the created beings had He done so. Variations and distinctions among creatures only occurred as the result of the remaining nine creative utterances.

5. Every creature in the universe possesses its own spiritual source above. Both categories — animals on the dry land and fish in the sea — at their source,

represent two worlds: hidden and revealed. Hidden worlds obtain their vitality from hidden powers such as letters of thought within the soul of man by way of example, while revealed worlds are created and maintained by revealed powers, when the letters of thought become revealed from their state of concealment as letters of thought. When they are revealed and become the source of creation, they are called *maamorot* ("utterances"), or the "word of God," or the "spirit of His mouth." (*Shaar Hayichud v'haemunah*, Ch. 11)

6. See *Midrash Talpiot* (Section on *Adam HaRishon* 20:4) in the name of *Sodi Raza*: "Creatures of the seas do not become ritually impure because man never named them." This means that since they never took on a final "form," they never become impure. Moreover, there is an opinion that fish never died in the flood, since they did not fall under the decree to "destroy all flesh." (Rashi on Genesis 7:22, Gemara *Sanhedrin* 108A)

7. According to the *Shaar Hayichud Vehaemunah*, which states that the vitality of every creature comes through the letters of its name, and originates from the ten creative utterances as they descended to create physical creatures, we have to conclude that the names of marine creatures, such as fish, are not so revealed. Indeed, the only name of fish that is mentioned in the Torah (in Isaiah 27:1, Psalms 74:14 and elsewhere) and in the works of the sages (Rashi in *Parshat Breishit* 1:29, *Baba Batra* 74B, in *Breishit Rabba* 7:4) is the "Leviatan," which is a name stemming from a word meaning *hithavruth*, or "joining." (see *Parshat Vayeitzei* 29:34 regarding Levi — "this time my husband will 'join with' me").

Righteous Is Relative

Noach 6:9

In the beginning of this week's Torah portion — *Parshat Noach* — we read that "Noach was a righteous man in his generation." Rashi tell us this implies that, "relative to his generation, Noach was righteous, but had he been born in Avraham's generation, he would not have been considered important at all."[1]

However, it is difficult to understand Rashi's comment, since Noach did live, at least for a time, in Avraham's generation. Indeed, when he did pass away at age 950, it was 58 years after the birth of Avraham. While it's true that, in his early years, Avraham did not have the spiritual stature that he later attained, nonetheless, during those 58 years, he had already discovered God and made the service of God his way of life.

In fact, Avraham used this time very well. Without the benefit of a teacher or spiritual guide, Avraham discovered the Creator by himself. All by himself, using his reason alone, Avraham figured out the existence of God and began to grow into the *tzaddik* that he would eventually become. This occurred during the lifetime of Noach, so it's difficult to understand why Rashi and the Midrash suggest that they were of different generations.[2]

But, by looking deeper into the life of Noach, we can find a clue.

Noach was a grandson of Chanoch and Metushelach, who operated a *Beit Midrash* ("study hall") as well as a *Beit Din* ("court of law").[3] Thus, Noach most probably learned all that he knew about God from them.

This knowledge didn't come from inside himself, as it did with Avraham, but from his family members who were his teachers.

In contrast, we can see how Avraham figured out, without any teachers, the existence of God. It appears his learning process took place in three stages.

1. There were his formative years in the Babylonian city of his birth, Ur Casdim, during which time he discovered his Creator and argued against the local idol worshipers. This earned him the wrath of the local king, who sought to execute him.
2. He then proceeded to another city, Charan, where he became famous for persuading people to forsake idol worship and adopt monotheism.
3. His crowning achievement, however, did not occur until years later when entered the land of Canaan, "and proclaimed the name of God, Lord of the universe, until thousands and tens of thousands gathered around him and they became the people of the house of Avraham, in whose hearts he successfully implanted this great principle." (Rambam, *Hilchot Avoda Zara* 2:3).[4]

Thus, Avraham's first steps in Ur Casdim were to successfully refute the arguments of the idol worshippers, and his second steps in Charan were to convince others of the correctness of his own monotheistic conclusions. But all of that wasn't equal to what he achieved in Canaan. Indeed, what Avraham managed to achieve in Canaan was beyond intellectual. He did more than merely convince the people to believe in one God. As a charismatic leader and spiritual luminary, he managed to start a revolution in the Holy Land.

People who came in contact with him were not merely persuaded by his towering intellect, as if it were an "external force" working on them from the outside. Instead, they acknowledged the truth of Avraham's philosophy from the very essence of their own beings. Using their own intellects, they arrived to Avraham's conclusions. Thus, his principles of monotheism became "implanted in them" and became part of their own outlook.

This is what the Rambam means when he says that Avraham was successful in "implanting this great principle" in the souls of the people of Canaan. Like Avraham himself, the people of his generation arrived at the appropriate intellectual conclusions of their own volition just like he did, which is why they were called the "generation of Avraham."

And that is what Rashi meant when he said that if Noach had lived in the "generation of Avraham," he would not have been important. Rashi pointedly did not say "during the lifetime of Avraham," but "during the generation." The "generation" of Avraham was comprised of those who came to accept his way of life because they, like Avraham, were convinced of the oneness of God.[5] They were not persuaded by Avraham's intellectual arguments alone, but by their own searching and reasoning, which led them to the same conclusion.

This occurred a long time after Noach passed away. Noach was alive only during the early years of Avraham's life, when Avraham was in Ur Casdim and in Charan, beginning on his path. It was a path that Noach was never to know because his own approach was different. Noach accepted God matter-of-factly, as he was taught, not because he found God on his own initiative. Therefore, unlike Avraham, he did not leave a lasting spiritual impression on his or any generation.

We find that it is the person whose belief system stems from his own understanding and analysis who is considered "important."[6] That's what Rashi means when he says that if Noach had lived in the "generation of Avraham," he would not have been important at all.

Adopted from Likutei Sichot of the Lubavitcher Rebbe,
vol. 20, pp. 13–24

NOTES

1. See the commentators on Rashi here (R' Eliyahu Mizrachi, the Gur Aryeh and others) who unanimously agree that had Noach lived in a generation of true *tzaddikim* and maintained the same level of righteousness that he achieved in his own generation, he would not have been considered significant at all. Their disagreement is over whether the Hebrew word *dorotav* ("in his generation") was meant to be praiseworthy or disgraceful.

2. The *Nitzutzei Zohar* (a commentary on the Zohar) suggests that the early days of Avraham's life were not called the "generation of Avraham" because at that time he was still called "Avram," and not "Avraham." However, we do not find that the sages made such a distinction — they referred to him as "Avraham" even when they mentioned him regarding the early period of his life (see *Brachot* 13a). Moreover, if we made such a distinction, we would find that it did not apply merely to his "early life," but to the majority of his life, since he did not receive the name Avraham until he was ninety-nine years old (Genesis 17:1)

3. Later the *Acharonim* could not find a source for this. Perhaps it is from the *Midrash Avchir*, found in the *Yalkut Shimoni, Breishit remez* 42, that Noach "recited 900 sets of Mishnah." The source that Metushelach had a *Beit Din* may be from *Pirkei d'Rebbi Eliezer* which mentions *ibur hodesh*, or the process of declaring a second day of the new month — which is a process that may only occur in a *Beit Din*.

4. The original edition of Rambam's *Mishneh Torah* (Kushta, 1509) calls this section, *Hilchot avoda zarah v'chukot hagoyim* — "Laws of idol worship and rules of the non-Jews." Later censored editions (including the editions that we possess, from Warsaw and Vilna) write, *Hilchot avodat cochavim u'mazalot v'chukot ha'acum* — "Laws of those who worship stars and constellations and rules of the non-Jews." Similar changes were printed in several places within the text of the *Mishneh Torah* itself (not only in the titles and headings).

5. See the Meiri in his introduction to *Pirkei Avot*: "[Avraham] turned the spirit of most of the world to faith in God." See also what the Meiri writes in connection to the education of Chanoch, Metushelach and Noach, before his comments on Avraham.

6. In this manner, we may explain Rashi at the beginning of *Parshat Lech Lecha* on the first verse: "And there I will make you into a great nation, while here you will not merit to have children, and moreover I will inform the world of your nature." Rashi does not mean to merely explain that Avraham will become famous and known in the world, but that his "nature" — as one who recognizes and publicizes Godliness (Avraham's "brand," so to speak) — will have an impact on the entire world. At that point, the generation is called the "generation of Avraham." And, of course, we know, because the Torah tells us, that at that point Avraham was already seventy-five years old (Genesis 12:4).

Windows for the Ark

Noach 6:16

In this week's Torah portion — *Parshat Noach* — God instructs Noach in the intricacies of building the ark that will house all of the species for the duration of the Flood.

Among other instructions, Noach is told, "Make a *tzohar* for the ark" (Genesis 6:16). Rashi gives us two possible translations for the Hebrew word *tzohar*: "window" or "precious stone."

Tzohar — implies "light," as in the *tzaharayim*, meaning "afternoon," the time of day when it brightest outside. Accordingly, Rashi focuses his commentary on what would produce light in the ark. The Torah verse seems to instruct Noach how to build the ark so that there would be light inside, and, within that framework, Rashi suggests that it will shine either through a window, or from a precious stone that will illuminate the ark.

However, if we are to understand Rashi's commentary as an explanation of the simple meaning of the text, there are several questions we are forced to ask:

1. The command is issued in the singular: "Make a *tzohar*..." indicating that whether this was a window or a shining stone, there was only one of them. And, therefore, we have to ask, how could one window or one shining stone have been sufficient to illuminate the entire ark which was 150 meters long, 50 meters wide and three stories high?[1]
2. Among the other instructions to Noach was one to build cubicles within the ark — enough cubicles of various sizes and shapes to

house all the various animals and species to be brought onto the ark. Even if the illumination from the window or the shining stone was intense and brilliant, how could it have lit up all of the various nooks and crannies of so many cubicles?[2]

3. There is a known principle of Rashi's commentary: If Rashi mentions more than one explanation of a Torah verse, then his first explanation is closest to the "simple meaning" of the text. Nevertheless, there must have been an issue regarding the first explanation that made it necessary for Rashi to seek a second explanation. The second explanation apparently resolves the issue, but it is further away from the "simple meaning" of the Torah text. So then we are left to wonder: What bothered Rashi initially that he sought to resolve with his first explanation, and what was the issue that necessitated a second explanation?[3]
4. When the first two explanations offered by Rashi are insufficient, he will often offer a third explanation that, while even more difficult than the previous two explanations will resolve the questions unanswered by the first two explanations. In this case, there is such an explanation, but it is not Rashi who mentions it. Another Torah commentator, Chizkuni suggests that the word *tzohar* is related to the word *yitzhar*, meaning "oil," and that the command to Noach was to bring oil onto the ark for the purpose of illuminating the ark. This explanation is hard to accept as the command was not to "bring *yitzhar* onto the ark," but rather to "make a *tzohar* for the ark." Nevertheless, the Chizkuni's explanation answers the big question: How can one window or shining stone illuminate the entire ark? His answer is that Noach lit up the ark by bringing in oil and wicks to make lamps. So, why does Rashi fail to mention this as a third plausible explanation in his commentary?

Later in *Parshat Noach*, the Torah tells us that "[the cycle] of day and night will not cease" (Genesis 8:22), and Rashi explains, "the implication is that during the Flood, the cycle of day and night did cease, since the heavenly bodies ceased to orbit, and it was impossible to distinguish between day and night."

Here, we see that our original question takes on even more relevance: There was no light at all during the Flood, so what would have been the purpose of a "window" that let in light? There was no light at all in the world for the entire forty days of the Flood!

But here is a way to resolve all of our questions regarding Rashi's commentary and then some:

While giving instructions to Noach as how to build the ark, God did not go into all of the details of the building. For example, when the rain subsided, the Torah tells us that, "Noach removed the covering of the ark" (Genesis 8:13). Yet, we do not find anywhere that God told Noach to make a covering for the ark. Similarly, we do not find anywhere that God commanded Noach to construct the hatch or opening that he used to send out the raven or the dove. Nor do we find that Noach was commanded to build a door to the ark. The reason is simple — when commanded to build the ark, it was assumed that Noach would include the normal components that are present in any "house" — such as a covering, a door and a window. It was not necessary to instruct Noach in all of the details, but rather to give him general guidelines (such as the size), and then Noach himself would be able to reason out what components were needed to complete the ark. It was only necessary to instruct Noach about the details that he could not have figured out by himself.

Accordingly, it was not necessary for God to command Noach to prepare illumination for the ark. It was understood and obvious to Noach that such illumination was necessary. The animals were all dependent upon Noach for their food and sustenance and, moreover, each species lived in its own cubicle. So, it is clear that Noach must have prepared either candles or oil, etc. to provide light on the ark, without needing to be prompted from Above.

But, if so, then still another question arises: Why did God command Noach to make a *tzohar* for the ark? Since, in any case, Noach knew to provide light, why was it necessary to command him to build *tzohar* if that was its purpose? We are forced to conclude that Noach was commanded to bring *additional* light into the ark.[4] Aside from the illumination that Noach naturally prepared, he was commanded to make a separate source of light (*ohr* from *tzohar*), in order to create even more illumination inside the ark.

And it is in relation to that additional light that Rashi provides his two explanations. The first of those explanations is that the additional light came from a window (because, after forty days of rain, the cycle of day and night was renewed). Even though this light did not add a lot of illumination to the ark, the window also had other functions, such allowing for the bringing in and taking out various items, or providing ventilation.

However, this explanation lacks credibility, since the word *tzohar* implies that its major function was to shed "light" and not to serve as a ventilator, etc. Moreover, as discussed above, light coming through a window could not possibly illuminate the entire ark, and light was not present at all until after the forty days of the Flood. And, therefore, Rashi brings a second explanation — that the *tzohar* was a "shining stone." A shining stone is a movable object, and it could have been taken from one place to another throughout the ark, much like we would use a flashlight to illuminate what it is necessary at any time.

Yet, this explanation also has its drawbacks — the verse says, "Make a *tzohar* for the ark, and not, "bring a *tzohar* into the ark," which would have been more appropriate language if this was the case. Moreover, why would God have commanded Noach to do something so unusual as to bring a precious shining stone onto the ark for the purpose of adding illumination? Since this explanation does not fit well with the simple meaning of the text, Rashi mentioned it as his second explanation, with the "window" as the first explanation.

There is another reason why Rashi chose "window" as his first explanation. Rashi's intention is to answer *all* questions that arise regarding the simple level of the Torah text. Yet, at first glance, he failed to resolve an obvious question — he did not explain why it was necessary to make a window. If it was there for the purpose of sending out the raven after the Flood, it was redundant, as it was possible to do so without it, by utilizing the main opening to the ark.

The answer is that, of his own volition, Noach would not have made a window. God had told him that the entire world would be destroyed in the Flood and even mentioned all the details of the destruction, including the cessation of normal cycles of day and night — so what point was there in making a window? There was nothing to see and no light to allow into the ark.

That is why it was necessary for God to issue a command to Noach to "make a window (*tzohar*) for the ark." In reality, the initial rains descended softly, in the hope that the people of Noach's generation would do *teshuvah* — that is, repent and return to God. At least for that initial period of time, the window did allow more light into the ark.

Additionally, the window made it possible to observe if the world did *teshuvah,* in which case the rains would turn into "rains of blessing" (*gishmei brachah*) — and there would be no devastation. But Noach could not know ahead of time how the rains would initially fall — if it would a soft or hard rain — and that is why it was necessary to issue a command to him to make a window.

Of course, this explanation only applies if the definition of *tzohar* is "window." It does not apply if the explanation of *tzohar* is "precious stone." In that case, when there was nothing to observe outside of the ark and no light to let in, the shining stone would have provided the necessary illumination.

Finally, within Rashi's two explanations, we find pearls of wisdom that reveal the inner structure of the Torah and its secrets. The difference between the light streaming from a window and the light of a shining precious stone is the difference between light from the outside and light emerging from within. Each category of light symbolizes a unique style of serving God. The ultimate purpose of fulfilling the mitzvoth of the Torah is to "make a *tzohar* for the ark" — to shed light and reveal Godliness in the world. This can be achieved in two different ways:

1. *By making a window.* The light already exists, it is present in the world, ready to be revealed. Businessmen, for example, run across examples of Divine Providence in their work, even more so than do Torah scholars who sit and learn Torah all day long. But in order to reveal this Godliness in the course of their work, they must remove the concealment that hides it. They have to tear asunder the "garment" of nature that hides Godliness. That is the first step in serving God — to create an opening or "window" in the garment of nature in order to reveal the Godliness concealed in the world.
2. After revealing Godliness in the world by creating a "window" in the garment of nature, we are able to ascend to a higher level of divine service. In the words of Rashi: "and there are those who say that the *tzohar* was a precious stone that shone." These are the people who have successfully created a "window" in the garment of nature. They showed that it is not only possible to reveal Godliness in nature, but it is possible to transform nature itself into something luminous that reveals Godliness. Through our divine service, we not only reveal Godliness but we and the

world become divine receptacles and together we reveal Godliness everywhere, just like a precious stone from which light emanates.

From Likutei Sichos of the Lubavitcher Rebbe, vol 10, page 19–23

NOTES

1. This question is especially strong in light of the fact that Rashi's comment is at variance with his commentary on the Talmud. There, (*Sanhedrin* 108b and *Yerushalmi Pesachim Perek* 1, *Halachah* 1), Rashi says that *tzohar* means "precious stones and pearls," in plural. Ibn Ezra suggests that although the terminology of the Torah is singular, the Torah really means plural, as in the language of Yaakov, "I have oxen and donkey…" (beginning of *Parshat Vayishlach*). However, if that were Rashi's intention, then Rashi should have written, "windows" (plural) in his explanation, rather than relying on language the occurs later in the Torah. Moreover, the fact that Rashi changes from his commentary in the Gemara proves that he really intended what he wrote — one window.

2. If the explanation of *tzohar* is "precious stone," then the simple understanding is that it was a shining stone that could be carried from one cubicle to another for the purpose of shedding light wherever necessary. But it would be very difficult to suggest that this was all the light that was present on the ark, especially since not only Noach but his children, as well were involved in feeding the animals, each one needed light, wherever they were.

3. Several commentators (*Gur Aryeh, Mizrachi, Levush Haorah*) ask, "According to those who say that *tzohar* means a "window," why didn't the scripture use the word "window" (*chalon*)?" Further on (Genesis 8:6), the Torah does mention "window": "And Noach opened the window of the ark (*chalon*)." But on the simple textual level, this is not a question, since the original commandment was about "light" (and not about ventilation or bringing objects in and out of the ark), and that is why the Torah uses the word *tzohar* that is indicative of light. But, after the *tzohar* was already present, it could also be used for other matters, such as sending out the raven, since it was, after all, a "window."

4. According to the opinion that *tzohar* means "window," it is doubtful whether Noach would have made the window without the command from God. Since he prepared candles, etc. to provide light in the ark especially during the forty days of the Flood, that would have made the extra "window" extraneous. Since making a window would have weakened the protection that the ark provided against rain and water, it was unlikely that Noach would have made this window of his own volition. But according to the opinion that *tzohar* means "precious stone," (Genesis 8:6), "And Noach opened the window of the ark," proves that Noach *did* make a window of his own volition.

Come into the Ark

Noach 7:1

In general, when we quote from Chassidic literature, it is from one of the Chassidic masters who developed a court of thousands of disciples, all of whom clung to his words and literally lived by his Torah. Occasionally though, we go back to the very source and quote something from the Ba'al Shem Tov, the founder of the Chassidic Movement. The Ba'al Shem Tov did not have a court in the normal sense; the entire Jewish world was his court. Like our forefather, Avraham, he did not wait for people to come to him — he went to them. He delivered the inner dimensions of Torah to the masses in one location, and then he moved on to another Jewish population center and repeated the act. That is how the Chassidic Movement got started. We will quote from him this week regarding our weekly Torah portion — *Parshat Noach.*

The Ba'al Shem Tov did not have a court in the normal sense; the entire Jewish world was his court.

Of course, the big event of *Parshat Noach* is the Flood — the boiling[1] water that covered the earth for forty days and forty nights, erasing all forms of terrestial life (except for the fauna and flora that Noach took into the ark with him), and purifying the earth, much like the 40 units of water of the *mikveh* purify man. The Hebrew word for "ark" — *teivah* — also means "word." And that is the basis of the Ba'al Shem Tov's explanation of the Torah portion for this week.

When the flood waters hit, God told Noach, *Bo el ha'teivah* — "Come into the ark" (Genesis 7:1). But the Baal Shem Tov tells us that the deeper meaning of this verse is: "Come into the words of Torah and prayer."

When the waters of the Flood washed over the earth, they came from two sources — from the *t'hom rabah* ("great chasm") and from the *arubot ha'shamayim* ("portals of the heavens").[2] That is, they came from both below and Above, threatening to overwhelm Noach. But God told him to enter the ark and bring with him his wife and children and his children's wives, together with all kinds of animals, plants and even minerals.

How are we to understand this in terms of our everyday activities in serving God? What is the equivalent of the "flood" in our everyday lives, and what is the "ark"?

In general, water that descends from Above in the form of rain is a blessing. It provides us with irrigation for our crops and supplies us with water to drink. But, the overwhelming waters of the Flood were a threat to mankind. Chassidic teachings refer to such waters as *mayim rabim* — "colossal waters." The "colossal waters" are the worries and anxieties of making a living. Even so, we say that such "colossal waters are unable to extinguish the love." All of the confusing thoughts and worries that wash over us, as we struggle to make a living, are still unable to overcome the love for God that exists in the Jewish heart.

In particular, such worries about making a living are divided into two categories: 1) they either come from the "great chasm," referring to worries about physical matters, or 2) they come from the "portals of the heavens," referring to worries about spiritual matters, such as supporting a Jewish school, for example.

Both categories of worry carry the potential to disturb our prayers and Torah study. If the worries come from "higher matters," such as how to support an educational system, they need not disturb our ability to learn or fulfill mitzvoth. Torah and prayers are what connect man to God and draw Godliness into the world. If that is missing, what benefit is there in all of the work on behalf of the public? If we claim that we are too "busy" with "higher matters" and cannot learn and pray as he should, then we are making a grave mistake. If all of our worries prevent us from doing what the Code of Jewish Law tells us to do, this means that we are not doing our job properly, and our so-called justification (that we are involved in "higher matters") is merely an "excuse," coming from our animal soul and not from our divine soul. And if we fail to take care of our own spiritual needs, by praying and learning properly, then our success with the "higher matters" of public service will also suffer.

The resolution to both cases (whether the Flood came from the "great chasm" or the "heavenly portals") is: *Bo el ha'teivah* — "Come into the words of Torah and prayer." For, as the Baal Shem Tov explained, *teivah* refers to this precisely. And his advice to us is to enter into these words, to be surrounded by them, and then without doubt nothing can overwhelm us, and our families will be safe.

"Entering the words of Torah and prayer" begins from the moment that we awaken in the morning, reciting *Modeh Ani* — "I acknowledge" — and continues through the morning blessings, when we recite the blessing *Malbish arumim* — "He who clothes the naked." Why should we recite such a blessing, when our clothes are placed before us and all that we need to do is to put them on?

From elsewhere in the teachings of the Baal Shem Tov, we know that "the one who is wise is the one who sees what is about to be born" — meaning, the one who is wise is the one who sees the future. Indeed, Chassidic teachings tell us that the wise man is the one who is able to detect the Godly energy in every object. The Godly energy renews that object every day, at every hour and at every instant. This Godly energy re-creates the world instantaneously, and our goal is to become aware of this constant, ongoing process.

In the Zohar (part 1, p. 199b, as well as part 2, 62b), the story is told of Rabbi Yeisa Sabah, who would pray every day for food, even though his food was already placed before him. Nevertheless, he would not eat before reciting his prayer requesting food. The obvious question is: Why pray regarding what is already placed in front of you? Why request what you already possess?

The answer is that the food (as well as the clothes we wear) has no existence of its own. If it were not renewed at every instant, it simply would not exist. If it weren't for the fact that God, in His eternal goodness, renews creation at every instant, there would be no food or clothes (or any other object of creation). And, therefore, it is appropriate to pray for the very food and clothes that we get, since whatever exists now is not the same as what existed one moment ago. It was re-created by the grace of God, and over that we must make a blessing as well as pray so that the process continues and we always receive what we need.

What enables us to develop this ability to "see what is born" — to detect the inner vitality that enlivens future creation?

It is *tefillah* — "prayer" — at the beginning of the day. Before we pray, we operate under the assumption that the universe "exists," that it is an independent entity that maintains itself with its own rules and principles. And, therefore, when we ask ourselves whether it is permitted to act in this or that way, we might say to ourselves, "as long as I do not know that it is forbidden, I will assume that it is permitted." But, after prayer — which includes meditation upon the principles of Godliness that enliven the world — we realize that the world is not independent and does not maintain itself. Only the One Above determines if and how the universe is created and re-created. The entire creation does not really and truly exist, since all that really and truly exists is God Himself.

And, therefore — after prayer — when questions arise whether it is permissible to do this, that, or other activity, we are likely to reach a conclusion that is opposite of the one just mentioned. Rather than assuming that the action is permitted unless we know otherwise, we assume that it is forbidden unless expressly permitted by Jewish law. Moreover, even matters that are permitted but unnecessary in our lives become boundaries that we do not wish to cross, since they do not further the goal of turning the world into a dwelling place for God. After prayer that reminds us of the true nature of creation, we become more precise in our observance, since we are aware of the presence of God and that nothing takes place without His constant supervision. As the Chassidic saying goes, "What is forbidden is forbidden. And what is permitted — we don't necessarily need."[3]

Another message that emerges from our parsha is not to become overly involved in our own spiritual well being, to the extent that we ignore others. The verse (Gen 6:18) reads, "...you will enter the ark, yourself and your children and wife, and the wives of your children with you." Your "children," according to our sages, is interpreted to include "students" — those whom we have taught so they are like our "children." This verse then instructs us not to neglect others, but to teach them and bring them as well "into the ark" — into the world of Torah and mitzvoth. We cannot become so wrapped up and absorbed in our own spiritual search and journey that we neglect others.

This, then is the message of the Baal Shem Tov:

"Come into the *teivah*" means to be totally immersed and surrounded by words of Torah and prayer at all times. And once this has penetrated our awareness — that nothing but Torah and prayer are important since nothing truly "exists" aside from God Himself — then our involvement in physical matters itself becomes a path of spiritual growth. At that point, there is no possibility for the *mayim rabim* — the "colossal waters" — to overwhelm us. If nothing exists but holy matters, and all of our needs are met and permeated with Godliness, then what is to stop us from fulfilling the words of the verse (in Proverbs 3:6): *Bekol derachecha da'eihu* — "In all of your ways, know Him."

From Torat Menachem, vol. 18,
page 156 of the Lubavitcher Rebbe, ztz'l

NOTES

1. From the Midrash we know that the water coming from the *t'hom*, or depths of the earth, was boiling water.

2. Gen 7:11

3. From the letters of the Frierdiker Rebbe, the *Rayatz*, vol 4, Page 74 (and published in *Hayom yom*, 25 Adar Sheni)

Go Out of the Ark

Noach 8:16

There is something strange about the end of the Flood story. After the waters receded and it was clear that the flood had run its course, Noach didn't want to come out of the ark. Indeed, God had to tell him, "Go out of the ark, you, your wife, your sons, and your sons' wives with you" (Genesis 8:16). Why was that command necessary?[1]

After a year being cooped up with hungry animals and restless beasts, Noach could have been expected to rush out of the ark with tremendous relief and gratitude, and yet we see that he was reluctant to leave. Not only that, but a command was also necessary in order to remove the animals from the ark — "Bring out with you every living thing, all flesh that is with you…" (Genesis 8:17).

The Midrash (*Tanhuma Noach* ch.8) says that, since Noach received permission from God to enter the ark, he did not want to leave the ark without explicit permission to disembark as well. However, Rashi does not mention this Midrash, which is a sign that it is not an explanation on the simple level. In addition, Noach never really wanted to enter the ark in the first place, which is why a special command had to be issued for him to do so. And, therefore, it is reasonable to assume that, after the Flood, he would have wanted to leave as soon as possible.

Perhaps the commandment to leave the ark was not about the departure but about the details of life within the ark. For example, upon boarding the ark, not only Noach and his wife but all the creatures were forbidden to have sexual relations. Normal relations were again permitted only after they left the ark. Perhaps that was why the command to leave the ark was necessary; it made sexual relations once again permissible.

However, Rashi makes it clear this was not the case. Regarding the command to remove the animals from the ark, Rashi comments, "Take them out ... if they don't want to go, bring them [even against their will]." So, even if one of the *reasons* to leave the ark was for the animals to once again engage in reproduction, it is clear that the *command* itself applied only to leaving the ark, but not to anything afterward.

An explanation found in Chassidic literature, where it says that the situation in the ark was similar to what we will experience in the future, when the Mashiach arrives. The Mashiach will usher in an era of peace, when "the wolf will dwell with the lamb ..." (Isaiah 11:6–9). It seems that this was already the case on Noach's ark, where all species of animals dwelt together. This is also evident from the simple meaning of the text. The Torah verse tells us that Noach built "nests" in the ark (Genesis 6:14), and Rashi explains that each animal and beast had its own cubicle.[2] Nevertheless, it's difficult to believe that for a full year, such beasts were able to remain in their own cubicles and avoid harming or destroying other animals. Moreover, it takes a full team of trainers, veterinarians and maintenance men to care for a zoo, and yet, on the ark, we find only Noach and his sons caring for multiple representatives of all the animals in the world![3]

It must be that something about the ark changed the nature of the wild animals, allowing them to live harmoniously with each other, similar to the situation that we are told will exist in the Messianic Era.

So, it must be that something about the ark changed the nature of the wild animals, allowing them to live harmoniously with each other, similar to the situation that we are told will exist in the Messianic Era.[4]

But, if so, why doesn't Rashi say so in his commentary? Rashi's task is to explain the simple meaning of the text, so why doesn't he tell us that a miracle occurred which allowed all of the animals to peacefully co-exist on the ark? The answer is that Rashi did hint at this miracle earlier on (in his commentary on Genesis 6:20), when he explained that the animals who boarded the ark were "only those who bonded with their own species, without mixing with other species, and who came of their own volition onto the ark; all that the ark was capable of sheltering were brought in."

So, Rashi said that: 1) only certain chosen animals entered the ark; 2) even before entering the ark, the chosen animals were recognizable because they refrained from harming any other animals; 3) the very fact that they came onto the ark of their own volition and entered was a miracle; 4) the ark itself "selected" which animals were allowed, and the permitted ones prevented the entry of the others.

Since this change in their nature occurred as the animals entered the ark, it is reasonable to assume that it continued during their entire period while they were aboard the ark. All of the time that they were on the ark, the animals retained their tame nature, refraining from hurting or harming any other animal.

(Rashi, in his commentary on Genesis 7:23, mentions a Midrash which relates that, at one time, Noach was late in bringing a meal to a lion, which then mauled him in anger. However, this was a one-time event that was the fault of Noach. Moreover, Rashi mentions it only as a secondary explanation, meaning that he doesn't believe that it is the primary explanation of the simple meaning of the text.)

Now, we can understand why specific commands were necessary in order to get both Noach and the animals to leave the ark. Noach found himself in a situation similar to what will be in the Messianic Era. He experienced a high spiritual illumination on the ark, as if the Messianic Era had already arrived. That is why Noach was reluctant to disembark. Leaving the ark implied a spiritual descent. This applied to the animals as well who, while on the ark, lived peacefully among themselves. Why would they desire to return to the "wild," to their former nature as malicious predators or as vulnerable prey? Therefore, a commandment was necessary to compel both Noach and the animals to overcome their reluctance to leave the ark and venture back into the world.

Not only that, but that very commandment must have opened up for Noach and for the animals a new spiritual world, one that surpassed even what they experienced on the ark.

Life was good on the ark, as previously mentioned. All the needs of the animals were taken care of, and they had no need to search for food. As for Noach and his family, they worked hard, but they also experienced a spiritual level beyond what they had known before the Flood. There was only one thing missing — the ability to reproduce. Forbidden while on the ark, marital relations resumed upon leaving. In fact, the first thing that Noach and the animals were commanded to do when they left the ark was to be fruitful and multiply. As their first commandment, it was clearly not a side-issue, but the main issue. It was time to re-populate and re-build the world destroyed by the Flood.[5]

Everything physical has a spiritual counterpart Above. The ability to "be fruitful and multiply" — to give birth - is similar to creation itself. Creation is dependent upon the infinite light of the Creator, as is the process of bringing offspring into the world.

During his time on the ark, Noach was exposed to high spiritual revelation, concomitant with his ability to absorb Godliness. This could only take place within the confines of his own soul, which was limited by his body. But, the ability to bring offspring into the world, as well as to illuminate the world with Godliness, came from the Creator Himself and was, therefore, unlimited. It was this Godly energy that Noach was commanded to reveal in the world after the Flood. So, while he was reluctant to leave the ark, with its spirituality reminiscent of the Messianic Era, he was pulled into the brave new world after the Flood by the promise of revelation of the infinite light of God, corresponding to the mitzvah to "be fruitful and multiply."

Our generation has also emerged from another kind of flood — the Holocaust which destroyed a full third of world Jewry. It is incumbent upon us to rebuild the world, to re-populate the Jewish people. Again, as in Noach's generation, we have to place the emphasis on the first mitzvah of *peru u'revu* — "be fruitful and multiply."

Our generation has also emerged from another kind of flood — the Holocaust which destroyed a full third of world Jewry. It is incumbent upon us to rebuild the world, to re-populate the Jewish people.

The sages said that the Messianic Era will arrive when all the Jewish souls have been brought down into a body, in order to completely fulfill all 613 mitzvoth. Even if we wonder why we should bring children into this world, not only because of the Holocaust, but because of the difficulties inherent in raising children and providing them with their spiritual and physical needs, the answer is that it's not for us to ask questions — it's up to us to fulfill the commandment and, thereby, bring the infinite light of God into revelation in the low physical world in which we live.[6]

From Likutei Sichot of the Lubavitcher Rebbe,
vol. 25, pp. 28–37

1. The question is especially pertinent in light of the fact that all that took place before this command was at the initiative of Noach. For example, it was Noach who opened the ark and sent out the raven and the dove to examine whether the waters had receded (though it is possible to distinguish between testing the waters and actually exiting the ark).

2. R' Mizrachi on Rashi wrote, "There were *kilin* — "rooms" — for each and every animal to dwell in on its own. (See also Ibn Ezra and Radak on the verse.) However, from *Breishit Rabba* (31:9), it is not necessary to assume that each and every animal and beast had its own dwelling inside the ark. This seems to be proven further on in *Breishit Rabba* (31:11), where we find a difference of opinion regarding how many rooms there were, though obviously, there was no difference of opinion about how many animals and beasts were present on the ark [although, see the *Pirkei d'Rebi Eliyhau* here; "from here we learn that there were 32 species of fowl, and 365 insects"]. (Also see Rashi on *Breishit Rabba* where he explains that *kilin* are large rooms, while *madorim* were compartments within each large room containing the needs of the animals. But in his commentary on the Torah, Rashi says that there were "rooms for each and every animal and beast.) In *Ohr HaTorah* of the Tzemach Tzedek (p. 637b), "They did not have special rooms for each one of them," and in the series of Chassidic discourses, *Vechacha* of the Rebbe Maharash (p. 154), he writes, "Although Noach was commanded to make rooms within the ark, the command did not require the rooms to be specific to particular species, such that one animal could not enter the space of another." And in the Rebbe Rashab's set of discourses of the year 5677/1917 p. 47, after mentioning that according to Rashi, "rooms for every animal and beast," he says, "It's possible that there were a great number more animals (than 900)." But Rashi does not mention how many rooms were in the ark, and the simple understanding of his comment is that there was a room for each and every beast and animal.

3. According to the Ramban (on *Noach* 9:5, *Bechukotai* 26:6, and also according to the Radak on *Breishit* 1:25), before the sin of Adam and Chavah, the animals did not attack one another, so what occurred in the ark was not new, but a return to the situation that existed before the sin. But it is very difficult to claim that Rashi shared this point of view because, if so, Rashi should have stated so explicitly. On the other hand, we cannot suggest that there was no change of nature at all, since the animals ate only vegetables (as Rashi explains in *Breishit* 1:29–30: "all animals were equal and were permitted to eat all vegetation"). Rashi explains explicitly that there was no such a thing as a wild beast who did attack (see Rashi on *Breishit* 1:22, 4:15, *Noach* 9:5). See also *Likutei Sichot* of the Lubavitcher Rebbe, vol. 20, p. 7.

4. This is the reason that it was necessary for the animals and beasts to leave the ark and return to their former nature. Their exit from the ark paved to way to return to "be fruitful and multiply," which reveals the infinite power of the One Above. See *Likutei Torah* (*Shir haShirim* 40a): "The animals have the ability to reproduce because their sustenance comes from vegetation growing from the

ground, in which is found the power to reproduce, since 'The beginning is wedged into the end.'" (*Sefer Yetzira*)

5. This is the true content of *bitachon* (trust in God). See *Cad Hakemach* in the section on *bitachon*. And see the letter of the Previous Rebbe (*Igrot Hakodesh*, vol. 6, p. 399). *Likutei Sichot* vol. 3, p. 883, as well as vol. 26, p. 97 and vol. 31, p. 3.

Atmospheric Change

Noach 8:22

There are times that we have to stretch our imagination, in order to adapt to the timeframes of the Torah and gain a true understanding of events recounted therein. This week's Torah portion — *Parshat Noach* — is a case in point. As we come to learn, the Flood occurred at an important nexus in time, which shifts us from one epoch to the next.

To grasp this concept, first let us analyze the situation of the world before and after the Flood. On the one hand, the Torah tells us that, after the Flood, "Never again ... will sowing and harvesting, cold and hot, summer and winter, day and night cease" (Genesis 8:22). God promised that the cycles of time — that did not function during the Flood, when God unleashed the roiling waters that engulfed the earth — will never again cease functioning, under any circumstances. He made a covenant with creation after the Flood that He would never again destroy the world. This, of course, added a new dimension to creation.

Although at the time when He created the world, God had pronounced it "very good" (Genesis 1:31), nevertheless, until the Flood, there was always the potential that man's transgressions would result in destruction, as indeed took place when the floodwaters engulfed the earth. But, afterwards, the covenant that God made with creation ensured that the seasons of the solar cycle and of the orbit of the earth would never cease.

That said, we find that man's life span shortened after the Flood. As the Ramban (commenting on Genesis 5:4) wrote, "Prior to the Flood, men lived long lives," but after the Flood, "their days were shortened and minimized." This seemingly diminished the status of creation — since man is its apex, the entire universe was diminished when his days were shortened.

We may understand this apparently contradictory set of circumstances — a promise of no further wholesale destruction but a shortened lifespan — by considering a deeper transformation that took place in the world after the Flood.

The purpose of creation was for the Torah — which existed before creation — to be put into action, which would happen when the Jews started fulfilling its mitzvoth. Therefore, it was necessary that, at the time of the giving of the Torah, creation contain the same elements that were present within it from the start. Since the purpose of the Torah is to join the higher spiritual levels with the lower physical levels of creation, both had to be present in creation — both higher and lower elements had to be built *into* the creation, in order for them to "come together" when the Torah was given. In order that "the lower world would ascend to the upper world and the upper would descend to the lower" (*Midrash Tanhuma Va'era* 15), both "upper" and "lower" had to exist. And it was precisely regarding these "upper" and "lower" elements of creation that a transformation took place after the Flood.

We can best understand this transformation by examining the rainbow. The rainbow was the "sign" that God gave after the Flood, signifying His intention to never again destroy the world. Biblical commentators tell us that the rainbow is a "natural" phenomenon — when the sun's rays strike clouds in a certain manner, the result is a rainbow. If so, they ask, how could the rainbow be a sign of God's divine intention to never again destroy the world? How could a naturally occurring phenomenon be a divine sign?

Their answer is astounding — they tell us that before the Flood, there was no such thing as a rainbow. The circumstances that allow for a rainbow occurred only after the Flood. Prior to the Flood, the conditions leading to a rainbow just did not exist.

So what changed? The atmosphere changed.

Prior to the Flood, the vapors that arose from the earth to form clouds were thick and impenetrable. They were not capable of reflecting sunlight. Indeed, the entire physical universe was coarse, which is why the clouds were thick as well. The physical creation reflects a higher spiritual reality, and since the spiritual reality at the time was that what was "higher" did not descend, the "lower" realm remained "thick" and impenetrable to spirituality. The effect of the Flood was to refine and purify the earth, as well as the entire physical universe. And, for that reason, the vapors arising from the earth to form clouds after the Flood were more highly distilled than previously. In fact, they were fine enough to refract the sun's rays in the manner that we see today — to form a rainbow.

Prior to the Flood, the entire world existed on a lower level that was not subject to refinement and purification, and that is why the Flood occurred. After the Flood, the world became a place that could be uplifted and purified through man's divine service. Therefore, the rainbow serves as a sign from Above, since it expresses the new purity and refinement that imbued the world after the Flood.

Nevertheless, not all is clear here. The Flood had the effect of rendering the earth refined enough to sustain a rainbow. But, the very reason the Flood occurred was because of man's transgressions. It was man's deeds that lowered the earth to the state of impurity and coarseness that could be rectified only by the Flood. But the Flood lifted the earth even above its previous level — to a new status that it did not possess even at the time that the earth was created. So, the rainbow not only indicated the new purity and refinement of the earth, it also indicated a new level that was not present before the Flood, or even at the beginning of creation when its physical condition did not permit the existence of a rainbow!

The way to grasp this is as follows:

The perfect and elevated status of the world, upon creation, had nothing to do with its own qualities. It had everything to do with the will and desire of the Creator, who created a beautiful world including animals, plants and minerals of all sorts. It was a complete and perfect world as created, but its status was not due to any inherent qualities of its own, but rather due to the Creator alone. It was only because of the kindness of God that His creation possessed any status whatsoever.

The quality of refinement presently found in creation arrived only after the Flood.[1] That is when, after purifying the world, God instilled a new element in creation, enabling it to ascend and become refined. And that is why the rainbow occurred at precisely this juncture in history. Even though a rainbow is the product of both clouds and sun's rays, the main element is the clouds. The sun's rays all appear identical until they encounter the clouds, which refract them into the spectrum of colors that we see in the rainbow. The clouds themselves are the product of mist and vapor that arise from the ground. Only if the mist and vapor are sufficiently refined do they reflect the sun's rays in a manner that results in a rainbow.

The potential for refinement of the earth — which, in turn, gave rise to a more refined vapor that forms the clouds — was a novel element that was introduced to the world only after the Flood. That is precisely the reason that the rainbow made its appearance in the world at that time. God instilled in the clouds the potential to form a rainbow. The "mist arising from the earth" (Genesis 2:6) became more fine and, therefore, capable of reflecting the light of the sun.

Now we can understand why God's supernal will that created the world in such a perfect and amazing manner (so much so that God found His creation to be "very good") could not, nevertheless, prevent the Flood. Yet this same Creator who allowed His creation to descend to such a level of depravity that it had to be destroyed, now announced that even if the world returned to such a low state, He would "never again cut off all life"?

How could such a dichotomy exist?

Once we understand that, initially, creation attained its status only because it was formed by God (and not because it possessed an inherent status of refinement), we can also understand that man's sins could lower the status of the creation so much that no "fixing" was possible. At that point, the Flood became necessary. The sins of the generation of the Flood so coarsened creation that no rectification could undo what they had done. (And this is why Noach's rebuke to his neighbors, warning them that "God is about to bring a Flood" had no effect on them and failed to arouse them to do *teshuvah*, i.e. repentance.[2]) The world reached such a state of corruption and impurity that there was simply no reason to maintain it any longer.

God desired a perfect world. Once it turned into a world that was foreign to His will, He destroyed it. But after the Flood, the One Above instilled within the world the potential for refinement and purification, so that even if it did descend into a deep state of corruption, the possibility existed for it to emerge from this state via *teshuvah*. Because the world had the potential to return to what God wants it to be, it became a world in which He has a permanent and eternal interest. At that point it became reasonable for God to declare that He would never again destroy His creation under any circumstances.

Now, we may finally answer our initial question: How is it that, on the one hand, the Flood strengthened the status of creation, since God promised afterwards that He would never again destroy the world, and that He would never allow the cycles of day and night to cease, while, on the other hand, we see an apparent weakening in the status of creation as people began to live shorter lives?

With our newfound understanding that a new epoch in the history of the world arose after the Flood, we can conclude that these two outcomes are not opposite to one another. Indeed, both stem from the same cause. Both are a result of the new condition that prevailed after the Flood — for the first time, the world had the potential for *teshuvah* and, therefore, its own refinement.

Before the Flood, the world was maintained simply by God's kindness. After the Flood, the world continued to exist not only because of God's kindness but mainly because built into it was a mechanism for spiritual ascent. After the Flood, God has continuously re-created the world because of the world's own qualities, which include a built-in potential for refinement and elevation. In other words, after the Flood, the world can continue to exist forever, for reasons that are built into the world itself.[3]

And that is the reason for both outcomes that were described earlier. God "adjusts," so to speak, the nature of the energy that goes into re-creating the world:

1) Since the world itself became a more hospitable place for God (who is unchanging and invariable), He now maintains it in a way that is unchanging and invariable by promising not to destroy it.
2) The world became inherently "weaker" because it became entirely dependent upon God's creative "input" in order to remain in existence. Without His constant "input," the world would disappear. Therefore, God adjusts the level of energy and grants to the world the level that is necessary to maintain it. It is no longer the perfect world that God originally created, and one of the results is a shorter life span for man.

The two epochs mentioned above — first the epoch prior to the Flood, during which the world was sustained from God's kindness and will alone (not due to any traits of its own), and the second epoch following the Flood, when the world was (and continues to be) sustained based upon its own potential for refinement — served as an introduction to the third epoch, called the "two thousand years of Torah" (*Sanhedrin* 97a). This epoch began in the days of Avraham. It was during Avraham's life that the joining of the "upper realms" with the "lower realms" began to occur, as an introduction to the giving of the Torah. This also explains why Avraham and Sarah gave birth to Yitzchak after they were already well advanced in years (Avraham was 100 years old, and Sarah 90 years old). Yitzchak's late birth gave expression to the nexus between the two epochs.

Even though Avraham's advanced age was considerably less than the ages of the generations that preceded him (since his post-Flood generation was no longer sustained from above nature, by God's kindness alone, but rather from a level that was natural/inherent in creation), nevertheless, he fathered Yitzchak at this advanced age.

The connection between the two epochs came into expression specifically at the birth of Yitzchak, who was the first person born Jewish (Avraham became Jewish only after intellectual investigations which led him to disavow idol worship), whose descendants received the Torah, which captures the concept of joining the "upper" with "lower" realms.

From Likutei Sichot, vol. 15, pp. 49–57

NOTES

1. This is the reason that eating meat was not permitted until after the Flood (*Sanhedrin* 59b, Rashi on *Bereishit* 1:29, *Noach* 9:3). One who is ignorant of Torah matters (an *am haaretz*) may not eat meat (*Pesachim* 49b), "because he is unable to spiritually elevate the meat," and the meat "will make him coarse" (*Likutei Torah* of the Alter Rebbe *Behaalotcha* 31, col. 3, as well as p. 33 and elsewhere…)

2. Adam and Kayin both lived many generations before the Flood, and yet they did *teshuvah*, and their *teshuvah* was so effective that it removed the decree from them. But that may have been as a result of their association with *Gan Eden* (both Adam and Kayin were born in *Gan Eden*) which transcends the physical world.

3. This is not in contradiction to what is written, that "All twenty-six generations prior to the giving of the Torah were sustained by the kindness of *Hashem*" (*Pesachim* 118a) because, within this, there were several levels.

Avraham's Intellectual Development

Lech Lecha 12:1

There are several opinions about Avraham's age when he "discovered" God. One opinion says that he was three years old (*Talmud Nedarim* 32b), another says he was forty (*Radak parshat Toldot 26:5*), yet another says he was forty-eight (*Breishit Rabba* 30:8), and still another says fifty (*Pesikta Rabati*).

However, the Rambam (*Hilchot Avoda Zarah* 1:3) says that Avraham was forty years old when he recognized God,[1] and this leads us to ask: a) why did Rambam choose forty, when there were other opinions, and b) why was it necessary for him to mention any age whatsoever?

Upon looking closer and analyzing what the Rambam writes about Avraham (in his *Mishneh Torah*, at the very beginning of *Hilchot Avodah Zarah*, "Laws of Idol Worship"), we see the following progression:

1. At the outset (in the first *halachah*), the Rambam states, "In the days of Enosh, people committed a grave error…" He goes on to say that they knew God had created the universe, but thought that He imparted independent existence to His creations. Therefore, they concluded that it was appropriate to praise and honor those creations as "intermediaries." The Rambam explains that this intellectual error led people "to build edifices for the worship of the heavenly bodies, to serve them offerings, to praise them verbally and to bow down to them. They did all this in an attempt to manipulate God's will … and this was idol worship."

2. Then (in the second *halachah*), the Rambam states, "as time went on, there appeared false prophets who claimed that God commanded people to worship a particular celestial host, etc. ... As the days passed, God was forgotten and no-one recognized Him ... aside from isolated individuals such as Enosh, Metushelach, Noach, Shem and Eiver, and so time went on until that pillar of the world was born — Avraham our father."
3. Finally, (in the third *halachah*), the Rambam explains at length how Avraham came to recognize his Creator, and how he implanted in the hearts of thousands upon thousands of people the "main principle" of recognizing and serving the one God. Avraham also succeeded in passing this on to his son Yitzchak and his grandson Yaakov. Ultimately, God chose the descendants of Avraham, by then the Nation of Israel, and gave them the Torah through Moshe our teacher.

Why such a lengthy treatise on history?

The *Mishneh Torah* is a legal code, an explanation of the mitzvoth and *halachot* to help Jews properly conduct themselves in everyday life. In such a legal code, what place is there for stories and biographies?[2] What instruction for everyday life comes from this long digression about how idol worship got started and what Avraham did about it?[3]

It seems that the Rambam wrote the first chapter of *Hilchot Avodah Zarah* as an introduction to the rest of the laws of idol worship. Although the main body of his work deals with prohibitions against specific actions, firstly the Rambam establishes that idol worship begins with thoughts of the mind and stirrings of the heart. When a person begins to equate a creature, an angel or a planet with God, or even to consider it an independent intermediary, he has already committed a serious sin, because "he knows that God is the Creator, yet he serves this creature as did Enosh [who also knew the truth but was nevertheless an idolater]." As the Rambam goes on to explain in the first *halachah*:

> "This is what the Torah warned about, meaning that we should not cast about in our heart arguing that this or that has influence on the world the world and that God put them here ... [so we can] serve and bow down to them. About this He commanded us and said that we should not err in the thoughts of our [mind and feelings of our] heart

to serve these entities as if they were intermediaries between us and the Creator."

Further on, the Rambam says that this is why "God commanded us not to read books [about idol worship] at all and not to think about this subject at all ... and not only is thought about idol worship forbidden, but any thought that causes us to part with the ways of the Torah is forbidden."

From this it is understood that in order to properly obey the laws against idol worship, it isn't enough to know how not to act. It is first and foremost necessary to beware of our thoughts — and that is why the Rambam writes at such length about it in the introduction to *Hilchot Avodah Zarah*. First and foremost, we must know and understand in our mind that all the creatures and creations of the world possess no independent existence, and that, therefore, there is no good reason to impart to them any importance, or worse, to serve them. Furthermore, this introduction is relevant to the fulfillment of all the commandments, since denying idolatry is "the foundation" of serving God (end of fourth *halachah*).[4]

In the first two *halachot*, the Rambam explains the grave intellectual error of Enosh and his generation, which ultimately led to entire generations worshipping idols and forgetting about God. In the third *halachah*, the Rambam traces the history of the reversal of this trend. This began with Avraham, and the story of his awakening corresponds inversely to the process that led to idol worship:

1. While still among idol worshippers in Ur Casdim, Avraham started to "grasp the true path and understand the right direction." At this point, Avraham did not yet negate idol worship, even though he was having doubts. This stage corresponds inversely to the process that Enosh underwent, since Enosh began to worship idols while still among those who served the one God.
2. How did Avraham pursue his intellectual search? The Rambam writes: "He wondered how it was possible that a planet could continue eternally on its path, without anything moving it. Who was moving it along, for is it possible for anything to move itself? ... His heart was inquiring and starting to understand." That is, Avraham came to a tentative conclusion that even if the planet (or any other creature) truly exists, it is still under the dominion and sway of the one God. Here also we see how Avraham's process corresponded in an inverse fashion to the process that Enosh

underwent. Enosh claimed that even if God is one, it was still possible to serve intermediaries because they possess independent existence.

3. And finally, Avraham came to the conclusion that "there is only one God who moves the planet and created everything." That is, no aspect of creation has a truly independent existence of its own, and the only reality is the one God. Again, in this conclusion of his thought, Avraham stood in diametric opposition to the conclusion of Enosh's train of thought, which led people to forget about God completely, while Avraham's conclusion led people back to the certain knowledge that there is only one God and everything else owes its existence to Him.

If we follow Avraham's intellectual process, it becomes clear that idol worship should be totally unacceptable to anyone because it defies logic. In fact, it is observation of creation that leads us to the correct conclusion, as occurred with Abraham.[5] It is clear that creation possesses no independent existence of its own; it is entirely dependent upon and subservient to the One Above. This is how Avraham ultimately concluded that "there exists only one God who moves the planets and created everything."

So, as an introduction and basis for all of the *Hilchot Avodah Zarah*, the Rambam establishes that it is not enough for us to merely avoid actual physical practice of idol worship. It is vitally important that, in our heart and mind, we recognize the truth. There should be no room for intellectual error — we need to *know* that none of the inhabitants of the universe have true existence of their own. To even think anything else is already to plant the seeds of idol worship.

And now, we can also understand why the Rambam chose to mention Avraham's age at the time that he came to this knowledge — forty years old.

Pirkei Avot ("Ethics of the Fathers") tells us that, at forty, man reaches *binah* ("understanding") because it is at this age that man reaches the peak of his intellectual maturity and he experiences validation and confirmation of all that he knows to be true. Although Avraham's pursuit of truth certainly began much earlier, the Rambam wanted to emphasize the intellectual nature of Avraham's conclusions and, therefore, he cited the age at which Avraham completed his process. If the Rambam had cited the age at which he began, we might have understood that Avraham's conclusions were not associated with his intellect, but with the miraculous events of his search (such as being saved from Nimrod's furnace, etc.).[6] Instead, the Rambam cited not the age at which Avraham began, but the age at which he attained full recognition of his Creator — forty years old. Without doubt, Avraham's quest continued after this age but, since forty also corresponds to a natural milestone in intellectual maturity, that is the age that the Rambam cited. In so doing, he emphasized and underscored the intellectual nature of the mistake that led to idol worship, as well as what can be done to prevent it.

Of course, even when he reached the peak of his intellectual prowess, Avraham did not stop there. The Rambam tells us that Avraham immediately began preaching to his fellow man: "He travelled, called and gathered the people from one city to the next," persuading them of the truth of his path, "gathering around him thousands and tens of thousands, who became the 'people of Avraham's house,' and he implanted this great principle in their heart." With his intellectual proofs, Avraham succeeded in uprooting idol worship and converting many people to the path of truth, which he "instilled in their hearts." All of this emphasizes the power of the truth that Avraham revealed, which countered idol worship.

But then, we need to understand the continuation of the Rambam's narrative (in the third *halachah*), in which he informs us that after Yaakov's sons became a "nation that recognizes God, although they lived on in Egypt," they "learned how to serve idols like [the Egyptians], and almost uprooted the principles that Avraham had instilled within them."

This passage in the Rambam seems to contradict the entire content that was mentioned previously in which he established that man, through his own intellectual devices, rejected idol worship and recognized God. Yet, here, he states that "even the nation that knew God," went back to learning the ways of idol worship and engaging in it as well!

But, this becomes clarified when we continue reading what the Rambam says:

> "Out of love for us, God sent Moshe, our teacher and master of all prophets. Then Moshe prophesied and God chose the Jewish people as His inheritance, crowning them with mitzvoth and informing them how to serve Him in all ways, obeying the laws against idol worship and what to do regarding those who err in this regard..."

Previously, in his introduction, the Rambam emphasized that any form of idol worship whatsoever had no place and no "existence." He noted that this is an intellectual point that man is capable of grasping, as well as a natural conclusion to any logical investigation. Yet — and here is the important point — man cannot rely solely upon his own intellect to protect himself from idol worship. Intellect is not and cannot be the only basis on which to rely in our attempts to negate idol worship, nor the basis on which to recognize the one and only Creator and worship Him. As we have seen regarding what happened to the Jews in Egypt, it is possible to recognize God, and then to return to idol worship. In order to avoid this error, it is necessary to add another ingredient — the teachings of Moshe:

"Out of God's love for us — He sent Moshe our teacher and directed him to us give us [the Torah and its] mitzvoth and informed us how to serve Him."

From this we learn that not only recognition of God, but also how to serve Him (which in the days of Avraham was known only to specific individuals) comes from God Himself, via His prophet Moshe. It is possible that this is more than a philosophical point, but also a halachic ruling — even one who fully negates idol worship and recognizes God as the only one to serve, must do so not because he himself decided this out of logic, but because so he was commanded to do so by God, through His prophet Moshe.[7]

Just as the fulfillment of the positive Torah commandments, starting with belief in God, cannot be based on man's intellect alone (since man is limited and can only grasp the level of Godliness that descends to enliven the limited world), so fulfillment of the negative injunctions against idol worship cannot be based on intellect alone. It is not enough to become convinced intellectually that idols have no real existence and that they are truly nothing. This intellectual persuasion can be worn down with time and with exposure to the world that we live in.

Intellect itself exists — it is a created entity — and, therefore, it lacks the power to absolutely negate the independent existence of the rest of creation. Only when fulfillment of the injunctions against idol worship is combined with the command from God, and imbued with faith, does our belief system become permanent. Only then does it become clear that no one but the One Above truly exists.

From Likutei Sichot of the Lubavitcher Rebbe, vol. 20, pp. 13–24

1. A commentary on the Rambam suggests that Avraham began to philosophize about God when he was three years old and continued until he reached unmistakable conclusions when he was forty years old (*Keseph Mishneh*).

2. The question of "Why does the Rambam write at length?" does not apply to his *Moreh Nevuchim* ("Guide for the Perplexed"), in which he did write at length about idol worship in the third section, Ch 29. There, Rambam explains, "The primary intention of the entire Torah is to eradicate idol worship and the very essence of its memory" (Ch 29), and "The very purpose of the Torah is to remove this [idol worship] and to erase the descendants of those who worshipped it" (Ch. 30). From Rambam's language there, it would seem that information about idol worship, its various cults and manner of worship that existed until the day of Avraham, is important in order to properly understand the Torah's commandments regarding the subject. The purpose is to distance and remove such false opinions and practices, which had been common in the world as explained at length in the *Moreh Nevuchim*. However, (aside from the fact that, if so, the emphasis should have been on knowledge of the subject and not a lengthy description of Avraham and his role — both here in *halachah* 3 there and in the *Moreh Nevuchim*), the description gives reasons for the mitzvah. This is appropriate for the *Moreh Nevuchim*, but not for the *Mishneh Torah,* which is a book of *halachot,* which does not mention "reasons" for the mitzvoth.

3. The question is especially strong because the "error" mentioned in the first *halachah* regarding Enosh was not the halachic transgression of idol worship that is forbidden to Noachides. It was an error called *shituf* ("partnership") in which the worshipper pairs his worship of God with another deity or intermediary. The Rambam (in *Sefer Hamitzvoth*, positive mitzvah *beit)* mentions that *shituf* is forbidden for Jews, but not that it is forbidden for non-Jews (Noachides). See *Derech Mitzvotecha* of the Tzemach Tzedek, at the beginning of the mitzvah *Achdut Hashem* ("Unity of God").

4. The division of Rambam's *halachot* is not merely chronological. That is, the *halachot* do not merely trace a historical process, beginning with Enosh, followed by "the passing of generations," and then finally culminating with the arrival of Avraham. Rather, the division of *halachot* follows, first and foremost, a mental process by which man comes to recognize and negate the error of idol worship. In *halachaa aleph*, we come to recognize the nature of idol worship as an error in human thinking. In *halachah beit*, this mental error leads to "false prophets and other lies." Finally, *halachah gimmel* is about how we come to recognize Godliness (and, therefore, that idol worship is out of the question) as an intellectual process.

5. This is not contradictory to the Rambam in Ch.2, *halachah* 3, where he writes, "Because man's grasp is limited, and not everyone is able to clearly grasp the truth, and if every man is drawn after the thoughts of his heart, he will 'destroy the worlds' due to his limited grasp." In this passage, the Rambam specifically mentions that man "should not turn to idol worship, and not only idol worship itself is forbidden, but any thought leading to it is forbidden." However, it is obvious that man is permitted and encouraged to contemplate and grasp Godliness within

creation. And quite the opposite — that is the path to achieve divine love and fear, as the Rambam writes in *Hilchot Yesodei HaTorah*, beginning of Ch. 2.

6. This may be the basis for the Rabad's difference of opinion with the Rambam. On what the Rambam wrote, "At forty years old, Avraham recognized his Creator," the Rabad (R' Avraham ben David) writes, "There is an *agadah* that states at three years old." If Avraham recognized his Creator at three years old, it was not the result of intellectual effort and philosophical investigation, but as a gift from Above. And that is why as proof of his opinion, Rabad cites the Torah verse, "Avraham listened to My voice." This verse emphasizes that Avraham's recognition of God and his fulfillment of the mitzvoth was the result of listening to "My voice" — that is, he was commanded from Above.

7. Possibly, the reason that Rambam wrote, "Since Moshe prophesied and God chose the Jewish people as His inheritance and crowned them with mitzvoth and informed them…" — when he could have simply written that "God crowned them with mitzvoth and informed them…" — was to emphasize that the establishment of divine service came after 1) the prophecy of Moshe, which is revelation of the word of God from Above, and not as during previous generations "because God chose the Jews as His inheritance" meaning that the Jews were chosen by God and not, as during previous generations when "there came about [as if spontaneously], through a nation that they knew God." This factor ("the prophecy and chosenness") adds to our understanding that His crowning them with mitzvoth and informing them of how to serve Him is the result of faith in Him.

Avraham on the World Stage

Lech Lecha 12:3

Once Avraham came onto the world stage, he began to "illuminate" creation with Torah, even though it had not yet been given. What does that mean?

Prior to Avraham, God had patience with the world and provided everyone with their needs and physical sustenance even though they sinned and transgressed against His will. However, with the advent of Avraham, the principles of Torah began to descend to the world (as a result of Avraham's recognition of the one God) and that is when man became responsible for his actions. From that point onward, sinners could expect to be punished and those who followed God's will could expect to be rewarded.

Looking at the passage in *Pirkei Avot* ("Ethics of the Fathers") that discusses world history prior to Avraham, we see mention of two epochs:

> "There were ten generations from Adam until Noach to inform us of the patience of God. They angered God perpetually, until He brought upon them the Flood. Then there were ten generations from Noach until Avraham, in order to inform the world of the patience of God. All these generations angered God continuously until Avraham arrived and received the reward of all of them." (*Pirkei Avos* 5:2)

Apparently, even before Noach, there were ten generations who were sinners that angered God. But Noach did not receive their reward. And, moreover, they were destroyed in the Flood. So what does it mean that Avraham received the reward of the next ten generation who also angered God? What reward was there for Avraham since these generations were no different from the preceding ones?

There are those who answer that since Noach didn't pray for his generation, he received no reward.[1] But, Avraham not only prayed for his generation, but actively sought to educate everyone around him. Consequently, Avraham received the reward that would otherwise have gone to his generation (if they hadn't sinned), while Noach received no reward.

However, if Noach did not receive the reward (in the afterlife) of his generation, then who did? There is a reward in the "Garden of Eden" for every soul after it leaves the body, in accordance with the role that it played in this world.[2] If this reward didn't go to Noach in his generation, then to whom did it go?

We're forced to conclude that there never was a reward available to the people of Noach's generation. But if so, what was the difference between the way that they angered God (so much so that they received no reward whatsoever) and the way in which Avraham's generation angered Him?

In addition, it must be asked: What is the point of this statement in *Pirkei Avot*? If it is to inform us that God is patient, then that is already stated in the Torah — "God is patient" (Exodus 34:6) — and Rashi explains that His tolerance extends both to the righteous and to sinners. It would seem that *Pirkei Avot* wants to tell us just how patient God is — up to ten generations. But, what exactly does that mean? What is the significance of ten generations of patience?

Like much of the Torah, this statement of the sages is best understood by placing it in context and looking at what *Pirkei Avot* says previous to this. At the very beginning of Chapter 5, we read:

> "With ten utterances the world was created. God could have created the world with one utterance, [but He created it with ten] in order to punish sinners, who act to destroy the world that was created with ten utterances, as well as to reward the righteous, who maintain the world that was created with ten utterances." (*Pirkei Avot* 5:1)

After this follows the passage quoted earlier about the early generations of the world. However, if the only point is to teach us history by giving us a chronological account of what happened from creation until the present, then there's a later statement (in *Pirkei Avot* 5:6) which ought to be inserted here. That statement describes ten items that were created at the end of the sixth day of creation, before the ten generations from Adam to Noach began. It would have been logical to insert that statement here, after the creation narrative but before the mention of the generations. So obviously, the sages weren't trying to teach us history at this juncture. And if not, then what's this all about?

When we look closely, we see a parallel between the first and second statements. The first speaks of the ten utterances of creation that were created in order to punish the wicked (who destroy the world with their deeds), and to reward the righteous (who uphold the world with their deeds). And then the second statement speaks again about reward and punishment. The first ten generations from Adam to Noach were sinners who destroyed the world and were therefore destroyed by God in the Flood. That was their punishment. The second set of generations from Noach to Avraham were also sinners, but Avraham was able to sustain them. Avraham's prayers and efforts on their behalf were enough to transform some of their evil deeds into good and to inspire some good in them, though they eventually returned to their sinful ways. Ultimately, Avraham received their reward. Thus, the second statement follows in the footsteps of the first. While the first tells us that God created the world with ten utterances in order to mete out reward and punishment, the second tells us who was rewarded and who was punished.

Still, what was the difference between the sins of the first ten generations, and those of the second ten? Why were the first ten destroyed by the Flood and the second ten left unpunished?

This is best explained by way of example. When a nation goes to war, it has at least two paths to victory — one is by destroying the enemy, the other is by capturing the enemy fighters.[3] When we must, we destroy. However, there are situations when the most efficient path to victory is by incapacitating or capturing the enemy. Both approaches occurred in Jewish history:

We are told to totally destroy and eradicate the nation of Amalek (1 Samuel 15:3) whose entire existence is devoted to annihilating the Jews. Since Amalek's only purpose is to destroy Jews, the only way to "transform" and "rectify" them was by eradication. The command was not only to kill the entire nation, but to destroy all of their property as well. Yet, on other occasions (such as the war against Midian described in Numbers 31), the Jewish army was permitted to take possession of the defeated enemy's property. Thus, we see that when there is no good present, the command is to eradicate, but when there is even a spark of good present that may be liberated and transformed, then we are commanded to capture.

The same applies to the first and second set of ten generations. The first generations were such sinners that there was no hope of rehabilitating them. So, God destroyed them. But, the generations that culminated with Avraham could be transformed by being taught the general principles of monotheism. There was some good in them, and destroying them would not have redeemed the good that was present. Since it was Avraham who revealed the good in his generation, it was he that received their reward.

It remains only to explain why *Pirkei Avot* chose to demonstrate God's tremendous forbearance with the number ten? This is because "ten" in the Torah represents completion. Where the Torah counts to ten (as in a *minyan* or prayer quorum, or in the ten powers of the soul), that means a whole is there, complete with all of its (ten) parts. The number ten here in *Pirket Avot* also represents completion. God restrained His anger for ten generations, hoping that they would return to Him by doing *teshuvah*. The ten generations represented the completion of God's patience. But, after this much time passed, it became clear that there was no good whatsoever in those generations, and they would have to be destroyed.

This principle also applies to our own lives. When we come from a place that is negative — that is the opposite of Torah — we have to respond to our own past exactly the way that God responded to the generations of Noach. We have to destroy it. It may seem to us that "all is well," and that there is no problem to maintain connections with our negative past, even though we know that our environment is opposed to Torah and holiness. But, at some point, Hashem's patience may end or we may backslide. Therefore, it may be better to avoid our past and eradicate it, because if we allow it back into our lives, it will control us rather than the other way around. Some of the negative aspects of our past may still exert control and influence over us and, therefore, it may be preferable to avoid it completely.

However, once we have achieved absolute separation from the negative aspects of our past, there is something else we can do. We can elevate the past. We can do such a high level of *teshuvah* that we actually remove the good parts from our past and transform them.

The greatest level of healing is not the eradication of an unhealthy past but its transformation. By approaching the past with this attitude, we can uplift it and, by doing so, transform ourselves into new human beings, closer to the One Above. But, sometimes in order to achieve that transformation, we have to first separate ourselves until we're on firm enough ground to remain unaffected. Afterward, the sky's the limit.

Like Avraham himself, we have to leave "your land, birthplace and the house of your father," and journey "progressing steadily to the south," to the land that God shows you. And then, "it will be for a blessing," and we will not only elevate ourselves, but many others as well, with the help of God.

From Likutei Sichot of the Lubavitcher Rebbe, vol. 15, pp. 70–74

NOTES

1. Even though Noach "told them that in the future, God will bring a flood upon the world, [and he did so] with the intention that perhaps they will do *teshuvah*" (Rashi on Genesis 6:14), and Tractate *Sanhedrin* 108ab states, "Noach rebuked [the people of his generation]," nevertheless Noach was not actively involved with his fellow men. Only when they came to him and asked him about the ark that he was building did he say anything (see *Likutei Sichot*, vol. 2, p. 322).

2. It is logical to assume that the portion that anyone assumes in Gan Eden is in proportion to his service of God during the days of his life that were allotted to him.

3. This is comparable to the difference between the two explanations on the verse, "And I will neutralize the wild animals from the land" (Numbers 26:6): 1) "neutralize" may mean either "destroy" the wild animals, or 2) prevent the wild animals from doing any damage. (See the Rogachaver Gaon in *Tzafnat Paneach* on *Parshat Bechukotai* there.)

Avraham in the Holy Land

Lech Lecha 12:7

Looking in the Torah, we find not one, but many references promising the Land of Israel to the Jews.

To begin with, Rashi explains at the very start of his commentary (Genesis 1:1) that although the Torah is a book of laws, it opens with the creation narrative in order to teach that the Land of Israel belongs to the Jewish people. Nonetheless, the first scriptural promises don't come until later, when Avraham enters what was then the land of Canaan. At that time, God tells him, "I will give this land to your descendants..." (Genesis 12:7). The promise is reiterated later when Avraham is separated from Lot, and God tells him, "I will give the land that you see to you and to your descendants forever" (Genesis 13:15).

When Avraham first arrived in the land of Canaan, he traversed its entire length and breadth in response to a command from God: "Arise, walk the length and the breadth of the land, for it is to you that I will give it" (Genesis 13:17). Translating this verse into Aramaic, the Targum Yonatan writes that, at that time, Avraham "took possession" of the Land of Israel.[1] And the *Ohr Hachaim*, one of the major commentaries on the Torah, states that, when Avraham walked around the borders of the Land, he thereby established ownership of it.[2]

Furthermore, God's promise did not remain merely verbal — it was sealed by Avraham with a sacrifice (described in Genesis 15:18–21). As directed by God, Avraham slaughtered some animals, divided the carcasses in half and walked between them in what became known as the "covenant between the pieces" (*brit ben habetarim*). While perhaps not pleasing to the imagination, this event represented the sealing of God's promise that, come what may, the Land of Israel would always belong to the Jewish people.

The *brit ben habetarim* was different from former promises because it was not just a promise but a covenant. When someone merely "promises" to give something, it's usually because he likes or feels an attachment to the recipient. But, if times change and their relationship sours, he may come to regret his gift, and perhaps renege on the promise. The significance of a "covenant" is that, even if the relationship goes bad at some point, the promise of the gift remains intact. The covenant establishes that neither side may back out of the agreement. So as a result of the *brit ben habetarim*, the Land of Israel remained a Jewish possession, even after the Jews fell out of favor with God and were exiled from their Land.

Thus far, we have found three instances in which God promised the Land of Israel to the Jewish people:

1. "And God appeared to Avraham, saying, 'I will give this land to your descendants...'" (Genesis 12:7)
2. "This entire land that you see, I will give to you and to your descendants, forever..." (Genesis 13:15), and "Arise, traverse the length and the breadth of the land, for it is to you that I will give it." (Genesis 13:17)
3. "I am God who brought you out of Ur Casdim to give you this land as an inheritance..." (Genesis 15:7), and "On that day, God made a covenant with Avraham, saying, 'To your descendants I have given this land, from the River of Egypt all the way to the great river, the Euphrates." (Genesis 15:18)

When we look closely at these three instances, we find some differences between the first two promises and the third. The first two are in the future tense, while the third is expressed in the past tense, as if the land had already been given. Moreover, the first two promises do not come in response to any question or request from Avraham; they are promises that came from Above, at God's initiative. The third promise, however, occurs in response to Avraham's question after the "covenant between the pieces" when he asks God, "How do I know that I will inherit it?" (Genesis 15:8), and God answers, "To your descendants I have given this land..."

The Rogochover Gaon presents an interesting analysis of the differences in the language of these promises.[3] He suggests that the first two promises to Avraham — characterized by the word "give" — correspond to a later event, when the Jews (led by Joshua) first entered the Land of Israel as a nation returning from Egyptian exile. And the third promise — characterized by the word "inheritance" — corresponds to the second time that the Jews (led by Ezra) entered the Land as a remnant returning from Babylonian exile.[4]

From a Jewish legal perspective,[5] all of the promises (including "the covenant between the pieces")[6] indicate only one aspect of the Jews' connection to the Land of Israel — physical ownership.[7] Whether they came to it by way of a gift or inheritance, the Jews took possession of the Land of Israel in the same way that an individual acquires any piece of land — he becomes the proprietary owner and gains physical control.[8] However, there is another aspect of the Jewish connection to the Land. By entering and settling it, the Jews not only became its physical owners, they also imbued it with holiness (*kedushah*) and elevated it to a higher level. While the Torah tells us that keeping the mitzvoth is the key to living and thriving in Israel, even by merely entering the Land, the Jews already imbued it with a higher level of holiness.[9]

And here we find an interesting distinction, according to the Rambam. When the Jews were exiled from Israel after the destruction of the first Temple (some 850 years after entering it with Joshua), the Land did not retain the holiness that the Jewish presence had instilled in it. Any holiness that was present after the Jewish conquest under Joshua did not remain after the Jews left the Land. Practically, that meant that any isolated Jews who did remain after the bulk of the population was exiled were not obligated in the mitzvoth of tithing and of keeping the Sabbatical year. Since the Jews *as a nation* no longer resided on their own soil, it wasn't necessary for the few remaining Jews to keep the mitzvoth associated with the Land.

Then, seventy years after the destruction of the first Temple, a small group of Jews — only about ten percent of the exiled population — returned to Israel. This happened when the Persian king Cyrus (also known as Corush) and later, his son Darius gave permission for the Jews to return to Israel and build the second Temple under the leadership of Ezra. But, that small group was enough to re-establish the Jewish connection with the Land and to imbue it with *kedushah*.

The Temple they rebuilt stood for 420 years. During that period, the Jews had a very tempestuous relationship with their kings and spiritual leaders. They led less than exemplary lives from the Torah point of view, and so, once more, the Temple was destroyed and they were exiled, this time by the Romans. But on this occasion, the spiritual situation was very different. Rather than losing its holy status (as it did after the destruction of the first Temple), the Land of Israel retained its *kedushah*. The few Jews who remained after the Roman exile were obligated to fulfill the agricultural mitzvoth of tithing and of the Sabbatical year (as commanded by the rabbis). Even though the bulk of the Jewish nation was in exile, the holiness that the Jews of the second Temple had re-introduced remained.

What accounts for the difference? Why did the Land lose its *kedushah* after the destruction of the first Temple, but retain it after the second?

The Rambam answers (in *Hilchot Beit Habechira,* end of Ch. 6):

> "[The first sanctification of the Land] only occurred as part of a conquest, so when the Land was forcibly taken away from the Jews [by the Assyrians and Babylonians], the first conquest was nullified, and the Torah obligations to give tithes and keep the Sabbatical year were also nullified … And then, when Ezra [and his group] came to Israel and sanctified it, they did so not by military conquest but by taking peaceful possession based on presumption of previous ownership (*chazaka*). And, therefore, every place that the Jews returning from Babylonia settled became sanctified … and it remains holy today, even though the Land was later removed from Jewish hands. And [the Jews dwelling here] are still obligated in the mitzvoth of the Sabbatical year and tithing."

The *Keseph Mishneh* (a commentary by R' Yosef Caro) asks the following questions regarding the Rambam's statement:

1. What is the advantage of peaceful possession based on presumption of ownership over military conquest, and why was the sanctity of the Holy Land not nullified when the Land was taken away from the Jews the second time?
2. When the Land was conquered militarily the first time, did the Jews not also "take possession"? In what way is peaceful possession

based on presumption of ownership stronger than military possession via conquest?

There are a number of answers to these questions. One (from the Radbaz) is that, in the days of Joshua, the Jews conquered the Land but failed to verbally sanctify it, while, in the days of Ezra, the Jews took possession and also sanctified the land verbally. However, there is no hint regarding "verbal sanctification" in the writings of the Rambam. Quite the opposite, the Rambam states that the sanctification of Ezra and his group lasted because it involved a "peaceful" act of possession, and not because it was "verbal."

Another answer is offered by the *Tosfot Yom Tov* (R' Yomtov Lipman Heller). He said that when the Babylonians conquered Israel [and destroyed the first Temple], they nullified the first conquest of the Jews. However, when the Jews returned with the full permission and encouragement of the Persian king, their peaceful takeover could not be uprooted by the later Roman conquest. Even though the Romans drove the Jews out of the Land, the Jews retained ownership.

However, this still does not satisfactorily answer the questions raised by the *Keseph Mishneh*. What is stronger about the peaceful possession of the Land than possession by conquest? Why is it that when the Romans conquered the Land and destroyed the second Temple, that did not uproot Jewish ownership or the holiness of the Land?

Regarding the second question we find that, even in the days of Joshua, there were peoples — the Gibonim[10] — who voluntarily gave up their lands to the Jews. Yet, although the Jews took possession of their land peacefully and with their permission, the Rambam does not single out their part of Israel as retaining holiness. He simply says that all of Israel was devoid of sanctity after the non-Jews re-conquered it. So, the questions of the *Keseph Mishneh* remain in place...[11]

The following explanation provides possible answers to all our questions:

As previously noted, the physical ownership of the Land of Israel was determined by the promises made by God to Avraham, as per our Torah portion. However, the manner in which holiness was imparted to the Land of Israel depended upon later commandments, as per the Torah and the Prophets. For example, when Joshua first entered Israel with the Jews, it was in response to a command of God to "enter as pioneers" (Deuteronomy 3:18), and to "pass in front of your brothers armed as soldiers" (Joshua 1:14), in order that "the land be conquered before you" (Numbers 32:29). Since God told the Jews that they must enter Israel and conquer it, the *kedushah* also took hold as a result of their conquest.[12]

However, Ezra and his group entered in an entirely different manner. The Prophet Jeremiah (29:10) said, quoting God, "I will command you ... in order to return you to this place." The command was not to conquer, but to simply enter and settle the Land. It was not necessary to wage a military campaign, because there was no-one there to contest the Jewish presence, and also because the Jews were permitted by the Persian king to return and re-establish control over what was already theirs. Therefore, this was also the manner in which the *kedushah* "took hold" in the Land. There was a seamless transition from exile in Babylonia [which by then was Persia] to reclamation of the Land of Israel. Since the command was not to conquer, but to "settle," the *kedushah* took hold naturally and organically as the Jews re-entered and re-settled the Land.

The distinction between these commands also determined what happened to the *kedushah* of the Land during each of the exiles, when the Jews were forced out after the destruction of the first and second Temple. Since the *kedushah* of the first entry was the result of their coming "as pioneers," the holiness disappeared when the Jews were driven from the Land. The initial conquest of Israel remained in effect as long as the Jews were present and maintained control of the Land. As long as they lived in Israel, the command of God to conquer the Land (and thereby instill *kedushah*) remained in force, and the *kedushah* also remained. However, as soon as the Jews were exiled from the Land by another conquering force, the original command to Joshua was no longer operative. Since the Land was re-taken by force by the "other side" (the non-Jews), the Land returned to the "other side." Therefore, the *kedushah* of the Land dissipated as the Jews moved elsewhere, and the few Jews who remained were no longer obligated in tithing and in keeping of the Sabbatical year. The *kedushah* that was imposed by force did not remain.

However, the *kedushah* that permeated the Land after the arrival of Ezra was not established by conquest. Rather, it was established by the command to return and re-settle the land. And that is why the *kedushah* that his group instilled in the Land remained indefinitely. In Ezra's case, there was a seamless connection between physical possession (already established in the days of Avraham) and *kedushah.*[13] It was not necessary for the Jews to do anything (such as conquering) other than settle the land. By merely settling, the Jews exercised their presumption of ownership (*chazaka*), took possession, and also established holiness within the land. Since the *kedushah* accompanied the Jewish return to Israel, it remained even after the Jews were exiled following the destruction of the second Temple.[14]

Even though the Romans arrived many generations later and uprooted the Jews, the *kedushah* of the Land remained nonetheless. That is why, until to this day, those who live in Israel are obligated by the rabbis in the mitzvoth of tithing and of the Sabbatical year, even though there is not yet a majority of world Jewry living in the Land.

According to this explanation, we may now answer the first question of the *Keseph Mishneh* on the Rambam: What is the advantage of peaceful possession over military conquest, and why was the sanctity of the Holy Land not nullified when the Land was taken away from us the second time?

The answer is that, when the Jews conquered the Land by force, the holiness that came into the Land also came in by force. Therefore, as soon as the Land was taken away from the Jews by force, the holiness itself dissipated. Since there was nothing keeping the Land holy except the command to conquer it, when the conquest ceased, the *kedushah* of the land also ceased.

But, when Ezra and his group entered Israel and took peaceful possession, there was no conquest involved; they were not conquering but returning and resettling. As a consequence, not only did they retain physical ownership, but they simultaneously facilitated the sanctity of the Land. When the Jews returned, their mere presence in the Land is what imbued it with *kedushah.*

At this point, we may also answer the second question of the *Keseph Mishna*: When the Land was conquered militarily the first time, did the Jews not also "take possession"? The answer is "yes," however, since the possession was forceful, it did not last. The physical possession remained, but the *kedushah* dissipated when the conquest ceased.[15]

We might also understand this process from the perspective of personal *avodat Hashem* ("service of God"). During the first Temple, the

Jews were comparable to *tzaddikim* ("righteous people") whose path of worship caused refinement and elevation of the "lower worlds" by bringing down holiness and Godliness from Above. However, their style of worship did not bear much connection with the lower physical world. Such a style of worship is not sustainable, because it is not grounded in the physical world. Therefore, it is prone to change and interruption. Similarly, the *kedusha*, or "holiness" of the land of Israel was ultimately interrupted by the conquest of the Babylonians and Assyrians and the destruction of the First Temple.

And so it is in our individual lives — when our spiritual efforts take place on a spiritual plane alone, divorced from worldly matters, our *avodah* lacks a solid foundation. As soon as some sort of test comes along from the side opposed to holiness, there is no certainty that we will withstand the test. However, when the *avodah* takes place from below to Above is has a greater chance of withstanding challenges from the side opposed to holiness

The spiritual status of the Jews during the second Temple was comparable to today's *ba'alei teshuvah* (those who seek to return to God after having strayed off the path). The *ba'al tshuvah* seeks to refine and elevate the world by making it into a "vessel" for holiness, infusing the world with holiness that is permanent and does not undergo variation. And in their personal *avodah*, *ba'alei teshuvah* do not change; after they have gotten involved in the world, or even after they have fallen for the tricks of the evil inclination, *ba'alei teshuvah* pick themselves up and continue along the path of Torah and its mitzvoth. This is a sign that Torah and its mitzvoth have so permeated them that even a spiritual fall cannot tear them away from God. The connection of a true *ba'al teshuva* to God is stable and without any limitations. In this, *ba'alei teshuva* bear similarity to the holiness of the second Temple that was established through peaceful possession of the Land of Israel. After the first Temple was destroyed and the Jews were exiled, they picked themselves up and returned to Israel (or at least a small number of them did). They did not treat the Land of Israel as a land to re-conquer, but as a land to which they were always and permanently connected.

At this point, we can return to the Rogochover Gaon and his references to the words "give" and "inheritance." Earlier, we demonstrated how his suggestion that when the Jews entered the Land of Israel under Joshua, their first entry was similar to a "gift," but when the Jews re-entered under Ezra, it was similar to an "inheritance." Now we can show how his analysis is also reflected in the legal level of the Torah.

One of the halachic differences between a "gift" and an "inheritance" is that a gift may be rescinded, but an inheritance may not be rescinded.[16] The reason for this is that a gift is dependent entirely upon the "giver." Although the giver usually does not give his gift unless the recipient finds favor in his eyes, nevertheless that itself can change. If, at a later stage, the giver is no longer impressed or happy with the recipient, he may ask for his gift back again. The recipient has no claim on the gift — the whole process is dependent entirely on the giver. When the Jews entered the Land of Israel under Joshua, this was a "gift" from Above. In this case, the granting of the Land to the Jews was solely dependent upon the giver and the recipients (the Jews) had no independent claim to the Land whatsoever.

An inheritance, on the other hand, takes place precisely because there is a connection between the recipient and the grantor and often a claim from the recipient as well. Since the recipient is (usually) a family relation of the grantor, he has a natural claim to the inheritance. Moreover, just as family relations cannot be altered, the claim of the recipient also cannot be altered. Unlike a gift, an inheritance cannot be rescinded. Once it has been set in motion, the inheritance may not be reversed. Not only may it not be reversed, but the grantor may not stipulate that "after the inheritance passes to one person, it will pass on to someone else when the first one dies." Because of the natural claim of the heirs to the family wealth, it is as if they step directly into the shoes of the grantor, and the inheritance becomes theirs forever. In that sense, then, when the Jews re-entered Israel under Ezra, their entry was much more similar to an "inheritance" than to a "gift." The giving of the inheritance from Above (indicated by the command from God through the Prophet Jeremiah for the Jews to return and re-settle the Land of Israel) revealed the ongoing connection of the Jews as the owners and masters of the Land, from the time of Avraham our father.

Now, it is possible that the distinction between the first entry (under Joshua) and the second entry (under Ezra) is also hinted at in the words of the Torah verses themselves. The first two verses articulating the first two promises, using the word, "give" are stated in the future tense (as noted earlier). This is because they refer to the Jewish connection to the Land, which was only actualized later when the Jews conquered the Land from un-holy ownership and instilled the Land with holiness. However, the third promise is expressed in the past tense. This is because with their action of returning and again taking possession of the Land, the Jews merely revealed their innate connection to the Land, which already belonged to them.

However, we still find that, after all that, the second Temple [as rebuilt by Ezra and expanded by Herod] was destroyed. Something must have been lacking in the approach from below to Above, as well.

As long as the dynamic is in one direction alone, whether it be Above to below or the opposite, the results can only be temporary. Only when both are present — revelation from Above together with an effort from below — can the results be eternal.

When we realize and recognize that the Land of Israel — within its entire biblical boundaries — belongs to the Jewish people because it was both given and bequeathed to us from Above, then we are successful in peacefully settling the Land. And that also brings with it fulfillment of the prophetic verse, "And kings will be your craftsmen and princes will be your servants" (Isaiah 49:23). This means that the nations of the world will assist the Jews in fulfilling the word of God, both in general and in the specific matter of settling the Land of Israel within all of its Torah-ordained borders.

Based upon Likutei Sichot of the Lubavitcher Rebbe, vol. 15, pp. 100–109

NOTES

1. As a result, the Talmud suggests that this is one way of establishing ownership of a piece of land (*Baba Batra* 100a).

2. *Ohr Hachaim* on Genesis 13:17. See also the Alter Rebbe's *Shulchan Aruch HaRav, Hilchot Hefker, Kuntres Aharon S"K* 1 toward the beginning: "[Israel] was acquired by taking possession (*chazaka*) in the required manner … and so is stated in *Baba Batra* 110…"

3. The Rogochover Gaon (R' Yosef Rosen) was one of those rare Torah scholars who appears on the scene once or twice in a century, and whose intellectual scope encompasses the entire Torah. The Torah of such giants from our recent past (including not only the Rogochover, but R' Yosef Engel and others) constitutes a unique genre in Torah literature. Neither *pshat* ("simple" textual meaning typified by Rashi's commentary) nor *drosh* (the exegetical portion of the Torah expressed in Gemara and *halachah*), their novel insights nevertheless shed light on how to

understand both *pshat* and *drosh*. Perhaps as a consequence of his vast erudition, the Torah of the Rogochover Gaon transcends the traditional "categories" of the Torah, yet simultaneously illuminates them. See his *Tzafat Paneach* on the Torah.

4. The *Talmud Yerushalmi* (*Baba Basra* Ch.8 *Halachah* 2) asks, "If the land was given as a gift, why was it [also] given as an inheritance?" The Jerusalem Talmud answers, "After He gave it to [the Jews] as a gift, He returned and gave it to them as an inheritance." Thus, we know that there were two types of grants of the Land to the Jews, associated with the two entrances.

Basing ourselves on the above analysis of the Rogochover Gaon, we might go further and say that the "covenant between the pieces" (during which the third promise occurs) also alludes to the seventy-year period of exile between the first and second time the Nation of Israel entered the Land. How so? At the "covenant between the pieces" Avraham asked God, "How do I know that I will inherit it?" The sages suggest that Avraham's question indicated doubt (as if Avraham were questioning God). It is possible to compare such doubt to the exile, during which the Jews experienced distance from revealed Godliness and see an allusion to it in Avraham's question.

The Ramban says, "In addition, God established a covenant, just in case they would sin. And when He commanded Avraham regarding the *brit milah*, He mentioned "a permanent portion" to indicate that if the Jews were exiled from the Land, they would yet return and inherit it."

5. The three promises we have been discussing were made by God to Avraham many centuries before the events to which they allude (if we accept the Rogochover Gaon's thesis). The first time the Nation of Israel entered the Land with Joshua, after having wandered in the desert for forty years, occurred some 400 years, or eight generations, after Avraham passed away. When the Jews entered Israel at that time, they conquered and settled the Land and eventually built the first Temple.

The building of the first Temple took place some fifteen generations after Avraham passed away. It stood for 410 years before being destroyed by Babylonians and the Jews were exiled. They remained in exile for seventy years before a small group returned with Ezra to build the second Temple, which stood for 420 years. (These are the two times the Jews entered the Land — one approximately 400 years after Avraham, and the other some 1,300 years after Avraham — that the Rogochover Gaon mentions in commenting on the promises of our Torah portion.)

6. It is noteworthy that while the first entry to *Eretz Yisrael*, with Joshua, was commanded in various verses in the Torah (as quoted within), the second entry, with Ezra, was promoted and enabled by a non-Jew (Cyrus/Corush, king of Persia). Moreover, the conquest of *Eretz Yisrael* by Joshua took place in a miraculous manner, without the loss of a single Jewish soldier. The second entry with Ezra did not require conquest or war, but merely the return of the Jews to their land. These two factors lend support to the perspective that the first entrance was similar to a gift "from Above to below," while the second was similar to inheritance, "from below to Above." See the Rebbe's *biur* in *Inyanei Beit Habechira, Sicha* 5, p. 149 of *Chidushim U'biurim al Rambam (Hilchot Beit Habechira)*.

7. From the language of Rashi on the first verse of *Bereishit* — "If the nations of the world will say to you, 'You are robbers, you conquered the land of the seven Canaanite nations…' etc." it seems that the physical acquisition of the Land took place only after it was conquered (and not before) — [it's then possible that Rashi's opinion in his commentary on the Torah disagrees with the view we are elaborating here], even though it could be explained that that is only according to their opinion — the opinion of the "nations of the world."

8. "Even so, the Jews acquired the Land only by means of a proper possession, as stated in *Kiddushin* 26, "How did you inherit? By settling." And so is stated also in *Baba Basra* 110. See *Kuntres Aharon* in *Shulchan Aruch Harav, Hilchot Hefker* at the beginning. And in the *Makneh* on *Kiddushin* there, "possession (according to the school of R'Yishmael) consisted of dividing the Land among them, and each one acquiring from the other, and not from the Canaanites."

9. This halachic discussion follows the viewpoint of the Rambam in *Hilchot Beit Habechira.*

10. Joshua 9. Moreover, the city of Jebus (later to become Jerusalem) was not conquered by Joshua (see Joshua 15:36, Judges 1:21, 2 Samuel 5:6) and David later acquired it from Aravna by paying the full price (2 Shmuel at the end, 1 Chronicles 21:22). The *Minchat Chinuch*, mitzvah 284 (section 6) suggests that "since this place was acquired only by conquest, therefore it became holy for *trumot* and *maasrot* and *challah*, and its sanctity was not nullified after the destruction of the first Temple and the subsequent exile" (even though the sanctity of the rest of the Land of Israel was nullified).

11. There is no room to suggest that the sanctity of the Land of Israel is all one and indivisible, since the language of the Rambam proves otherwise. During the second entrance of the Jews, they only succeeded in sanctifying "every place that they settled" (*Hilchot Beit Habechira and Hilchot Terumot*). And it is difficult to suggest that the first entrance and conquering was "different," since it applied to the entire Land, as mentioned in *Hilchot Terumot, Halacha* 2 (if we assume that only the areas that were conquered became sanctified). But see later in this *sicha.*

12. The Rambam (*Hilchot Trumot* 1:2) writes, "Joshua and his *Beit Din* divided all of Israel among the tribes even though they had not yet conquered the Land, so that their conquest would not take place piecemeal as each tribe conquered its own portion." As the Rambam states there, this was in order to "call it *Eretz Yisrael* in regards to fulfillment all of the mitzvoth." Thus, the obligation of performing the mitzvoth occurred as each tribe conquered its portion in *Eretz Yisrael* (if this were not the case — and the obligation of the mitzvoth occurred only after the entire Land was conquered, that would not have happened until the end of the days of King David — but from several sources it is understood that the obligation occurred as each area was conquered). Nevertheless, the sanctity of the entire Land applied immediately after the conquest began, with the conquest of Jericho which was the "key to the entire Land," even though the mitzvah obligations occurred later.

13. The return of the Jews and their re-settlement of the land of Israel under Ezra also constituted a legal *kinyan*, or "acquisition" of the land, known as *chazaka.*

According to the gemora (*Kiddushin* 26), there are three ways by which to acquire land; one way is to acquire land by settling it — this is called *kinyan* by *chazaka*. In the gemora there, two verses are brought in support of this manner of acquisition: Hizkiya mentions a verse from Yirmiya the prophet (40:10) — "And settle in the land which you have taken." And R' Yishmael mentioned a verse from Deuteronomy (11:31) — "Inherit it, and settle it." One way to understand the difference between the first and second entrances to the land of Israel was that the first entrance, under Joshua, required taking the land by force (because so the Jews under Joshua were commanded from Above). When the Jews did so, they also established the holiness of the land — by force. The second entrance, under Ezra, did not require force. Possession of the land took place concomitantly with the establishment of holiness — both occurred together, and the holiness remained permanent.

14. Possibly, the *kedushah* after the second Temple remained also because there was always a remnant of Jews remaining in the Land, even after the Roman conquest. There was never a period in which there were no Jews living in the Land of Israel, even after the destruction of the second Temple, and throughout most of that two-thousand-year exile, the Jews formed a "plurality," meaning they were the largest minority living in the Holy Land. If the reason for the *kedushah* that was established with Ezra's entrance was that the Jews returned and settled the land without conquest, then their continued presence may be a factor in the continued presence of *kedushah* in the Land.

15. This explanation provides an allegory for understanding Jewish history. The Torah was given to the Jews at Mt. Sinai as a set of instructions imposed from Above to below. However, that was only the beginning. The Jews soon began to accept the Torah, but this took some time, through the period between the first and second Temples. It was then that the Purim story took place, while the Jews were in exile. The Book of Esther tells us that, at that time, the Jews "accepted what they already fulfilled." The Jews had been keeping the mitzvoth ever since Mt. Sinai, but only after the destruction of the first Temple did they fully accept the Torah. Their full acceptance was an act coming from below to Above, and it paved the way for their re-entry into the Land of Israel. It was soon after the Purim story that Ezra was granted permission by the king of Persia (a grandson of Queen Esther) to re-enter the Land of Israel. This typified the approach from below to Above, the approach of acceptance and agreement. Therefore, when Ezra and his group reentered the Land, it was in order to take peaceful possession of it, not to conquer it.

16. See Tractate *Baba Batra* 129b and 133a.

Three Stages of Milah

Lech Lecha 17:1

In this Torah portion we read about Avraham's circumcision (*milah*) which he performed on himself. It may sound like a simple physical action. But, it's really much more than that — the number of times that the Torah mentions *milah* and the subtly different language that it uses each time tells us that much more is going on here…

The Mishnah (in *Nedarim* 31b) says, "Circumcision has special status, since despite all the commandments that Avraham fulfilled, he wasn't considered complete until he circumcised himself, as it says (in Genesis 17:1), 'Walk before Me and be *tamim* (complete).'"[1]

The Gemara (in a *Beraisa*) elaborates, "Circumcision has special status, since nobody was as involved in the commandments as Avraham, and yet he was called perfect only after his circumcision, as it says (in Genesis 17:1), 'Walk before Me and be *tamim* (perfect).'"

Although it may appear that the two statements say the same thing, that is not the case. The Mishnah describes Avraham after the *milah* as "complete," while the Gemara describes him as "perfect." Both are translations of the same Hebrew word (*tamim*), but the Mishnah interprets it one way while the Gemara interprets it in a different way.

What the Mishnah means is that every mitzvah that Avraham fulfilled contributed to his "completeness," but he wasn't fully "complete" until he underwent circumcision. However, the Gemara states that circumcision contributed to Avraham's "perfection" — without mentioning the contribution of the other mitzvoth. According to the Gemara then, Avraham was "perfect" because of his *milah* (and not because of any other mitzvah).

Perhaps these two interpretations have to do with the two results of circumcision. The foreskin represents a sort of barrier, a physical obstacle that prevents the Jew from making spiritual progress. And the *milah* has two effects: 1) it removes the obstacle, and 2) it allows the person to grow spiritually. That might account for the two ways that the Mishnah and the Gemara interpret the Torah verse: "Walk before Me and be *tamim*."

On the same page, the Mishnah speaks negatively about the foreskin, and concludes with a statement of R' Elazar ben Azariah, "the foreskin is loathsome…" So, it would seem that the Mishnah places emphasis on the first result of circumcision — the removal of the foreskin, which is like a blemish.

The Gemara, on the other hand, describes the positive effects of circumcision — it frees the Jew to grow spiritually — and, therefore, the language it uses specifies that circumcision leads not only to completion (as if previously something were missing) but to perfection.

However, this explanation fails to explain other subtle differences in the language. The Mishnah says: "After all the commandments that Avraham fulfilled, he wasn't considered complete…" implying that not only circumcision but also the other commandments led to his completion. But, the Gemara says, "nobody was as obedient to the commandments as Avraham, and yet he was called perfect only on account of his circumcision," which implies that it was only the *milah* that led to his perfection, regardless of the other mitzvoth he fulfilled.

So, we must refine our search for another possible explanation. As happens frequently, light is shed from another angle — specifically from the way the word *tamim* is used in other contexts. We see it applied in two different ways: 1) to negate of any kind of lack or blemish, or 2) to indicate a higher level of completion, which not only lacks nothing, but actually implies a higher level of integration.

For example, we see this in the Torah's description of the sacrifices (*korbanot*). Sacrifices are called *tamim* when they are lacking any blemish that would make them unfit to be offered on the altar. But, *tamim* also indicates "highest quality," as the Rambam writes in the beginning of *Hilchot Issurei Mizbeach* ("Laws of Prohibited Altar Offerings"), "it is a positive commandment for all the sacrifices to be *tamim* and of the choicest…" We find this as well in the Torah's references to the yearly cycle. A normal Jewish year contains twelve months, and a year in which the months *Cheshvan* and *Kislev* have thirty days is called *shalem* ("complete"). However, a leap year, in which there is a full extra month, is called *tamim* ("fully complete").

This leads us to conclude that there are two levels to *tamim*: 1) one implying that nothing is lacking, and 2) the other implying a greater level of completion, in which not only is nothing lacking, but something greater than the sum of the parts is present.[2]

Consequently, we might interpret the Mishnah and the Gemara on the basis of these two meanings of the word *tamim*.

The Mishnah uses the first interpretation of *tamim* — not lacking anything. It tells us that upon circumcising himself, Avraham was no longer lacking anything. And that's why it says that Avraham fulfilled all the commandments, but it was the circumcision that led to his completion — "he wasn't called complete until he circumcised himself." It wasn't the circumcision alone that led to his completion, but once he was circumcised, he was complete.

The Gemara, however, refers to *tamim* in the sense of something additional, something choice and superior. So, the language indicates that it was the *milah* alone that brought Avraham to this condition. Nobody obeyed all the commandments as did Avraham, and yet "he was only called perfect on account of the *milah*."[3] It was precisely the *milah*, and not the other mitzvoth, that led to his new level of perfection.[4]

However, there is a third definition of *tamim* in the Talmud — one who grows spiritually by wholeheartedly fulfilling the will of God. As it states (in *Nedarim* 32a): "Those who make themselves *tamim*, God is *tamim* with them, as He said to Avraham, 'Go before me and be *tamim*...'" That is, one must progress rather than remain on one level, and then one is *tamim*. It is not enough to achieve completion and perfection on a one-time basis, rather one must continually work on achieving new levels of completion and perfection. And the way to do this is by fulfilling the will of God wholeheartedly, without raising questions.

This is similar to the command in *Parshat Shoftim* (Deuteronomy 18:13), "Be *tamim* with the Lord your God" — which Rashi interprets as follows: "Go with Him wholeheartedly and wait for His will to unfold, don't look into the future and don't ask questions, but accept whatever comes your way wholeheartedly." Since this definition of *tamim* is cited in the Gemara where it discusses Avraham's circumcision, we understand that it applies to him, just as the first two definitions did. Therefore, there is likely to be a causal relationship as well. It is likely that the mitzvah of *milah* induced, or elicited, this level from Avraham, causing him to "walk" wholeheartedly with God, progressing in spiritual completeness and perfection.

These three definitions of *tamim* apply to all three of our forefathers — Avraham, Yitzchak and Yaakov. However, each of them "specialized" in one of the three forms. Each was complete in fulfilling the will of God, with an emphasis on one of the three definitions described above.

Avraham was the son of idol worshippers. He used his intellectual acumen and sense of independence to take himself out of this morass. He was surrounded by people who accepted and worshipped idols but, by asking questions and analyzing his environment, Avraham concluded that there is only one God and it is appropriate to worship only Him. So, he fulfilled the word of God as one who has overcome a deficiency in his environment. His initial surroundings in life were not holy, but he became *tamim* by rejecting a flawed milieu and accepting the will of God. Thus, he was *tamim* in the sense of "complete," as in not lacking anything.

Yitzchak was born in a holy environment and raised to know that there is only one God. He is described by the Torah as an "*olah temima*," a perfect offering, and he never left the Land of Israel. He spent all of his time in Torah study and prayer. Thus, Yitzchak fulfilled the second definition of *tamim* — one who is "perfect," in possession of an added measure of wholeness and integration. However, since Yitzchak never left the Holy Land, his faith in God was untested and unchallenged. He lacked the wholeheartedness of one who has withstood tests in his life and overcame them.

Finally, Yaakov is described by the Torah as an *ish tam*. He was the epitome of one whose life was filled with hardships but who "soldiers on," without asking questions. Although the events of his life confronted him with many different situations, under radically different circumstances, he always maintained his commitment to God. He never wavered nor doubted his task in life, which was to obey God's commands. Whether in the house of his father-in-law, Lavan, one of the greatest con artists of all time, or while coping with the loss of his son Yosef, or while dealing with the immoral inhabitants of Shechem, Yaakov not only maintained his faith, but increased and deepened his connection with God. He exceeded the divine service of his father Yitzchak, who served God under one protected set of circumstances (in the Land of Israel).

Yaakov stood "above the fray" and maintained his faith and commitment wherever he went and, in this respect, he exemplified the third definition of *tamim* — as one who grows spiritually while accepting the will of God wholeheartedly, under all circumstances, without asking questions.[5] (Incidentally, this was also one of the most prized traits of the Baal Shem Tov and the Chassidic Movement — it is called *hishtavut*, meaning "equanimity.")

To delve even deeper into our explanation of what it means to be *tamim*: Whether it means "complete" (lacking nothing) or "perfect" (possessing an added measure of positive qualities), our definition relates to the details. For example, when referring to sacrifices, *tamim* either means that the offering is complete in all of its details (unblemished), or that its details lend it "perfection" (meaning that it has a quality that transcends its details). In both cases, the definition relates back to the details. The same is true of the yearly cycle of time. If the year is *tamim* in the sense of "complete," it simply means that it is missing no details — all twelve months are present. If it is *tamim* in the sense of "perfect," then it possesses even more details; it possesses a thirteenth month and is a "leap year." The same applies to us as people. One person may be *tamim*, or more "complete" than others because he has rid himself of faults and blemishes that are still present in other people. Or, he may be *tamim*, or "perfect" because he no longer needs to work on his faults, but instead focuses his energy in trying to be a better person, constantly improving his service of God. In either case, his situation relates to the details that make up his personality.

But, there is a third level of *tamim* that transcends details, and that is the level of *kaballat ohl malchut shamayim* ("accepting the yoke of heaven"). In this case, *tamim* means that, regardless of details, we unflinchingly and wholeheartedly accept what God wants from us. Without asking questions, and without looking into the details, we do what is required of us. It is not the details of our personality, nor any extra qualities that we possess, that motivate us. It is our simple desire to do what God wants that motivates us. And, for that reason, our divine service is direct and unchanging at all times.

Regarding *milah*, the three definitions above are expressed in three different elements of the mitzvah. First of all, the circumcision frees the person from certain aspects of the *yetzer harah* ("the evil inclination"), making him "complete." Second, the *milah* helps him to improve upon and embellish his connection with God in all sorts of positive ways, leading to "perfection." Both of these elements are associated with "details, parts and components" of the person, namely, his intellect and emotions. However, the third element of circumcision is the deed itself — the act of taking a knife and cutting away the foreskin.[6] Obviously, this was not something that Avraham wanted or chose to do of his own volition. The act required an ability to put aside his own desires and simply do what God told him. Since it is not based upon intellect or emotions, this act transcends the "parts" of the person and penetrates to his very essence. The circumcision produced in Avraham another level of *tamim* — *kabalat ohl malchut shamayim*, or the ability to connect to God by doing what He wants under any and all circumstances. This is the highest expression of *tamim* — the ability to walk in God's way wholeheartedly, without flinching and without asking questions.

We tend to think that the greatest achievement of a human being is in the realm of intellect and the effect that he has upon the rest of the world. However, the truth is that it is usually the person who puts himself to work and doesn't waver in his path of divine service who achieves the most. When enough of us do that, it's sure to bring about the Final Redemption (Translator's emendation).

From Likutei Sichot of the Lubavitcher Rebbe, vol. 30, pp. 44–52

NOTES

1. In handwritten manuscripts of the Mishnah, the following verse (from Genesis 17:2) is added, "I will establish my covenant between Myself and you." And so it appears in Rambam's *Mishneh Torah, Hilchot Milah* 3:8. See also the *Tosfot Yom Tov* on the Mishnah.

2. We find a similar distinction in regard to other matters in the Torah: In Tractate *Yoma* (24a), the priestly service in the Temple is considered *tamah* ("complete") only if there is no other aspect left to perform. Rashi explains there, complete *avodah* "finishes and completes (*metamemet*) the matter, without leaving anything else to do, such as slaughtering, collecting the blood, and bringing it [to the altar]." A similar concept applies to giving *tzedakah* (*Ketubot* 67b): One may give enough *tzedakah* "to fill [the poor person's] necessities that he is missing" or he may give (but is not obliged to do so) "enough to make him wealthy" — which is more than what he is missing.

3. Given this understanding, the language of the *Braisa* (in the Gemara) becomes clearer. The *Braisa* states, "There was no one as involved in the mitzvoth

as Avraham…" and we do not find this terminology — "involved with" in regard to anyone else whose *avodah* was "complete." But once we grasp that it was the mitzvah of *milah* that "completed" his *avodah*, we also understand that he was more "involved" with the mitzvoth than others, even though they also kept the mitzvoth.

4. This perhaps allows us to understand the continuation of the Gemara there (*Nedarim* 32a) — "When God said to Avraham, 'Go before me and be *tamim*,' Avraham was seized with trembling and wondered, 'Perhaps there is something loathsome about me?' But when God said, 'And I will establish My covenant between you and Me,' Avraham relaxed." At first glance, what changed between the two statements from God to Avraham? But, if we understand that "Go before me and be *tamim*" suggests the first meaning of *tamim* — meaning without blemish, we understand why Avraham was seized with trembling — it suggested to him that perhaps he had a blemish. The second statement from God though, allayed Avraham's fears; "I will establish My covenant" refers to the second meaning of *temim*, "added completion," and not to any blemish.

5. Perhaps this is the reason that only "Yaakov's bed was perfect" — all of his children were *tzaddikim*, or "righteous."

6. Even though Yaakov was born circumcised, the third definition of *tamim* (one who works on himself to be *tamim*) still applied. The main expression of this third level is the act itself, and yet Yaakov didn't need full circumcision since he was born circumcised. Nevertheless, he underwent *hatapat dam* ("taking a drop of blood" from the place of circumcision). Perhaps the fact that he was born circumcised showed that the first two expressions of *temim* — "lacking the foreskin" and "possessing an "added measure of perfection" — did not apply to him (because he already possessed these traits from birth). All that was necessary was the deed itself — and that was the *hatapat dam* that he underwent. [Possibly the same applies to King David, who was also born circumcised (see *Sotah* 10b). As the Gemora says there, "King David was *tamim* in every respect." (Rashi: "*Tamim* in all his ways"). Just as he made himself "small" before all those who were greater than him when he was a child, so he also did when he grew up.

Milah and the Land of Israel

Lech Lecha 17:8

There is an implicit relationship in the Torah between the mitzvah of circumcision (*milah*) and the Land of Israel. It is expressed in our Torah portion — *Parshat Lech Lecha* — although the exact nature of the relationship is not explained. It remains for us to try to understand why the two appear together — the commandment to undergo circumcision, and the granting of the Land of Israel to the Jewish people.

First, Avraham was promised the Land of Israel by God, who said: "And I grant to you and to your descendants this land where you dwell, the entire land of Canaan, for an everlasting possession" (Genesis 17:8). And immediately after this he was commanded as follows, "And now you must keep My covenant ... make sure that every male is circumcised" (Genesis 17:9).

Earlier, God had commanded Avraham, "Walk before Me and be complete (*tamim*)," (Genesis 17:1), which Rashi interprets as referring to the mitzvah of *milah*." And then, God said, "And I will establish a covenant (*brit*) between Me and you." (Genesis 17:2), which Rashi interprets as referring to "a covenant of love and of the Land, which God promised to bequeath to Avraham by way of this mitzvah."

Even more explicitly than Rashi, the Midrash (*Breishit Raba* 46:9) states, "If your descendants will keep the mitzvah of *milah*, they will enter the Land, and if not, they will not enter ... so said God to Avraham, 'And I gave [the Land] to you and to your descendants after you ... on condition that you fulfill my covenant.'" And as the Zohar (Vol 2, p 23A) says, "All who remove the foreskin inherit the Land."

However, this brings up a big question in the logical flow of the Torah text. The Land was promised to Avraham and to his descendants much earlier, when Avraham was seventy years old (Rashi, Ex 12:40) at the *brit ben habetarim* ("covenant between the pieces"). There, Avraham fell into a trance and walked between the pieces of his offerings (Genesis 15:18). The Torah states, "On that day, God established a covenant with Avram, saying 'To your descendants I have given this Land...'" Yet, our verses (in Ch 17) mentioning the land and the *brit milah* occurred thirty years later, when Avraham was already one hundred years old! And if so, what does the Torah add by telling us here that the promise is dependent upon the mitzvah of *milah*?[1]

One possible answer might be that the earlier covenant (*brit bein habetarim*) represented a promise to the Nation of Israel that the land will be given to them, while the later one was to individuals, informing them that they will be able to enter the Land of Israel. That is, firstly the Land of Israel was promised to the Jews collectively, while later God qualified that only those individuals who had undergone circumcision would be allowed to possess it.

However, the Zohar — commenting on a verse in the Book of Exodus (Exodus 6:4) which states, "And I also fulfilled my covenant with them, granting them the Land of Israel" — makes clear that it is the entire Nation of Israel (not just individuals) that is being addressed here. States the Zohar, "All who cut off the foreskin inherit the Land." Since all heirs of Avraham (through Yitzchak) inherited the Land, it is clear that the later promises (in Chapter 17) were also addressed to all Jews. Without a doubt, the inheritance of the Land of Israel is associated with the *milah*.[2]

To clarify this matter further, let us look at the comments of R' Levick [the Rebbe's father, *ztz'l*] on the Zohar. There, he says, "The Zohar uses the Aramaic word *yarit*, meaning 'inheritance,' to translate the Torah verse, 'And they will inherit the Land.'" He points out that the choice of words is precise, as "inheritance" implies "forever." (One who bequeaths cannot stipulate, "Today I bequeath to so-and-so, and tomorrow to someone else." Once property is inherited, it passes only to the designated recipient.)

Inheritance of the Land took place in conjunction with the *milah*. And just as circumcision is forever (it cannot be "undone"), so inheritance is forever. And, therefore, the inheritance of the Land is forever.

Although the Jews were exiled from their Land, they were never disinherited. As R'Levick points out, the exile was for a limited amount of time after which the Jews would be allowed to return, and the exile was on account of their sins and transgressions, which seems to imply that the eternity of *milah* can be interrupted.

What does this mean? The first explanation (that the exile was for a limited amount of time) implies that the inheritance of the Land of Israel is everlasting. However, the second explanation implies the opposite — that the inheritance of the Land may be interrupted. And, if so, what is the connection with *milah* which is forever?

We are forced to conclude that with *milah*, as with the promise to inherit the Land of Israel, there are two aspects: 1) there is one aspect that is similar to inheritance and therefore permanent; 2) there is a second aspect that is comparable to a gift, which may turn out not to be.

A covenant between God and humanity is different than a contract between two people. Two people are more or less equal regarding any contractual agreement — either one of them may renege, and that is the reason that they make it binding — in the hope of preventing that from happening. But, in a covenant between God and humanity, although any human may renege, God will always uphold His end of the deal.

Therefore, in the covenant between God and Avraham, there were two sides. There was Avraham's side in which, as a human being, he could be expected to uphold it as well as he could, but he was not infallible. And then, of course, there was the side of God, who could be relied upon to uphold His side of the deal at all times. That is why R' Levick gave two explanations for the exile. Even though the *milah* was permanent and everlasting, it was a covenant between man and God. From the Godly point of view, any exile from the Land will always be temporary and the Jews will always return — and so, there is no interruption in the fulfillment of the covenant. But, from the human point of view, we are fallible and, since we are prone to sin, there may appear to be an interruption in the way we uphold the covenant. Therefore, as R' Levick mentioned, *milah* is an acronym for "a gift that may be interrupted" — our sins may get in the way of the complete fulfillment of the covenant between us and God.

The same concept may be applied to the two separate commandments to fulfill the mitzvah of *milah* — before and after the giving of the Torah. The first commandment, "And you must keep my covenant..."

was given before Mt. Sinai. Even though it was stated as a command from Above to below, from God to Avraham, nevertheless, historically, this commandment preceded the giving of the Torah at Mt. Sinai, when the decree separating the upper and lower realms was annulled.[3] It was only then that the spiritual and physical worlds could be truly fused together. And, therefore, the mitzvoth that preceded this fusion did not have the same status as what they later attained at Mattan Torah. Even the mitzvoth of the forefathers were compared in their time to "fragrances." Just as a fragrance is nothing more than a hint of something and its effect quickly dissipates, so the mitzvoth of the forefathers had no permanent effect upon the world. They could temporarily draw Godliness down to the world but, soon after, the world would continue as before. And so, the *milah* of Avraham lacked the element of permanence characterized by any *milah* performed after the Torah was given.

Therefore, the command, "And you must keep my covenant" placed emphasis on the side of Avraham, who as a human being was fallible. That's why his *milah* was a "gift that may be interrupted."

However, when the Jews were commanded later, after the giving of the Torah, to circumcise themselves on the eighth day (Leviticus 12:3), this was a command from Above to below. Then, the spiritual realms from Above could descend to the physical world and have a permanent effect. Therefore, the Torah command to circumcise on the eighth day represents the Godly side of the covenant, which is permanent, without interruption.

This explanation applies to the Land of Israel as well since although the Land was given permanently and immutably to Avraham and his descendants, nevertheless its distribution and allocation to the Jewish tribes and their families occurred in three different modalities that bore a resemblance to 1) a sale, 2) a gift, and 3) an inheritance.

A "sale" requires that the buyer meet certain requirements — he must come up with the money and, if he fails to do so, the sale does not go through. The "covenant between the pieces" (*brit bein habetarim*) had elements of a "sale" — God promised the Land of Israel to Avraham, but only after informing him that his descendants would have to undergo a four-hundred-year sojourn in a foreign land. The torment and discomfort of living in Egypt was a sort of "payment" for entering Israel a few hundred years later. The implication was that if Avraham did not agree to this "payment," the Jews would not receive the Land. Thus, it was an acquisition that could be interrupted or stopped. It could even be stopped before it occurred, if the "buyer" (Avraham) did not guarantee that the Jews would pay the price (exile).

However, subsequent transactions, associated with the *milah* were permanent as they involved a gift and then an inheritance from God.

In the beginning of *Parshat Lech Lecha*, after the commandment to "walk before Me and be complete (*tamim*)," God says, "I will establish My covenant between Myself and you." This, of course, implies a "gift," which although granted freely by the giver, usually implies the recipient has done something to deserve it. Indeed, we see that Avraham had caused God to look favorably upon him and his descendants. That is a situation that could change, which is why exile from the Land of Israel could be considered an interruption (but not a cancellation) of the gift.

But the next transaction, taking place a few verses later in *Parshat Lech Lecha* can be characterized as permanent and can be called an "inheritance." Here God says, "And I grant to you and to your descendants this land where you dwell, the entire land of Canaan, for an everlasting possession…" (Genesis 17:8).

That is, here God bequeathed the Land of Israel to the Jewish people without any conditions whatsoever, in a manner that is permanent and unchanging. Just as the inheritor enters into and permanently occupies the place of the benefactor, so the Jews in this case become the permanent recipients of the Land of Israel. That is why, even though the Land of Israel had previously been given to Avraham and his descendants, at the covenant of *milah*, it became theirs forever.

It emerges then, that these two latter acquisitions of the Land of Israel — by way of gift and by way of inheritance — correspond to the two aspects of the mitzvah of *milah*:

1. The first is a conditional grant dependent on the recipient (the Jewish people) finding favor in the eyes of the giver (God). This corresponds to the aspect of *milah* which is "reversible."
2. The second is an inheritance, totally unconditional, in which the recipient simply enters the "place" of the benefactor — the One Above. This corresponds to the covenant of *milah* from the side of God, not subject to any change or variation whatsoever.

From Likutei Sichot of the Lubavitcher Rebbe, vol. 35, pp. 45–52

NOTES

1. The promise at the beginning of our Torah portion, to give the Land of Israel (Genesis 12:7, 13:15) occurred after the "covenant between the pieces," which took place when Avraham was seventy years old (see Rashi on Exodus 12:40). The above promise occurred when Avraham was seventy-five years old (Genesis 12:4) — see the *Shaloh* on *Lech Lecha* p. 277a.

2. The Jerusalem Talmud (*Nedarim* Ch.3 *Halacha* 9) counts the thirteen "covenants" in the Torah as associated with the *brit milah.* The very first to be counted is the *brit bein habetarim* — the "covenant between the pieces" but the Rambam at end of *Hilchot Milah* does not consider it associated with the *brit milah.* (See *Likutei Sichot* vol. 25, p. 54). However, the Tanhuma (*Lech Lecha*, Ch. 20) does associate the *brit milah* with the verses of *brit bein habetarim.* The Tur (*Yoreh Deah* 260) writes, "In merit of the *milah,* a covenant was made to give the Land," and the Beit Yosef comments, "It seems this is because the Torah verse (in Genesis 15:18) says, "On this day God made a covenant (*brit*) with Avraham, saying "To your descendants I have given the Land..." See also the Bach on the Tur there ... For a Chasidic explanation of the connection between *brit milah* and theLland of Israel, see *Likutei Torah Eikev*, p. 16 col. 3, as well as the Alter Rebbe's *Siddur* 111a.

3. Before the Torah was given, even though the forefathers "figured out the Torah," nevertheless it did not descend "from the upper realms" in order to have a permanent effect upon and transform the physical world (the "lower realms"). Only when the Torah was given to the Jews at Mt. Sinai did the 613 mitzvoth begin to have an effect upon and permanently transform the world.

Two Stages of Torah Learning

Lech Lecha 17:9

A topic of interest that arises frequently is the Torah learning and mitzvah fulfillment of our forefathers — Avraham,[1] Yitzchak and Yaakov as well as Yaakov's sons, the Twelves Tribes of Israel — versus that of the Jews after the giving of the Torah at Mt. Sinai.

Since the Torah learning of the forefathers and the Tribes preceded Mt. Sinai and, therefore, preceded the command to learn Torah, their fulfillment of the mitzvoth was self-motivated. Since they were not commanded to do so, but nevertheless learned, they studied the principles of the Torah in accordance with their own abilities and potential. This meant that they were unable to reach those levels that transcend creation. The best they could do was to grasp the Torah principles as these were connected with the created world and pertained to their own spiritual needs in their divine service.

After the Torah was given though, in conjunction with the command to learn Torah and fulfill its mitzvoth, the Jews attained the ability to access the Creator and to connect with the very essence of the Torah, as it completely transcends creation. That's why the Rambam states:

> "All that we do or refrain from doing these days is only at the command of God through Moshe our teacher, and not because God gave these commands to the prophets who preceded Moshe. For example, we avoid eating the limb of a live animal (*aiver min hachai*) not because Noach was commanded to avoid it but because Moshe forbade us to do so, since we were commanded not to eat a limb of a live animal when the Torah was given at Mt. Sinai. Similarly, we do not undergo

circumcision because Avraham circumcised himself and his household members, but rather because God commanded us through Moshe to circumcise ourselves at Mt. Sinai just as Avraham did. The same applies to the injunction against eating the sciatic nerve — we do not follow this command because of Yaakov, but rather because we were commanded by Moshe."[2]

If so, we have to ask: Since every aspect of Torah is pertinent to the divine path of every Jew, what is the lesson emerging from the lengthy stories about our forefathers, which appear in both the written and the oral Torah (as well as in Chassidic teachings)? Since all of this history precedes the giving of the Torah at Mt. Sinai, what does it have to do with our divine service after that momentous encounter? After all, whatever happened, happened already...[3]

The Ramban (*Parshat Lech Lecha*) offers a solution. He explains that the Torah writes at length "about the journeys and the well-diggings and other events in the lives of the forefathers ... to teach us about the future." And as the Midrash (*Tanhuma Lech Lecha* 9) adds, "The acts of the forefathers were signposts for their descendants." Thus, we might say that the Torah and mitzvoth of the forefathers (as explained in Chassidic teachings as well[4]) provided their descendants with the preparation and ability to accept the Torah at Mt. Sinai and bring down Godliness through the fulfillment of the mitzvoth.

However, neither one of these explanations is sufficient. Since the stories of the forefathers and their actions are a part of the Torah itself, which is eternal, they must be more than indications or preparation for the future. They must be eternal instructions that also affect our divine service after the giving of the Torah.

Just as we ask about the stories of the forefathers, we might also ask about the long narrative concerning the Egyptian exile: What instruction does it contain for the Jews after the giving of the Torah? Here, the question is especially pertinent since we know there will never be a repeat of the Egyptian exile (see *Gevurot Hashem* from the *Maharal* of Prague, Ch. 61).

It is also insufficient to explain as the Alter Rebbe did (in *Torah Ohr*, p. 74) that the bitter exile in Egypt was preparation for the giving of the Torah (since the Egyptian exile served as a sort of "furnace," refining and purifying the Nation of Israel). Since the Egyptian exile and Exodus narrative occurs in the Torah, it must mean that it contains a lesson for all Jews, whenever and wherever they are, after the giving of the Torah as well as before. It must be that the stories of the forefathers, as well as the stories of the Egyptian exile, serve as preparation of what will occur at Mt. Sinai. At the same time, they contain lessons for all time, including after the giving of the Torah, as will be elucidated in the coming paragraphs...

The difference between the spiritual path of the forefathers and the spiritual path of the Jews after Mt. Sinai is two-fold. It concerns both the forefathers themselves and the Godly illumination that they were capable of drawing down to the world. 1) First, the path of worship of the forefathers was from below to Above. As a result of the spiritual work that they did on themselves, they attained a great level of refinement and purification that transformed them into "vessels" to contain the divine light that they drew down. 2) Second, since that light was within range of creation (the physical world in which they lived), the light shone within them in a revealed manner.

We Jews who live after the giving of the Torah at Mt. Sinai are not as refined and pure as our forefathers (who were "vessels" for the expression of Godliness) or as the original Twelve Tribes of Israel. And so, we are not capable of drawing down the same level of revealed Godliness as they attained. However, through our mitzvoth, we do draw down Godliness that is beyond this world and that transcends the creation. Because it is such a high, transcendent level of Godliness, it remains concealed. It does not shine within us as did the illumination that was brought down by the forefathers.

The background explanation for this is the following. Prior to the giving of the Torah, there was a "disconnect" between the higher (spiritual) and lower (physical) realms. "The higher could not descend to the lower realm, and the lower could not ascend to the higher realm" (*Shmot Rabba* 12:3). Godly illumination that was totally beyond creation could not descend into the world. After the giving of the Torah at Mt. Sinai, though, the "disconnect" was rectified, so to speak, and it was possible for the lower realm (our world) to fully unite with Godliness that is transcendent and completely beyond this universe.

The events at Mt. Sinai took place from Above to below. The world at the time was not in any kind of condition to accept or recognize the transcendent Godliness that descended at that time. For that reason, Godly light did not illuminate the lower world during the giving of the

Torah (it only "shone" from Above). Also for that reason, the illumination was temporary, and thereafter, it ceased. In order for us to access the transcendent light that was present at Mt. Sinai and to become vessels that reveal the Godly light from beyond creation, inner work (*avodah*) is needed — we must refine ourselves and improve our divine service. It is necessary for us to polish, refine and uplift our character traits, in order to transform ourselves into "vessels" to receive the revelation of Mt. Sinai in a permanent fashion.

Now we can understand what the stories of the forefathers, who preceded the giving of the Torah, can teach us Jews who are living after this awesome event. Just as the forefathers were required to work on themselves and refine themselves to receive Godly revelation even before the Torah was given, so too, we must work on ourselves and refine ourselves in order to receive the Godly illumination that descends to us as individuals as a result of our learning Torah and fulfilling its mitzvoth.

During the lead-up to giving of the Torah, it was necessary for the forefathers to reach the highest perfection that was possible, including absolute nullification of their egos to the One Above, in order to bring down the Godly light that was appropriate for their spiritual level.[5] Our individual refinement after Mt. Sinai is also necessary in order to bring down illumination (from Above to below), to unite with and illuminate the world. As we learn Torah and fulfill its mitzvoth, our initial goal is to attain the highest levels of refinement — in relation to the Godliness in our world — in our individual frame of reference. Only afterward might we succeed in ultimately uniting with the highest levels of Godliness that are out of range of our world, by transforming ourselves into "vessels" for the revelation of Godliness of the Torah, as He gave it to us at Mt. Sinai, totally transcending this world.

[This is similar to the process described in the statement, "At all times, man should be involved in Torah and mitzvoth even if not for the sake of Heaven, because eventually he will come to learn Torah for the sake of Heaven" (*Pesachim* 50b). From the phrase, "at all times," we understand that this saying of the sages applies to learning Torah on whatever level the student may be holding at that time. By learning Torah not "for its own sake" (even if the goal of our learning is very high, such as in order to know how to observe the mitzvoth), we will eventually arrive to learning "for its own sake" — for the inherent value that is present in the Torah. Even learning on the highest levels that are not "for its own sake," we Jews becomes united with the Torah on whatever levels of Godliness that concern us in this world.[6] And this serves as an introduction to eventually learning the Torah "for its own sake." We eventually become connected to God alone, through His Torah, as it exists completely above and beyond investment in the world.]

Although the encounter with God at Mt. Sinai produced a revolution in Torah learning that applied (and continues to apply) on all levels, that doesn't mean that we are conscious of it. The revolution that occurred means that one who learns Torah now accesses a level of Godliness that is far beyond the creation. "Every Torah scholar who reads, recites and is involved in Torah, God sits across from him, reading and reciting with him" (*Tana d'vei Rebi Eiezer Rabati*, Ch. 18). And this applies to one involved with the mitzvoth as well.

This level of intimacy and proximity to God did not occur before the Torah was given. And although it takes place now, it does so in a concealed manner. In order for this very high level of Godliness to become revealed, it is necessary for the Torah scholar to first achieve perfection on his own level. Completion of his own personal connection to the Torah on his own lower level is a pre-requisite to accepting and learning the Torah on its higher level. Only after he learns the Torah on his own lower level can he reveal the Torah as it is, far beyond any connection to this world.

To illustrate:

Consider a child of five years old, learning Torah for the first time. When the teacher mentions God's "great hand," or "strong hand," and similar expressions that appear in the Torah, he translates and explains to the child that the phrase refers to a "big" hand, one that is "stronger" or "bigger" than what the child is aware of. As much as the teacher tries to explain to the child that the Torah is referring to the abstract concept of "hand," the child will still picture a physical hand in his mind, but one that is "bigger" and "stronger" than his teacher's hand. Here of course it could be asked if such an explanation is not opposed to a very important general principle of the Torah — that God is not physical and cannot be reduced to any physical representation. Yet, the teacher is not lying to the child or misleading him, because the child, even at this young age, understands what a hand is, and he knows that the strength and size of a hand is not due merely to its physical attributes, but due to the energy and vitality that is present in the hand and that comes from

God. The child understands then, that Torah expressions such as "great hand" or "strong hand" certainly do not refer to physical quantities or traits, but to a spiritual quality that is present in the "hand." It emerges, then, that every level of learning Torah, including a small child learning the simple textual level is "true." The child understands as a five-year-old can just beginning to learn Torah. Later, according to the order that is part of Torah itself, the child will learn the oral Torah (first Mishnah at ten years old, followed by Gemara at fifteen years old), and finally he will learn, on the most abstract level of all, the mystical secrets of the Torah which are completely divorced from the physical world.

In summary, all of us must first learn Torah according to the origins of our own soul level. In this regard, our learning is similar to the learning of the forefathers — i.e. learning Torah as it is associated with this world and with creation. And, thereafter, we can attain the highest level of Godly revelation, beyond creation and beyond our soul level. We can attain revelation of Torah similar to how it was given at Mt. Sinai.

In summary, all of us must first learn Torah according to the origins of our own soul level.

The reason that the forefathers were required to first learn Torah on their level (Godliness as it relates to creation) before moving on (to learn Torah on its own Godly level beyond creation) is not merely because they had to "build themselves up" to the necessary spiritual level, from below to Above.

This sequence is also a requirement of the upper spiritual realm. Revelation does not descend to the world in one "fell swoop." To the extent that it descends, it does not do so (to begin with) as absolute revelation of the very essence of Godliness. First, only a contracted ray of illumination descends, which becomes invested in creation. Only afterwards does full revelation of the very essence of Godliness descend earthward.

So it is with the Torah in its own "spiritual habitat," beyond creation. Before the Torah was "given," only a ray and reflection of it descended from Above to the forefathers. They brought down the level of Torah that pertained to them personally and that was within range of creation. And so it is after the giving of the Torah — before it can become revealed to us as it exists above creation, the Torah must first descend to us in a manner that is appropriate for us personally and for the world that we live in. Only afterward can the Torah as it truly is — beyond creation — descend to us.

This is also reflected in the order in which the Torah descends to the world — the simple/literal (*pshat*) level descends from the hinted/implied (*remez*) level, which descends from the comparative/allegorical (*drosh*) level, which in turn descends from the secret/hidden (*sod*) level.[7]

But even after all this, the learning process reflected in the divine service and inner work of the forefathers is not sufficient to apprehend the Torah as it exists beyond creation. It was necessary for the descendants of the forefathers to also undergo the process associated with the exile and slavery of Egypt. The spiritual efforts of the forefathers had to be followed by the slavery of the Jewish nation in Egypt, as preparation for the giving of the Torah at Mt. Sinai. Since the Torah as given at Mt. Sinai is so far above and beyond creation, it is not sufficient for us living in the lower world to reach our own highest personal levels of spiritual attainment. To reach levels that are beyond creation, it is not enough for us to attain our own highest personal levels. An internal transformation is necessary — there must be a change in our lower nature. Egyptian exile was "work in mud and bricks and all manner of labor in the fields … during which the Egyptians forced the Jews to do backbreaking labor" (Ex 1:14). The same process of "backbreaking labor" is present in the intellectual process of Torah learning after Mt. Sinai. We must work with "mud" (*chomer*, which the sages likened to *kal v'chomer*, which is a form of apriori argumentation) and "bricks" (*levana*, which the sages likened to *livun halachah*, or working out a halachic decision), in a process that is "backbreaking" on an intellectual level. The exile in Egypt is compared to the difficult intellectual work that the Torah scholar must undertake, "breaking his head" over Torah concepts until he understands them, working through seeming contradictions and arriving at appropriate halachic conclusions. All this reflects labor that is the very opposite of his nature and the opposite of what man is accustomed to, but through this labor against his will, he achieves transformation of himself and submission to the will of the One Above. And then he becomes a proper vessel, capable of receiving a revelation of the Torah as it exists Above — the "Torah of God."

With this foundation, we can perhaps understand a story about the third Lubavitcher Rebbe, the Tzemach Tzedek, that is otherwise somewhat puzzling. As a child prodigy, the Tzemach Tzedek was offered a "gift of Torah insights" as a present from his grandfather, the Alter Rebbe. The Tzemach Tzedek (even at this young age) refused this "gift," explaining that he preferred to receive such knowledge on his own, as the result of his own efforts to understand the Torah. And, therefore, he turned down his grandfather's offer. Many years later, the Tzemach Tzedek expressed remorse over his decision, noting that, had he taken his grandfather up on his offer, he still would have been able to continue to "work" and "labor" in Torah, arriving to yet higher levels, since the Torah is unlimited.

At first glance though, what was the Tzemach Tzedek thinking? Obviously if the Alter Rebbe wanted to give him a "Torah gift," it meant that even at that time, the Tzemach Tzedek was on a special spiritual level. He already knew what he expressed later — that even with his grandfather's "gift," there was still room to reach higher levels through his own efforts. So, what was he thinking at the time, and why did he change his mind later?

It seems that the Tzemach Tzedek was not expressing "regret" over his earlier refusal to accept the Alter Rebbe' offer. At the time that the offer was made, the Tzemach Tzedek felt that he was not yet on a level to accept a "Torah gift" from his grandfather. He felt that he had not yet worked hard enough and labored in Torah to deserve such a gift. He was not yet a vessel for such knowledge and that's why he turned down his grandfather's offer. Later though, having undergone the necessary preparations to receive that level of knowledge, the Tzemach Tzedek felt that he was now a vessel for his grandfather's "gift," [but of course by then it was too late, and therefore he expressed "regret" that he did not receive the "gift" in his present situation].

Possibly, this preparation and toil in Torah serves as an illustration of why the slavery in Egypt was a necessary "introduction" to the giving of the Torah on Mt. Sinai.

From Likutei Sichot of the Lubavitcher Rebbe,
vol. 15, pp. 75–82

NOTES

1. "Avraham sat and taught in yeshiva in his advanced years" (*Yoma* 28b) and "Avraham fulfilled the entire Torah even before it was given" (*Kiddushin* 82a).

2. *Pirush Hamishnayot*, end of Ch 7 of *Chulin*.

3. Rashi answers this question on the simple textual level in his very first comment on the Torah in *Parshat Bereishit*: There, he explains that in order to provide a response to the non-Jews who claim that the Jews "stole the land of Israel from

the seven Canaanite nations," the Torah includes sections that precede the first mitzvah of the Torah (sanctification of the new month). According to some commentators, that includes not only the creation narrative but also to the stories of the forefathers. They were included in the Torah so that the Jews could tell the nations of the world that the Land belongs to God and He gave it to whom He sees fit (the Jews) (see *Likutei Sichot* vol. 5). From Rashi's comment, it is possible to infer that — according to the simple textual level of the Torah — there must be a lesson from every verse of the Torah that is eternal and applicable to all times.

4. See *Torat Chaim* of the Mittler Rebbe, *Parshat Lech Lecha*, p. 83, end of *seif* 3. *Parshat Chayei Sarah* 135, Ch 29, as well as p. 137a , Ch 34. *Ohr HaTorah* beginning of *Parshat Lech Lecha* p. 72b.

5. This is not in contradiction to what is written elsewhere (*Kol Ha'am Roim* 5678, *Lereach Shemanecha* 5706, Ch 7), that the purpose of the forefathers was to draw down revealed Godliness to the world, rather than to "rectify" the worlds. And the purpose of the revealed Godliness was to later enable the rectification to take place (i.e., first God emanated the infinite light that revealed Him, followed by the light that illuminated the world). For it is possible that the above was about revelation of Godliness in the world in connection with physical objects, upon which the *avodah* of the forefathers had no bearing, as opposed to revelation to the forefathers themselves. [Perhaps the revelation to the forefathers discussed in this *sicha*, while having no bearing on the physical world, was the preparation that later enable the "rectification" of the physical world to take place — through revelation of the Torah at Mt. Sinai.]

6. In this regard, even learning for the sake of "knowing what to do" (knowing the *halachah*) is not the ultimate goal, which is learning in order to glorify and elevate the Torah itself (*Chulin* 66b).

7. According to the *Eitz Chaim* (mentioned in *Nagid u'metzaveh* in the beginning).

Avraham's Journeys

Vayera 18:1

Looking at early Jewish history, we may be able to detect patterns. Earlier, we discussed what took place during the first ten generations of man — from Adam to Noach, and in the second ten generations, from Noach to Avraham. Both epochs were dark periods in which people displeased God and sent His indwelling Divine Presence (*Shechinah*) further into exile from the physical universe.

Yet, there was a difference — the first ten generations possessed no redeeming value and therefore were destroyed in the Flood during Noach's generation, while the second ten generations possessed a minimal level of spirituality that was redeemed by the emergence -- almost two thousand years after the world was created — of Avraham as a spiritual beacon.

The beginning of Avraham's journey, when God called upon him to leave his land, his birthplace and his family, was also the beginning of preparation for the eventual giving of the Torah. For, when this *tzaddik* reached the Holy Land, he preached monotheism and began the process of bringing God's presence back down to earth once more. Thus began the period of preparation for the Torah, the culmination of which took place six generations later, when Moshe brought the *Shechinah* back down to earth, and the Torah was given to the Jewish people.

But prior to that, during the era of Avraham, there were actually two different sub-periods that we can discern, and they correspond to this week's Torah portion (*Parshat Vayera*), as well as last week's Torah portion (*Parshat Lech Lecha*). By understanding the difference between these two sub-periods, we can gain more insight into the life of Avraham and what he achieved for the Jewish people.

But first, let's establish the "big" picture. During the first ten generations of man, from Adam to Noach, there was no one in the world who could illuminate it with spirituality. There was no one to rebuke those who did wrong, nor to encourage those who tried to get closer to God. If there were any people who served God or tried to do what He wanted, they did so as private individuals, who expressed no concern for their communities or fellow men. Those individuals were motivated by divine inspiration from Above, but they were not motivated from within, from their own desire to reach others and, therefore, they had little or no influence over their generation. The prime example was Chanoch (Enoch), who was removed from the world before he could succumb to temptation and sin (Genesis 5:24). When there is illumination from Above without any participation from the world below, the illumination dissipates. As a result, the world became so depraved that God destroyed it. However, this destruction was also a purification process; the Flood cleansed and purified the world so that, hopefully, the generations that followed could start from a higher level and begin to serve God.

In private life, this might be compared to the person who takes care of himself, learning, studying and meditating in order to get closer to the One Above. He works from Above to below, nurturing his soul, but doing nothing to refine and uplift his body. Because of this, he may sometimes succumb to physical urges that distance him from God and spirituality. Unless it becomes clear to him that he must also discipline his body, and curb his physical appetites, all of his divine service leads nowhere, because his physical nature pulls him in the opposite direction. When there is only illumination from Above, with no involvement from below, the illumination dissipates.

After the Flood, the physical world existed on a higher, more refined level, which could be more easily uplifted. The people of Noach's generation and all the subsequent generations were capable of hearing a divine message. So, for 120 years, as he built the ark, Noach rebuked his generation, warning them to change their violent ways which were damaging and distancing God's presence from creation. In Noach, we have an example of someone who cared about his fellow human beings, but only insofar as he could rebuke them.[1] In truth, he was not interested in their spiritual good, but in his own. He did not want to live in a world of corruption and misdeed and, therefore, he rebuked his generation. His real concern was not with others but with his his task as commanded from Above. And so he engaged others not with a positive message of spirituality, but with a negative message of doom. Ultimately, Noach did not succeed because people generally respond only when they feel they are the object of true personal concern, so his message did not have the desired impact.

The same is true today when we try to influence others. If we limit ourselves to merely rebuking them (as Noach did) because that is what we believe we are commanded to do, we will have limited success. Only when we demonstrate that we truly care about the other person will success come within our reach. In order to influence others, it is not sufficient to issue commands. It is also necessary for the other person to see and feel that we are concerned about their personal welfare.

Part of Avraham's spiritual contribution was to combine the two. He not only worked upon himself from below, but managed to bring down Godliness from Above, thereby elevating himself even higher to become totally unified with God. And this is what we see in the two Torah portions focused on Avraham's life — *Parshat Lecha Lecha* and *Parshat Vayera.*

In *Lech Lecha*, we read how Avraham traveled, first from his own birthplace and home in Ur Casdim to Charan and, ultimately, to the Land of Israel. *Lech Lecha* is all about Avraham's spiritual journey, in which he pursued Godliness with his mind and intellect. By thinking about and meditating upon Godliness, he was able to draw conclusions and reach spiritual levels that had never before been attained. Nevertheless, the Zohar describes Avraham's spiritual vision as a *machazeh*, which is Aramaic for a "partial vision." At this stage in his spiritual development, Avraham did not yet have full appreciation of the essential nature of Godliness. He was still working on himself, using his own spiritual powers, while ascending from level to level and, therefore, he was not yet ready to attain a full measure of prophecy.

The catalyst that enabled Avraham to catapult to the highest, most essential level of prophecy occurred at the end of *Parshat Lech Lecha*. There, the Torah states that Avraham circumcised himself. This experience, the cutting away of the foreskin, is what facilitated revelation of the *Shechinah* to Avraham and enabled him to begin to reveal Godliness to the rest of the world around him. That's why our Torah portion begins with the words *vayera eilav Hashem*, meaning, "And God appeared to him...." Not in a "partial vision" (as before the circumcision), but in His full essence.

In other words, until his circumcision, all of Avraham's service of God had been from below to Above, based upon his own experience and intellect. However, after his circumcision, Avraham began to serve God based on revelation from Above to below, thereby elevating himself to become totally unified with God. The mitzvah of *milah* which he performed on his own flesh is what lifted Avraham out of his own existence and put him into an entirely different category. Therefore, after his circumcision, Avraham's teachings took on a new dimension, as they were imbued with added faith in God that came to him from Above to below.

That is the difference between what we read in *Parshat Lech Lecha* and *Parshat Vayera*. Though both deal with the events of Avraham's life, *Lecha Lecha* is pre-circumcision and *Vayera* is post-circumcision. Before his circumcision, all of Avraham's divine service was about him and his personal journey. His *avodah* was intellectual, limited to the bounds of his own mind and abilities. But, after his circumcision, Avraham no longer possessed a personal life. And as the opening words of *Vayera* indicate, Avraham's service took on a new dimension — that of "seeing."

Intellect is similar to "hearing" — we deduce conclusions from what we hear, or receive, from other sources. Some of those sources are more direct while others are less, but none of them have the immediate impact of "seeing." God gave us intellect in order that we use it to get closer to Him, but it is limited because it doesn't include direct experience of "seeing" Him. However, the level of revelation that Avraham achieved after his circumcision included direct perception of Godliness, similar to seeing, that transcended his previous divine service which was only based on the intellect.

More precisely, the maximum that human intellect may impart is the ability to receive Godly revelation "as if" visualizing Godliness — that is, our intellectual perception may be so great that it gives us an experience "as if" we are seeing Godliness. This is the *machazeh* ("partial vision") that Avraham achieved before his *milah*. It is sometimes compared to *aspkelaria sh'aino meira* ("a lens that is not transparent"). The culmination of Avraham's *avodah* from below to Above was this "as if" level. However, his spiritual level after the *milah* was far greater. It included authentic direct perception of Godliness, not "as if" but as real, in that he was actually visualizing Godliness. This level is sometimes described as *aspeklaria sh'meira* ("a lens that is transparent").

This distinction in Avraham's *avodah* explains why *Vayera* is a separate Torah portion — it deals with Avraham's new spiritual level after his circumcision, when he achieved a much higher spiritual attainment. In *Lech Lecha* he progressed from below to Above, using his intellect. In *Vayera* the direction was from Above to below, based upon his spiritual eyesight or direct spiritual experience. All along, Avraham preached what he practiced, combining intellectual pursuit with outreach, while introducing monotheism to the world.

In our personal lives, we take the time to develop our own powers and talents, getting closer to God, while going out to find those with whom we can share our knowledge, lifting up not only ourselves, but also illuminating others in the process. We succeed when our message is not merely a rebuke (as was Noach's) but one that also uplifts and inspires.

However, there was something missing even in Avraham's superior *avodah.* As accomplished as he was, Avraham was capable of connecting with only some of the people of his generation. He could not and did not try to reach all of them. We see that clearly in *Parshat Vayera*, when he "bargained" with God over the destruction of Sodom and Gomorrah. In that episode, he sought to persuade God not to destroy the twin sin cities if there were as few as ten *tzaddikim* who could serve as spiritual defense and protection. Receiving a positive response to his request (God promised not to destroy the cities if as few as ten righteous men could be found), Avraham backed off. He did not go so far as to request that the cities be saved on behalf of the sinning inhabitants themselves. He did not see any good that would warrant saving them, nor did he pray on their behalf. His ability to enlighten and illuminate his generation extended only to those who could accept his teachings. However, he was unable to reach those who had no spiritual identity whatsoever. Those whom he could reach, he sought to uplift. But he didn't have the ability to influence and transform everyone in his generation. That would have to await for another time — the generation of Moshe and the giving of the Torah at Mt. Sinai.

When, after the sin of the Golden Calf, God came to Moshe and proposed eradicating the entire generation and creating a new people from the descendants of Moshe alone, Moshe refused. He went so far as to tell God, "if so, then erase me from Your book." And, as the Zohar states, "he didn't budge until God said, 'I forgive them as you requested'" (Zohar sec. 1, p. 106a).

Moshe wanted nothing to do with a Torah that was for *some* Jews, but not all of them. His commitment to the divine spark present within every Jewish soul was so total and absolute that he could see the spiritual potential in every Jew, including those who were currently sinners. Therefore, he refused to even consider abdicating what he saw as his responsibility to every last Jew alive. Moshe's attitude was one of complete and total love for every member of the Nation of Israel. Such love is not predicated on reason, such as the other person's intellectual level, or even because "perhaps it will be possible to draw him closer to Torah." Rather, it is motivated by unconditional, essential love for the other person just because he is a Jew. Therefore, there is no need or reason to differentiate between one Jew and another — all are worthy of love.

Moshe wanted nothing to do with a Torah that was for some Jews, but not all of them.

Similarly, when the Torah was given to the Nation of Israel through Moshe, it wasn't given to one Jew in one place at the exclusion of another Jew. The Torah met every person, wherever he or she stood, on whatever level he or she existed.

But, such unity didn't come into the world until six generations after Avraham. In the meantime, *Parshat Lech Lecha* and especially *Parshat Vayera* form the beginning of the preparation for giving of the Torah, during which time a human being began not only to elevate and refine himself, but to bring spiritual revelation from Above to below, to the entire universe.

From Likutei Sichot of the Lubavitcher Rebbe,
vol. 15, pp. 83–92, and vol. 10, pp. 49–54

NOTES

1. Some say that Noach did not rebuke his generation of his own will, but only because he was commanded to do so by God (see *Likutei Sichot,* vol 15, pp. 40 and 89).

Are Non-Jews Required to Give Tzedakah?

Vayera 18:17

A unique event occurs in our Torah portion — *Parshat Vayera* — that gives us an opportunity to delve into the world of *tzedakah*, commonly translated as "charity," but also meaning "justice." When a Jew fulfills the mitzvah of *tzedakah*, he not only gives "charity," he also acts with justice, leveling the uneven playing field that may have developed in the world, between the "haves" and the "have-nots."

We correct injustice by giving, since the discretionary money in our possession is not really ours — it was given to us by God in order to help others.[1] Otherwise, why should any of us have two houses, for example, when others have no house at all? In answer, the mitzvah of *tzedakah* provides us with an awesome responsibility to alleviate the difficulties of others.

Indeed, Jews give huge amounts of *tzedakah*, both in Israel and in the Diaspora. But, what about non-Jews? Is there also an obligation for non-Jews to give *tzedakah*, or is it merely a "good deed" that everyone can do, but no one is required to do?

Part of the answer to this question emerges from a powerful event that is described in our Torah portion. After Avraham recovered from his circumcision, and God informed him and his wife Sarah that they would have a child, God then asked of Himself (so to speak) a question, "How can I conceal from Avraham what I am about to do?" (Genesis 18:17). He then informed Avraham about His plan to destroy the cities of

Sodom and Gomorrah. In response, Avraham "negotiated" with God in an effort to save the twin sin cities and their populations, but it emerged that if there were less than ten righteous people inside, the cities would have to be destroyed.

Actually, in addition to Sodom and Gomorrah, there were others — in total there were five such cities. These cities were situated near the Dead Sea on a large plateau which was to be overturned in a spectacular display of fire and brimstone which no human was allowed to observe (Gen 19:17). While the first destruction of the world (the Flood of Noah's generation) took place with water, this destruction took place with fire.[2] And it had an interesting name — *calah* or "total destruction."

It is unusual for the Torah to apply a specific term for an event of destruction. There are general categories of punishment, but to apply a term such as *calah* means that there was an unusual level of iniquity involved, so that God had to respond with an unusual level of punishment — in this case, destroying the cities in a spectacular fashion and incinerating their populations. What could they have done to deserve such a fate?

It is unusual for the Torah to apply a specific term for an event of destruction.

Their sin was failure to give *tzedakah*. This transgression is clearly identified in the Book of Yehezkel, "this was the sin of Sodom … they failed to support the poor and needy" (Yehezkel 16:49).

Although the Gemara (*Sanhedrin* 109b[3]) states that the destruction was God's response to "a great cry" emanating from Sodom (Genesis 18:20) which it identifies as the cry of the young woman (who violated the by-laws of the city by attempting to help someone), this is not a contradiction. They failed to support the poor and needy, and they persecuted those who did. They were so distant from proper behavior that a simple act of kindness by a young woman caused them to put her to death in an abnormal manner, smearing her with honey and leaving her to be bitten to death by bees.

In short, their extreme conduct led to *calah* — total destruction.

It should be obvious that the citizens of Sodom were obligated to give *tzedakah* because, if not, the One Above would not have killed them, and especially not in such a harsh manner.[4] But the mitzvah of *tzedakah* is not one of the Seven Noachide Laws! So why is their failure to "support the poor and needy" considered a sin, and in particular such a serious sin that they were annihilated for it?

The Torah seems to imply that Avraham — who had the halachic status of a *ben Noach*, as did all people before the Torah was given — was not obligated to give *tzedakah*: "For I have cherished him since he instructs his sons and his household to keep the way of God, acting with charity and justice." (Genesis 18:19) That is, the added love and attention that God showered upon Avraham was because of his willingness to act with charity and justice (and instruct his household to do so as well), even though he was not commanded to do so. And, if he was not, neither were the citizens of Sodom.

However, the Talmud (*Sanhedrin* 57b) tells us that the *bnei Noah* are obligated to give charity and to maintain courts of justice. In particular, both men and women among the *bnei Noach* are obligated: the way the Gemara interprets the above Torah verse is that "Avraham's 'sons' were obligated to maintain courts of justice and his 'household' (i.e. the women) to give charity." And that is why some early commentators on the Gemara (the Ran on *Sanhedrin* 56B) state that the city of Sodom was punished for neglecting the obligation to "support the poor and needy" — because the *bnei Noach* are obligated in this mitzvah.

However, if so, why is this mitzvah not counted among the Seven Noachide Laws? To this, the commentators answer that the "counting" only includes those commandments that are passive (requiring them to "refrain" from doing something), but not those commandments requiring pro-active behavior (such as giving *tzedakah*). However, this answers the question only according to one of the conclusions of the Gemara (that the counting of the Noachide laws includes only passive commandments), but not according to the original hypothesis which holds that the Seven Noachide Laws include the positive pro-active commandments as well as the negative passive commandments. And so the question still begs an answer: Why is *tzedakah* not mentioned among the Seven Noachide Laws?

Other early commentators — Rashi and the Rambam in particular — are of the opinion that the *bnei Noach* are not obligated to give *tzedakah*. Rashi (commenting on *Sanhedrin* 56b) states that the word *tzedakah* in the Torah verse (Genesis 18:19) does not refer to "charity" but to "compromise" — meaning a peaceful and just resolution of two opposing claims. Very often, in a civil case, the two opposing parties will choose to reach their own agreement, rather than rely on the decision of a judge. By reaching such a compromise, both sides may minimize their losses, and Rashi claims this is the meaning of the word *tzedakah* in that Torah verse. A later commentary — by the Maharsha — supports Rashi's interpretation, saying the fact that *tzedakah* is not counted among the Seven Noachide Laws is proof that Rashi is correct.[5] The Rambam (*Hilchot Melachim* 10:10) also suggests that the *bnei Noach* are not obligated to give *tzedakah* — he writes that the *bnei Noach* can fulfill optional mitzvoth in order to receive extra reward and he gives *tzedakah* as an example of such an optional mitzvah.

All this means that there is serious discussion among the sages regarding whether the *bnei Noach* are obligated by the Torah to give *tzedakah* or not. If they are obligated, then why is the mitzvah not counted among the Noachide laws? And if they are not obligated, then why were the people of Sodom guilty of failing to support the needy and were totally destroyed because of that?

The Rambam and the Ramban differ in their interpretation of the Noachide commandment to establish courts of justice. This requirement, called *dinim* ("laws") is one of the Seven Noachide Laws, according to all opinions (in fact, it is the only positive pro-active commandment among the seven). But the Rambam opines the requirement of *dinim* is simply to establish courts of justice in order to adjudicate and enforce the other six Noachide laws, while the Ramban (in his commentary on Genesis 34:13) offers a much broader interpretation. He holds that this mitzvah includes an obligation to judge the *bnei Noach* in all forms and categories of the law: fraud and extortion, wages and employment, rape and seduction, as well as the main categories of torts — damages, loans, contracts, etc. That is, *dinim* encompasses all categories of law.

Accordingly, we might conclude that, in the Ramban's eyes, *tzedakah* is not counted separately as one of the Seven Noahide Laws because it is part of the category of *dinim*, which include all those matters associated with "running the world" (*yishuv haolam*) in a just manner. *Tzedakah* is certainly part of running the world with justice. And if so, we can also understand why the people of Sodom and Gomorrah were punished for failing to "support the needy and poor." However, even if this resolves the issue according to the Ramban, nevertheless it remains an issue as far as the Rambam is concerned.

So, in order to make sense out of this web of seemingly contradictory opinions, we need to first of all understand the difference between the Seven Noahide Laws and the mitzvoth that the Jews were commanded to observe (such as the mitzvah of circumcision), even before the Torah was given, and all the more so, the mitzvoth that the Jews were commanded to observe after the Torah was given.

The universe was created for a reason. The sages (see *Midrash Tanhuma, Bereishit, pesikta* 3 and 5) tell us that all creation exists in order to make it possible for the Jews to fulfill their task of illuminating the world and connecting it to the One Above. Therefore, the seven mitzvoth that the *bnei Noach* must fulfill are not merely for their own sake, but for the sake of a higher purpose. While the 613 mitzvoth by which the Jews are obligated have intrinsic value and Jews fulfill them for the purpose of the light that they bring to the world, the Seven Noahide Laws are for the purpose of "settling creation" (*lashevet yatzra*) — that is, establishing a civilized society. For the Jews to fulfill their task, it is important that the non-Jews do what they can to establish a world that is free of negative influences and corrupted environment. For such a world to exist so that it can eventually become refined and perfected, it is necessary for the non-Jews to keep the Seven Noahide Laws. This includes the Noahide commandments that pertain to relationships between man and his neighbors (such establishing courts of justice) and those that pertain to the relationship of man and God (such as utterly rejecting idol worship). In this manner, non-Jews prepare and establish the world which the Jews must then refine, perfect and elevate to a state that is "beyond creation" — so that it becomes a "Torah world," a dwelling place for the One Above.

From this we can understand why, when a non-Jew transgresses one of the Seven Noachide Laws, he becomes deserving of the death penalty. Since his entire purpose is to make the world a just place, when he behaves in the opposite manner by transgressing his own commandments, he uproots his own purpose and undermines the entire basis of his own existence. When he acts in a manner that is counter to his own purpose, it is understood that his very life is called into question, and he becomes subject to capital punishment. With this understanding, we can comprehend how, even according to the Rambam, the people of Sodom deserved to die. Although it is true that they were not obligated to give *tzedakah*, and therefore their failure to do so could not be considered a transgression, nevertheless when the refusal to support the poor and needy takes on such an extreme form that they do not even permit another person to give *tzedakah* (and they condemn that person to a bizarre and cruel form of death), such behavior is certainly a transgression. It is the diametric opposite of "settling creation" — the very reason they were put on this earth — and that is why the inhabitants of Sodom and the other cities like it had to be destroyed.

From this analysis, it emerges that while both the *bnei Noach* and the Jews are commanded to give *tzedakah*, the reasons are different in each case. Since the *bnei Noach* are commanded to create a civilized society, it is necessary for them to give *tzedakah* in order to support the poor and needy, and in this way fulfill the function of running the world in a just way. But *tzedakah* given by a Jew has a higher purpose. It is for the purpose of transforming the world into a Godly world, thus elevating it beyond the bedrock foundation of civilization. As the Alter Rebbe writes in Tanya,[6] when a Jew gives *tzedakah,* it is comparable to planting a seed in the ground.

When we place a coin in a *tzedakah* box or in the palm of a poor person, our gift produces results that are far beyond our expectations. That is because every mitzvah that a Jew fulfills moves worlds and brings about a fusion of the upper spiritual realms with the lower physical realm. The mitzvah joins the infinite light of God's world with the physical creation and that turns civilization into a "dwelling place for God below."

From Likutei Sichot of the Lubavitcher Rebbe, vol. 5, pp 155–160

NOTES

1. See *Likutei Sichot*, vol. 2, p. 410.

2. Possibly this distinction is due to the different nature of their sins. Noach's generation was guilty of sins of pleasure, associated with the element of water (see the Tanya, *Likutei Amarim*, end of Ch.1), while the five cities were guilty of failure to give *tzedakah. Tzedakah* is an act of kindness (*chesed*) and with their failure to act kindly, they exhibited a very high degree of the opposite trait (*gevurah*), which is associated with fire.

3. *Sanhedrin* 109b: "A certain maiden gave some bread to a poor man ... When the matter becoming known, they daubed her with honey and placed her on the parapet of the wall, and the bees came and consumed her. Thus, it is written [in Genesis 18:20], 'And God said, "The cry of Sodom and Gomorrah ... it is great (*rabah*)," whereon R' Judah commented in Rav's name: 'On account of the maiden (*ribah*).'"

4. Like all of the Noachide Laws, murder was punishable by death by the sword, not by *calah*, and not even if the entire city took part in the murder.

5. The Maharsha writes that Rashi is correct, because compromise (*peshara*) is something that cannot be commanded (which is why *tzedakah*, as *peshara*, is not included in the Seven Noachide Laws). However, the Maharsha also indicates that Rashi's line of thought does not parallel the Gemara, which explains that God commanded all of Avraham's household, including the women, to give *tzedakah*.

6. Tanya, Section 4 (*Igros Hakodesh*), Ch 8

Avraham "Negotiates" with God

Vayera
18:23

The life of our forefather, Avraham, initiated the era of Torah. With him began the process of bringing the Torah down to earth in order to connect the upper realms with the lower realm — to connect spirituality with the physical world. We see this process in the sequence of weekly Torah portions:

1. First, *Parshat Breishit*, speaks of God's creation of the universe (from Above to below).
2. Next, *Parshat Noach*, speaks of the Flood, which had the effect of purifying the world (from below to Above).
3. Finally, *Parshat Lech Lecha*, *Parshat Vayera* and *Parshat Chayei Sarah* speak of the life of Avraham whose entire mission was to connect the upper and lower realms, elevating himself and his generation, bringing down spirituality from Above, and generally paving the path for unity of both dynamics (below to Above, as well as Above to below) that was to take place later, at the giving of the Torah.

Avraham's journey began with God's instruction, "Go forth, from your land, from your birthplace and from the house of your father..." (Genesis 12:1).[1] The command was from Above, as was the goal — to bring down Godliness into "the place that I will show you." But the action Avraham took was his own — from below — and, as a result, we immediately see the initial joining of upper and lower realms.

The tentative joining of upper and lower realms is also evident in the Midrash (Rabbah 39:6) which sees a connection between Avraham's leaving his father's house in Charan and his conduct regarding the people of Sodom. Unlike Noach who failed to pray for his generation, Avraham prayed for the people of Sodom, even though they were evil. However, Avraham did not pray for them for their sake but only in the merit of the "righteous" among them (and he ceased praying once it was clear that there was not even a quorum of ten righteous men in Sodom). Therefore, it is not clear how this act characterized the path of generosity and kindness that he later pioneered. The Zohar (Part 1, 106a) even claims that, in this respect, Avraham acted improperly. If so, how can we reconcile this with his ability to connect the upper and lower realms?

The answer is that the *true* connection between the spiritual and physical realms did not take place until the Torah was given at Mt. Sinai. Thus, Avraham's divine service (*avodah*) was only a preparation and precursor to the connection that was yet to be achieved. Since the connection did not yet fully exist, it was impossible to connect the wicked people of Sodom (the lowest place on earth spiritually) with the One Above. It was possible only to connect those who were already a vessel for spirituality — the *tzaddikim*, or righteous people — in whose merit Avraham prayed. As far as the others, all Avraham could do was to pray for mercy for them.

What this indicates, then, is that the conduct of Noach, Avraham, and Moshe in their respective generations corresponded to the eras in which they lived:

1. the era preceding the preparation for receiving the Torah (Noach)
2. the era of preparation for receiving the Torah (Avraham), and
3. the era of receiving the Torah at Mt. Sinai (Moshe)

During the era preceding the preparation for receiving the Torah, there was no connection between the upper and lower realms. This is why Noach did not pray for his generation. During the next era, when the preparation for receiving the Torah began, Avraham prayed for his generation, but only in the merit of the *tzaddikim* among them. But when the full integration of the upper and lower realms finally took place after Mt. Sinai, Moshe did pray not only in the merit of the righteous of his generation, but even on behalf of those who worshipped the Golden Calf.

An example of a teacher instructing his students will help illustrate the principle at work here. A teacher may…

1. present the material as it is — from above to below, so to speak — expecting the student to absorb the subject verbatim, without any indication that the student should use his own mind, or…
2. instead of giving over the material, the teacher may impart an approach that enables the student to figure it out for himself — from below to above, or…
3. the teacher may employ a combination of the two methods above, giving the student enough of the material to get him started, but also imparting the principles of how to make his own deductions; in that manner, the teacher raises the student to his own level and enables him to approach the subject matter much as the teacher himself does.

The first approach — in which the teacher teaches the material by rote, expecting the students to remember it — has the advantage that the student receives and preserves the material as it is given to him, without changes. This approach also preserves the material on the same high level as the teacher presented it. Of course, it has the disadvantage that the student does not develop his own intellectual capabilities, but rather learns by rote. The second approach emphasizes the student's own capabilities, but sacrifices the full scope of understanding of the subject matter as it could have been taught by the teacher. It sacrifices faithfulness to the material in favor of emphasis on developing the abilities of the student. It is only the third approach that contains both advantages of the previous two approaches — it allows the student to develop and use his own faculties, while also preserving the accuracy of the material. It is this approach that eventually allows the student to reach a level of understanding similar to that of the teacher.

The three pedagogical approaches described above correspond to three epochs in Jewish history.

1. The first approach, in which the teacher gives over the material regardless of the abilities of the student, corresponds to the first ten generations from Adam to Noach. It was at that time, for example, that Chanoch was taken prematurely from the world (Genesis 5:24). He was a *tzaddik*, but only because he was born

that way. A high illumination shone on him from Above but, left to his own resources, he would have sunk to the level of others and the high light would not have shone on him. Since he would not have been able to withstand the temptations of the physical world, God took him away prematurely. In other words, he was given special spiritual status by God that didn't correspond to his role in the physical world, much like a student receiving instruction from a teacher who fails to take into account the student's limited abilities.

2. The second approach corresponds to the ten generations from Noach to Avraham, when all was dependent upon the initiative of man living in the lower realm. Thus, it was up to Noach to rebuke and warn his contemporaries, and that he did. However, since the warning was limited by Noach's human capabilities, it did not go far in helping his generation. Noach was known to be among the *katnei emunah* or those who were lacking full-fledged faith in the One Above. He relied more upon human intellect and, therefore, the influence that he had on his generation was limited. He lacked the belief in God that transcends logic and affects us from Above and could not pass it on to his generation. This is similar to the second method, when the student proceeds according to his own abilities, which may fall short of what the teacher himself has to offer.
3. Finally, the third approach applies to the generations from Avraham to Moshe, during which time the process of connecting the upper spiritual realms and the lower physical realms began. At this juncture, the righteousness and intelligence of the forefathers started to bring the spiritual realm down to the physical, and vice versa. And so, we find in Avraham's path both advantages. The beginning of his approach was based upon his own intellectual investigations but, ultimately, he did not question God's actions and served Him wholeheartedly in full faith. Thus, what he brought to the people of his generation was a combination of intellect and faith.

Avraham's actions were characteristic of the third pedagogical method previously mentioned. What the teacher imparts to the student has a powerful effect on the latter. It encourages the student to tackle the subject with his own abilities and to ascend to the level of the teacher himself. In the third approach, we see the beginning of the connection between below and Above, wherein the lower realm seeks to ascend and the upper realm begins to raise the lower realm higher, up to its own level.

But there is something missing even in the third approach, which is why it applies to the era preceding the giving of the Torah, but not to the era of Torah itself. If a student seeks to be taught, it means that he is ready to receive something from the teacher. The very fact that a student would come to class means that there exists some kind of connection, or potential for connection, between the teacher and student. Simultaneously, when a student comes to study, he presents only that side of himself that can develop intellectually. He doesn't make all of himself available — for example, for social or emotional counseling. He comes to learn, period. It is not his essential self that is changed by the educational experience, but rather his intellect. These two factors — that the student is capable of learning, but that he only opens his intellectual side, and not his entire self — do not correspond to the experience of receiving the Torah.

The situation preceding the giving of the Torah was such that there was no connection between the spiritual and physical realms — indeed, aside from the preparations of the forefathers mentioned above, there was an absolute rift between them. Only the One Above in His infinite wisdom could heal the rift, and then, when the connection took place, it was with the whole lower realm, not only with certain elevated dimensions of it.

This unique dimension of Torah — that it heals rifts previously thought to be beyond healing, and that it encompasses the essence of the world — surpassed the experience of Avraham and the other forefathers. It was achieved only by Moshe, whose love for his fellow Jews was so great that he prayed for his entire generation, including those who left Egypt as converts (the *erev rav,* or "mixed multitude") and who succumbed to idol worship during the sin of the Golden Calf. He prayed for them not only in the merit of the righteous of his generation (like Avraham) but for their own sake.

The Torah has the ability to reach even those who are so far that they seem to be in absolute conflict with spirituality and to transform their very essence. For such a power to be brought down, the world had to wait for the generation of Moshe, who connected heaven and earth during the giving of the Torah at Mt. Sinai and thereafter.[2]

These levels are also found today in our respective paths of divine service. It is our responsibility to spread and disseminate Torah but not like one who loves spirituality but doesn't care about the physical world (like the first ten generations from Adam to Noach); and not like one who teaches Torah because he has been told to, but rebukes others because he was commanded (as in the generations from Noach to Avraham); and not even like one who cares about others and wants to elevate their spiritual level, but only when he sees that they are capable of learning and elevation (like Avraham until Moshe). Rather, we should spread and disseminate Torah like one who loves his fellow Jews "like himself," without any kind of accounting of how or why or in what fashion, but only because he cares.

We should care about others not only because we want to get them involved in the Torah and its mitzvoth, but mainly because of our essential love for our fellows. By so doing, we will reach others on whatever level they may stand right now and bring them into the fold. And that is what will bring the Mashiach, speedily in our days!

From Likutei Sichot of the Lubavitcher Rebbe, vol. 15, pp. 83–92

NOTES

1. Even though the beginning of the "two thousand years of Torah" occurred when Avraham was 52 years old, when he was still in Charan, the beginning of preparation for giving of the Torah at Mt. Sinai began only after he left Charan. Even the "souls that he made in Charan" — whom he "connected to the Torah" — (Genesis 12:5 and Targum there), at the beginning of the "two thousand years of Torah" is mentioned in *Parshat Lech Lecha* even though it occurred before then.

2. Even though the revelation of the Torah at Mt. Sinai was only from Above, "and the lower realms remained in place, meaning that they demonstrated no elevation or refinement" (from the series of discourses of the year 5672 (1912) of the Rebbe Rashab, vol. 2, p.931 and see *Likutei Torah* of the Alter Rebbe *Parshat Re'eh* 28:2) and if so, then the giving of the Torah at Mt. Sinai seems to be illustrative of the first dynamic of revelation of a teacher to a student. Nevertheless Mt. Sinai gave the power and potential to the lower realms to afterwards become a *keli* or "vessel" (and not only for the illumination that was appropriate for the world, but) also for the infinite light of God that is unlimited, until the future when the world will be a "dwelling place" for the One Above. And since then as well, the world will

remain a physical world and yet it will be a *keli* and a "dwelling place," unlike the connection between a teacher and student as in the third manner (in which the level of the student rises to that of the teacher, leaving his former status behind), it emerges that Mt. Sinai imparted the power for the lower realms to join up with the upper realms, not only because of the influence of the "upper," but because the lower realms themselves could ascend (as "vessels" for the holy illumination).

Avraham's Desert Hotel

Vayera 21:33

Toward the end of our Torah portion — *Parshat Vayera* — Avraham's life seems to be building to a crescendo. He finally has a son (Yitzchak), and due to his wealth and success, he is the envy of all the families and nations surrounding him in the land of Canaan. In truth though, his only real interest is connecting with the One Above and sharing that with others. With that in mind, the Torah tells us that Avraham "planted an *eshel* in Beer Sheva and campaigned there in the name of the Lord, Master of the universe." (Genesis 21:33).

Some Torah commentators explain that an *eshel* is an orchard, while others say that it is an inn, a place for wayfarers to rest. In support of the latter interpretation, they interpret the Hebrew word *eshel* as an acrostic for "eating, drinking and sleeping" (*achila, shtiya, lina*).

As for the second part of the verse which refers to Avraham's "publicity campaign," the Talmud (*Sotah* 10a) tells us, "Do not say 'campaigned,' but 'caused others to campaign.'" Avraham used his inn (or orchard) to provide hospitality to wayfarers; once they finished eating at his table, they would stand and bless him. And then he would say to them, "Did you eat from my provisions? No. You ate from the provisions of the One Above. Give thanks and praise and bless the One who spoke and the world was created."

The Midrash (*Breishit Raba* 49:4) elaborates further on this. It tells us that some of Avraham's guests refused to bless God. In response, Avraham would demand a large payment from them, much larger than the cost of what they consumed (he justified his demand by saying that, in the desert, it was difficult to find the produce that he was feeding them). Of course, upon hearing his demand, they would immediately decide to bless God: "Blessed be the Lord of the Universe, from whose provisions we have eaten."

Here, though, we must ask a fundamental question. If some individuals did not wish to bless God of their own accord, then what was achieved by coercing them? They certainly did not really mean what they were saying; they blessed God in order to avoid payment and not really to give thanks to the One Above. Regarding those who agreed to bless God, it is possible that, by doing so, they publicized God's name in the world, but regarding those who did not believe in God, what was the point in persuading them to bless God when all they were really doing was avoiding payment?

Regarding the fulfillment of the mitzvoth after the giving of the Torah, the Rambam says that even a Jew who fulfills a commandment under duress is considered to have done the mitzvah "out of his own will." As an example, the Rambam mentions the concept of coercing a man who refuses to grant a divorce (to give a *gett*) to his wife (even though a Jewish court has decreed that it is the right course of action). Since, underneath his rebellious veneer, there lurks a Godly soul that really desires to do the mitzvah, he is considered to have done the mitzvah even if he was coerced to do so. The Rambam writes: "He desires to be considered a Jew and, as such, he wants to fulfill all of the mitzvoth and to distance himself from transgressions, but his evil inclination has led him astray. And after he is beaten to the point that his evil inclination is weakened so that finally he says 'I want,' he is considered to have divorced his wife of his own free will."

The law that the Rambam cites (in *Hilchot Girushin*, end of Ch. 2) is couched in terms of divorce, but applies to all other mitzvoth as well. Since inwardly a Jew truly prefers to do mitzvoth, the mitzvah is valid even if he fulfilled it under duress. However, in our case, the Torah was not yet given, so we cannot say that the travelers who enjoyed Avraham's hospitality really wanted to fulfill mitzvoth.

There are those (for example, the abridged *Yafeh Toar*, on the Midrash Rabbah[1]) who wish to explain that although some travelers did not bless God honestly, nevertheless Avraham had done his part. That is, Avraham did what he was supposed to do in accordance with the will of God, and if some people blessed God without really meaning it, that was not his problem. Still, what did he achieve by coercing them to bless God? Moreover, elsewhere the Midrash (Bereishit Rabbah Ch.43) says that by his actions, Avraham became a "partner with God in the creation of the universe," and made God's name known in the world. Nowhere does the Midrash distinguish between those who blessed God honestly and those who did not — it simply states that by having his guests bless God, Avraham increased awareness of God in the world. If the blessing was not sincere though, how did Avraham's conduct "increase awareness of God" in the world?

There are three different ways to elicit a positive response from those who fail to respond appropriately, and which approach to use depends upon where they are holding — how deeply buried or concealed is their true desire to do what they know is truly right.

1. With most people, who function according to intellect and emotion, and who usually do what they are supposed to do according to the Torah, it is sufficient to simply "show them the light." As a general rule, such people are not coarse, and all that is necessary is to point out to them the proper course of conduct. No negative reinforcement is necessary. Even if such people stray off the path occasionally, positive reinforcement — such as "eat and drink for free, just bless God" — is sufficient to bring them back onto the path. Most of Avraham's guests meant well and wanted to do the right thing; they just needed Avraham to show them the way, and then they were willing to "bless the One who spoke and the world was created."
2. However, there are some people for whom positive reinforcement is not sufficient. Such was the case, for example, when the Jews refused to enter the Land of Israel, after having been led astray by the spies in the desert. Moshe responded by delivering a harsh speech which caused them to recall their true purpose and inner identity. After his speech "the nation was very regretful," and they said, "we ready to go ascend to the place of which God spoke" (Numbers 15:39–40). Here was a case in which positive reinforcement was not sufficient, but some brief harsh words turned them around.

   The same is true regarding learning Torah. The Mishnah in

Ethics of the Fathers states, "Every day, a voice comes from Heaven, saying, 'Woe to the world for disdaining Torah. For everyone who fails to learn Torah should be rebuked" (*Pirkei Avot* 6:2). If the point of the Mishnah is to encourage us to learn Torah, why does it not simply show us the sweetness, light and wisdom that is the Torah? Why focus on the negative consequences, emphasizing that one who fails to learn Torah should be rebuked. But, since these words are directed at all Jews, including those who do not normally act in an enlightened and spiritual manner, the Mishnah adopts a negative tone. For those who normally fulfill the mitzvoth of the Torah but occasionally suffer a lapse, some positive reinforcement from Above will be sufficient to remind them of their true purpose in the world. But to bring out the best in those Jews who do not act spiritually, it is necessary to go beneath the surface and reach their Godly soul. In such a case, positive reinforcement may not be sufficient. It is necessary to bring their spiritual side out of concealment, and toward this end, sharp and negative words may be more effective. Hence, the heavenly voice is couched in negative terms, "everyone who fails to learn Torah should be rebuked."[2]

3. But, there is a third kind of person — those whose spiritual side is so concealed that even tough words are not sufficient to bring it out from its state of concealment. It is necessary first to shatter the exterior of vanity and coarseness that buries their divine soul. The critical words of Moshe and the heavenly voice mentioned in the *Pirkei Avot* are effective when there is a concealed divine soul and it needs only to be "actualized and enabled." Such people are sensitive to Godly issues, but sometimes their evil inclination leads them astray, and then sharp words of rebuke are sufficient to bring them back on the path.[3] But when the people possess no innate spirituality, or it is so buried under vanity and physical temptation so that their soul is inoperative, it is then necessary to shatter the veneer, and only then will it be possible to reach them in an appropriate fashion.

Two examples illustrate this concept. One is a story from the Gemara (*Taanit* 20a-b): "R' Elazar bar Shimon … once met a man who was extremely ugly… and said, 'What an empty man! How ugly is he!' … to which the man replied, 'Go and tell the Craftsman who made me how ugly is the vessel that he created!'" Here, we may ask the question, what was R' Elazar thinking? Did he not know that God created this ugly person? Moreover, how was it possible that R' Elazar should speak in such a derogatory manner to another human being? But, the truth is that as a great rabbi, R' Elazar was not merely exchanging "pleasantries" (or lack thereof) with the man. Upon seeing the ugly man, R' Elazar grasped immediately that his spiritual soul was so buried that there were no pleasant words that could elevate his spiritual status. In calling him "empty" and "ugly," R' Elazar was declaring that he could find in him no positive spiritual quality whatsoever. By referring to him in these surprising terms, R' Elazar meant to shock and shatter the man. By so doing, he hoped to break through the man's outer vanity and access his buried spiritual side.[4] And this is what happened. By replying "Go and tell the craftsman who made me…." the man showed that he was aware of God and acknowledged His existence. At the very least, he admitted to the existence of his Creator. Thus, R' Elazar's words had the intended effect of shattering the man's external veneer and revealing the spark of Godliness inside.[5]

"R' Elazar bar Shimon … once met a man who was extremely ugly… and said, 'What an empty man! How ugly is he!' … to which the man replied, 'Go and tell the Craftsman who made me how ugly is the vessel that he created!'"

Another example comes from the Rebbe Rashab (the fifth Lubavitcher Rebbe). Once a Jew, in very poor and desperate circumstances, came to the Rebbe to ask for a blessing to take him out of his difficult situation. The Rebbe refused to bless him, saying that there was nothing he could do to help him, and the Jew left the Rebbe's office sobbing in great distress. The Rebbe's brother (R' Zalman Aharon) asked the Rebbe, "Is this the proper way? Someone comes to ask for your blessing and you say to him that you cannot help him? And he leaves shedding tears out of great distress?" The Rebbe then stood up and had the man brought in again, whereupon he blessed him. After the Rebbe's blessing, the man's circumstances underwent a transformation and his situation improved dramatically. Here then the question is, why did the Rebbe not bless him to begin with? Why did he put him through the torment of saying he could not help, only to bring him back to the room and bless him?

And if the Rebbe truly could not help at first, why did he not at least give him some encouraging words, rather than allowing him to exit in great distress? The answer is that the Rebbe saw that the man needed a huge blessing, coming from a very high spiritual place, but that in his current spiritual condition, he simply was not capable (and perhaps not worthy) of receiving it. That is why the Rebbe told him that he could do nothing to help. However, his words had such a powerful effect on the man that they shattered him completely, transforming him into a vessel that could receive the blessing he needed. In other words, after the Rebbe's statement, the man was so broken-hearted that he became even more committed to God, thus becoming a fitting vessel to receive the blessing of the One Above through the Rebbe.

In these two illustrations, the intention behind the words was not merely to reveal the otherwise hidden aspect of the men's souls. Rather, the idea was to deal with their hardened veneer, to break through and shatter it and, in so doing, to transform each man into a vessel to reveal Godliness. The same was true of Avraham's words to the passers-by who initially refused to bless the One Above. The difference is that, since the giving of the Torah, Jews possess a divine soul, however revealed or concealed it may be. It may be necessary to provide positive reinforcement to reveal it, or it may be necessary to shatter their egos with strong words. In either case, the result is the revelation of the divine spark inside the Jew.

However, in the case of Avraham, before the Torah was given, there was no divine soul to reveal among the travelers whom Avraham entertained. Nevertheless, especially after the Flood, everyone had some ability to recognize the Creator and express gratitude to Him. Most of the time, simply by requesting them to bless the One Above whose food they had eaten, Avraham was able to elicit from them the appropriate recognition that God was the Creator. Since Avraham was occupied with publicizing monotheism and busy explaining spiritual concepts, the masses generally understood him. But, when that did not happen, and some people refused to accept Avraham's explanations and teachings about the existence of God, Avraham had to use more forceful techniques. The point was not to reveal their divine soul, because at that point in history it just did not exist. The point was to break their external resistance so that they would acknowledge the presence of God.

Our lesson for today is that, like Avraham, we have to reach every Jew. Even if what is needed is food and drink (and that is usually the case), whatever steps are necessary must be taken to reach out to all Jews and teach them about God and Torah. The question may arise: Is it permissible to "force" a Jew to do a mitzvah? And, if we use "coercion," are we really achieving anything? The answer is that pressure can be good or the opposite. We have to have the sensitivity to know when powerful persuasion will have a positive or a negative effect on a particular person. If it had a positive effect on the travelers Avraham hosted and persuaded them to acknowledge God's existence, it may certainly work now, after the giving of the Torah at Mt. Sinai, when the world is a much better vessel capable of receiving Godliness. Inside, every Jew wants to do a mitzvah. Nevertheless, any persuasion must be tuned to the individual to bring out his or her divine soul and not the opposite.

We have to have the sensitivity to know when powerful persuasion will have a positive or a negative effect on a particular person.

From Likutei Sichot of the Lubavitcher Rebbe, vol. 15, pp. 122–128

NOTES

1. The unabridged *Yafeh Toar* says, "Even though this was coercion, and the person might not mean what he was saying while blessing God, that was not a problem, because all Avraham required was that the table where his guests ate should not be a low and disgusting place, and for that purpose it was sufficient if the guests would verbally bless God. Moreover, the majority of his guests were his company and friends, so they blessed whole-heartedly."

2. From the fact that "the voice from Heaven" has an effect on him, we know that the *Pirkei Avot* is talking about the kind of person whose soul-source makes itself "heard" in his conscious soul as it is enclothed in a body. The higher levels of the soul that are not enclothed in the body "hear" the heavenly voice and transmit the message to the lower levels that are enclothed in the body, so that the person "wakes up," so to speak. See *Keter Shem Tov* in the *hosafot, seif* 79, and in *Sefer Haredim* in the conclusion.

3. Such as, for example, the words mentioned in the Tanya, Ch. 29: "You are evil, and wicked, and disgusting!" However, the Tanya concludes with the words, "How long will you hide and contradict the truth?!" from which we understand that Tanya is speaking of someone who is disturbed by his distance from God. Here, on the other hand, we are suggesting that the strong negative words are only "You

are evil, etc...." without the conclusion mentioned in the Tanya. Similarly regarding the rebuke and heartbreaking words to the "spies" (cited in the Tanya there, Ch. 29): the subjugation of their heart occurred not because they were far from God, but as a result of the words themselves. Accordingly, we might suggest that the intention of the Alter Rebbe in the Tanya (Ch. 29) by mentioning the "spies" is not only to bring a proof to what he mentioned earlier ("this is mentioned openly in the Torah"), but to allude that the benefit of the rebuke is not only among those who are far from God at the ultimate distance," but to whom the rebuke matters (touches them in their soul), but even to those who claim openly not to believe in God. Even such people, once they are "broken," reveal the true inner nature of their soul.

4. The conclusion of the Gemara there is that the ugly man forgave R' Elazar, "as long as he does not [rebuke in this manner] on a regular basis." It does not say, "as long as one no longer rebukes in this manner." That is because the usage of sharp words of rebuke is acceptable, but not necessary in most cases. Most people do not require this kind of rebuke in order to achieve remorse for their conduct, even if outwardly it might appear that they need it.

5. In the continuation of the story, R' Elazar apologized to the man for having been so quick to criticize and insult him. From the quick response time of the man's retort ("Go tell the Craftsman who made me"), it is evident that he was not on the very low level that R' Elazar originally assumed him to be. It would have been more difficult and taken more time to "break through" to someone on such a low level. Moreover, by mentioning the "Craftsman," the man made it clear that he was a *keli*, or "vessel" for Godliness, not as previously assumed by R' Elazar. Therefore, R' Elazar recognized his mistake and apologized.

The Test of the Akeida "Sacrifice"

Vayera 22:1

Looking at the three weekly Torah portions of Genesis in which Avraham is the protagonist, there is so much happening there that we have to pay close attention to avoid missing any of the details of his eventful life. This week, in *Parshat Vayera*, the main theme is the sacrifice of Yitzchak — better known as the *Akeidah*, or the "Binding."

Let's look carefully at the *Akeidah*, which was a seminal event in Jewish history. One of the medieval sages — Abarbanel — described it thus: "[It represents] the entire prestige of the Jews and their merit before their Father in Heaven, which is why we recite it before our prayers every day."

But, when you think about it, throughout Jewish history, there have been plenty of Jews who were willing to give up their own lives for the sake of God. And, indeed, many of them unfortunately did so, yet few (if any) of them heard a direct command from God. Avraham had direct communication with God, who told him to sacrifice his son. How is this greater than what all these other Jews did, voluntarily giving up their lives, without any kind of command or communication from Above?[1]

For example, in the time of the Talmud, R' Akiva and nine other major sages of the Talmud were executed by the Romans for the "sin" of spreading and teaching Torah. There was no command from Above for them to give up their lives; they could have resisted and perhaps used their spiritual powers to totally avoid this punishment. But they understood that it was a divine decree, even without being told by God. How was their self-sacrifice less than that of Avraham?

There are some who answer that giving up one's own life is not as dreadful as giving up the life of your child. However, many generations after Avraham, we find that Chanah [who lived in the time of Greek persecution of the Jews and whose story is recorded in the Book of the Maccabees] did just that, giving up her seven children for the sake of God. And, as she herself said speaking of Avraham, "You tied [your son] on one altar; I tied mine on seven altars" (*Gittin* 57b). In fact, Jewish history is rife with stories of Jews who not only gave up their own lives, but also their children's lives.

Ikarim (a medieval work of philosophical investigation into Judaism) attempts to explain that Avraham had a choice. He could have said to God, "Wait a minute, You just told me that my descendants would come from my son Yitzchak. How can you now ask me to sacrifice him?" And since Avraham could have (at least theoretically) prevented the sacrifice in this way, his self-sacrifice was greater than that of others in later generations who had no choice in the matter. Moreover, *Ikarim* adds that Avraham was asked by God to give up his son Yitzchak; he was not commanded to do so. Therefore, he had a very reasonable way of avoiding the sacrifice, by simply refusing God's request, and yet Avraham did not refuse. On the other hand, the holy Jews of later generations were obligated by the commandment of the Torah, "And I should be sanctified among the children of Israel" (Leviticus 22:32). Avraham was under no such halachic obligation (since his act preceded the giving of the Torah).

Aside from the fact that from Avraham's perspective, a direct command from God did constitute an obligation (for even a request from God seemed like a command in Avraham's eyes, since he knew that is what God wanted from him), we find many instances in later generations when righteous Jews could have found halachic leniencies in order to avoid giving up their lives to sanctify God. And yet, even under those circumstances, they sought to do just the opposite — to demonstrate their devotion and determination to sanctify God's name even if it meant death by cruel means.

The answer that is mentioned in Chassidic literature (in a book of discourses of the Rebbe Rashab for the year 1918, p. 283 and also from the book of discourses of the Rebbe Rayatz for the year 1928, p.102) is that the path of serving God by giving up one's life (under the narrowly proscribed circumstances mentioned by the Rambam) was initiated by Avraham. That is, the reason that later generations found it relatively easier to give up their lives to sanctify God's name was because Avraham already opened up the path. If he had not done so, then later generations would have had much more difficulty in doing so.

Every path of serving God is difficult until the spiritual channels are opened up. Once they are opened, then the path is a "two-way street," so to speak, and God clears the way for the person who wants to sanctify His name in this manner. It is the initial step that was difficult because, until Avraham demonstrated his willingness to give up his son's life, it was not apparent that this was a way of serving God. But, once Avraham initiated it, the holy Jews of later generations found that path open and gave up their lives when the situation called for it.

Every path of serving God is difficult until the spiritual channels are opened up. Once they are opened, then the path is a "two-way street," so to speak

However, there is another question that comes up here, this time from the life of Avraham himself. Long before the test of the *Akeidah*, Avraham went through another test. Way back in Ur Casdim, where Avraham grew up, he became an agitator against idol worship. As he grew in knowledge and comprehension of the existence of the one God, he simultaneously rebelled against idol worship. He did so quite publicly, demonstrating in no uncertain terms to the people of his town that he was a threat to their idolatrous way of life. As a result, the Mesopotamian ruler Nimrod decided to have Avraham executed; he threatened him that, unless he bowed to idols, he would be thrown into a furnace. When Avraham stood steadfast in his rejection of idolatry, he was thrown into the furnace but was miraculously saved. Here, then, was an example of self-sacrifice that was not commanded from Above. No one told Avraham to reject Nimrod's demand to bow down to idols. He did so on his own, and this was well before the test of the *Akeidah*, when he was asked to sacrifice his son. So, the question remains: What was so special about the test of the *Akeidah*? It seems that the path to serving God by giving up one's life was opened up by Avraham long before then![2]

Based upon the earlier explanation — that Avraham pioneered the spiritual path of self-sacrifice — it is understood that, without his initial act, it would be impossible to serve God in this fashion even now. Avraham created the channel. Self-sacrifice means giving oneself up for a higher cause — in this case, for the sake of sanctifying God. Quite literally, it means giving up one's own existence — and this is impossible without divine help from Above. Man was created and, in his own subjective experience, he "exists," therefore he cannot be expected to erase his status as a creature of God of his own volition. "A prisoner cannot free himself" — for that, divine intervention is necessary.

However, it may be argued that we find situations in which non-Jews also gave up their lives in service of God. In fact, there is an opinion that non-Jews must give up their lives if challenged to violate the Seven Noachide Laws. [And, in the last few years, it has unfortunately not been unusual for non-Jews to kill themselves as "suicide bombers" an act which they, and others, justify in the name of their religion. The Torah is far from such barbarity, but how do we distinguish philosophically between our own self-sacrifice and that which we see among the non-Jews of the world?][3]

The truth is that not all self-sacrifice is worthy of the name. The mere fact that a person takes his own life "for the sake of God" does not necessarily qualify his act as true self-sacrifice according to the Torah. It is possible that the person took this step after weighing his options and concluding that it was the only step that made sense in his situation. He could have made an intellectual calculation and decided that he had more to gain by taking his own life than by remaining alive. His intellectual accounting may have led him to the conclusion that he will have a higher existence in the next world if he takes his own life [as in the Muslim calculation that he will get "seventy virgins in the world to come," and the like — translator's note]. This kind of calculation is found among the non-Jews, wherein they are convinced that taking their own lives will lead them to a higher form of existence afterward. Or, inversely, they think that they have no reason to remain alive — this, as well, is a calculated pretext for taking one's own life.

Real self-sacrifice occurs when one gives himself up — gives up his "I," his ego — to God without making any kind of calculation or intellectual accounting whatsoever. He gives himself up completely in a way that indicates that his own existence means nothing to him whatsoever — only the existence of God matters. And that, we might say, was the path of Avraham. In fact, we can see clearly that this was the case regarding the *Akeidah*, but it is not as clear regarding the test that Avraham underwent in Ur Casdim with Nimrod.

The test of Ur Casdim was a public contest pitting monotheism against idol worship. Avraham was, of course, totally committed to getting the message of monotheism out to the world; indeed, his motivation in all of his activities at that time was to denounce idol worship and promote the recognition and worship of the One God. This is why his self-sacrifice in Ur Casdim, as noble as it was, seemed to be for a reason. He acted to remain true to his ideals and promote monotheism.[4]

But the same cannot be said of the *Akeidah*. Here, there was no reason, other than this was what God said to do. And God sent him this test to see if Avraham was "God fearing." And, concurrently, there was no publicizing of the miracle; no one other than Avraham and Yitzchak knew what happened. As the Ibn Ezra (commenting on Genesis 22:1) said, "At the time of the *Akeidah*, even the assistants [Avraham's servants] were not around." Quite the opposite — his act of binding his son on the altar would have likely erased any chances he had of spreading monotheism in subsequent generations. It would have contradicted the very principle that Avraham strove so mightily to establish — the existence of the One God. The only purpose of the *Akeidah* was that it was requested by God and, therefore, Avraham complied.

A new principle was established at the *Akeidah* — Avraham was asked to undergo a test of self-sacrifice that occupied no place whatsoever in human intellect. It was nothing less than the will of God. Automatically, then, it required total self-nullification.[5]

Now, we can explain why the Talmud (*Sanhedrin* 89b) says that Avraham was asked to undergo this test so that no one would be able to say that the previous nine tests were for naught. If Avraham had not undertaken this test, then the world might have claimed that the only reason that Avraham passed the previous tests was on account of his own intellectual calculations. His thoughts and intentions were holy but, since they were still in the category of intellect, they only served his own purposes. But, were he to be tested in something that did not mesh with his own calculations, then it was not clear if he would "pass the test."

But pass the test he did.

Indeed, by passing this test, Avraham proved retroactively that even the previous tests were undertaken with self-sacrifice. Even though it was possible to apply intellect and calculate a holy reason why it made sense to stand up to these tests, nevertheless, Avraham passed them for the *right* reason — because he was totally committed to the One Above. And that also is why Avraham opened new channels by passing this test — the *Akeidah* — and not by passing the previous nine tests.

The point of opening up a new path of worship — any holy, Torah path — is so that Jews in all subsequent generations will be able to serve God in the exact same manner as those who established that path. That means, in this case, that all Jews who served God with true self-sacrifice passed their tests in the same way that Avraham passed all of his tests.

Even if it is possible to make a calculation and see that there is a reason — a good and holy reason — for us to undertake a given test, nevertheless we pass the test for the same reason that Avraham did, because of our inner attitude of total sacrifice to God. That is the true meaning of opening up a new path in divine service.

From Likutei Sichot of the Lubavitcher Rebbe, vol. 20, pp.73–78

NOTES

1. At first glance, it is possible to explain that the *Akeidah* produced a "change in the nature of Avraham's character," as expressed in Chassidic discourses such as *Zeh Hayom* 5694 (1934) of the Rebbe Rayatz and others. Until the *Akeidah*, Avraham served God only out of love, but after the *Akeidah*, he served out of fear as well (which is why in the verses following the *Akeidah*, God said, "Now, I know that you are God-fearing"). However, this does not change the original motivation of God to test Avraham with the *Akeidah*, since "the previous tests were not substantive." For even if the *Akeidah* changed Avraham's essential nature (previously he "loved God" naturally, now he also feared God), the previous tests were also tests — in particular, the test of Ur Casdim which demanded Avraham's physical self-sacrifice.

2. In *Sefer Hasichot* 5703 (*Sichat Chag HaPesach*, p. 94 and in *Likutei Diburim*, vol. 3, p. 430b), the Rebbe Rayatz wrote that Avraham "opened the conduit" with his self-sacrifice in Ur Casdim. And so, he states in the discourse, *Padah b'Shalom* 5684 (1924): "When Avraham was thrown into the furnace, he did not think about self-sacrifice, but remained committed to his path and, in this manner, he opened the conduit of *mesiras nefesh* for those who followed after him." And so is understood from *Sefer Hasichot* 5702, p.30 (*Hayom Yom* of *Gimmel* Mar Cheshvan) — the *mesirat nefesh* that Avraham bequeathed to the world was in order to publicize Godliness in the world, which is what occurred at Ur Casdim. See also *Likutei Sichot*, vol. 10, p. 205 and vol. 13, p. 209. But in *Sefer Maamorim* 5677 (1918) of the Rashab, and 5688 (1928) of the Rayatz, the opening of the conduit of *mesiras nefesh* occurred at the *Akeidah*.

3. This section of the translation is not from the *sicha* of the Rebbe.

4. Nevertheless, Avraham's *mesirat nefesh* in promulgating belief in One God, even if for a "reason," was not comparable by any stretch of the imagination to the abhorrent practice of non-Jews who explode themselves in the presence of innocents,

taking not only their own lives but the lives of countless others. Such deviants are motivated by a selfish interest, such as "seventy-two virgins" or a "better life" in the world to come — and not by any principle of faith or belief. The need to kill others (and the "more the better") belies their commitment to any principle or religious belief — if they really meant to sanctify God in their name, it would be sufficient to take their own lives. The need to kill others demonstrates that their real motivation is senseless hatred.

5. In this manner, it may be possible to resolve the various explanations for the *Akeidah*: In *Igeret Hakodesh* 21, the Alter Rebbe explains that, with the *Akeidah*, Avraham demonstrated special speed and alacrity, and that was the reason it took place. The Alter Rebbe does not explain, as we do here, that Avraham "opened the conduit" to serve God with *mesiras nefesh* at the *Akeidah*. And elsewhere, it is explained that "opening the conduit" occurred at Ur Casdim, and not at the *Akeidah*. Yet, as explained here, 1) the test of Ur Casdim was not similar to the test of the *Akeidah* and 2) the discourses mentioned above state clearly that the "opening of the conduit" is the explanation for the *Akeidah* ... [So, there seem to be several contradictions here], but if we explain that the *Akeidah* proved retroactively that the *mesiras nefesh* of Ur Casdim was real, then all falls into place. All the other explanations were applicable when the event (Ur Casdim and the other tests) occurred. But once Avraham proved his devotion with *mesiras nefesh* at the *Akeidah*, it became clear what was his underlying motivation all along, during all of the ten tests that he underwent previously, including Ur Casdim.

Life of Sarah?

Chayei Sarah 23:1

It is known that the name of the weekly Torah portion gives us clues as to its true content. But when we look at *Parshat Chayei Sarah*, we find that the stories related therein contradict its stated theme — "Life of Sarah."

First, the purchase of the burial cave for Sarah (*Maarat Machpelah*) took place after her death. Then, we read that the subsequent marriage of Yitzchak and Rivkah brought solace to Yitzchak after his mother's death (Genesis 24:67).[1] As well, we learn that, after Sarah's death, Avraham married Keturah and had six children with her before sending them all off to the "east" with "gifts." (Genesis 25:6) According to the Midrash (*Breishit Rabba* 61:4), Keturah is another name for Hagar, Sarah's maid-servant who gave birth to Avraham's first son, Yishmael; he also figures after the death of Sarah, returning to the path of his father after having strayed. None of these events happened during Sarah's life — they were all associated with her death in one way or another — and yet the Torah portion is called *Chayei Sarah*, meaning "Life of Sarah."

How can we make sense of this?

The sages (R' Yohanan, Taanit 5B) say about our forefather Yaakov/Israel that "Yaakov did not die." (The Torah only records that he "was gathered to his people." It does not say that he "died," as it does regarding Avraham and Yitzchak). The sages explain that because his progeny (the Jews) are still alive, so Yaakov himself is "alive," since the Jews — the Children of Israel — maintain and carry on his beliefs. Similarly, we may say about Sarah that, since her progeny live on, she herself lives on.[2] In fact, the main fruits of Sarah's life became apparent only after she passed away, and this is why our Torah portion is called *Chayei*

Sarah, the "Life of Sarah." In it are recorded the most important fruits of Sarah's labors, all of which became evident after her death.

In order to understand this better, it is instructive to look at the offspring of Avraham and Sarah. Avraham is described in the Torah as "father of many nations," and indeed his first son, Yishmael, gave rise to the predominantly Arab peoples who have populated many nations of the earth. But with Sarah, Avraham sired only Yitzchak, who took his place as one of the forefathers of the Jewish people, without giving rise to any other nations. So, while Avraham is the "father of many nations" as well as of the Jews, Sarah is the "mother of the Jews" alone. And although Avraham spoke to and attempted to influence all people, his wife Sarah sought to establish the exclusive hegemony of the Jewish line; when Yishmael misbehaved, she insisted, "Expel this maidservant and her son; the son of this maidservant will not inherit along with my son…" (Genesis 21:10) Her emphasis on exclusivity is expressed throughout our Torah portion in various ways, since Sarah's purpose in serving God was to establish the Jewish people as separate and distinct from the rest of mankind.

That she succeeded we see beginning with her burial site, *Maarat Machpelah*. Avraham sought to purchase this specific cave for Sarah because Adam and Eve were already buried there. As their final resting place, this cave had a connection to all of mankind. But, once Sarah was buried there, it became the sole possession of the Jewish people, without any connection to any other nation. (This also demonstrates that the Jews were the most significant progeny of Adam and Eve.[3])

The next development in the unique status of the Jewish people is found in the search for Yitzchak's wife. The story of this mission, as undertaken by Avraham's servant Eliezer, makes it clear that the distinction between Yitzchak and the rest of his family applied not only to Avraham's immediate family but also to his extended family.

The Gemora (Yoma 28B) tells us that Eliezer "disseminated Avraham's Torah" to others (Rashi on Gen 15:2). And yet, when Eliezer sought to marry off his daughter to Yitzchak, Avraham refused. He distinguished between the descendants of Ham (from whom Eliezer descended) and the descendants of Shem (from whom he and his family descended). Since the descendants of Ham were "cursed" (on account of Ham's misdeeds) while the descendants of Shem were "blessed," Avraham would not allow his son to marry the daughter of Eliezer.[4] Despite Eliezer's obvious positive qualities, it was impossible to mix the two nations. Yitzchak could marry only someone from his own family line. This is part of the distinction that his mother Sarah established in order to set apart the Jewish people from all others.

Finally, at the end of our Torah portion, we see the distinction between Jews and non-Jews taken to a new pinnacle. Avraham has children with Hagar/Keturah, but sends them off to the "east" with "gifts." This is because, as Sarah said regarding Yishmael, "the son of this maidservant will not inherit along with my son…" Again, she wished to distinguish the Jews from the non-Jews. Even though offspring of her maidservant, Hagar/Keturah, were also sired by Avraham, it was Sarah who established that Yitzchak would sire the Jewish people exclusively and guaranteed that they would be forever separate.

And, indeed, we find that when enumerating the descendants of Yishmael, the Torah first mentions that he is "the son of Avraham," and then immediately adds, "born to Hagar, the maidservant of Sarah." Moreover, when Yishmael did *teshuvah* at the end of his life, he recognized Yitzchak's primacy in relation to Avraham's inheritance. This happened because, throughout her life, Sarah's divine service was to establish and maintain the exclusivity of the Jewish people through her son Yitzchak, even though this became clear only after her passing.[5]

But, we may understand this theme on a deeper level as well. The ultimate purpose of the Jews is to serve God by fulfilling the mitzvoth of the Torah. Even the basic Seven Noachide Laws (prohibiting theft, murder, incest, idol worship, blasphemy and animal cruelty, as well as mandating the establishment of courts of law to enforce these laws) are for the purpose of establishing a civilized world. However, Jews fulfill a completely different role: Their purpose is to draw Godliness down into the world, thereby improving and enhancing the world with spirituality.

Therefore, non-Jews must strive to do their part. From the events of our Torah portion we see not only that during her lifetime Sarah established the exclusivity of the Jewish people, but that she exemplified the notion that when a non-Jew raises obstacles to fulfillment of the will of God, he is removed from the scene. And now, after her death, that is exactly what happened.

When Avraham first approached Ephron the Hittite regarding the purchase of *Maarat Machpelah*, he described himself as a "visitor and resident among you." At first glance, he was either one or the other — a visitor or a permanent resident — so why does Avraham describe himself as both? Rashi (on Gen 23:4) explains Avraham's words citing a Midrash (*Breishit Rabba* 58:6) that recounts Avraham's thought process: "If you are willing to sell the cave, then I am like a visitor and I will pay fully. But if you refuse, then I will exercise my right of citizenship and take the cave from you rightfully by law, since it was promised to me by God..."

The entire Land of Israel was promised to Avraham and his descendants, but it came to them in stages. It was conquered by Yehoshua when the Jews entered the Land after wandering in the desert for 40 years, but even prior to that, *Maarat Machpelah* was acquired by Avraham privately.[6] The divine intention was for the Land of Israel to come into Jewish hands but, in the meantime, it had come into Ephron's hands for the purpose of transferring it to Avraham.[7] So, if Ephron had attempted to prevent the transfer, then Avraham would have displaced him, nullifying his ownership and thereby also uprooting his whole reason for existence. The Torah does not specify how, but Rashi (based on the Midrash above) implies that if Ephron had gotten in the way, he would have somehow been removed from the picture.

The same was true of anyone who would have tried to prevent the marriage of Yitzchak and Rivkah.[8] In fact, Rivkah's father, Betuel, did attempt to prevent the match from taking place. Rashi (basing himself on the Midrash in *Bereishit Rabba* 60:12) says that he was killed by an angel, so the marriage could go through. When someone tries to stand in the way of the divine will, he loses his reason to exist and is removed from the scene.

And finally, Yishmael, who did *teshuvah*, giving open recognition to Yitzchak as the true first-born and inheritor of Avraham, did so only toward the end of his father's life. His *teshuvah* was in response to Avraham's prayer, "Would that Yishmael would 'live' before You" (Genesis 17:18), meaning "live a life of Torah." Yishmael's *teshuvah* lasted while Avraham was alive, but Rashi on the final verses of our Torah portion (Gen 25:18) tells us that, after Avraham died, Yishmael "fell" (from Bereishit Rabba 62:5). Even though Yishmael remained a tzadik, nevertheless he was no longer spiritually "alive" in the same sense that he was when his father Avraham was still alive. While Avraham was alive, Yishmael recognized the true place of Yitzchak as Avraham's heir. But, upon Avraham's death, he "fell" spiritually. The implication is that he no longer recognized Yitzchak as the sole heir of Avraham — and therefore he "fell." The Torah does not specify what exactly occurred, but the Midrash (Rabba 62:5) suggests that Yishmael lost his spiritual status. Once again, when someone fails to fulfill the role for which he was created, he no longer has any significance in the scheme of things, and no longer truly "exists."

This effect on the world — recognition that any creature's true existence is dependent upon fulfillment of the will of God — comes not from Avraham, but from Sarah. Avraham, as "father of many nations," maintained and developed connections with non-Jews, and they gained recognition and identity through him. When they became members of his community (the "souls that Avraham made"), they took on newfound spiritual status and identity by recognizing the one God, Creator of the world. However, Sarah's divine service was different. Her job was to separate Jew from non-Jew, and to make sure that it was her son Yitzchak who received Avraham's inheritance and continued his legacy. This is reflected in her name as well — Sarah from the word *srarah* meaning "having dominion over," and the word *sar*, meaning "minister." It was Sarah who established the principle of Jewish dominion over the nations of the world. Through Sarah, it became clear that the Jews were the main reason for creation so that they could create a dwelling place for God on earth, and the point of non-Jewish existence is to create the appropriate environment in the world for Jews to accomplish their purpose by fulling the mitzvoth of the Torah.

Avraham, as "father of many nations," maintained and developed connections with non-Jews, and they gained recognition and identity through him.

There is an important lesson for us here regarding the claims of non-Jews to the Land of Israel. When the Arabs claim that we have usurped their residence and, as the descendants of Yishmael they are the real owners, the response must be that, first of all, the vast majority of Arabs are not descendants of Yishmael (since Sennacherib, the Assyrian ruler, moved all the nations around and relocated them).[9] But aside from that, Yishmael's true lineage comes from Hagar, the maidservant of Sarah. As such, he was not the heir to God's promise to Avraham that his descendants will inherit the Land. That promise applied only to Yitzchak, son of Sarah, and to his descendants through Yaakov.

So, when anyone comes with wild claims that Israel belongs to them, they need to be reminded firmly and clearly that the Torah, in which they also believe, says that it is the descendants of Yitzchak, not of Yishmael, who inherited the Land of Israel. In that way, they will peacefully accept their real status, as the descendants of Sarah's maidservant, and fulfill their true purpose which is to make the Land of Israel a fitting place for Jews to learn Torah and fulfill its mitzvoth.

From Likutei Sichot of the Lubavitcher Rebbe, vol. 15, pp. 145–154

NOTES

1. The very concept of Yitzchak getting married occurred to Avraham only after the *Akeidah*, and, according to Rashi, the news of the *Akeida* is what caused Sarah's passing. See Rashi's commentary on Genesis 23:2.

2. The Zohar (part 1, 122b) says that, "Sarah arrived, descended [to a place of impurity in Egypt], ascended [back to Israel] and the impurity did not cling to her ... she merited a supernal life for herself and her husband ... clinging to life and that is why her Torah portion refers to 'life.'"

3. The Arizal states (see *Likutei Torah*, Psalm 32), "When God created Adam, all the souls who were included within him were Jewish souls, and if he had not transgressed, no other nations would have emerged."

4. Yishmael, as well as the subsequent sons whom Avraham sired with Hagar, could also be considered "Semites," since Avraham was from Shem (progenitor of all "Semites") and descendants took on their father's blood line among *bnei Noach*. But since God told Avraham to "listen to the voice of Sarah" and drive Yishmael out of his house, and that the continuation of the Avrahamic line would come from Yitzchak and not from his other sons, we see that it was Sarah, not Avraham, who established the exclusivity of the Jewish people.

5. Although it was Avraham who performed these actions, he did so under the influence of Sarah. For example, it was Avraham who sent Yishmael away, but he did so at the express demand of Sarah.

6. From *Bereishit Rabba* 79:7 — "[There are] three places that the nations of the earth cannot extort the Jews and say, "You stole this from us" — *Maarat Machpela*, *Beit Hamikdash*, and the tomb of Yosef." Moreover, the sages (*Pirkei d'Rebi Eliezer*, Ch. 26) say that Pharaoh gave the land of Goshen to Sarah. The Radak (on Joshua 11:16) says, "And it [Goshen] is included among the cities of the Jews." Also see the Tosefot noted there, and the Radal, as well as p. 407 of *Likutei Sichot*, vol 15.

7. The Maggid of Mezeritch (cited in *Ohr HaTorah* of the Tzemach Tzedek, *Vayeitzei* vol. 5, p. 869a) writes, "Since Yaakov left 'letters' with Lavan that were not yet extracted [and spiritually elevated)], Lavan ran after Yaakov to 'give' him the letters that Yaakov had left with him. This resulted in an added episode in the Torah,

composed of those letters." Similarly, the episode in which Ephron sold *Maarat Machpelah* to Avraham resulted in an additional narrative in the Torah, demonstrating once more that the purpose of creation is for the Torah.

8. In addition to the fact that Eliezer was in need of the family's agreement in order to take Rivkah with him to marry Yitzchak (and thus was added an entire episode to the Torah), this event also contributed the known principle that "the conversation of the servants of the forefathers is more valuable to God than the Torah of their sons." [Thus, our Torah portion not only singles out and elevates the Jews, but also the Torah itself].

9. See Rambam *Hilchot Issurei Bia* 52:21 and R' Avraham ibn Ezra on Gen 27:40 (at the end). Ibn Ezra states clearly that there are few if any Yishmaelim left in the world, and that was during his generation, 900 years ago.

Avraham Acquires Hebron for the Jews

Chayei Sarah 23:4

Previously (in our discussions of *Parshat Vayera* and *Parshat Lech Lecha*), we examined God's promises of the Land of Israel to the Jewish people. One of those was the promise to give the Land to Avraham and his offspring as a gift, while another presented it as an inheritance. In this week's Torah portion, *Parshat Chayei Sarah*, we see that the same concept applies to public and private ownership of the Land.

Parshat Chayei Sarah starts with the negotiations between Ephron the Hittite and Avraham over the purchase of a burial cave, which today is known as *Maarat Machpelah* ("Cave of the Double Tombs" or "Cave of the Patriarchs"). Avraham sought to buy this cave in order to bury his recently deceased wife, Sarah.

According to the *Pirkei d'Rebi Eliezer* (Ch 36), the Hittites who held possession of the area knew that the entire Land was promised to Avraham and his descendants. However, they were not about to let it go easily. Therefore, Avraham devised a strategy. This is how the Midrash relates his thought process: "If you are willing to sell the cave, then I am like a visitor and I will pay fully. But if you refuse, then I will exercise my right of citizenship and take the cave from you rightfully by law, since it was promised to me by God…" As the negotiations went on, the Hittites said to Avraham: "We know that in the future God will give to your offspring all of these lands. Take an oath with us now that they will not take the city of Jebus (Jerusalem) against the will of the Jebusites (who were also Hittites)." Avraham agreed to take an oath and so they sold him the cave.

There are a number of questions that must be asked about this Midrash:

1. If the entire Land, including the city of Jebus/Jerusalem had been promised to Avraham and his descendants, how could he agree not to conquer it? God made a covenant many years earlier with Avraham to give him the Land — how could Avraham go against his covenant with God?[1]
2. Why did the Hittites inject the issue of Jebus/Jerusalem at this point, as Avraham sought to buy *Maarat Machpelah* which is located in Hebron? It would have made more sense to treat the two locations as different issues rather than complicate the transaction.
3. Rashi's commentary quotes Avraham as saying, "If you refuse, then I will ... take the cave from you rightfully by law for God has promised it to me (in Genesis 12:7): 'To your descendants I will give this Land...'" But, since it was Avraham himself who sought to buy the cave, and not his descendants, wouldn't it have made more sense to cite God telling him (in Genesis 13:15) "To you [Avraham] I will give this entire Land..."?

In order to explain, we must draw a distinction between public and private ownership. When a nation takes possession of a country, the entire land is associated with every citizen of that nation — this is called public ownership. Into this category falls the principle of "eminent domain," in which a king or government can confiscate private land for public needs or build a road through private land for the purposes of the nation as a whole. However, this does not contradict the concept of private ownership, in which an individual, even from another nation, may come and buy a piece of property for his own use. In such a case, the land is rightfully his unless dictated otherwise by the needs of the public.

In the time of Avraham, the Hittites were the public owners of the Land. The area of *Maarat Machpelah* in the city of Hebron, as well as the city of Jebus, fell under their jurisdiction. Although this land was to eventually come into the hands of Avraham and his progeny, that had not yet taken place; at this point in time, the Hittites were the rightful public owners. However, Avraham knew that this was the correct place to bury Sarah, because Adam and Eve were buried in *Maarat Machpelah.*

So, he reasoned that if the Hittites were amenable to a private purchase, he would establish private ownership over this piece of property under their jurisdiction. But if they were unwilling to sell, then Avraham realized the time had come to establish Jewish public ownership over this Land, in order to bury Sarah. In that case, he was willing to take the land "rightfully," since in any case it was to become Jewish. If the Hittites were unwilling to sell, then the time of God's promise had arrived, and God would help transfer the ownership to Avraham now.

That is why Avraham quoted God as saying, "To your descendants I will give this Land…" This statement emphasized the public possession by Israel. When God made that promise, He addressed Avraham as leader of the Jews,[2] while when He said, "To you will I give this entire Land…" God addressed Avraham as an individual. If Avraham would have quoted the latter promise, placing emphasis on him as an individual, it might have been construed as referring to private ownership of the Land being transferred from owner to his heirs. Therefore, he quoted God's promise which does not mention him and mentions only his offspring. In this manner, Avraham wanted to indicate that he could establish public ownership of the Land for the entire Jewish people (not only for himself).

But still, why did the Hittites inject the city of Jebus into the negotiations? To answer that question, we have to look more closely at what took place.

In the *Pirkei d'Rebi Eliezer* (where the story of Jebus/Jerusalem is narrated), we learn that "when the Jews entered the Land of Israel [under Yehoshua] … they couldn't enter the city of Jebus because of the oath of Avraham…" But several generations later, King David was advised by the Jebusites that it was not permissible for him to take possession of it unless he removed "all the idols that have written upon them the oath of Avraham." From this, it would appear that it was permissible to conquer Jebus, at least under certain circumstances. And that was exactly what David did — "he announced to his soldiers that whoever could ascend first and remove the idols would become a leader, and the first to go up was Yoav ben Tzruya…" whereupon David proceeded to take the city. But afterwards, "David bought the Jebusite city for the Jewish people, committing that in writing forever."

If, in the time of King David, Avraham's deal with the Hittites was still in effect, what benefit was there in removing the idols? How could that alone cancel any oath that Avraham made?[3]

The Jebusites apparently made their statement sarcastically, as if to say, "you cannot change history by merely removing any mention of the oath." But if so, why did David take them seriously and undertake to remove the idols? And what changed between the time of Yehoshua and the time of King David that permitted David to conquer the city?[4] Moreover, when David purchased the city from the Jebusites, didn't that indicate that the city was in their hands and that it was necessary to appease them? Finally, if it was sufficient to purchase the city, why was it necessary for David to first remove all the idols through conquest?

The explanation is as follows:

When the Jews entered the Land of Israel under Yehoshua and conquered it, they established Jewish public ownership over all sections of the Land that they conquered. However, the public ownership did not negate the possibility of non-Jewish private ownership within Israel. Indeed, Yehoshua gave the local inhabitants the option of escaping or surrendering before he conquered their cities. Since they could stay, it is clear that — under some circumstances (that included fulfillment of the Seven Noachide Laws) — non-Jews were permitted to live in Israel and establish private ownership.

In our case, the establishment of Jewish public ownership did not prevent the Jebusites from maintaining their private ownership of the city of Jebus. Moreover, Avraham's oath, applied only to their private ownership. He could not make such a commitment regarding future Jewish public ownership. God had already promised all of the Land, including Jebus, to the Jews as a people, and it was not possible for Avraham to abrogate that. The Hittites themselves admitted as much, when they said, "We know that in the future God will give to your offspring all of these lands. Take an oath with us now that they will not take the city of Jebus (Jerusalem) against the will of the Jebusites…."

If the Land was promised to the Jews, how could Avraham swear not to take it from the Jebusites? Clearly, his oath was in regard to their private ownership of the city. That could remain in place even as the Jews took over the public ownership. But the promise by God to Avraham that the Land would eventually belong to his descendants took precedence over all, and no oath could abrogate it.

Now, we can understand why the Hittites made this stipulation regarding Jebus when Avraham was buying *Maarat Machpelah*. In their minds, this was a case of "one good deed deserves another." The Hittites were saying, "Just as we are willing to sell you private ownership in our land (Hebron), do the same for us in your land. When you take public possession of Israel, leave us with the private possession of Jebus (Jerusalem)."

This was acceptable as long as the Jews did not need Jerusalem for their public, national needs. Therefore, when Yehoshua conquered the Land and the Jews settled it, he did not conquer Jebus. The time had not yet come when the Jews needed to build the Temple. The portable Tabernacle rested in various places in the Land, and it was there that the Jews would bring their sacrifices and pray.

However, things changed in the time of King David. When it came time to build the Temple in Jerusalem, the principle of "eminent domain" became applicable. That meant the Jews had to take the city of Jebus, and establish it as a Jewish city. According to the oath of Avraham, it would have been forbidden for a private Jew to take private ownership of Jebus away from the Jebusites. However, when it came time for King David to build the Temple, it was necessary to establish the Jewish public claim over the city, and that's something the Jebusites could not object to.

When it came time to build the Temple in Jerusalem, the principle of "eminent domain" became applicable.

However, the Jebusites did object. They wrongly claimed that Avraham's oath also applied to public ownership, and therefore it was forbidden for the Jews to take the city at all. They made sure that their idols, with Avraham's oath written on them, were placed strategically throughout. That was the reason that David commanded his soldiers to first remove the idols. He did not want it even to appear as if he were taking the city improperly and, therefore, he had the idols removed first. Furthermore, even though he was justified in exercising the right of "eminent domain" and simply confiscating whatever territory he needed, David did not want to even give the appearance of "stealing" anything from the Jebusites and, therefore, he paid the inhabitants, in effect buying their city as if it were private property. (In doing so, he acted in a similar manner to a government that reimburses its citizens for land appropriated while building public infrastructure, such as a highway or dam.)

Jerusalem has been public Jewish property ever since and, God willing, so it will remain!

From Likutei Sichot of the Lubavitcher Rebbe, vol. 30, pp. 82–89

NOTES

1. In *Parshat Re'eh* (Genesis 12:17), Rashi explains that the Jews could not conquer Jebus because of the deal that Avraham made with the Hittites when he bought *Maarat Machpelah.* Yet, according to Rashi's commentary on the Book of Yehoshua (15:63), the Jews were unable to conquer Jebus because of the oath that Avraham swore to Avimelech. However, by the generation of King David, the years mentioned in Avraham's oath to Avimelech had already passed. Therefore, it is assumed that it was Avraham's oath to the Hittites that prevented the Jews from conquering Jebus.

2. Indeed, at this point in history, Avraham himself was *clal Yisrael* — the Jewish people — since until his son Yitzchak was born, Avraham was the only Jew in the world.

3. The Radal (R' David Luria) commenting on *Pirkei d'Rebi Eliezer* suggests that, "In truth, the oath was not nullified and that's why King David was unable to inherit their land … until he bought it from them afterward." And King David did not remove the idols because of the oath that was written on them, but because "he detested hearing and seeing the idols close to him." But, aside from the fact that the simple understanding of the *Pirkei d'Rebi Eliezer* indicates that King David removed the idols because of the oath written on them, there were idols in general (of all types), as we see from various verses of Scripture.

4. The Radal suggests that, "Since the Torah commanded the Jews (in Deuteronomy 20:16) 'not to allow any of the Canaanites to remain alive,' therefore the covenant that Avraham made with the Hittites (one of the Canaanite nations) was no longer valid." However, this needs investigation, since if so, the oath was already invalid in the days of Yehoshua (even before the seven years that it took to conquer the land), and how was it possible that "Yehoshua could not dis-inherit them [was not allowed to conquer the Jebusites]?" It would be hard to suggest that Yehoshua was allowed to conquer them, but did not want to do so because of the "disgrace" that it would cause [making it appear as if Yehoshua was abrogating the deal made by Avraham], because the simple language of the *Pirkei d'Reb* Eliezer does not support such an explanation, but rather indicates that Yehoshua did not conquer them because of the oath itself. The *Zayit Ra'anan* on the *Yalkut Shimoni* suggests that, "the Jebusites abrogated the treaty first by fighting against the Jews" (and therefore it was permissible for the Jews to conquer their land). But see the Radal there, who states that we don't find that the Jebusites abrogated the treaty.

Eliezer's Stunning Success

Chayei Sarah 24:4–7

From this week's Torah portion (*Parshat Chayei Sarah*) — which relates the long story about Eliezer, the servant of Avraham who was sent to find a wife for Yitzchak — our sages learn that "the conversation of the servants of our forefathers is preferable to the Torah words of their descendants [that is, us]." (Bereishit Rabba 60:8))

How so? In answer, let us examine that story.

Eliezer received instructions to go to Avraham's birthplace in order to find a suitable wife for Yitzchak. When Eliezer asked, "What happens if the woman doesn't want to go with me to this land? Should I then bring your son there?" Avraham answered him, "Make sure that you don't bring my son there ... He [God] will send His angel *before you* and you shall take a wife for my son from there." (Genesis 24:4–7)

However, later, when Eliezer recounted the conversation he'd had with Avraham to Betuel, Rivkah's father, he changed it a bit and said, "[God] will sent an angel *with you* ..." (Genesis 24:40). That is, Eliezer switched from "before you," to "with you."

Now, it could be argued that this is an inconsequential deviation, except that Rashi sees it as very significant. When the Torah related that God walked "with Noach" (Genesis 6:9), Rashi commented that, although God walked *with* Noach, Avraham walked *before* God. Rashi attributes the difference to the fact that "Noach needed support, but Avraham relied on his own righteousness." Clearly, then, there is a significant distinction between "before you" and "with you."

The difference is simple. If, as Eliezer described, the angel went "with" him, it meant that the angel accompanied him and helped him to accomplish his mission. If, however, the angel went "before" him, it means that the angel prepared his path in order to guarantee the success of his mission. But here is the key point — if it is "with" him, then the effort and success belong to Eliezer, while the angel merely helped. But if it is "before" him, then the angel not only helped, but actually prepared the ground for the successful completion of the mission. In the latter case, the success of the mission was not dependent upon Eliezer; his presence was needed as a catalyst, a passive ingredient, but it wasn't his effort that produced the results — success was guaranteed from Above.

What we see in these Torah verses is that the angel truly preceded Eliezer on his mission. The narrative is replete with examples of how the success of Eliezer's mission was guaranteed from Above, and we are convinced that the angel walked "before" him.

For example, clearly Rivkah left her house before Eliezer started to pray since she arrived there before he was finished (Genesis 24:10–15). This alone demonstrates that her appearance at the well was not the result of his prayers.[1] Rivkah was meant to marry Yitzchak; in fact, she was pre-ordained to do so. That is what is meant by "[God] will send His angel *before you*..." The angel paved the path for Eliezer's incredible success.

After meeting Rivkah at the well, Eliezer went to the house of her parents and talked with her father, Betuel, about what had just occurred. But Betuel began putting up resistance to his daughter leaving so quickly to marry Yitzchak. Here, Rashi (basing himself on the Midrash) comments that an angel came and killed Betuel. Whether or not this was the same angel who walked "before" Eliezer is not mentioned, but an angel was present to remove this obstruction to the marriage. Again, it is evident that the success of the match was guaranteed beforehand, and that is why any obstacles were so promptly eliminated.

Finally, even though we don't find that Eliezer spoke previously with Rivkah about the match (he only gave her gifts and jewelry at the well), nevertheless when asked, Rivkah answered that she wished to travel immediately to marry Yitzchak. The normal procedure in those times would have been for Rivkah to take her time in preparing for the wedding. Yet, the match was so ready to happen this was not necessary, nor was it necessary for Eliezer to put any effort into the arrangements. The presence of the angel guaranteed the success of Eliezer's mission in every respect.

But, if so, then we return to our question: Why did Eliezer, when speaking to Betuel, change the language to say that the angel went "with" him rather than "before" him? If the success of Eliezer's mission was so obviously because the angel went "before" him, why did Eliezer change the wording to "with" him?

In order to answer this question, we have to put ourselves in Betuel's place and look at the proposed match from his perspective. If the point of the conversation with Betuel was to convince him to agree that Rivka marry Yitzchak, then there was no point in telling Betuel that the match was pre-ordained. If Eliezer had said to Betuel, "Look, you can see that this whole process is miraculous, so please allow your daughter to return with me," then Betuel would have logically replied, "If it is pre-ordained, why are you asking for my permission?" In other words, there was no point in trying to convince Betuel if, in fact, it was already evident to everyone that the match was a "done deal." Further, if the match was pre-ordained, then there was nothing to be gained by seeking Betuel's agreement.

This is why Eliezer changed the language when speaking to Betuel, saying only that the angel was "with" him (that is, only helping him). Ultimately, as Rashi tells us, Betuel resisted the match and was killed. But before that took place, Eliezer naturally tried to convince him in order to win his support. Therefore, he refrained from telling him that the match was pre-ordained, leaving him free to engage in a conversation about the process.[2]

The above explanation resolves another detail in which Eliezer deviated from the actual events. At the well, Eliezer gave Rivkah gold jewelry as a gift even before asking her who she was. Yet, when speaking with Betuel, he mentioned first that he asked her who she was and that only afterward gave her the jewelry. But once we understand that Rivkah's arrival at the well, even before Eliezer finished praying, was a sign that the angel had already gone "before" him, and the match was set, then we understand why Eliezer was prepared to give her the gifts even before he actually knew who she was. Since Rivkah's prompt appearance was enough to convince Eliezer of the success of his mission, he had no hesitation in giving her the gifts even before he knew who she was. Of course, while speaking with Betuel, he could not reveal how he knew the match was pre-ordained. So that Betuel would not ask, "How could you give her gifts before even asking who she was," Eliezer changed the order of events and told him that he first asked who she was, and then gave her the gifts.

Although Eliezer could not inform Betuel that the match was preordained, he did try to provide a hint. When he told Betuel that Avraham said the angel would be "with" him, he added another few more words that Avraham did not say. To wit, Avraham, when speaking with Eliezer, never mentioned the word "success." But in recounting Avraham's words to Betuel, Eliezer quotes him as saying, "[God] will send His angel with you and make your journey successful" (Genesis 24:40). What Eliezer was trying to suggest to Betuel was that there was a supernal aspect to this process which guaranteed his success and there was no point for anyone to resist it.

True success is not the result of our efforts below. True success is a gift from Above. This we see in many places in the Torah. For example, regarding Yosef, the Torah says that "God was with Yosef and he was a successful man … God brought him success … and all that he did was successful" (Genesis 39:2–3). While it is true that, "He who says he labored and succeeded is believed," (Talmud *Megila* 6B) the degree of success may far outstrip any degree of effort, because true success is not predicated on effort — in fact, it is a gift from Above.

True success is not the result of our efforts below. True success is a gift from Above.

Thus, when Eliezer told Betuel that the angel was "with" him and was making him "successful," Betuel was meant to understand that, "there's something going on here, and God is making it happen." He was meant to grasp that this level of success was not solely associated with Eliezer's efforts. It was a gift from Above, and Eliezer was merely the vehicle for it. His success was part and parcel of the process that started when the angel went "before" Eliezer, and was "with" him throughout his journey. And from Betuel's response — "This matter is from God, and nothing good or bad can be said about it" (Genesis 24:50) — we know that he did get the hint.

Armed with this explanation, we can return to Avraham's original instructions to Eliezer and explain something else that is puzzling. When Eliezer asked, "What happens if the woman doesn't want to go with me to this land? Should I then bring your son there?" Avraham answered, "Make sure that you don't bring my son there … He [God] will send His angel before you and you shall take a wife for my son from there." The obvious question is: How could Avraham have been so sure that Eliezer would return with a wife for Yitzchak? At this stage, when Avraham was giving instructions to Eliezer, there did not seem to be any guarantee that the trip would be successful. And, why would any girl be expected to agree to marry Yitzchak sight unseen?

The answer is that since Avraham knew that the mission was to take place with an angel going "before" Eliezer, Avraham knew that the mission was a pre-ordained success. He knew that the efforts of Eliezer were not the significant factor, and that true success was a gift from Above. Thus, he had no problem in answering Eliezer as he did.

However, if that is the case, why does Avraham even mention the potential for failure, as indicated at the end of his directive to Eliezer, "If the woman does not want to come back with you, you are absolved of your oath to me..." (Genesis 24:8). If the success of Eliezer's mission was guaranteed, then why was it necessary to even entertain the possibility of failure?

Although the presence of an angel guaranteed Eliezer's success, it did not guarantee that Rivkah (or that any other specific woman) would want to marry Yitzchak. Rivkah had free choice, as did all other potential candidates for marriage, and any one of them could refuse. And if so, Eliezer was absolved from his oath to Avraham to find a wife for Yitzchak.[3] Nevertheless, Avraham knew that Eliezer's success was guaranteed, and that some woman would marry Yitzchak, and therefore he sent Eliezer on his way to facilitate the process.

And that may be why "the conversation of the servants of our forefathers is preferable to the Torah words of their descendants [that is, us]." In all that we do, including our divine service, we have free choice. Whether we are learning Torah, fulfilling its mitzvoth, or pursuing a livelihood, we make choices about why, how and what we are doing. But our forefather's servants were guided by angels. They didn't have a choice in the matter. Their divine service was so lofty that its success was guaranteed by angels that went "before" them.

Even though the "the conversation of the servants of our forefathers is preferable to the Torah words of their descendants," nevertheless the Torah words of their offspring (us) include the conversations of the servants of our forefathers. In fact, the conversation of Eliezer constitutes an entire section of the Torah, and from it we learn that the experience of a servant of one of our forefathers is relevant and provides an eternal instruction for us.

We can also attain the spiritual level of the servants of our forefathers. However, for that to occur, there are two pre-conditions:

1. We have to become "servants of our forefathers," meaning that we have to become as devoted to the One Above as a servant who does not exist for himself but only for his Master.
2. We have to engage in a "conversation" — that is in prayer, which is directed to the One Above by Jews who know that we are dependent upon our Master, the Creator of the world.

By means of total ego-nullification and prayer, we make ourselves into vessels for God, so that He can send us angels, the kind that go before us and lead to true success!

Adapted from Likutei Sichot of the Lubavitcher Rebbe, vol. 25, p. 99

NOTES

1. One could ask, if the angel were truly preceding Eliezer, why did Rivkah arrive as Eliezer was praying, and not before he began praying? The answer is that she did not appear before Eliezer began praying because he requested her appearance as a "sign" in answer to his prayers.

2. Another possibility is that Eliezer was following "protocol." Even though the match was pre-ordained from Above and there was no question that Rivkah would follow Eliezer home to marry Yitzchak, nevertheless, it was necessary for Eliezer to follow the normal protocol of asking for Rivkah's hand in marriage on behalf of Yitzchak. Yet a third possibility is that despite the pre-ordained nature of the match, Eliezer was afraid that Rivkah's parents would resist it (as Betuel her father actually did), and therefore he tried to obtain their agreement beforehand. (Elsewhere, the Rebbe makes it clear that Rivkah was determined to go with or without the agreement of her parents — see vol. 10 of *Likutei Sichot*.)

3. This could have meant that Eliezer was completely free of his oath after the first suitable woman declined to marry Yitzchak, or it could have meant that he was free of his oath regarding Rivkah, but should continue to look for another candidate from Avraham's family. Finally, Avraham's words may have indicated that since the angel was proceeding "before" Eliezer, success was guaranteed, but perhaps the girl's family might raise obstacles, thereby preventing her from following Eliezer. And in that case as well, Eliezer would be exonerated from his oath. (In *Likutei Sichot* vol. 10, the Rebbe indicates that Rivkah was prepared to accompany Eliezer even against the will of her family).

Whose Prayers Are Answered?

Chayei Sarah 24:15

When Avraham returned from the *Akeidah*, or the "binding" of his son Yitzchak in response to God's command to offer him as a sacrifice, he thought about how to marry him off. He reasoned that since Yitzchak had not died, then God's promise that he would have many descendants through Yitzchak would need to be fulfilled. Therefore, it was necessary to find a soul-mate for Yitzchak, as soon as possible. In short order, Avraham sent his servant, Eliezer, to his former homeland to find a wife for Yitzchak.

Laden with gifts from his master, Eliezer arrived in Charan and uttered a prayer for success. Before he even finished his prayer, Rivkah appeared and offered to water his animals and provide hospitality. Since that was the sign he had prayed for, Eliezer knew that Rivkah was the pre-ordained match for Yitzchak.

The Midrash (*Midrash Rabba* 60:4) states: "Three were answered while saying their prayers: Eliezer, the servant of Avraham ('He didn't yet finish speaking and Rivkah appeared' Genesis 24:15), Moshe ('And as he finished speaking … the ground opened up' Numbers 16:31), and King Shlomo ('And as Shlomo finished praying to God, fire descended from the heavens' (2 Chronicles 7:1)."

Since all three — Eliezer, Moshe and Shlomo — are mentioned in the Midrash, it's obvious that there is a common thread between them. And yet, what did Eliezer, a servant, have in common with Moshe and Shlomo, both of whom were leaders in their respective generations? Even more so, how is it possible that Eliezer was answered faster than Moshe and Shlomo? Yet, that is what the Scripture says — Eliezer was answered even *before* he finished praying, while the others were answered only *after* they finished praying.

We could take these same questions even further: What was the unique quality shared by these three that led to such a quick response (whether during or right after) from Above? Why does the Midrash single them out? Were there no other *tzaddikim* throughout the Tanach whose prayers were answered immediately?[1]

Since they are so different from each other and yet all were answered quickly, perhaps it wasn't that *they* had something in common, but *their prayers*. Perhaps all of them prayed in a way that demanded an immediate response from Above. So what was special about their prayers that they were answered immediately?

That special quality is defined by the Rambam in his discussion of *teshuvah*, the process of returning to God through repentance after having committed a transgression. Two of his statements (in *Hilchot Teshuvah* 7:6–7) are most pertinent:

1. "*Teshuvah* brings people close to God. Yesterday, one may have been … far, while today he is close…"
2. "How tremendous is the benefit of *teshuvah*; yesterday, one may have been distant from God … praying without being answered … and today he is cleaving to the Divine Presence (*Shechinah*) … praying and being answered immediately."[2]

The Rambam is very precise in his choice of words, so it is puzzling why he would divide this subject into two, when both describe the *baal teshuvah* returning to God after having strayed. But, in truth, the Rambam is describing two different levels of *teshuvah*. In the first statement, he describes one who was far from serving God, but who came "close." But, in the second, he describes one who not only came close but who is also "cleaving" to the Divine Presence. And this is why the Rambam says that when the latter person prays, he is "answered immediately." It is the cleaving to God that brings an immediate answer to his prayers. In short, one who comes close to God receives an answer to his prayers, sooner or later. But, one who cleaves to Him receives an immediate answer, without having to wait at all.

From this we learn the reason why someone praying might be

answered only after a delay, if at all. When the person and God are two separate entities, then there is distance between man and the Creator. Since they are two entities, even though one might strive to draw near and approach the other, there is a separation between them and, therefore, there is a delay in a response. However, when the person who prays cleaves to the One Above, the distance is erased.[3] It is then that the supplicant receives his answer from God immediately, without any delay.[4]

Just as it is true of physical proximity, the closer we are to someone, the faster and easier we can communicate with him or her, so in spiritual terms, the closer we are to God, the faster we can expect to communicate with Him. Each one of us immediately affects the other.

This helps us explain the difference between Eliezer, Moshe and Shlomo and why only these three were mentioned and not many others, who cleaved to God in prayer.[5] And here is where the subject of their respective prayers comes in. When we examine the content, we find that their prayers correspond to three different modes in which the world cleaves to God: 1) unity of man and God (Moshe); 2) unity of physical creation and God (King Shlomo); and 3) unity of Torah and God (Eliezer).

Upon examination, we find that this explains why the prayers of Moshe (corresponding to the unity of God with man) and those of Shlomo (corresponding to the unity of God and the world) were answered immediately. However, the Scripture tells us that they were answered *after* Moshe and Shlomo finished praying while Eliezer was answered *before* he finished praying. And here is why:

Unity of God and man takes place during prophecy. As the Rambam wrote (in *Hilchot Yesodei HaTorah* 7:1), "One of the foundations of our faith is that God causes men to prophesy." And as the Alter Rebbe said,[6] Godliness "is manifested in the prophets' mind and intellect as a prophetic vision, as well as in their thought and speech." Through prophecy, God reveals His secrets to human beings, and that is when the greatest unity of God and man occurs. And that's why the Midrash quotes Moshe as saying, "by this you will know that God sent me to do all these things..." Then the earth immediately split and swallowed Korach and his group (Numbers Ch. 16), and it became clear that God had made Himself known to Moshe in prophecy, just as Moshe had predicted, thus demonstrating the unity of God with man.[7]

Unity of God with the physical creation takes place where the *Shechinah* comes down to earth — at the location where the Temple (*Beit HaMikdash*) once stood. As the Midrash mentions, it was there that Shlomo prayed, "I have built a house for you, a place for your eternal dwelling" (2 Chronicles 6:2), and "the heavens and the heaven's heavens can't contain You, and how can this house that I built [contain You]?" (1 Kings 8:27 and 2 Chronicles 6:18). As Shlomo finished his prayers, he received his answer — a fire came down from Above to consume the offerings he had brought, demonstrating the ultimate unity of God and the physical creation.

Eliezer's prayer represented the unity of God with the Torah, which began with Avraham. Before the Torah was given at Mt. Sinai, there was a gulf between the upper spiritual realm and the lower physical realm, but with the advent of Avraham (and the other forefathers and their wives), the two began to approach one another. The forefathers were able to bring spirituality down into the world, as well as uplift the physical creation, even if only temporarily. As they did a mitzvah, Godliness came down to permeate the physical object at hand. However, immediately after, the spirituality disappeared. This continued until the generation of Moshe, who enabled the Jews to permanently fix spirituality in the physical world and elevate creation. The catalyst enabling this unity of God and the world is the Torah and its mitzvoth, which facilitated permanent transformation. Nowadays, when we Jews fulfill a mitzvah, we bring Godliness to n the world in a way that is permanent and everlasting. But, the time of the forefathers was a time of preparation for the revelation of the Torah, and the first time that such true unity between the upper and lower realms occurred was during the lifetime of Yitzchak and Rivkah. Their marriage — arranged by Eliezer — was the very first opportunity for Godliness to become fixed in the physical world.

Yitzchak was from the upper worlds. He was brought up in the house of Avraham and Sarah, in a state of holiness, which he never abandoned or diminished. Moreover, he was an *olah temima* — an unblemished offering who was not allowed to leave the Land of Israel. He attained this state as the result of his total willingness to give up his life as an "offering" at the time of the *Akeidah*. Rivkah, on the other hand, grew up among idol worshippers and in an atmosphere of impure spirituality outside of the Land of Israel. She was a spiritual gem trapped in impure circumstances. Because of the gulf between Yitzchak and Rivkah, their match required intervention in the person of Eliezer, the servant of Avraham. When he prayed, it was for the sake of Torah, for the sake of creating the first real match between the upper spiritual (represented by Yitzchak) and the lower physical realms (represented by Rivkah).

The match between Yitzchak and Rivkah was a meeting of the upper and lower worlds, and it began to produce a permanent, lasting bond between them. (This was not true of Avraham and Sarah, both of whom came from impure circumstances, from the homes of idol worshippers. They both completely rejected their circumstances and established a holy household together, but it cannot be said that they began to unite the upper spiritual realm with the lower, since they both came from the latter.)

The match between Yitzchak and Rivkah was a meeting of the upper and lower worlds, and it began to produce a permanent, lasting bond between them.

And that's why Eliezer was answered even before he finished his prayers. His quest to find the right match for Yitzchak symbolized the beginning of bringing Torah down to unite with the lower realms of creation.[8] The Midrash[9] relates that during the six days of creation, God made a pact — if the Jews accept the Torah, creation will be maintained, and if not, He would destroy it. From this we see that the necessity of Torah and its mitzvoth is built into creation. There can be no creation without them. The unity is built-in and innate; one cannot exist without the other. Therefore, the unity of God and Torah is qualitatively different than the unity of God and man and the unity of God and His physical creation. And therein lies the difference between the way Eliezer's prayer was answered and the way Moshe's and Shlomo's prayers were answered.

In biblical times, when a prophecy would come to a prophet, he was a different person before he began to prophesy than afterward. He never remained in a permanent state of prophecy, but changed before, during and after the event. He and the prophecy were always two different entities. The same is true of the revelations in the Temple which were not permanent, and indeed, the Temple was ultimately destroyed (though the holiness of the site remains). This indicates that God and man, as well as God and His creation, are two entities separate from one another, which can sometimes unite through prophecy or through the Temple. However, God and the Torah cannot be separated ever. From the onset, they were "one," as the Zohar says, "The Torah and God are one." (Zohar

3, 73A) The Torah is the very essence of God, as symbolized by the acrostic of *Anochi* ("I wrote Myself [into the Torah] and gave it"). And that's why Eliezer's request to find Yitzchak's soul-mate (corresponding to the unity of God and Torah) was answered even before he finished praying. If he had been answered when he finished (as were Moshe and Shlomo), it would have implied that God and the Torah were separate entities — united but nevertheless two.

Put slightly differently, Godliness is something "new" to man, but it is not "new" to the Torah because God is one with His Torah, and they are inseparable.

The lesson for us is obvious — to achieve the greatest possible unity with the One Above, we must put aside our own egos and let God in. And the more we are capable of praying while cleaving to the One Above, the more quickly we will be answered. May we be answered with ultimate speed as we pray for the building of the third and permanent Temple and the renewal of prophecy among all the Jewish people immediately![10]

From Likutei Sichot of the Lubavitcher Rebbe,
vol. 20, pp. 91–99

NOTES

1. The Midrash (*Hagadol*) continues: "Not only these [three], but all *tzaddikim* are answered immediately, as it is written "...before they call, I will answer..." (Isaiah 65:24), and also David said, "Listen to my voice..." even before I express myself." But based on the fact that the Midrash divides them into two categories, and even more so that these are the three concrete examples that we find in the Torah, we understand that the main advantage is to be found in these three prayers.

2. The Rambam continues by citing the verse, "And even before they call, I will answer" (Isaiah 65:24), which at first glance is not equivalent to "praying and being answered immediately" (since the verse from Isaiah implies that he was answered even before he finished praying, as occurred with Eliezer). But see note 4.

3. From the language of the Rambam (in *Halachah* 4) — "he is beloved and delightful before the Creator as if he never sinned at all..." [which differentiates between a *baal teshuvah* and a *tzaddik*] it seems that the person described (in *Halachah* 6) is a *baal teshuvah* whose spiritual level is "like" a *tzaddik*, while the language later (in *Halachah* 7), describes a *baal teshuvah* who clings to God on an even higher level than a *tzaddik*. The sages tell us that "a total *tzaddik* cannot approach the level of a *baal teshuvah*," [which could be construed to mean] that the *ba'al teshuvah* (described in *Halachah* 7) is on a higher spiritual level than the *baal teshuvah* who is "like" a *tzadik* (described in *Halachah* 6). We might also suggest

that their two spiritual levels are dependent on two different levels of *teshuvah* out of love: 1) If one's *teshuvah* out of love is so great that his sins are totally uprooted and eradicated (see Rashi on *Yoma* 86a), then he is comparable to the *baal teshuvah* (who is "like" a *tzaddik* as described in *Halachah* 6). But, if his level of *teshuvah* out of love is so great that he manages to convert his sins into meritorious deeds (see *Yoma* 86b), then he is comparable to the *baal teshuvah* (described in *Halachah* 7) who exceeds the *tzaddik*. Regarding this topic, see *Likutei Sichot*, vol. 17, p. 185. In any case, there are many levels of "cleaving" to God, and everyone [whether a *tzaddik* or a *baal teshuvah*] is commanded to cleave to Him, as the verse says, "And you should cling to Him" (Deuteronomy 11:22) and "To Him you should cleave" (Deuteronomy 13:5). And "You [referring to all those entering the Land of Israel], are clinging to Him today" (Deuteronomy 4:4). From all the above, it is understood that there are *tzaddikim* who "pray and are answered immediately" as stated in the Midrash (see footnote 1). Moreover, the Tzemach Tzedek (in *Ohr HaTorah* on *Parshat Nach*, vol. 2, p. 874) quotes from the book, *Emek Hamelech*, "And there are *tzaddikim* who always cleave, 'spirit to spirit,' about whom God says, 'even before they call, I will answer' (Isaiah 65:24)."

4. Possibly, the reason that the Rambam quoted the verse, "And even before they call, I will answer" (Isaiah 65:24), is to indicate that there are many levels within "cleaving to the *Shechinah*." There are higher levels than he who is "answered immediately," and "even before they call..." is one of those higher levels. And between them there are also levels. See *Ohr HaTorah* (quoted in previous footnote) on the verse, "And even before they call..." where the Tzemach Tzedek writes, "When a person is doing *teshuvah ila'ah* ("supernal *teshuvah*"), he is united with his *mazal*..." (*Likutei Sichot*, vol. 2,p. 70, footnote 28).

5. Accordingly, it makes sense that the sage who said, "Three were answered..." was the Rashbi — R' Shimon bar Yochai. The special quality of "being answered immediately" is not due to prayer per se, but to the quality of Torah that the person learns, as we find regarding the Rashbi himself (Zohar sec. 3, 59b) who, by saying words of Torah, caused rain to fall immediately and in a useful manner (unlike Honi Hamagel who also prayed and brought down rain, but only after several requests did the rain descend in a useful manner (*Taanit* 19a). See *Hithalech Liozna* of the Alter Rebbe, p. 210, *Ohr HaTorah* on *Parshat Acharei* (vol. 1, p. 254), as well as *Torat Shmuel* 5627 of the Rebbe Maharash, p. 267.

6. *Sha'ar Hayichud v'haemuna*, Ch 2, citing the *Arizal* in *Sha'ar Hanevuah*

7. This event was not about proving the truth of the Torah that Moshe taught — that was known and agreed upon. Rather, the issue was regarding Moshe himself (as a man, not regarding his teachings) and his accurate representation of God's will in all of his deeds, including appointing his brother Aharon as the High Priest.

8. The one mitzvah performed by Avraham that was similar to mitzvoth performed after the Torah was given was the mitzvah of *milah*, or "circumcision." With this mitzvah (unlike all others fulfilled by Avraham), the holiness that was brought down remained even after the event (see *Likutei Sichot* vol. 5, p. 89). When Avraham instructed his servant Eliezer (Genesis 24:2) to take an oath on his "thigh" that he would bring a wife for Yitzchak only from Avraham's family,

Eliezer's action was proof that the *milah* was a *heifetz shel mizvah* ("an item with which a mitzvah is performed") and it may have been the first example of an "item of mitzvah" having a revealed effect upon the world.

9. *Bereishit Rabba* 5:5, *Shemot Rabba* 21:6, *Zohar* 2, 198B

10. This paragraph of conclusion is from the translator, not from the original *sicha*.

Avraham's Golden Years

Chayei Sarah 25:1

At the end of our Torah portion — *Parshat Chayei Sarah* — we are told that "Avraham took another wife and married a woman whose name was Keturah, and she bore him [six sons]..." (Genesis 25:1). This is surprising because, by that time, Avraham was 140 years old. Forty years earlier, when Yitzchak was born, this was described as a miraculous event for both Avraham and his wife, Sarah (Genesis 17:17 and 18:11–12). So why does the Torah say nothing about the miraculous birth of six sons to Avraham and Keturah?

However, the Ramban (commenting on Genesis 17:17) states that the birth of Yitzchak was not miraculous. Men often sire children at an advanced age, and indeed forty years later, Avraham fathered six sons. The Ramban claims that the birth of Yitzchak was miraculous only because Sarah was 90 years old. However, the relevant verses of the Torah do not differentiate between Avraham and Sarah, implying that Yitzchak's birth was miraculous not only from Sarah's point of view, but also from Avraham's perspective. And Rashi explains (in his comments on Genesis 17:17), "even though people of the early generations would have children at age 500 and more, in the days of Avraham human beings lived shorter lives and began to weaken — see what happened during the ten generations from Noah until Avraham when people began to have children earlier, at 60 and 70 years old..."[1] So it seems that, according to Rashi, it was just as miraculous for Avraham to have a child at 100 years old as it was for Sarah to give birth at 90.

Theoretically, we might say that Avraham was not weak and tired at 140, since at 100 years old we find that Avraham and Sarah "returned to the days of their youth."[2] However, after the birth of Yitzchak, the Torah tells us a second time that "Avraham was old, getting on in days..." (Genesis 24:1) So, after his late "youth," Avraham once more experienced old age. Consequently, if the birth of Yitzchak (when Avraham was 100) was miraculous, the birth of six sons later (at age 140) was certainly miraculous — so why does the Torah fail to mention this?

We can begin to understand this by looking at what happened in the world — not just in the private world of Avraham and Sarah, but in the world at large — when Yitzchak was born. About the birth of Yitzchak, the Torah tells us, "And Sarah said, 'God has made me laugh' — all who hear about this will laugh..." (Genesis 21:6). Rashi explains, "Many barren women became pregnant at that time, many sick people were healed that very day, many prayers were answered together with hers, and there was much laughter in the world." So, it is evident that the birth of Yitzchak brought salvation and cure to much of the world, leading to much happiness and joy.

Soon after, when Sarah weaned Yitzchak, there was a "party." According to Rashi (commenting on Genesis 21:7), "on the day that Yitzchak was weaned, various noblewomen brought their children with them, and Sarah nursed them all. This she did because there had been rumors that she did not really give birth but only had taken in a foundling from the street." However, since only a woman who has actually given birth can nurse, Sarah demonstrated that she could nurse all of the young children who were present and quelled the rumor that her son Yitzchak was not hers.

But if the reason that God enabled Sarah to nurse many children was in order to quell the rumors that she did not really give birth, then it would have been sufficient for her to nurse Yitzchak alone. Once all the noblewomen saw that Sarah was nursing her son, they would have known that Yitzchak was her true biological son, and not a foundling from the street. Why was it necessary for Sarah to actually nurse all of the children?

The fact that Sarah nursed all the other children of the noblewomen of the region was an indication that something much bigger was playing out here that affected the entire world. And that was why Sarah made a point of nursing not only Yitzchak, but also the other children. The fact that Sarah was able to nurse the other children was only a small hint of the real achievement. The really big event was that Yitzchak's birth heralded a new dawn of global joy in the world.

And just as the birth of Yitzchak heralded the advent of a new positive spirit in the world which came down in the merit of Sarah, it also heralded the advent of miracles to come 40 years later in the merit of Avraham, when six more sons were born to him. Those sons were not Jewish, but were part of the nations of the world. The fact that their birth was not mentioned as "miraculous" was because their birth was an extension of the original miracle — the birth of Yitzchak. Once Yitzchak was born, the blessing of joy and happiness was brought to the world, and the birth of six more sons much later in Avraham's life was merely an extension of that.

The really big event was that Yitzchak's birth heralded a new dawn of global joy in the world.

Nevertheless, more explanation is needed. For one, what was the reason that Yitzchak's birth added miracles to the world, such that now the world was "full of mirth"? For another, why is there a difference between Sarah's effect on the world and Avraham's? For we see that Sarah's impact on the world was immediate — as soon as Yitzchak was weaned, the various noblewomen came and Sarah nursed their children. Moreover, many prayers (resulting in many pregnancies) were answered immediately at that time. But Avraham's effect on the world did not occur until much later — only after 40 years do we find that he had six sons with Keturah. As well, Sarah's effect on the world happened automatically — it did not require any special effort on her part, but was rather a direct result of her giving birth to Yitzchak, whereas Avraham's impact came through an investment of effort and energy.

The answer to the above questions is connected with the influence that Jews in general have on the world. And the interesting point is that it began with the very first Jews — Avraham and Sarah — more specifically, it began when Yitzchak was born.

Even before that happened, we see that God changed their names from Avram to Avraham, and from Sarai to Sarah. The reason, in both cases had to do with what was coming. Avram would now be called Avraham, because "I have made you the father of many nations..." (Genesis 17:5). And Sarai, whose name means "my princess," became a princess/leader for the entire world (see Rashi on Genesis 17:15). But what is the connection between the change of names, and the birth of Yitzchak?

Obviously, the birth of Yitzchak had something important to do with the various ways Jews would be able to influence the world — one associated with Sarah, and the other associated with Avraham.

We'll be able to grasp this better by looking into the *Mishneh Torah* (*Hilchot Melachim* 8:10–11), where the Rambam speaks about the Seven Noachide Laws and how Jews must enforce them in the world:

> "Moshe our teacher commanded in the name of God that Jews must persuade all of the nations of the world to accept the Noachide laws ... All those who accept the seven commandments and who are careful to fulfill them are among the 'righteous people of the world,' and they have a portion in the world to come. This is on condition that they accept and fulfill them because God commanded them in the Torah, as handed down by Moshe our teacher ... but if they fulfill them [merely] of their own volition ... they are not among the righteous of the world."

Now, this needs explanation. Moshe brought God's Torah to the world and handed it down to the Jews alone. What do non-Jews have to do with the giving of the Torah to the Jews? And why must the Jews persuade all nations of the world to accept the Seven Noachide Laws, precisely because God commanded them in the Torah?

Obviously, the birth of Yitzchak had something important to do with the various ways Jews would be able to influence the world — one associated with Sarah, and the other associated with Avraham.

In order to explain, we need to look carefully at the Rambam's language. He states:

1. Jews are commanded by God through Moshe to persuade the non-Jews to keep the Noachide laws.
2. Non-Jews must keep the Noahide commandments because they were commanded by God, as transmitted through Moshe.

It is notable that these points are covered in two separate *halachot* in the Rambam's work. At first glance, we would think that the two details should be part of one directive (since non-Jews are required to observe the Noachide laws, they must also do so because they come from God). However, the fact that the Rambam separates them into two *halachot* suggests that they are two separate commandments, independent of one another. Perhaps the way to understand them is as follows:

1. The first *halachah* establishes the obligation of Jews to educate and persuade non-Jews to keep the Seven Noachide Laws, without necessarily convincing them that the commandments are from the Torah.
2. The second *halachah* tells us that the fullest observance of the Seven Noachide Laws occurs when the non-Jews observe them because they come from the Torah. And only then are they described as the "righteous of the world."

It follows then, that although Jews are obligated to persuade non-Jews to keep the Seven Noahide Laws, they are not obligated to persuade non-Jews regarding their origins. Nevertheless, since the second *halachah* follows immediately upon the heels of the first, it suggests that even awareness of the origins of the Noachide laws is the result of Jewish activity. For how else would non-Jews know about such requirements, if it weren't for Jews engaging them in conversation on that matter? Therefore, Jews fulfill their duty by merely persuading non-Jews to fulfill the Noachide laws. Nevertheless, Jews help non-Jews fulfill their obligation to the fullest by persuading them to keep the Noachide laws because they come from the Torah.[3]

Moreover, perhaps we could extend our thesis further by suggesting that there are two ways in which Jews may have an effect on the non-Jewish world:[4]

1. Either directly — by compelling (through coercion if necessary, but preferably by using verbal persuasion) non-Jews to fulfill the Noahide laws,
2. Or indirectly — after non-Jews are persuaded to fulfill the Noachide laws, Jews must work indirectly to persuade them that the fullest fulfillment of these laws is because they were commanded by the Torah

We can see these two approaches elsewhere in Rambam's writing (see the final two chapters of his *Hilchot Melachim*), where he writes: "[The Mashiach] will gather together the exiled Jews … and rectify the entire world to serve God together … At that time, there will be no hunger … goodness will be everywhere … nothing but knowledge of God."

Note that the Rambam first speaks of action (the Mashiach will "rectify the entire world") and then of the more passive results of that action ("there will be no hunger," etc.). This corresponds to the two paths of influence that the Jews have upon the world — one, by persuading the non-Jews to keep the Noachide laws, and the other, by way of example, showing the non-Jewish world how to live according to the precepts of God as commanded in the Torah.

Now, we can understand why in order for Yitzchak to be born, there had to be a change in the names of Avram and Sarai, to Avraham ("father of many nations") and Sarah ("princess/leader" of the entire world). And why, at the same time, miracles occurred that had an open effect on the rest of the rest of the people of the world. When Sarah demonstrated her influence, "many barren women became pregnant ... many sick people were healed ... and there was much laughter in the world..." Avraham demonstrated his influence later, by siring six more children with Keturah, a non-Jewish woman. In both cases, their purpose was to influence the world and demonstrate that, through the Jews, God instills holiness into the world.

In general, God does not perform miracles for "no reason." God cherishes the laws of nature that He Himself created and wishes to maintain the order and harmony of His "dwelling place in the lower worlds." It requires events of major significance for Him to change the rules of nature and produce a miracle. Therefore, the "additional" miracles (whether in association with Sarah or with Avraham) that took place after Yitzchak was born were not "new" miracles but were natural extensions of the miraculous birth of Yitzchak. His birth was a global event, intended to publicize the effect that the Jews already had upon and would subsequently have upon the world. The accompanying events of many barren women becoming pregnant, many sick being healed, and many prayers answered were a continuation of the effect of Yitzchak's birth on the world in two key respects — one associated with Avraham, the other with Sarah:

1. Sarah's effect upon the world was spontaneous and indirect, and therefore, immediate. Directly after Yitzchak's birth, prayers were answered and miraculous healings occurred. And only a couple of years later, at the weaning of Yitzchak, she miraculously nursed other babies. That was because as a "princess," she affected the world automatically by her mere presence. The immediate effect of her giving birth to Yitzchak was to bring many blessings to the nations of the world as well.[5]

2. Avraham took a proactive stance by siring more children, even at the age of 140. This corresponds to the proactive stance of Jews regarding the non-Jews of the world — to persuade them to accept the Seven Noachide Laws. And that is why it took time — it was 40 years after the birth of Yitzchak that Avraham finally had this effect upon the world.

From Likutei Sichot of the Lubavitcher Rebbe, vol. 35, pp. 94–100

NOTES

1. According to several commentators on Rashi (including R' Eliyahu Mizrahi on Genesis 17:17), there was nothing miraculous about Avraham's ability to sire children at the age of 140. However, according to the *Gur Aryeh* (the Maharal's commentary on Rashi, see Genesis 17:17), the *Be'er Besadeh* and other works, Avraham's ability to sire children at this advanced age was indeed miraculous. See *Likutei Sichot*, vol. 20, p. 80. In any case, it is possible to explain Rashi in any number of ways since Rashi on this subject is not clear, and Rashi himself offers more than one explanation of the simple meaning of the text in many instances. And even if we posit that Avraham's ability to father children at 140 was not miraculous since, even at that age, he had not weakened, that itself is was a wonderful blessing that deserves mentioning. See Rashi on *Parshat Lech Lecha* 17:17.

2. Bereishit Rabba 53:9, also 48:16

3. The Rebbe concludes this section with a remark in brackets, "More investigation is necessary to determine whether there is an obligation for Jews to persuade all non-Jews to become righteous people of the world."

4. And so, Jews have had an effect on the nations of the world throughout history in two different ways: 1) By way of war and conquering land, after which the conquered nations were subdued and taxed (Deuteronomy 20:11), and compelled to accept the Seven Noachide Laws (Rambam *Hilchot Melachim* Ch 6). Or, 2) as occurred during the reign of King Shlomo, when "Shlomo sat on the throne of God" (1 Chronicles 29:23), and war was not necessary. Rather, the leaders of various nations came to see and meet the Jews, as when "the Queen of Sheba brought Shlomo [gifts]..." (1 Kings, 10:1, 2 Chronicles 9:1). According to the language of Chassidus, "refinement and elevation" (*birur*) can take place either by way of war, or peace — see *Likutei Torah* of the Alter Rebbe, *Parshat Bamidbar* p. 3, col. 4, *Sefer Maamorim* 5659 (1899) of the Rebbe Rashab, p. 162 and *Sefer Maamorim* of the Rebbe Rayatz, 5704 (1944), p. 106.

5. See Tanya, *Likutei Amarim* end of Ch. 36 regarding the End of Days: "At that time the physical nature of the body and of the entire world will become sufficiently refined to accept the revelation of Godliness that will illuminate to the Jewish people ... and this higher illumination to the Jews will enlighten the darkness

of the nations as well, as is written, 'the nations will go in Your path' (Isaiah 60:3) and 'the house of Yaakov...' (Isaiah 2:5)." Even though the simple understanding of these verses is that the removal of darkness from the nations will be a result of illumination to the Jews, meaning that the removal of darkness will occur spontaneously, nevertheless, the enlightenment of darkness may occur in the same two manners mentioned, which is why the Alter Rebbe cited more than one verse in Tanya. See *Likutei Sichot*, vol. 23, p. 170.

Who Is a Jew?

Toldot 25:19

The sages do not consider Yishmael, the son of Avraham, to be Jewish. But they accept as such Esav, the son of Yitzchak, even though Esav — unlike Yishmael — remained a sinner his entire life. Why? One way to solve this riddle is to look at their mothers.

Yishmael, Yitzchak's half brother, was the son of Avraham and the maidservant, Hagar. Esav, Yaakov's twin brother, was the son of Yitzchak and his wife Rivkah, who was one of the matriarchs and not merely a maidservant.

It makes sense that the Jewish line was continued through Rivkah (a matriarch) but not through Hagar (a servant). However, when we look further into Jewish genealogy, we see that this is not the deciding factor. When Yaakov married two sisters and also had offspring from their maidservants, we don't see any difference between the children of the servants (Bilhah and Zilpah) and the children of the matriarchs (Rachel and Leah). All were equally considered the progenitors of the Twelve Tribes of Israel. So, we need to adjust our theory in order to solve the riddle of Yishmael and Esav.

After the Torah was given at Mt. Sinai, Jewish identity was determined by the mother. But, before that time (in other words, during the generations of the patriarchs and the matriarchs), it was the father who determined Jewish identity. So, in our case, it was Avraham and Yitzchak who determined their respective sons' identities. And yet, in the case of Avraham and his sons, one of them — Yishmael — was disinherited, so to speak. We know that because the Torah tells us so. In *Parshat Vayera* (Genesis 21:12), God tells Avraham, "through Yitzchak your descendants will be called" — through Yitzchak and not through Yishmael.

Although Yishmael did *teshuvah* during the lifetime of his father, he was not considered the true heir of Avraham and, therefore, he was not considered Jewish. So why would Esav, who remained a sinner, merit different treatment?[1]

In the case of Yishmael, although he returned to the path of following the one God, he never fully accepted and internalized the path of his father, and therefore he was not considered "Jewish." His deeds were always "external" and did not reflect Avraham's "internal" spiritual attitude. But, in the case of Esav, although he left the path of Judaism, his mindset remained "Jewish" like the mind of his father, Ytizchak. That is, his body rebelled, but he — in his intellect and essence — remained Jewish. Therefore, even though Yishmael did *teshuvah*, since in essence he never fully accepted the path of his father, he could not carry on the line of Avraham. Esav, on the other hand, accepted the path of his father, but his evil inclination (*yetzer harah*) prevented him from acting accordingly. Therefore, he is considered a "sinner" (*Yisrael mumar*) but nonetheless "Jewish."

If that sounds difficult to accept, consider the concept of *shlichut* ("mission/agency"). *Shlichut* is a halachic construct that has no counterpart in secular law. It may be used to determine culpability when one sends somebody — the agent or emissary (*shaliach*) — on a mission and that person fails to fulfill the assigned task. For example, if A sends B to do a job, their relationship may be looked at in one of two ways:[2]

1. Either A and B are two separate people, in which B does what he is asked to do while maintaining his own independent existence. In that case, B remains independent, but the Torah determines that since B is the agent of A, his actions are attributed to A.
2. Or, we might consider that the appointment of B to undertake A's task turns B into an extension of A, as if they are really the same person. In that case, it is not the action of B that is attributed to A (because if they are one and the same, then B's action *is* A's action); it is the appointment of B that turns him into A's extension, and A is responsible for B's action.

In our analysis, Avraham and Yishmael fit the first model of *shlichut*. Yishmael acted as an "independent" agent to fulfill the will of his father Avraham. Whether he failed or succeeded, his deeds reflected back and were attributed to his father. When he followed in his father's path (as a result of his father's influence), Yishmael followed the model of an emissary who was acting independently of his father. Whatever mitzvoth he fulfilled, he did so with his father's motivation, and therefore his action reflected back to his father. When he failed to follow his father's directives, his failure was also attributed to his father for he did not "own" his own actions, so to speak, since he was no more than an agent of Avraham.

Yitzchak and Esav fit the second model of *shlichut.* Whatever Esav did was as if his father did it as well. Since Esau was an "extension" of his father, he was not only an agent. It was as if Esav "was his father." Therefore, Esav could fail at his task, but he could not fail to be Jewish. Since his father embodied all of the principles of monotheism and of the Torah, and Esav was one with him, even Esav's failure to fulfill his task did not separate him from his father. Esav could fail, but he could never escape his one-on-one identification with his father, as he was considered one and the same as Yitzchak. Therefore, despite his failings, he was still considered Jewish.

However, all of the above still leaves us with the question of why there should be such a difference. Why does Yishmael seem to lack full identification and essential connection with Avraham, while Esav is part and parcel of Yitzchak? The answer lies in the respective styles of the forefathers in serving the One Above.

Avraham's mission was to illuminate the world — drawing down light from Above to below. His task was to go to places of spiritual darkness — of idol worship and paganism — and introduce the concept of one God, ineffable, indivisible and omniscient. Avraham even left the Land of Israel in order to promulgate his mission. Thus, he persuaded the world to recognize the one God who rules creation. However, the moment he was not present, the world reverted to paganism and idol worship. This was a sign that it was only because of Avraham that the world began to recognize God. The world itself — the idol worshippers and even the spiritual searchers — did not change. They remained the same idol worshippers even though they agreed that Avraham's views were correct. Even the converts that Avraham made in Charan only proclaimed the primacy of one God under the influence of

Avraham's mission was to illuminate the world — drawing down light from Above to below.

Avraham. They themselves never adopted his approach and, therefore, they eventually melted into the background and disappeared when Avraham passed away.

We cannot say the same about Yishmael, since he was Avraham's son and Avraham had more influence over Yishamel than he had over the other men of his generation. After all, unlike the passersby who had one meal in Avraham's tent and fell under his influence, Yishmael spent years with his father. Avraham taught him and brought out his inner light.[3] Nevertheless, the same principle applies — when Avraham was not present, he no longer illuminated Yishmael's awareness, and therefore "fell" and failed to live the spiritual life of his father (as we see at the end of parshat Chayei Sarah, Gen 25:18).[4]

Yitzchak had a different form of divine service however. His path was from below to Above. This is seen most clearly in the primary action that the Torah attributes to him — digging wells. In order to dig a well, one must remove dirt and stones, clearing away the unwanted obstacles until one arrives at and reveals the source of water. Yitzchak worked upon himself in this way in order to reveal his inner light. His task was not to illuminate the world in the same manner as his father, Avraham. It was not to go "outside," but to go "inside" — to work on himself. He did have an influence on his surroundings and environment, but only on those people who were prone to refinement and elevation, because they could detect the elevation within Yitzchak and were attracted to it. All others were immune to his light. Yitzchak showed the world what refinement means, but he was able to elevate only limited aspects of the "lower world" — those who were inclined to recognize his holiness and identify with it. On the other hand, those who were affected by Yitzchak, were truly affected in their souls, and remained uplifted even when Yitzchak was not present.

In the drawbacks of the respective paths of Avraham and Yitzchak is where we find the explanation for Yishmael and Esav. The advantage of Avraham's path is that his light met the inhabitants of the lower world in their own place. That is why Avraham could unite with Hagar, the maidservant and produce offspring. However, their son Yishmael, could not achieve Avraham's status. Although he eventually returned to his father's path, he did so only under Avraham's tutelage and remained there only as long as Avraham was alive. The drawback of Avraham's path was that it failed to elevate the world, even though it brought illumination to it. When Avraham wasn't there for Yishmael, then Yishmael "fell," and that's why he was not considered Jewish.

Esav was Yitzchak's son. He knew how to work on himself. He adopted his father's approach and accepted and accepted (when it suit him) that it was the correct way to elevate himself spiritually. And his father saw that from him would emerge great and exalted souls that would convert to Judaism.[5] What he failed to realize was that Esav also had a mighty *yetzer hara* that would forever prevent him from realizing his full spiritual potential. Instead of elevating himself spiritually, he was sidelined by lusts and wayward appetites. His mindset was Jewish, but his body was trapped by the temptations and illusions of the physical world.[6]

The disadvantage of Yitzchak's approach is that not everyone has the strength and self-control to make it work. Because of his high level of discipline, it was not appropriate for Yitzchak to marry a maidservant, nor for him to bring into the world a son who was by nature "separate" from him (as Yishmael was from Avraham). Therefore, Yitzchak married from within his own family. His son Esav was Jewish in essence, and he remained an heir to Yitzchak's fortune. In his head (mind), he was connected with Yitzchak, but his body drifted away. Ultimately, his body was not buried in *Maarat Machpelah* with his father and mother, but his head (that is, his mind and essence) did "roll" into the burial cave.[7]

The correct path to God in this world did not emerge until the third of the forefathers — Yaakov. Yaakov established the correct combination of illumination from Above, combined with labor and effort from below.[8] He worked on himself here below in the physical world, while bringing light to bear from Above, thus ensuring that the inspiration from Above would enable him to continue his work upon himself down below.

Everyone needs to feel the joy and sweetness of Godliness as they discipline themselves in their spiritual work.

Everyone needs to feel the joy and sweetness of Godliness as they discipline themselves in their spiritual work. Both hard work and inspiration are necessary, and the proper combination is vital. It was Yaakov who attained this balance and thus opened the path for the Jewish people who followed him. For this reason, all his offspring turned out well. Even though he had children with the maidservants of his wives, all of his children were *tzaddikim* who followed his path without straying as did the sons of Avraham and Yitzchak.

Now we can return to our original proposition — that Yishmael was not Jewish because he was the issue of Hagar, a maidservant, unlike Esav, who was born to Rivkah, a matriarch. And yet, the puzzling fact is that Yaakov's children by the maidservants nevertheless were not treated any differently than those that Yaakov sired with the matriarchs.

The reason that Yaakov's children from the maidservants (Bilhah and Zilpah) were considered Jewish is because Yaakov brought a new path of divine service to the world, in which he united light and illumination with discipline and refinement. This is how he managed not only to inspire the children of the maidservants "from above" (like Avraham), but also to elevate them spiritually "from below" (like Yitzchak) so that they were fully "Jewish."

And then there is something else that we can learn from Yitzchak and Esav. We see that despite all of his transgressions, Esav remained "Jewish," and his head (his essence) was buried with his father. This means that no Jew is totally lost. Esav knew the correct spiritual path but strayed, and yet he remained part of the Jewish people. If so, then we must be available to help the vast majority of Jews alive today, who know nothing about their Jewish heritage and yet they are Jews in every sense of the word. It remains for those of us who know at least *aleph-beit* to teach *aleph* to those who still don't know it and thus to illuminate their spiritual heritage for them. And then, God willing, all the Jews will come to serve the One Above.

The lesson is clear — when seeking to teach and to draw any Jew closer to God and His Torah, we must be careful to bring him up to the level of Torah, and not to "lower" the Torah to his level. The temptation may be great to compromise so that some people will feel more comfortable with the Jewish way of life. But, about this, our sages are clear — we must be like the students of Aharon, the first High Priest, and "love the people and draw them near to Torah." (*Pirkei Avot* 1:12) It is important to draw people near and uplift them, rather than compromise and lower the standards of Judaism. The most important advice that our rabbis (See Ch 32 of *Likutei Amarim Tanya*) give us in this regard is not to look at the "body" of each Jew, but at his "head" — his intellect and essence. But focusing on whom he is in essence, we can appeal to his best instincts and lift him up to a life of Torah study and fulfillment of its mitzvoth.

From Likutei Sichot of the Lubavitcher Rebbe,
vol. 15, pp. 191–199

1. See *Kiddushin* 18a — Esav was from Yisrael, though he was considered a *Yisrael Mumar.*

2. See the *sefer Lekach Tov* of R' Yoseph Engel, *Clal Aleph*. See also *Likutei Sichot*, vol 9, Page 323. Vol 12, Page 148. Vol 20, Page 303. In particular, there are three modes of *shlichut.*

3. And therefore, Yishmael remained a *tzaddik* and *baal teshuvah* until the end of his life, even after Avraham passed away (Bereishit Rabba end of Chayei Sarah). Even though Yishmael remained a *tzadik* after Avhraham passed away, he "fell," meaning that he no longer remained on the same spiritual level of *tzadik* as when Avraham was alive. See footnotes 49 and 52 of the sicha (vol 15, Page 191):

4. From *Ohr HaTorah* of the Tzemach Tzedek, *Parshat Chayei Sarah* (121a, 445a): "If Avraham had known that Yishmael would turn out so badly, he would not have wanted to extend any support to him. However, Avraham thought that Yishamel would also turn out well, although not as well as Yitzchak."

5. See *Torah Ohr* of the Alter Rebbe on *Parshat Toldot*, p. 20, second column.

6. That is why the Torah portion is called *Parshat Toldot* (and relates to Esav). The novelty of Yitzchak's *avodah* was his ability to reveal Esav's mindset, showing that Esav was indeed Yitzchak's son. This activity bore a similarity to the activity of digging wells in order to reveal the "living waters" that flow spontaneously, deep within the bowels of the earth.

7. Targum Yonatan ben Uziel on Gen. 50:13, Alter Rebbe's Siddur 22A, Torat Chaim of the Mittler Rebbe 89:4 (where it is brought in the name of the Zohar). See also Gemora Sota 13A. Pirkei deR' Eliezer end of Ch 39.

8. Possibly because Yaakov combined the approaches of Avraham and Yitzchak. This is what enabled Yaakov to refine and elevate the "lower world" on its level of existence. See *Likutei Sichot* vol, 20, pp. 341–2.

Spiritual Paths of Avraham and Yitzchak

Toldot 26:1

There is a well-known phrase found in the Midrash (*Tanhuma Lech Lecha* 9, *Bereishit Rabba* 40:6), "All that happened to the forefathers is a directive to their children."

The Ramban[1] writes at length about this statement of the sages and demonstrates with several examples how the events of the forefathers' lives served as directives for their descendants. Since the sages express the phrase in terms of "fathers and children," and whatever a father possesses, he passes on to his children via an inheritance, it is clear that the lives of the forefathers were not merely directives, but much more than that.[2] Whatever transpired in the lives of the forefathers empowers and inspires the rest of us.

In *Parshat Toldot*, the Torah tells us that, at a certain point, "There was famine in the Land." And then God instructed Yitzchak, "Do not descend into Egypt, dwell in the Land that I am telling you about. Live in this Land and I will be with you and I will bless you." (Genesis 26:1–2)

The sages[3] explain that Yitzchak was like an *olah temimah* ("perfect sacrifice") and therefore he had to stay within the boundaries of Israel.[4] Here, the "directive to the children" is clear. The true "place" of all Jews is not outside of Israel — in exile (*galut*) — but at the "table of our father [God]." (Gemora Berachot 3A)

Even during the current era when we have been exiled from our Land, we still have the status of "children." While we suffer in exile — because that is not where we truly belong — we beg God to bring us "to the table of our father," to the Land of Israel. This is why we pray three times per day that "the sprout of David shall germinate," and even on Shabbat and festivals, we pray that "our eyes shall behold [God's] return to Zion with mercy."

That may be one of the reasons that, in the future, we will point to Yitzchak (not to either Avraham of Yaakov but only to YItzchak) and say, "You are our father." For, at that time, we will clearly perceive the benefit of the *temimut* ("integrity/perfection") that is specifically associated with him (as an *olah temimah*). And that is the perception that will bring us to our true place at "the table of our father" in the Land of Israel.

The issue of never leaving the Holy Land is related only to Yitzchak among the forefathers. It does not arise regarding Avraham and Yaakov, who sometimes found themselves living temporarily outside of the Land.

There are only three biblical characters whom we call our "forefathers/patriarchs," and that is just as true now as it was in previous eras. From this it is understood that specific details associated with each of them — and the details lead to general principles — provide directives for their descendants. Such details provide inspiration not only for the Jews in general, but for each and every Jew in particular, and especially those who find themselves in exile.

By way of further explanation, let us examine two categories of Jews:

1. those who are dedicated mainly to learning Torah, as was the Tribe of Yissachar of whom it is written "Rejoice … Yissachar in Your tents" (Deuteronomy 33:18)
2. those who are devoted to going out to make a living, as was the Tribe of Zevulun of whom it is written "Rejoice Zevulun in your excursions" (Deuteronomy 33:18)

The Jews whose main occupation is Torah study are found inside their "tents" or academies. And those businessmen and professionals — who find it necessary to go outside of the world of Torah and deal with the world at large — do so in a manner of "All of your deeds should be for the sake of Heaven," (*Pirkei Avos* 2:17) and "Know Him in all of your ways" (Proverbs 3:6). This is how they spread holiness to all parts of the world.

The ability and power to undertake each of those paths comes from the forefathers.

Avraham uprooted himself from the Land of Israel and descended to Egypt (in Hebrew *Mitzrayim*, meaning land of "limitations/"), and there as well as in other places, he managed to persuade others to recognize and worship the one God, bringing them "under the wings of the *Shechinah*."[5] His divine service was to "call upon the name of the Lord" (Genesis 12:8) wherever he went, as the Rambam describes it,

> "He began to explain to the world that it was not appropriate to worship anything other than the God of the universe ... and he would call in a great voice to the people of the world to inform them that there is only one God and that He is the only one to serve. He would travel, call and gather the people from one city to another and one kingdom to the next..." (*Hilchot Avoda Zarah* 1:3).

This Avraham did until he succeeded in instilling awareness of God not only as, "God of the heavens," but also as "God of the earth," as Rashi puts it, explaining that Avraham "publicized God among the people" (Rashi on Genesis 24:7).

Yitzchak's divine service, however, was the precise opposite. He did not leave the Land of Israel. Since he was an *olah temimah* ("perfect offering"), he was obligated to remain in the Land of Israel. But even within Israel, we do not find that he left his home to deal with matters outside. His main task was "inside."

And it is from these two forefathers that we Jews have taken on the two categories of divine service described previously.

From Avraham, each and every Jew has received a clear directive and impetus to work "outside." All Jews, including those whose main approach is "inside," learning Torah, must also from time to time go out of their place of comfort and bring holiness to the outside. They must publicize the name of God until they draw Jews closer to God and His Torah, as the sages said, "All who are involved in Torah alone are considered as if without God..." (*Avoda Zarah* 17b) and "Anyone who says, 'I have only Torah,' does not have even Torah..." (*Yevamot* 109b).

And, from Yitzchak, each and every Jew has received a clear directive regarding "inner work," meaning that even those whose main focus is "outside," whose major involvement is with matters of the world, must sometimes separate and get involved "inside." Although they draw holiness into the world through their deeds, bringing the Torah to those Jews who for the moment are far away from God, they must take time out to learn Torah themselves and set aside their material concerns (like the Jews in the desert who ate manna and had no worries about making a living).

This we also learn from the name of our Torah portion — *Parshat Toldot.*

The name of a Torah portion — while generally referring to its opening words — also reflects its content. This is especially true according to the doctrine of the Baal Shem Tov, who taught that the name that an object is called in Hebrew is what animates and vitalizes it, bringing it into a state of "existence." A proof of this approach comes from *Parshat Toldot* — which begins "These are the offspring (*toldot*)..." (Genesis 25:19)

Now, our Torah portion is not the only portion to begin this way. Indeed, *Parshat Noach* begins with the exact same words, "These are the offspring (*toldot*)..." (Genesis 6:9) If the name of the Torah portions were based merely on their beginning, then *Parshat Noach* should be called *Toldot*, since the word *toldot* figures in the beginning. Or our Torah portion should be called *Parshat Yitzchak* since his name is as close to the beginning as is that of Noach. But since it doesn't, this proves that the name of the Torah portion expresses its essential content, and "offspring" is the focus here.

There is a spiritual instruction that emerges from this, which is that every Jew must produce "spiritual offspring" — that is, he or she must persuade other Jews to keep the Torah and mitzvoth. It is our obligation to bring them closer to God and His Torah, as it says, "All who teach the son of their friend Torah are considered as if they gave birth to him" (*Sanhedrin* 19b). In other words, this is the content of the mitzvah to "be fruitful and multiply" in the spiritual sense.

This is also hinted in Rashi's commentary for *Parshat Toldot*: "*Toldot* refers to Yaakov and Esav..." That is, *toldot* refers to both sons of Yitzchak — not just the holy Yaakov but also the sinful Esav. This teaches us that we must also ensure that not just those on the level of Yaakov but also those on the level of Esav should be brought closer to Torah and educated about its mitzvoth.

But if so, we are in need of explanation. We have previously explained that Yitzchak's divine service was the opposite of Avraham — he separated himself from the rest of mankind, living alone in the Land of Israel, "inside," rather than getting involved with others "outside," and raising "spiritual offspring" among those he might have encountered, as did Avraham.

Moreover, since the entire Torah portion is about Yitzchak and his divine service, why is it not called *Parshat Yitzchak* to emphasize his special nature?

His nature, as mentioned previously, was not to go out as his father did, but to remain in Israel. But since the Torah portion is called *Parshat Toldot*, we are forced to conclude that in some way Yitzchak was also involved in establishing "spiritual offspring." Moreover, since the Torah portion focuses on Yitzchak, and yet is called *Toldot*, we know that the concept of "spiritual offspring" is more specifically associated with Yitzchak than with Avraham.

We can resolve this riddle by examining what our divine service will be in the future when the Mashiach arrives, and we will all be able to point to Yitzchak and say, "You are our father." (Gemora Shabbat 89B)

The Rambam (in *Hilchot Melachim* 8:10) writes, "Moshe commanded us in the name of God to persuade all people of the world to accept the Seven Noachide Laws." The *halachah* in this case, as in all matters of Jewish law, is that such verbal persuasion is the best method — that is, Jews should actively try to convince all the people of the world to accept the Seven Noachide Laws.

Accordingly, we need to investigate the role of the Jews in the future, during the Messianic Age, for the Rambam indicates that the Mashiach will "prepare[6] the entire world to serve God together." The question is, since all the Jews at that time will have emerged from exile and will be found together in the Land of Israel and non-Jews will have already accepted the Seven Noahide Laws, in what manner will the Jews be involved, at that time, in teaching the non-Jews anything new regarding these commandments?

The words of the Prophets (especially Isaiah 2:2–5) are clear on the matter regarding the future redemption:

> In the days to come, the mountain of the Lord's house shall stand firm above the mountains and tower above the hills. And all the nations shall stream to it. And the many peoples shall go and say: 'Come, let us go up to the Mount of God, to the House of the God of Yaakov — that He may instruct us in His ways, that we may walk in His paths.' For instruction shall come forth from Zion and the word of the Lord from Jerusalem. Thus He will judge among the nations and arbitrate among the many peoples. And they shall beat their swords into plowshares and their spears into pruning hooks; nation shall not lift up sword against nation, and they shall never again know war. O House of Yaakov, come let us walk by the light of the Lord."

These verses tell us that what will occur in the future — when the non-Jews will learn the ways of God and serve Him — will not be the result of Jews going out from the Holy Land to the Diaspora in order to persuade them. Rather, since the status of the Jews, as well as of the

Land of Israel and of the holy Temple, will be at the highest level of perfection, the "light of Lord" will shine from Zion in a revealed manner and illuminate all living beings. It will automatically have an effect on the nations of the world and their non-Jewish citizens, to the extent that "all the nations shall stream to it, and the many peoples shall go and say: 'Come, let us go up to the Mount of God, to the House of the God of Yaakov ... that we may walk in His paths."

It emerges, then, that in the future, it will not be necessary for the Jews to get involved with all the nations of the world. Instead, the Jews will be "involved in Torah and its wisdom" — as the Rambam says (in *Hilchot Melachm* 12:4–5), "the Jews will be great sages, with knowledge of hidden matters, and an understanding of the Creator according to the abilities of man." Nevertheless, the Jews will hold sway over and influence the nations, so that they will be directed to "walk by the light of the Lord."

Rather, remaining in one place in the Land of Israel, Yitzchak attracted the people of the world to him, just like a large torch that attracts the smaller sparks to it.

Similar to this was the path and divine service of Yitzchak.[7] Yitzchak was all about establishing "offspring," without traveling from one city to another, or one kingdom to the next in order to publicize the name of God in each and every place like his father Avraham.[8] Rather, remaining in one place in the Land of Israel, Yitzchak attracted the people of the world to him, just like a large torch that attracts the smaller sparks to it. And that form of divine service is what is expressed in the content of our Torah portion.

When a famine occurred in the land, "Yitzchak's intention was to go down to Egypt just as his father had done during famine" (Rashi on Genesis 26:2). Yitzchak was fully aware of the principle that his father Avraham had implanted — that God runs the universe and controls all that happens in the world — and from this principle, Yitzchak understood that the famine had occurred by the will of God. And, therefore, Yitzchak understood that he, too, should leave the Land of Israel and go down to Egypt, where he would publicize the name of the One God, just as his father had done under similar circumstances. However, God told him, "Do not descend to Egypt, dwell in the Land..." And the sages interpret it as God saying, "Cause the *Shechinah* to dwell in the Land" (*Bereishit Rabba* 64:3).

Yitzchak's mode of serving God was not by leaving the Land of Israel for Egypt (the lowest spiritual point of the earth), but by remaining in the Land, so that the name of God would emanate from Israel to all the nations of the world. And that is exactly what took place. As a consequence of Yitzchak dwelling in Gerar, he "grew and developed until he was very wealthy" to the extent that it was said it was better to own, "the manure of a mule of Yitzchak rather than the silver or gold of Avimelech [the Philistine king of Gerar]." (Rashi on Genesis 26:13). As a result, Avimelech told Yitzchak, "Go away from us for you have become much more powerful than us" (Genesis 26:16). But after Yitzchak built an altar and "called out in the name of God," Avimelech reconsidered. The Torah relates that Avimelech came to him with a handful of his compatriots and said, "We have seen that God is with you ... let us make a covenant with you" (Genesis 26:28). From this, we understand that when the Philistines figured out that God was with Yitzchak, and this awareness filtered all the way up to their king, he then came of his own volition to establish a treaty of peaceful co-existence. It emerges then, that these were non-Jews who listened to and followed Yitzchak.

Now we can understand why it is our Torah portion is called *Toldot*, and not by another name.[9] When one uproots himself in order to deal with matters that are "outside" of *kedushah*, as did Avraham, it is not so clear that the results are in the category of "offspring." It's true that Avraham made converts wherever he went including in Egypt, but it is not as if he "sired" them, which would imply that there was a similarity between them and Avraham. [They never rose to Avraham's level. They never changed internally, even though they recognized God under Avraham's tutelage.] *Toldot*, however, implies that there can be such offspring. The divine service of Yitzchak was such that he remained in his place and elevated the population of the world to his level and status, so that in the process they became similar to him as if he had sired them.[10]

This then, is the eternal teaching that emerges from Yitzchak, that is alluded to in the name *Toldot*. True, there are Jews whose divine service is to go "outside," to journey from one place to another in order to publicize Godliness and establish "offspring" for God and His Torah. But they must also, from time to time, ensconce themselves "inside" in order to devote themselves to learning Torah in such a manner that says, "Torah is my profession." But that in no way means that they are interrupting their main work to draw Jews closer to God and His Torah. Quite the opposite; this continues to be a vital element of their mission.

All Jews are descendants of our forefathers — and that means we all have a spark of Yitzchak in our soul — our divine service "inside" also has the ability to impact our mission "outside" in the world, including also those Jews who are under our influence. And, in addition to the influence that we have over such people, whom we succeed in bringing "under the wings of the *Shechinah*," they also become our "offspring."

There is a similar teaching that emerges concerning those Jews whose task is to sit "inside" and learn Torah. In addition to the fact that they must from time to time emerge and bring Torah to others who are "outside" of the fold and draw them closer, their involvement in the Torah and its mitzvoth must be imbued with recognition that they are obligated to create "offspring" for the One Above. Their learning must be for the sake of teaching, which then ensures that their "offspring" remain faithful to the path.

By establishing "offspring" for God and His Torah in this manner, we emulate the divine service of Yitzchak and hasten the arrival of the true and final redemption. And in so doing, we engender perfect laughter and delight Above (as did Yitzchak whose name means "will laugh"), and the laughter and delight Above also descends to us enabling us to get a taste of the day when "the entire earth will be full of knowledge of God like the waters cover the seabed." (Habbakuk 2:14)

From Likutei Sichot of the Lubavitcher Rebbe,
vol. 25, pp. 123–130

NOTES

1. Ramban on Parshat Lech Lecha 12:6, as well as 14:1 and in Toldot 26:1, Vayishlach 32:4 and more.

2. The word *siman* that is here translated as "directive," is commonly translated as "sign." However, even according to the more common translation, a *siman* is more than symbolic. For example, the "signs" (*simanim*) that an animal is kosher do more than merely inform us that the animal is kosher — they actually cause the animal to be kosher. (See *Tzafnat Paneach* of the Rogochover Gaon on the Rambam's *Hilchot ma'achalot asurot* Ch 1. See also the Ramban on Genesis 12:6.

3. See the Midrash in *Breishit Rabba* 64, and Rashi and the Ramban in their commentaries on these verses in Genesis 26:1–2.

4. Just as an *olah temimah* had to stay within the boundaries of the Temple courtyard.

5. As it is written in the Torah, "the souls whom they [Avraham and Sarah] made in Charan" (Genesis 12:5) and as the Midrash explains at length (*Bereishit Rabba* 39).

6. The word translated here as "prepare" (*letaken*) is commonly translated as "to fix/rectify." In censored versions of the Rambam's *Mishneh Torah*, the word refers the Mashiach — he is the one who will prepare (fix/rectify) the world. In the uncensored versions, there is another phrase that had been removed, "and if he is not successful ..." and the word "prepare" (*letaken*) appears in the middle of the phrase. "And all of these matters (regarding Yeshua the Christian) and of the Yishmaelite ... only occurred in order to pave the path for the king, the Messiah, and to prepare (*letaken*) the entire world..." See also *Likutei Sichot* vol. 18, p. 283.

7. The verses cited in the previous paragraph (from Isaiah) refer specifically to the *avodah* of Yaakov, as the sages said (in *Pesachim* 88a) , "Not like Avraham ... but like Yaakov who was called a 'house.'" (See *Likutei Sichot* vol. 15, p. 240). Nevertheless, in general, these verses also apply to Yitzchak.

8. The difference between the *avodah* of Avraham and that of Yitzchak explained here is based upon and parallel to what is explained in Chassidic texts and discourses: Avraham's *avodah* was from Above to below and Yitzchak's *avodah* was from below to Above. See at length in *Likutei Sichot* vol. 15, p. 194.

9. The previous two Torah portions — *Vayera* and *Chayei Sarah* — mention Yitzchak as a detail in the overall narrative of Avraham. And in the following portions — *Vayeitzei* and *Vayislach* — Yitzchak is scarcely mentioned.

10. According to this distinction, we may possibly understand the two versions of the saying of the sages, "Anyone who teaches Torah to his friend's son is as if he 'made'" him, as it is written, 'The souls whom they made in Charan" (*Sanhedrin* 99b) or "as if he sired him" (*Sanhedrin* 19b).

Why Yitzchak Could Not Leave Israel

Toldot 26:2

After his twin sons, Yaakov and Esav were born and grew up, Yitzchak was confronted with a famine, and he took his family to the land of the Philistines (a region which was still within the boundaries of the land promised by God to Israel). At that point, God appeared to him and said, "Do not descend to Egypt, dwell in the land that I will tell you about … Settle in this land and I will be with you and bless you…" (Genesis 26:2–3).

Apparently, unlike his father Avraham, there was something about Yitzchak that prevented him from leaving Israel and dwelling elsewhere. Yet this sparks a controversy, as we see in the differing opinions of the sages quoted in the Midrash and the Torah commentator, Rashi.

The Midrash (*Breishit Rabbah* 64:3) says that Yitzchak was an *olah temimah*, "a perfect offering [since he had been nearly sacrificed by his father], and just as an offering becomes disqualified if it leaves or is taken out of its designated area of the Temple, so he would have been disqualified if he left the Land of Israel." Therefore, God told him to stay.

But Rashi (commenting on the words, "do not descend to Egypt") says, "It was Yitzchak's intention to descend to Egypt as his father did in the days of famine, but God told him not to do this since he was a perfect offering and leaving the borders of Israel was not appropriate for him."

In the contrasting explanations of the Midrash and Rashi, we see two main differences:

1. The Midrash says that leaving the Land of Israel would have make Yitzchak unfit, like a sacrifice that becomes invalid if it leaves its designated physical area. However, Rashi says only that it would be "inappropriate" for Yitzchak to leave the Land of Israel — he does not say that leaving would make Yitzchak unfit.
2. The Midrash focuses on the phrase, "Dwell in the Land…" while Rashi's commentary is focused on the phrase, "Do not descend to Egypt…."

We might explain these differences as follows: The Midrash chooses to emphasize the positive quality of the Land of Israel — if Yitzchak left, he would forfeit the heightened holiness of the Land. While Rashi chose to emphasize the negative side — if Yitzchak left, he was going somewhere that was simply inappropriate for him.

It's tempting to suggest that the difference between these two viewpoints is that, according to the Midrash, the Land was holy and that's why Yitzchak shouldn't leave. But according to Rashi, the Land was not yet holy because the Jews had not yet conquered and settled it. To elaborate, according to the Midrash, the innate holiness associated with the land of Israel made it forbidden for Yitzchak to leave the land. However, according to Rashi, the innate holiness existed only in potential, and would not be revealed for another several generations until the Jews entered and conquered the land with Yehoshua. While the forefathers kept all of the holy mitzvoth in Israel even before the Torah was given, it was only after they received the Torah that the mitzvoth became obligatory. And only by fulfilling the obligatory mitzvoth in Israel, did the innate holiness of the land become revealed, according to Rashi. Therefore, according to the Midrash, it was forbidden for Yitzchak to leave Israel. But according to Rashi, it was not forbidden, but only "inappropriate" for Yitzchak to leave. Exiting the land of Israel would not cause Yitzchak to become halachically unfit.[1]

However, it turns out that we cannot make this distinction. We saw already saw that Avraham would not allow Yitzchak to leave the Land of Israel for any reason, even to find his soulmate. When asked by his servant Eliezer what to do if the girl he found for Yitzchak would not follow him back to Israel, Avraham replied, "Be sure not to take my son [out of Israel]…" (Genesis 24:4–6). If the problem with leaving the Land of Israel was because (as the Midrash implies) Yitzchak would have lost his status as a holy offering, then Avraham would have cited that when speaking with Eliezer. The fact that Avraham did not mention this reason when speaking with Eliezer means that it was entirely permissible for Yitzchak to leave, but there were other reasons why Avraham would not let it happen.

Since there are no indications that it was because Yitzchak was a "perfect offering" that he couldn't leave Israel, we are back to "square one." Again we ask: Why couldn't Yitzchak leave Israel, and what is the difference between the two explanations of the Midrash and Rashi?[2]

It is evident that, in the time of the forefathers, there was no specific holiness associated with the Land of Israel, and the injunction against leaving it was not in effect. Even though the forefathers fulfilled all the principles of the Torah even before it was given at Mt. Sinai, the Land had not yet taken on the holiness associated with mitzvoth of the Torah, and that's why the forefathers were able to enter and leave the Land of Israel at will.[3]

The one exception was Yitzchak. Quite simply, the reason that Avraham did not permit his son Yitzchak to leave Israel was because the Land had been promised to him and his descendants. Since the Land of Israel belonged to Avraham and his descendants, he was not willing to permit his son Yitzchak to get married on foreign soil and remain there. However, we do see in *Parshat Toldo*t that when there was a famine, it was permissible for the forefathers to leave the Land and seek food elsewhere while the famine lasted.[4]

So, if there was no special holiness associated with the Land of Israel in the time of the forefathers, then why did Yitzchak's status as a "perfect offering" prevent him from leaving when there was a famine?

We can understand this by looking at how the Midrash and Rashi relate to Jewish ownership of the Land of Israel in the days of the forefathers.

When expounding upon the "covenant between the pieces," when God said to Avraham, "to your descendants I have given this Land" (Genesis 15:18), the Midrash states: "The word of God is deed … so it is as if the deed was already accomplished. The Torah does not state, 'I will give this Land,' but "I have given…" (Bereishit Rabba 44:22) Thus, according to the Midrash, ownership of Israel was already accomplished during the "covenant between the pieces" [which happened during Avraham's lifetime].

However, Rashi understands all this differently. Rashi says that "to your descendants I have given this Land," means "*as if* it were done already." That is, Rashi reads this Torah verse to mean that the Land had had not yet been given, but only promised to the Jews in the future. Their true possession would not occur until later, in the time of Avraham's descendants, when they would conquer and settle the Land.

The difference here is that, according to the Midrash, the Land of Israel was fully acquired by the Jews during "the covenant between the pieces," while according to Rashi, only a promise was made, and it was *as if* the Land was acquired.[5]

If, according to the Midrash, the Jews fully acquired the Land of Israel during "the covenant between the pieces," why did they not also acquire the ability to instill holiness into the Land?[6] And if a statement of God ("to your descendants I have given...") could produce ownership, why could it not also induce holiness?

We know already that there is a difference between the mitzvoth that the forefathers fulfilled (before the Torah was given at Mt. Sinai) and the mitzvoth that we, who live after Mt. Sinai) are commanded to fulfill. The difference is that, before the Torah was given, its commandments did not permeate and transform the physical world. The object of a given mitzvah — say *tefilin*, for example — remained the same as before. Before the Torah was given, Yaakov used sticks of wood to fulfill the mitzvah of tefilin (Zohar), but the holiness that he drew down to the sticks permeated them only as long as Yaakov performed the mitzvah. The minute he stopped performing the mitzvah, the holiness, like a pleasant aroma, dissipated. Whatever the mitzvah achieved only impacted the person who fulfilled it, but not the outer world.

However, the mitzvoth that we fulfill now, after the giving of the Torah, have transformational power. They actually induce holiness (*kedushah*) into the physical world and transform it, so that the object of a given mitzvah is no longer the same. With the Torah came the ability to transform certain physical objects into Godly objects. Not only the person, but also the object itself, become transformed. The reason for this is that, when the Torah was given at Mt. Sinai, the previously impermeable barriers between the upper and lower worlds were removed. After the giving of the Torah, Godliness could descend to the lower world, and man and his world could ascend. The giving of the Torah introduced a new category of creation — a physical object that is a vessel for Godliness.

The same applies to the Land of Israel. When God promised the Land of Israel to Avraham and his descendants, this provided them with physical ownership. But, before the giving of the Torah, the promise could not deliver holiness to the Land and transform it into an object of holiness. That could only take place later, after the Torah was given, and specifically when the Jews conquered and settled the Land.[7]

Before that era, because of the barriers that existed between the upper and lower realms, the potential to imbue the Land with holiness could not be actualized. With the giving of the Torah, the holy potential of the Land was triggered, and when the Jews then entered the Land, they imbued it with holiness.[8]

The above distinction (between physical ownership and holiness) applies to Rashi's commentary as well as to the Midrash. Rashi understands that a major change took place when the Land of Israel was given to the Jews. Unlike any other transaction — in which the item undergoing transition from one owner to another owner remains unchanged — the Land of Israel underwent a fundamental transformation once it came into Jewish possession.[9]

Unlike any other transaction — in which the item undergoing transition from one owner to another owner remains unchanged — the Land of Israel underwent a fundamental transformation once it came into Jewish possession

Before it was given to the Jews, the Land of Israel could come under the control of whoever conquered it. But after it was given to the Jews, and its very essence became "Jewish," it was no longer possible for any other nation to own it. It was the sole possession of the Jews. However, this distinctive transformation could only occur when the Jews received the Torah — before that, the Land belonged to the Jews only potentially and theoretically; it was not until they conquered the Land (under Yehoshua) that they truly transformed it. Only then could Jews say to non-Jews: "The Land belongs to God … and He gave it to us…" (R' Yitzchak in Rashi Gen 1:1)

Having established that the holiness of the Land of Israel was not an issue before the Jews actually conquered it, we can again compare the positions of Rashi and of the Midrash regarding Yitzchak's status.

The Midrash tells us that Yitzchak could not leave Israel because he was an *olah temimah* ("perfect offering"). But it is not referring to his level of holiness. The Midrash is not concerned that Yitzchak, when leaving Israel, would have descended from a higher level of holiness to a lower level. Rather, it is concerned with the "boundaries" of the Land, especially as they applied to Yitzchak.

There is a general principle in Jewish law that every category of meat has its own "boundaries." We learn this from the Torah verse, "You may not eat *treif* meat from the field" (Exodus 22:30). This mandate pertains to *treif* meat, but also has implications for kosher meat and is interpreted to mean that, once meat is outside of its boundaries, it becomes forbidden. For example, the meat of sacrifices categorized as *kodesh kedoshim* ("highest of holy") could not be taken out of the Temple courtyard. Meat that is *kodshei kalim* (of "minor holiness") could be taken out of the Temple courtyard but could not be eaten outside of the city walls of Jerusalem. The meat of the Passover sacrifice could not leave the group with which it was associated, and so forth (Ex 12:46).

Since, according to the Midrash, God's promise to Avraham was intended literally — that the Land was already granted to him and his descendants — therefore, at the very moment that Yitzchak became an *olah temimah* ("perfect offering") he took on "boundaries," so to speak. His boundaries were the boundaries of the Land of Israel, beyond which he was forbidden to pass. Again, this was not due to the holiness of the Land (which did not exist), but simply because at this point Avraham and Yitzchak gained full ownership of the land with all that entails. This meant that Yitzchak, as an *olah temimah*, gained "boundaries," beyond which he was not allowed to pass.

However, according to Rashi, the issue is not an offering and its boundaries, since God's promise to Avraham at the "covenant between the pieces" established neither ownership nor boundaries. For Rashi, the issue is awareness of God. As he explains (in his commentary on *Parshat Vayera*, Genesis 24:7), when Eliezer asked if he could take Yitzchak outside of Israel to get married, Avraham replied that, outside of Israel, God is known only as the "God of the heavens but not of the earth." That meant that awareness of God had not yet permeated creation outside of the Land of Israel. However, in Israel, Avraham's efforts had resulted in awareness of God on a conscious physical level, which is why God was called the God of the earth as well as of the heavens here. (Still this was only superficial, as a verbal expression alone. Therefore, Yitzchak could not marry the daughters of the Canaanites, and instead Avraham gave instructions that Yitzchak should marry only a daughter from his own extended family). True knowledge, fear and love of God occurred only after the Torah was given and the Jews settled the Land. For that reason, according to Rashi, it was inappropriate for Yitzchak to leave Israel, where God was known as the God of heavens and of earth, and go to a land where people recognized God only as God of the heavens and failed to acknowledge the Divine Presence on earth.

Underlying the distinction between the Midrash and Rashi is a fundamental difference in their approaches. The Midrash, which transcends the simple meaning of the Torah text, approaches ownership of the Land from a more spiritual perspective. Therefore, the Midrash holds that ownership of the Land began even in the era of the forefathers, and that is why Yitzchak, as a *olah temimah* could not leave Israel for another land. Rashi, however placed emphasis on the simple meaning of the text, according to which we don't see true Jewish ownership of the Land of Israel until the Jews conquered it under Yehoshua. Therefore, according to Rashi, the only reason Yitzchak couldn't leave Israel was because any other place was "inappropriate" for him. It was simply unsuitable for one who recognized God in his everyday life to go to a land where God was ignored.

Rashi was interested in the simple meaning of the verse, according to which only the conquest by the Jews established Israel as their possession. However, once that took place, it changed the entire nature of the Land, transforming it into a place that couldn't belong to any other people, since it was given by God to the Jews forever.

From Likutei Sichot of the Lubavitcher Rebbe, vol. 15, pp. 200–210

NOTES

1. Another reason that Rashi may not have accepted the explanation of the Midrash literally is that an *olah tmimah* is not invalidated as a sacrifice if it leaves its designated area. Nevertheless, it is understood that certain locations are inappropriate for such a holy object — akin to Lavan's statement, "I emptied the house of idol worship" in order to persuade Eliezer to enter (Genesis 24:31 and Rashi's commentary).

2. Hypothetically, we might answer according to *halachah*. There are a few reasons why it is permitted to leave Israel ("to marry … or to learn Torah" according to the Rambam in *Hilchot Melachim* 5:9), but then only if the plan is to return to Israel. However, when there is a famine, it is permissible to leave Israel and to stay away for an extended period of time, which was the case here in *Parshat Toldot* (but not

in *Parshat Chayei Sarah* when Eliezer inquired if he could take Yitzchak out of Israel). But, God issued a special command to Yitzchak to remain in Israel, and not to leave even because of the famine, since Yitzchak was an *olah temimah.* (Midrash Rabba 64:3) However, this line of reasoning is suspect for two reasons: 1) As the Rambam continues, "Even though it is permissible to leave, it is not considered pious behavior. Machlon and Chilion were two great Jews of their generation and for unfortunate reasons they left Israel and became 'guilty' before God." That being the case, it was highly unlikely that the forefathers, who kept all the principles of the Torah before it was given, would have left Israel. 2) We see that Avraham left the Land of Israel even when there was no famine. After the "covenant between the pieces," when God promised the Land to Avraham and his descendants, Avraham returned to Charan and to his father (some say that Avraham was permitted to leave in order to fulfill the mitzvah of honoring his father, but that is highly unlikely since he was commanded by God in *Parshat Lech Lecha*, "Leave the land of... your father's house..." (Genesis 12:1).

3. Aside from Yitzchak, who received a specific command to remain, while Yaakov left Israel. Although it "pained him" to do so, according to Rashi, and according to *Pirkei d'R'Eliezer* in Ch 39, he did not leave until commanded from Above to join his son Yosef in Egypt (Genesis 46:3–4). There was famine in Israel at the time, but the brothers had brought food back to sustain themselves and their father in the Land. Yet, when given the opportunity to join his Yosef, Yaakov did so, since at the time there was no injunction preventing the forefathers from leaving Israel if they deemed it important to leave.

4. The injunction against leaving Israel did not apply, not only according to the opinion (Rashbam on *Baba Basra* 91a) that the reason for the injunction is because by leaving, one eschews the mitzvoth that are possible to fulfill only in Israel — since this principle did not apply during the period of the forefathers. (See *Shu't Maharit* section 1:4, *Tashbatz* section 3 *sif katan* 98 and *siman* 200). But also according to the opinion (*Shu't Maharit Yoreh Deah* section 2:28) that the mitzvah of settling the Land of Israel is due to the holiness of the land itself — "and the mitzvah of settling the Land of Israel applies even now while in its state of destruction, as the Ramban writes" — the injunction against leaving did not apply, because the [holiness of the land] may also be dependent upon fulfillment of mitzvoth. (See *Kuntres Collel Chabad* of the Rebbe Rashab in his *Igros Kodesh* vol. 4, p. 179, sec. 7). At any rate, from the time that the Jews entered Israel and became obligated in the mitzvoth [of the Land], the holiness has not been nullified even after the destruction [of the second Temple].

5. Rashi's approach is evident in his very first comment on the Torah (Genesis 1:1). There he mentions the claim of the non-Jewish nations, "You are robbers, since you conquered the seven Canaanite nations," implying that the Jewish acquisition of Israel occurred only later when they conquered the Land. However, it could be argued that this claim was only "according to the opinion of the non-Jewish nations," and that in reality the Jews had already acquired the Land of Israel in the days of Avraham. Also, Rashi in *Parshat Lech Lecha* (Genesis 13:7) writes, "And the Canaanites and Perizites were in the Land at the time, and Avraham had no rights

to the Land yet." However, the Midrash (*Breishit Rabba* Ch. 41) on the same verse says, "Until now, the Canaanites were attempting to obtain rights to the Land," which could be explained as "rights," but not ownership, which had already been obtained by the forefathers even before the conquest.

6. Investigation is necessary to determine the level of holiness of Yitzchak himself after the *Akeidah*, as Rashi writes, "He was sanctified on Mt. Moriah as an *olah temimah*." During the *Akeida*, we could say that Yitzchak became a "holy object" (*cheftza d'kedusha*), since he was bound and nearly sacrificed according to the command of God. But investigation is necessary to determine if we may say this about Yitzchak after the *Akeidah*, since the conclusion of the episode was, "Do not extend your hand against the lad" (Genesis 22:12 and see Rashi's comment there). And moreover, no change took place on Yitzchak's body [Avraham's circumcision of course, did produce a change in his body]. Rashi writes about Yitzchak that he "did not want to marry a maid servant," but not that Yitzchak was unable to marry a maidservant [suggesting that after the *Akeidah*, Yitzchak's body did not remain on the same high level of holiness as during the *Akeidah*]. On the other hand, Rashi emphasizes that also after the *Akeidah*, there was an ongoing effect "for all generations ... the ashes of Yitzchak are gathered and remain as an atonement" (Genesis 22:14) — implying that only after the *Akeidah* and the burning of the ram did this high level of holiness take hold.

7. *Kedushah* — "holiness" — is mentioned regarding the Land of Israel even before the Torah was given. For example, in *Parshat Vayeitzei* (Genesis 28:16–17) in regard to where Yaakov placed his head to sleep that turned out to be the future location of the Temple — "God is found in this place and I did not know ... how awesome is this place, it is none other than the House of God" — but possibly these verses do not refer to imbuing and "fixing" holiness in a physical place. Similarly, several commentaries (*Moreh Nevuchim*, *Ikarim* and others) hold that even after the giving of the Torah, the presence of the *Shechinah* does not apply to "place" and produces no change in physical place, and its presence is only transient (see *Ohr HaTorah* of the Tzemach Tzedek *Vayeitzei* 178a). Take note also of the wording in Exodus 3:5, "Remove your shoes because the place on which you are standing is holy ground" — even though the verse is not referring to Israel, nevertheless since the *Shechinah* was present at that time [there was a command to remove the shoes]. And at the giving of the Torah itself, when "God descended ... onto Mt. Sinai ... all who touch Mt. Sinai will surely die" (Exodus 19:11–12), even though "at the blast of the shofar they will ascend the mountain" (Exodus 19:13 and Rashi there) [which demonstrates the presence of Godliness and holiness in a physical location].

8. This is the reason that the forefathers strongly desired to be buried in the Land of Israel. Even according to the opinion that the Land did not yet take on *kedushah*, the forefathers wished to be in the Land at the time when it would take on *kedushah* in the future (when the Jews would conquer it).

9. See the Rebbe's *sicha* in vol. 5 of *Likutei Sichot*.

Yitzchak on the Altar

Toldot 26:3

Our Torah portion — *Parshat Toldot* — mentions that Yitzchak was told by God not to leave the Land of Israel, even though there was a famine and his father Avraham had previously left Israel under similar circumstances. The sages quoted in the Midrash (*Breishit Rabba* 64:3, brought in Rashi, Gen 26:3) explain that, unlike Avraham, Yitzchak was like an *olah temimah* or "a perfect sacrifice" which it was forbidden to remove from the Temple courtyard. The whole of Israel was like the Temple courtyard in regard to Yitzchak, so he could not leave it.

But then, the sages of the Jerusalem Talmud took the comparison a step further and said something very puzzling: "The ashes of Yitzchak remain as if piled on top of the altar" (*Yerushalmi Taanit* 2:1)[1]

[As we well know, Yitzchak was never sacrificed by his father Avraham during the *Akeidah*. Although Avraham bound his son on the pyre in response to God's command, an angel stayed his hand and told him to sacrifice a ram instead. It was then the ram who was burned instead of Yitzchak. Furthermore, when Yitzchak died a natural death, he was not cremated. He was buried in the Cave of the Patriarchs (*Maarat Machpelah*) in Hebron, along with the other forefathers. So we are informed by the *pshat*, or simple narrative of the text. The rabbis though, give us another perspective of events, one that is allegorical]

The implication of the rabbinic allegory is that all the spiritual gains of the *Akeidah* remain with us and are analogous to "the ashes of Yitzchak" which "remain on the altar" forever. But, even if we accept this analogy, it does not seem to fit. The ashes of a sacrifice offered on the altar in Temple times were supposed to be removed and placed next to the altar and, if there was no more room, they had to be removed to another area altogether.[2]

On the simple level, we may say that in Yitzchak's case, there was no altar. The need to remove and take away the ashes of each Temple sacrifice was in order to make room for the next sacrifice that had to be brought. But, the *Akeidah* did not take place on an altar, so there was no need to remove Yitzchak's ashes.[3] Indeed, the Midrash says the ashes served as a sign for future generations. When the Jews built the Temple on Mt. Moriah, where Avraham had brought Yitzchak to be sacrificed, and looked for the proper location of the altar, they used Isaac's ashes as a guide (Gemora *Menachot* 62A).

When the Jews built the Temple on Mt. Moriah, where Avraham had brought Yitzchak to be sacrificed, and looked for the proper location of the altar, they used Isaac's ashes as a guide (Gemora Menachot 62A).

However, the Talmud Yerushalmi takes matters a step further. It suggests that his ashes remained on the altar because of Yitzchak's unique merit and qualities. But that is still problematic for two reasons: First, once something has been burned, the remaining ashes are no longer equivalent to the previous object (i.e., the "ashes" are not "Yitzchak"). And second, the benefit of a Torah offering comes from the fragrance and aroma that wafts from it, and this takes place only during the burning, not after it. So, what exactly was the benefit of leaving Yitzchak's so-called "ashes" on the altar?

To better understand this, we may look at the mitzvoth and how their fulfillment effects the future in various ways:

1. Usually, when a person fulfills a mitzvah, the act is done and a matter of the past, even if the merit accrues in the next world.
2. Sometimes, when a person fulfills a mitzvah, its impression lingers, even though the act is done and a matter of the past. For example, when a man puts on *tefillin* and prays, the spiritual elevation of his act may linger for the rest of the day although the mitzvah was done in the morning.
3. Finally, there are some mitzvoth whose fulfillment is an ongoing process, taking place at every instant. For example, when

King David entered a bathhouse and disrobed, he was distressed that he was not involved in any mitzvah, until he realized that he was accompanied by the mitzvah of circumcision (*Menachot* 43:B).[4]

It might seem that King David could as well have been comforted by the fact that he put on *tefillin* and prayed earlier that day, and that the effects of subduing his heart and mind associated with donning *tefillin* would have remained with him. But, King David wanted not only the ongoing elevation from a mitzvah done earlier in the day. He sought elevation at every instant, and this was why his circumcision gave him peace of mind: Although the physical act took place far earlier in his life, it was an ongoing process that was with him at every instant.

We can apply King David's reaction to the *Akeidah*. The merit of Yitzchak was so great that the effects of the Akeida continue as if he were being offered on the altar even now. Therefore, it is as if his ashes are still found on top of the altar, and he continues to provide the "pleasant aroma" of an offering.

Here is how we can apply this concept to our lives. In a sacrifice, the best of the animal becomes subsumed and elevated to the spiritual realms beyond. (In our case, the sacrifice is our "animal" soul.) What remains are only the ashes — the pure, meaningless physicality — which may be placed next to the altar, or if need be, removed altogether.[5] In our lives, we deal with the "ashes" in one of two ways: either we do nothing with them, leaving them to spontaneously degrade, or we remove them to a place that is far enough away that it has no effect on our daily lives. Leaving the ashes to spontaneously degrade symbolizes the divine service of a Jew who wishes to remain "close to the altar" (involved in Godliness) even while making a living and supporting his family. Removing the ashes altogether symbolizes the divine service of a Jew who must leave the "holy area" (any profession with a direct connection to Torah, such as a scribe, a Torah teacher, pulpit rabbi, etc.) in order to make a living, and yet he supports himself and his family in a manner that is elevated and may be utilized for holy purposes.

These are also the two ways in which we deal with everything in this world:

Sometimes we approach the physical world as a tool. It exists only in order to enable us to serve God — by doing mitzvoth. We learn a profession and practice it so that we will be able to place food on the table and raise a Jewish family. This is known as "all your deeds should be for the sake of heaven." (*Pirkei Avos* 2:12) This means that everything that we do should result in some sort of deed that is dedicated to God.

But, there is a higher way of dealing with the world (though it may not be a command from Above). And that is by following the precept of King Shlomo, "Know Him in all your ways." (Proverbs 3:6) Even while we are busy using the world to meet our physical needs, we must be conscious that it is enabling and facilitating our service of God. Our profession then becomes a way of bringing Godliness into the world. And, through it, we see greater and higher levels of Godliness in the world.

Still, what the sages meant by "the ashes of Yitzchak remain as if piled on top of the altar" was neither of the two interpretations above. Yitzchak's ashes were neither placed next to the altar, nor were they removed from the area altogether. They "remain ... on top of the altar." Yitzchak's divine service was so high that even his most physical element — his ashes — remained in the realm of holiness, on the altar. This is because Yitzchak, unlike Avraham, practiced real "self-sacrifice" (*mesirat nefesh*) not only of the soul but also of the body.[6] While Avraham allowed himself to be thrown into the furnace (by command of King Nimrod), the fire did not actually touch him. However, Yitzchak actually went through a "death experience." His soul actually left his body (though it returned).[7] And that is why his ashes remain on the altar. The most physical aspect of Yitzchak — his body as well as his soul — was also used for a mitzvah and elevated like the rest of a sacrifice, ascending to higher spiritual levels.[8]

The lesson for us:[9] The true place of a Jew is "inside" — within the realm of Torah learning and mitzvoth. However, sometimes it is necessary to make a foray "outside" — to a world that is not holy. Even so, the best path is to choose a profession that is "near the altar" — a way of making a living that at least serves holy interests, even if it does not itself entail fulfillment of the mitzvoth. Getting involved in matters that take one "outside" is not the best path for a Jew, but when there is no choice — as when there is no room on the altar for a new offering and the ashes have to be removed — a Jew may make a living away from the protective tent of *kedushah* in an elevated manner with Godliness in mind.

That is why we recite the story of the *Akeidah* every morning before prayer. It is to remind ourselves of the self-sacrifice of Yitzchak, which was so great that even his ashes were like a mitzvah and could ascend to the One Above. In a like manner, all of our activities for the rest of the day should remain elevated and dedicated to God.

From Likutei Sichot of the Lubavitcher Rebbe
vol. 25, pp. 131–138

NOTES

1. Also in *Torat Cohanim*, Rashi (Lev 26:42), *Midrash Tanhuma* end of Vayera, *Bereishit Rabba* 92:5. See also *Vayera* 22:14, *Berachot* 62B, *Taanit* 16A and other places.

2. This is even according to the opinions that removing the ashes from the altar was an activity that occurred every day, even when there was room on the altar for the new day's sacrifice (see the Rambam in *Hilchot T'midim u'musafim* 2:13). Even so, the content of the process was similar to the cleaning of oil from the Menorah — "cleaning" the altar (for the next offering). In our case, it is understood that since there was no more need for the altar, there was also no need to remove the ashes.

3. Even though the place where the *Akeidah* took place was the same place that was to become the location of the altar in the Temple, nevertheless at the time, the concept of *kedushat ha'azara* ("holiness of the courtyard") did not apply.

4. See *Likutei Sichot* Vol 3, Page759. Here the intention is to the mitzvah "to be circumcised," as opposed to the active mitzvah "to circumcise." See the letter of the *Tzafnat Paneach* in the *Sdeh Chemed*, end of his *Kuntres Hametzitza*. The commandment "to be circumcised" is renewed at every instant, and therefore it is considered as if the action of circumcision occurs every second.

5. The ashes themselves (without any consideration of how they became ashes) represent — "ultimate physicality." As the Alter Rebbe writes in Tanya (*Igrot Hakodesh* 15, Page 121B), "the ashes that remain after a tree has been burnt [are from] the foundation of "dust" that descends, over which the fire has no control...and dust (*ahfar*) is the most physical of all the physical elements."

6. See *Sha'arei Teshuva* of the Mitteler Rebbe, Sec. 1, Ch. 38, p. 46d — "Like *Akeidat Yitzchak* ... during which his soul actually left his body." See also *Hemshech Eyn-Beit* of the Rebbe Rashab, Ch. 62. But see *Sha'arei Teshuva* in Ch. 37, p. 46: "Even though *Akeidat Yitzchak* was like real *mesirat nefesh* ... and his soul flew out of his body out of fear of death," nevertheless, when the "actual act of taking a life is absent, then the main 'ingredient' of *mesirat nefesh* of the body is lacking."

7. In *Shaarei Teshuva* there (as well as Ch. 38 on p. 47a): "This is beyond the elevation of the body that was achieved by Chanoch and by Eliyahu, who retained their own "existence," but became very refined." But, during the *mesirat nefesh* of the body, also the "substance of the body...joins in the inclusion."

8. See the discourse, *Yonati* of the year 5640 (1880), pp. 51 and 56, in which the

Rebbe Maharash discusses the saying of the sages (*Pirkei d'Rebe Eliezer* end of Ch.31) that the ashes of Yitzchak's ram form the foundation of the "inner altar," on which the incense was offered [not the outer altar on which sacrifices were brought]. Thus the ashes represented *hitkashrut* (similar to the word *kitoret*, or "incense") — "unity" that results from essential *bitul* ("nullification") of the ego and of the self that is beyond the uplifting power of sacrifices.

9. See the Alter Rebbe's Siddur in the discourse, "To understand *terumat hadeshen* (Page 30, column 3), *Ohr HaTorah* parshat Beshalach (Page 435–6). And more...

YITZCHAK AND THE WELLS

Toldot 26:18

Parshat Toldot focuses on Yitzchak, who was the longest-living of our forefathers; he lived to 180, while Avraham lived to 175 and Yaakov to 147. But the Torah does not say a lot about Yitzchak's activities during those many years. One thing it does tell us is that he dug wells — three of them.[1] These wells were originally dug by his father, Avraham, but later were filled in by the Philistines. Yitzchak came along and reopened them and that carries a message for us. As the Ramban tells us (in his commentary on Genesis 26:20):

> "The scripture speaks a great deal on the subject of wells. There is nothing to be gleaned from the simple meaning of the narrative ... but there is a hidden meaning, because the scripture reveals the future. A well of 'living waters' alludes to the holy Temple that the offspring of Yitzchak will build ... as it is written, 'A source of living waters is God.' (Jeremiah 17:13)
>
> The first well was called *Esek* ("Discord"), and it alluded to the First Temple, [during which there was much discord between the Jews and their neighbors, as well as among themselves]. The second well was called *Sitna* ("Accusation"), corresponding to the second Temple [the building of the second Temple was delayed by false accusations about the Jews to the Persian authorities] ... and the third was called *Rehovot* ("Expanses") and it alludes to the third Temple that will be built soon in our days, without discord or accusations..."

The connection between the forefathers and the future Temples is also found in the Midrash[2] (*Breishit Rabba* Ch. 56), but there the connection is mentioned only in general. It is stated simply that the forefathers "saw the Temples" of the future, without detailing which Temple each one saw. Also, no mention is made of the wells. But, from the commentary of the Ramban quoted above, we understand that the wells in general were associated with the lifetime and behavior-pattern of Yitzchak, the second of the forefathers. Not only that, but the Ramban makes it clear that Yitzchak's re-opening of these wells contains a directive for us, just as all the actions of the forefathers show us how to act in our lifetime.

The forefathers were very precise in their actions. If there is a connection between the wells and the Temples, then it must be carefully analyzed. And one way to get to the heart of that connection is by analyzing how the Torah deals with water:

The Torah names two bodies of water which are to be used for purification purposes. The first is a *mikveh* — a man-made pool which is filled with a certain amount of rain water (or attached to a cistern containing a certain amount of rain water) to which drawn water, transported by human effort, may be added. The second is a *ma'ayan* — a spring created by God — the purifying capability of which is more potent than that of a *mikveh*. As long as even a minute amount of naturally flowing spring water from a source of "living water" is present, drawn water may be added, and it will remain a kosher purifying agent.

A well combines the qualities of both a *mikveh* and a *ma'ayan*. On the one hand, a well requires human effort, to dig and clear away the unwanted dirt and rocks. On the other hand, when water is finally uncovered, it is not a cistern of rain water to which drawn water was added. It is the potent purifying water of a *ma'ayan* that we uncover. The water that flows spontaneously into a well has the same power to purify as does a spring. Even a minute amount of such water will purify the worst impurities.[3]

This combination of effort from below and response from Above is what makes the well unique. The rain water plus drawn water of a *mikveh* symbolizes the effort that man invests, while the natural water of a *ma'ayan* corresponds to the response from Above. It is man who digs the well, but the water that he reveals in a well flows spontaneously like the waters of a spring. Man did not create the well water; he only revealed it. But once revealed, the water flows effortlessly. All that is required is the initial human effort to uncover the water.

In Jewish law, a well is considered to be a *ma'ayan*, and the slightest amount of its water purifies. And that, quite possibly, is the nature of the Temple as well.

This is evident in God's command to the Children of Israel to build the portable desert Tabernacle which later became a permanent Temple: "Make for Me a sanctuary, and I will dwell among you..." (Exodus 25:8). First, there is the commandment for man to act ("Make for Me..."), followed by the action of God ("I will dwell..."). When man works from below, he receives a response from Above. That's the inner meaning of both the wells and the Temples.

> *In Jewish law, a well is considered to be a ma'ayan, and the slightest amount of its water purifies. And that, quite possibly, is the nature of the Temple as well.*

Not only that, but the greater the effort and energy expended by man here below, the greater the response from Above. For that reason, every Jew had an obligation to participate in the building of the Temple. Although the obligation did not fall upon any particular Jew, but rather upon the congregation as a whole, nevertheless, the activity of building the Temple required the involvement of all Jews.

The relationship between man's effort and God's response applied to the physical location of the Temple, as well. Part of the command of building the Temple is to labor in finding the proper location, just as man has to labor to find the location of a well. Water is not found just anywhere, and the Temple as well, could not be built just anywhere. It was necessary to search for the proper place, and in response to that intense effort, God revealed the proper location to us.

And now, we can grasp the differences between the Tabernacle and the Temple, as well as the nuances relating to the Temples — the first and second Temples as well as the third Temple yet to be built.

In the case of the Tabernacle, there was no intense search for the proper location, because the location where the Children of Israel encamped was determined by command from Above. Moreover, there was no need for them to become involved in the plans and blueprints as again these were specified from Above. Finally, despite the fact that the Jews contributed the materials for the Tabernacle's walls and vessels, they did not become actively involved in building the Tabernacle as this was done by two expert craftsmen, Betzalel and Oholiav, who were appointed from Above.

Because there was little or no effort from man below to establish the Tabernacle, it lacked the elements of a well.

However, the first Temple demanded much effort on the part of man. King David searched for the right place to build the Temple. Only after he received confirmation, via prophecy, that he had indeed found the correct location, did he also receive instructions from Above how to build it, as he said, "All [the blueprints] were written by the hand of God, who instructed me..." (1 Chronicles 28:19). Nevertheless, the first Temple was actually built by King Shlomo, David's son, without the benefit of prophecy from Above to guide him. It is evident, then that much human effort from below went into the planning and building of the first Temple. That effort was not present in the construction of the Tabernacle.

Very likely, this is the reason that the Tabernacle was only a temporary structure, and it moved from place to place, while the Temple remained in one location. Since the Tabernacle lacked the element of human effort from below, it only stood temporarily. However, the Temple was designed to be a permanent structure, located forever on Mt. Moriah. The effort that was expended from below to build the Temple imparted a level of permanence never attained by the Tabernacle.

The element of effort from below to Above was even more pronounced in the second Temple than in the first. Although the initial command to build the Tabernacle applies to all of the Temples, there was no specific command to build the second Temple [which really consisted of re-building the first Temple]. Nor was there a specific prophecy dedicated to its location or its blueprints.[4] However, there was the desire of the Jews themselves to rebuild what conquerors had destroyed, and a helpful decree from the Persian kings — Cyrus and his son Darius — who also provided material assistance. Armed only with a strong will, Ezra and a handful of the Jews returning from exile rebuilt the Temple in Jerusalem. They built it to resemble the first Temple, following the plans found in the Book of Ezekiel. But, they had no precise directions from Above. [While they knew it had to be on Mt. Moriah, they did not know where to place the Holy of Holies and the altar, or its measurements as noted in *Zevachim* 62a.] It emerges, then, that the participation and effort of man from below was greater in the second Temple than in either the first Temple or the Tabernacle.

And because the permanence of the Temple is dependent upon the level of participation from below, we see that the second Temple achieved the greatest longevity of all. It stood for 420 years, ten years more than the first Temple, and longer than the Tabernacle as well. Ultimately (after Herod's expansion), it was also larger than the first Temple.

The principle of the greater permanence of the Temples is best exemplified by the spiritual path of Yitzchak. He was the forefather who emphasized prayer, coming from below but directed Above. His divine service was all about making contact with God from below, connecting the lower physical world to the One Above.

That was why he dug wells, which symbolize working on ourselves, removing the dirt and obstacles to divine revelation. When we remove these obstacles, we automatically reveal what lies underneath everything — Godliness. However, we must dig deep and mightily in order to reach the living, flowing waters of spirituality. That was Yitzchak's contribution — the example of man perfecting himself below to connect with Above. His digging was a sign that this must be a major component of our service of God.

An effort from below is also the most important factor in rebuilding the Temple, and that is the reason that the second Temple is associated with Yitzchak. Just as the second Temple was most exemplary of the principle of effort from below to Above, so Yitzchak, among the forefathers, was most associated with prayer and self-improvement, the reach from below to Above.

Still, we must ask: If human effort is the most important factor, then why do we expect the third and permanent Temple to come from Above?[5] Where is the effort from below that lends permanence if the third Temple is meant to descend upon us like a gift from on high?

The answer is that the effort from below in relation to the third Temple consists of the long years of exile, the nearly two-thousand years that we have spent in the Diaspora, exiled there after the destruction of the second Temple. The effort to make contact with God from below, to fulfill His mitzvoth and cleave to Him — despite all the trials and tribulations of life, all the persecutions and wars and internal discord — is what is necessary to build the third and final Temple.

No one can argue that this effort — the effort of the Jews in exile for over two-thousand years — is less than what went into building the first and second Temple. And that's why, when finally is is built, the third Temple will last forever. May it happen soon!

From Likutei Sichot of the Lubavitcher Rebbe, vol. 30, pp. 116–124

1. The Torah itself mentions three wells, but *Midrash Rabba* 64:8 brings a difference of opinion whether there were four or five wells that Yitzchak dug.

2. See also *Sifri* on *Parshat V'zot HaBrachah* Deuteronomy 33:12.

3. Not only that, but it has the power to purify even a *zav* (one who is spiritually impure because of a problem with his seminal flow), which no other body of water can purify. According to the Maharik (cited in the *Beit Yoseph* on *Yoreh Deah Siman* 201, as well as the Levush there and the Shach, *sif katan aleph*), "a well has the same law as (not merely an ordinary fountain that contains little water) "living waters," that even a *zav* may immerse in. In *Shu't Mishkenot Yaakov* on *Yoreh Deah* 45, in continuation of the words of the Maharik: "the verse says, 'And the servants of Yitzchak dug ... and they found there a well of living waters." From this it is clear that a well that is dug is called "living waters." See also the insight of the Tzemach Tzedek on the Mishnah (*Mikvaot* 1:6). The *Shu't Mishkenot Yaakov* continues on to say that not all wells have a law of "living waters," since some are found near to rivers and their water comes from those rivers.

4. In the *Shealot v'Teshuvot* of the *Chatam Sofer* on *Yoreh Deah, siman* 236 (as well as *Orach Chaim siman* 208, beginning with *ad cahn*), it is written that all of the variations from the first Temple that were built into the second Temple were according to prophetic instructions (see also the *Ohr Hachaim* on *Parshat Terumah*, Exodus 25:9). However, see the *Tosfot Yomtov* there (and at length in the introduction to *Tzurat Habayit*), where it is understood that several of the variations were implied and interpreted from the Prophet Ezekiel, and not everything originated from prophecy. See also the *Radak* on Ezekiel 40:13, and *Yoma* 51b and the Rambam in *Hilchot Beit Habechira* 4:2 regarding their questions on the building of the second Temple.

5. To understand both opinions — 1) the Rambam (*Hilchot Melachim* Ch. 11) that the third Temple will be built by Mashiach and 2) Rashi (*Rosh Hashana* 30a, *Succah* 41a, *Shavuos* 15b) that the Temple will be revealed from Above — see *Likutei Sichot* vol. 18, p. 418 as well as *Chidushim u'biurim* on *Hilchot Beit Habechira, siman* 19.

The Paths of the Forefathers

Vayeitzei 28:10

This week's Torah portion — *Parshat Vayeitzei* — tells us that when Yaakov left his parents' house, setting out on his spiritual journey, he spent the first night on Mt. Moriah. It was there that he slept and dreamt of the ladder with angels ascending and descending, and it was there that he realized that the Temple would someday be built in this very location. And perhaps this is why the Prophet Isaiah calls Temple "the House of the God of Yaakov" (Isaiah 2:3).

There are some Torah commentators who claim that the three appellations for the forefathers (in *Pesachim* 88a) — "mountain" (for Avraham), "field" (for Yitzchak), and "house" (for Yaakov) — also refer to the three Temples.[1] "House," the appellation for Yaakov, refers to the third Temple which is so-called because just as a house is secure, so the third Temple will be permanent. If so, then one would expect to find this quality of permanence reflected in the life of Yaakov. However, we actually find the opposite — Yaakov's life was anything but stable and permanent.

He fled from his parents' house and the wrath of his brother Esau to the house of his uncle Lavan, where he was not well treated; then he returned to Canaan, only to be beset by more problems. His daughter Dinah was defiled in Shechem; his son Yosef disappeared (presumably killed by wild animals), and then a famine descended on the Land so he had move to Egypt with his family. As he said to Pharaoh, "the days of my life have been few and difficult." (Genesis 47:9) So, what is the connection between the life of Yaakov and the permanent third Temple, which hopefully will be built speedily in our days?

To understand this connection, let us recall the prophecy of Isaiah which links the Temple with Yaakov:

> "In the days to come, the mountain of the Lord's house shall stand firm above the mountains and tower above the hills. And all the nations shall stream to it. And the many peoples shall go and say: 'Come, let us ascend to the Mount of God, to the House of the God of Yaakov — that He may instruct us in His ways, that we may walk in His paths.' For instruction shall come forth from Zion and the word of the Lord from Jerusalem." (Isaiah 2:2–3)

Now, three questions arise:

1. The prophecy refers to the third Temple, to which all of the nations of the world will come. But, why is it necessary to emphasize that this third Temple is the "House of the God of Yaakov?"
2. From the context, it does not seem that the nations of the world will ascend to the Temple in order to convert to Judaism. So, then why do they justify their desire to ascend by saying that God's instruction (i.e. Torah) comes from Zion and the word of God from Jerusalem?
3. It seems rather repetitive to say, "[God's] instruction from Zion" *and* "the word of God from Jerusalem." Aside from poetic license, why would it be necessary for the prophet to use both these phrases?

The truth is that there is a difference between "God's instruction" and the "word of God." The "word of God," according to the Talmud (*Shabbat* 138b) is *halachah* — which defines the legal parameters according to which a Jew should act in any given situation. But "God's instruction" or "Torah" comprises all of the teachings contained in the Five Books of Moses, as well as all that any Jew thinks of and aspires to in the Talmud, the Midrash, and other rabbinic sources.

In the realm of Torah, we can find all that we spiritually yearn for and love. We can utilize our intellect, follow our heart, and decide which practices and customs we prefer. We can argue according to our own conscience and logic. But, while on this path, we must bear in mind that our own investigations lead us to conclusions that are only approximations of Godliness. Even when our thought processes express Godly concepts, we cannot precisely describe the Godly realm. Since we retain our human existence in a physical body, even our Godly thoughts are only an indication or approximation of true spirituality and, for that reason, they are called Zion (which means "signpost" or "indication" in Hebrew).[2]

Within the realm of Torah, we can and must pursue our individual paths of love for and attraction to spirituality. With our own talents and abilities, we can try to approach Godliness. But, ultimately, we must come to the "word of God" — *halachah.* In the end, we have to be subservient to the "word of God" — to the law as defined by the myriad decisions of the Jewish sages. And for that, we need awe of God and ego-nullification.

"Torah" comes from Zion (*Tzion*) and is motivated by love of God.[3] But, the "word of God" is actualized by awe/fear and comes from Jerusalem (*Yerushalayim*) which means "complete awe" (*yirah shleimah*). In order to enact and fulfill the will of God, a higher form of consciousness is necessary. As opposed to the search for God, which is motivated by love and the intellect, the fulfillment of the will of God only happens when there is complete awe of God (*yirah*) and ego-nullification (*bitul*).[4]

The job of the Jews is not only to bring themselves closer to the One Above, but also to uplift the rest of the world. And, therefore, it isn't surprising that Zion and Jerusalem should have an effect on the non-Jewish world as well. The prophecy of Isaiah quoted above does not refer to non-Jews proceeding to Jerusalem for the sake of conversion to Judaism, but it does refer to non-Jews undertaking their own spiritual path, which also brings them to Jerusalem. But, unlike the Jewish path, which calls for fulfillment of 613 mitzvoth of the Torah, the non-Jewish path calls for fulfillment of the Seven Noachide Laws.[5]

The prophecy of Isaiah quoted above does not refer to non-Jews proceeding to Jerusalem for the sake of conversion to Judaism, but it does refer to non-Jews undertaking their own spiritual path, which also brings them to Jerusalem.

The effect of millions of Jews searching for God inevitably rubs off on non-Jews and causes them to begin their own search for spiritual meaning and fulfillment. And just as within the Jewish realm Zion and Jerusalem signify two approaches, so they signal two approaches in the non-Jewish context.

In the beginning, the search is for Zion is rooted in human faculties, understanding and intellect. That leads to the fulfillment of the first part of the prophecy: "In the days to come, the mountain of the Lord's house shall stand firm above the mountains and tower above the hills. And all the nations shall stream to it. And the many peoples shall go and say: 'Come, let us go up to the Mount of God, to the House of the God of Yaakov — that He may instruct us in His ways, that we may walk in His paths.'"

But having come that far, the non-Jews will see that they must accept the Seven Noachide Laws which come from the Torah: "For [God's] instruction shall come forth from Zion." Once they do so — acknowledging that their laws are also rooted in the Torah which was brought down by Moshe our teacher — the non-Jews will also be elevated to accept the "the word of God from Jerusalem."

The non-Jewish spiritual search will proceed from keeping the Seven Noachide Laws because they are spiritual and make sense (the experience of *Tzion*), to fulfilling them because they are the word of God (the experience of *Yerushalayim*). That is, the non-Jewish spiritual path will proceed in tandem with the Jewish path.

At some point, non-Jews will also tune in to Yerushalayim, and not merely to *Tzion*. Such a level will call for complete awe of God and subjugation to the will of God, to the extent that is required for fulfillment of the Seven Noachide Laws.

Now we can begin to grasp the correspondence between the three forefathers to the three Temples:

1. Abraham exemplified a spiritual path that was conducted "from Above to below." That is, he radiated kindness and light to the entire world. In fact, he was an "indication" (*Tzion*) of the Godly emanation of love (*chesed*) in the universe, and as such he represented Zion, the general aspect of Torah in the world. And so, he also corresponded to the first Temple, which came down "from Above to below" and which was built by King Shlomo following the original specifications found in the Torah. During the era of the first Temple, the open love involved in serving God had a direct and revealed effect on the world.
2. Yitzchak represented a totally different spiritual path — "from below to Above," and he corresponded to "the word of God from Jerusalem." Yitzchak worked on himself — removing all spiritual

impurities and revealing the light within — to become a spiritual magnet for all those who surrounded him. His service of God was highly disciplined (imbued with *gevurah*) and demonstrated awe and ego-nullification. The second Temple, which is associated with Yitzchak, also represented divine service "from below to Above." Its building was commanded by a non-Jew, a Persian king by the name of Darius (and his father Cyrus), and it lacked five important items that were present in the first Temple, which meant that the degree of revealed Godliness was less in the second Temple than in the first Temple. Therefore, the Jews had to work harder "from below to Above" while the second Temple stood, and their divine service was characterized by awe of God and ego-nullification as was Yitzchak's.

3. Ultimately, it was Yaakov who combined the approaches of his father Yitzchak and his grandfather Avraham. Yaakov's divine service demonstrated the middle vector — called *tiferet*, or "harmony" — because it combined the loving approach of Avraham with the disciplined approach of Yitzchak. Therefore, Yaakov's love of God was imbued with humility, and his awe of God was imbued with love and understanding. And that's why the third Temple is called the "House of the God of Yaakov" in the prophecy of Isaiah. It will be permanent because it will represent both paths of service of God — love (from Above to below) and awe (from below to Above). It will embody the pinnacle of Godly revelation (even more-so than in the first Temple/Zion) as well as an even greater sense of awe that characterized the second Temple/Jerusalem. While Yaakov's life was full of instability and insecurity, he eventually overcame all of the difficulties because of his ability to maintain equilibrium. His traits of love and awe combined for a stable approach, and all of his offspring turned out to be righteous people.

Now, we may understand the connection between the permanence of the third Temple and Yaakov, as well as his association with "house" in the writings of the sages and the prophets.

But there is one more consideration…

For each of our holy character traits, there is an opposite character trait which comes from the "other side" — the side opposed to holiness.

In opposition to the holy love associated with Avraham, there is the "foreign" love that can sometimes overcome us with "strange" desires for un-kosher food or forbidden sexual unions, by way of example. As well, in opposition to the holy awe of Yitzchak, we can develop a "foreign" temptation for idol worship, God forbid.[6] Therefore, it could transpire that the holy character trait will not last. (We see that this happened with the converts that Avraham inspired but who did not remain on his path).

And so it was with the first and second Temple — each one represented only one approach to the service of God (*avodat Hashem*) which is why the "other side" had some influence and effect over it, and eventually each Temple was destroyed. However, to the character trait of Yaakov — which included elements of both *chesed* and *gevurah* — there was no opposition. This is because when both vectors of *avodat Hashem* are present, they cannot be successfully opposed, which is why "Yaakov's bed was perfect" (*Shir Hashirim Rabba*, Ch 4), meaning that all of his offspring were righteous because nothing spiritually invalid emerged from Yaakov.

The same will be true of the third Temple. Since it will include elements of both *Tzion* and of *Yerushalayim*, it will be a fixed and permanent "House of the God of Yaakov."

That is also emphasized in the prophecy of Isaiah:

> "And the many peoples shall go and say: 'Come, let us ascend to the Mount of God, to the House of the God of Yaakov — that He may instruct us in His ways, that we may walk in His paths.' For instruction shall come forth from Zion and the word of the Lord from Jerusalem."

Note that the second sentence begins with the word "for" which clearly connects it with the previous sentence. This tells us that the beginning is connected to the conclusion. It informs us that just as we were successful in persuading non-Jews that we are sincere, so we will be successful regarding the future third Temple as well.

In order for the Jews to have a truly holy effect on the world, it is not sufficient for us to demonstrate only one of the above-mentioned approaches — either the approach of *Tzion* (inspiration and love), or the approach of *Yerushalayim* (awe and discipline). Both approaches must work together. Within both approaches, it must also be possible to see both the Torah and the *halachah*.

The love that we feel for God must be permeated with awe and humility, while our awe of God must also be imbued with love. When both approaches are present, then it becomes obvious that our divine service is "true" — and "truth" is the main ingredient of Yaakov's *avodat Hashem.*

Truth dominated Yaakov's entire being, which is why he is associated with permanence and immutability. Evincing this truth is what will enable the Jews to inspire non-Jews, so that they will say, "Come, let us go up to the Mount of God, to the House of the God of Yaakov — that He may instruct us in His ways, that we may walk in His paths."

Our truth is what will inspire the non-Jews to learn Torah (as dictated by their mitzvoth — the Seven Noachide Laws) and to achieve perfection in their own matters so that they may walk in the way of the Lord.

From Likutei Sichot of the Lubavitcher Rebbe,
vol. 15, pp. 231–242

NOTES

1. See *Maharsha* and *Iyun Yaakov* on *Pesachim* 88a, as well as *Tzror Hamohr* and the Alsheich on *Parshat Vayeitzei* and the Alsheich on *Tehilim* 24.

2. Note that within the category of *Tzion* are also found very high levels such as *Ana simana b'alma* — "I am no more than a sign," attributed to R' Shimon bar Yochai (redactor of the Zohar). His statement was an expression of his incredible *bitul*, or "ego-nullification" since he expressed no "existence" of self (see *Hemshech 5666* of the Rebbe Rashab p. 159 and elsewhere). And even higher levels are found (see *Tzion B'mishpat Tipadeh* 5735, Ch. 7 (within *Maamorim Melukat* vol. 1, p. 156, in footnote 58). Within *Hemshech 5666* of the Rebbe Rashab, see the distinction between *neshamot d'Mah* (from *z"a*) and *neshamot d'Bahn* (from *malchut*).

3. Within the category of "Torah," there is a distinction between learning Torah in general, and *halachah*. The *bitul* that is necessary to properly learn Torah is *bitul* of the ego of intellect so that, with our intellect, we are able to grasp and unite with the intellect of the Torah. But, to properly relate to *halachah*, it is necessary to completely and totally nullify all of our intellectual faculties, and only then do we become aware of the *ratzon ha'elyon* — the "will of God," which is beyond intellect.

4. For Chassidic and Kabbalistic explanations of *Tzion* and *Yerushalayim*, see *Likutei Torah* of the Alter Rebbe, *Bamidbar* 9a, *Devarim* 1:2, *Reshimot* of the Tzemach Tzedek on *Tehilim* (*Yahel Ohr*) 147:12. See also *Shivchei Yerusahalyim* from the Rebbe Maharash in *Torat Shmuel* 5627 (1867) p. 414, *Likutei Levi Yitzchak* on the Zohar sec. 2, p. 284. *Likuteim* on *Maamorei R'zl* p. 171.

5. As the Rambam (in *Melachim* Ch. 8) writes: "Moshe our teacher commanded, at the behest of God, [for us] to persuade the entire world to accept the Noachide commandments ... and to fulfill these laws because they were given by God in the Torah and passed down through Moshe."

6. As the sages said (*Pesachim* 119B), "Avraham — from whom Yishmael emerged" (who represented love from the "other side," opposed to holiness). And "Yitzchak — from whom Esau emerged" (fear from the "other side").

LADDER OF DREAMS

Vayeitzei
28:11–12

On his way from the Land of Israel to the home of his uncle Lavan in Charan, Yaakov dreamt of a ladder upon which angels were ascending and descending (Genesis 28:11–12). According to the Midrash (*Breishit Rabba* 68:12), the ascending angels were assigned to the Land of Israel and they could not leave to accompany Yaakov on his trip into the Diaspora. But the descending angels were from outside of Israel, and they came to the border specifically to escort and protect Yaakov on his journey. This is also Rashi's explanation.

However, at the end of our Torah portion — *Parshat Vayetzei* — we find a contradiction. When Yaakov returned to Israel, the angels of Israel did exit the Land in order to meet him and bring him back (Genesis 32:2). So we have two questions here:

1. If the angels were not allowed to leave Israel in order to escort Yaakov on his journey out, then why were they allowed to leave Israel in order to bring him back in?
2. In both places (Genesis 28:11 and Genesis 32:2), the text of the Torah uses an interesting word — *vayifga'a*, meaning "met unintentionally." As Yaakov left Israel, the Torah says that he "unintentionally met" the place (which would be the site of the future Temple). And as he returned, the Torah says that the angels "suddenly met" him. The wording of the Torah is very precise, so if the text contains the same word in both places, it suggests that there is a parallel meaning. What could that be?

Rashi does not explain the contradiction mentioned above (that the angels were not allowed to leave Israel in order to escort Yaakov out, and yet they were allowed to leave in order to bring him back in). From this, we can assume that Rashi was not puzzled by this, and the explanation must be simple enough for a child to understand. Possibly, it is as follows:

When leaving Israel, Yaakov needed the angels of the Diaspora to accompany and guard him as he began his long and dangerous journey. This is not something that the angels of Israel could do, since it was a journey into a foreign land. However, when Yaakov returned, the angels of Israel came out to meet him because, this time, it wasn't necessary to guard him, but only to accompany him. If this is the explanation, it could be that it is so obvious that Rashi felt he need not explain it.

All the dimensions of the Torah mesh together, even though each expresses a unique perspective. The above is an example of simple level of the text (called *pshat*). But, according to Jewish law which is derived from the second level of Torah interpretation (called *drosh*), one is allowed to leave the Land of Israel for a few reasons only: 1) to learn Torah, 2) to get married, or 3) to escape a dangerous person, or 4) to make a livelihood. So says Rambam (in *Hilchot Melachim* 5:9). And yet, we find that the Talmudic sages did leave Israel for other reasons — for example, in order to bring their parents back to the Land (*Kiddushin* 31b). If one is allowed to leave the Land of Israel only for the four reasons listed by the Rambam, then why did these sages leave?

The answer is that the Rambam's reasons are leniencies that the Jewish law permits in specific situations. However, there are other exceptions that are permitted — for example the need to escort one's parents back to Israel. In this case, *halachah* does not even consider the person to have left Israel at all (even if he or she has crossed the border). Therefore, the sages who left the Land in order to meet their parents and bring them back did not — in the eyes of *halachah* — leave at all.

It is only when people go out for an indefinite period (as is usually the case when seeking to get married or learning Torah, etc.) that they are considered to have left the Land [and that is when the leniencies apply]. But, when they leave for the purpose of escorting a parent, teacher or someone important back into Israel, it is as if they did not leave at all. It makes sense that upon his return, Yaakov was met by the angels of Israel for, by accompanying him back into Israel, it was as if they never left the Land at all. Thus, the *halachah* (based on *drosh*) supports the explanation above (based on *pshat*).

This leads us to another question regarding the angels. It seems that

Rashi's opinion (on the level of *pshat*) is that, before the Torah was given, there was nothing preventing the forefathers and their wives from leaving the Land of Israel. Back then, there was no special holiness attached to the land, so there was no reason why they could not leave. It wasn't until the Jews conquered the Land and settled it under Yehoshua that it became imbued with holiness. Although God promised the Land to Abraham and his descendants, it did not become holy until the Jews settled it and began fulfilling the mitzvoth of the Torah.[1]

But if the Land was not yet holy, why should there have been a problem for the angels leave? Why couldn't the angels of Israel accompany Yaakov outside of Israel?

The answer is that, even though the Land was not yet permeated with the holiness of the mitzvoth, the potential for that already existed. God created the Land with a special propensity for holiness, even before it permeated the physical Land. The angels, being denizens of the spiritual realms, were in contact with that potential, and that's why they could not leave. For these angels, the potential was real — they already lived an existence of holiness in the spiritual realms, even before it filtered down to the physical Land. They existed in the "spiritual Land of Israel" even before that spirituality descended below. And since the angels also existed Above, they could not be associated with Yaakov as he left Israel — that was a task for the angels of the Diaspora. However, that did not limit the forefathers or prevent them from leaving the Land before the Torah was given.

We can understand Yaakov's journeys from yet another angle — the inner dimensions of the Torah. The word *vayifga'a*, mentioned both as Yaakov left and as he re-entered Israel, implies a sudden, unexpected meeting. At the beginning of our Torah portion, such a meeting took place when Yaakov found himself on the Temple Mount (*Har HaMoriah*). At the end of the Torah portion, another surprise meeting took place as Yaakov returned to Israel and was met by the welcoming angels. In the first instance, it was only Yaakov who was surprised, after he dreamt and woke up to declare himself in a holy place without having realized it. But, at the end, neither side seems to have been prepared — not the angels and not Yaakov. What does that mean?

The sages tell us that while he was on the Temple Mount (the future home of the Temple), Yaakov established the evening prayers that today all Torah observant men pray daily. The evening prayers — unlike the morning (*Shacharit*) and afternoon (*Minchah*) prayers — are considered obligatory only because of custom. At their inception, the evening prayers were totally voluntary.

There is a spiritual distinction between prayers that are obligatory and those that are voluntary; obligatory prayers are associated with a spiritual level that is attainable by regular effort and service of God, while voluntary prayers are associated with a high spiritual level that is not readily attainable. While obligatory prayers are among the normal, everyday demands that are placed upon us, voluntary prayers are associated with higher spiritual levels that the soul thirsts for and searches of its own volition. Such voluntary prayers reach levels that are beyond those normally attained by our routine efforts, and they may result in unexpected responses from Above. And that is why the word *vayifga'a*, meaning "met unintentionally," is used in the context of Yaakov's experience.

As Yaakov established the voluntary evening prayers on Mt. Moriah, he experienced a sudden visitation of Godliness from a high spiritual level. It was totally unexpected. He did not know that he was on Mt. Moriah, where heaven meets earth. As he said, "In truth, God is in this place and I did not know it … How awesome is this place! This is none other than the house of God and this is the gate of heaven." (Genesis 28:16–17)

As Yaakov established the voluntary evening prayers on Mt. Moriah, he experienced a sudden visitation of Godliness from a high spiritual level. It was totally unexpected.

Yet, this high spiritual level came down to him as a sort of spiritual parting gift to support and reinforce him in his new service of God in a foreign land. The Hebrew term is *netinat koach*, meaning "a gift of strength and empowerment," and this gift came down to support and protect him in the Diaspora.

But, within the realm of voluntary prayer, there is an even higher level, and that is when the surprise occurs from both sides, not from one side alone. This is what happened at the end of our Torah portion, when Yaakov returned to Israel. There we once more encounter that word *vayifga'u* (this time in the plural form), as the angels of Israel came to meet Yaakov. This was a meeting of surprise for both Yaakov and for the angels. By this time Yaakov had completed his service of uplifting and purifying the Diaspora (through his labor tending the sheep of his uncle

Lavan),[2] and the spiritual level that he reached surprised not only him but also the angels who came to meet him. In fact, this was a spiritual level that Yaakov could not have prepared for — it came from beyond the normal order of "effort and reward." This spiritual level was a gift, and therefore, the angels did not arrive in order to protect and support him (for that wasn't necessary) — instead, they came to honor him by providing an escort back to the Land of Israel.

When we do all that we can to reach our highest spiritual potential, we are rewarded with an unexpected gift from Above that lifts us to heights of which neither we nor the angels knew we were capable.

The evening prayers — *Ma'ariv* — occur at the end of the day, after the standard morning and afternoon prayers. In this sense, *Ma'ariv* is like the gift that comes at the culmination of our *avodat Hashem*, after we have succeeded in all of our spiritual endeavors. As such, it may be higher than anything we could have expected.

But, the evening prayers are also the beginning of the next day, since according to the Torah, the new day begins at night. And, in this sense, the evening prayers are like a *netinat koach* — a gift of strength and empowerment that accompanies us into the next day, with all of its new challenges.

It was Yaakov who pioneered the path of *Ma'ariv* — voluntary prayer that takes us beyond the requirements of *halachah* — to the unexpected place that only the soul knows.

From Likutei Sichot of the Lubavitcher Rebbe,
vol. 25, pp. 150–158

NOTES

1. That is why, when Yitzchak was told not to leave Israel in the previous Torah portion (*Parshat Toldot*), Rashi does not explain that the reason was due to the holiness of the Land. Rather, he says that it is because the Diaspora was "not fitting for Yitzchak." It was not fitting for Yitzchak because, outside of Israel, people did not recognize God as the God of the heavens and the earth (but only of the heavens), but not because the Diaspora was "unholy."

2. Chasidic philosophy informs us that "sparks" of holiness fell from above into mundane physical objects, and it is our task to retrieve those sparks and return them to their rightful spiritual level above. Jews do that by fulfilling Torah and mitzvoth. Before the Torah was given, Yaakov worked with the sheep of Lavan to retrieve the holy sparks that fell within them, and return them to their spiritual source.

The Land Is Easily Ours

Vayeitzei 28:13

In *Parshat Vayeitzei*, during the famous dream of a ladder to heaven, God says to Yaakov, "The land which you are lying upon, I will give to you and to your descendants..." (Genesis 28:13)

According to Rashi, this was an important message to Yaakov, letting him know how easy it would be for his descendants, several generations later, to conquer the Land of Israel.

But the Talmud (*Chulin* 91b), in commenting on this verse, reads it differently. This is to be expected, because the Talmud is written from the perspective of rabbinic interpretation (*drosh*), while Rashi writes from the simple perspective (*pshat*) that any child could understand. The Talmud wonders about the purpose of this statement by God, since the entire Land had already been promised to Avraham and to Yitzchak and their descendants. So why, the Talmud asks, would it be necessary to reiterate this promise concerning the small piece of ground upon which Yaakov was lying?

The Talmud concludes that something miraculous occurred here — God folded up the entire Land of Israel and placed it under Yaakov so that he acquired not only the "four cubits" of personal space under him, but the entire Land of Israel, as he slept and dreamt. And this also enabled his descendants to easily conquer the Land in the future when they returned to Israel from Egyptian exile.[1]

This idea — that by doing something on or with the Land, our forefathers gained possession — appears elsewhere in the Talmud as well. At one juncture (in *Baba Batra* 100a), R' Elazar claims that by walking around a piece of land, one may acquire that piece of land. As proof, R' Elazar mentions God's directive to Avraham, "Arise, traverse the length and the breadth of the Land, for it is to you that I will give it." (Genesis 13:17)

However, for Rashi it is not so clear that this verse is talking about ownership. First of all, Rashi's comment on the Talmud (*Chulin* 91b) only mentions that lying down upon the Land "made it easy" for Yaakov's descendants to conquer it later. Rashi says nothing there about ownership. Most significantly, commenting on *Parshat Vayeitzei* (Genesis 28:13), Rashi says only that folding the Land under Yaakov served as a "hint" that it would be easy to conquer — again, nothing about ownership. Apparently, the concept of the Land coming into the possession of our forefathers with these acts of "traversing" (in the case of Avraham) or "lying upon" (in the case of Yaakov) does not fit the simple textual context that Rashi seeks to explain.

It seems that there are two difficulties that Rashi has with ownership as an explanation for the above-cited verses.

1. First, the Torah (Gen 12:7, 13:15) explicitly states that ownership will only take place in the future, when the Jews enter and conquer the Land under Yehoshua. To this way of thinking, it is not necessary to walk around the Land or lie down upon it. These are actions that the rabbis required for legal reasons, but any child knows that God is in charge, and if He gave the Land to us verbally, that is sufficient. The child will see right away that, in these verses, God does not give possession of the Land immediately to Avraham and to Yaakov, but to their descendants in the future, since that is what He says.
2. Second, it is difficult to explain, in the realm of *pshat,* that a miracle taking place in one era (folding the Land under Yaakov) can have a powerful effect generations later in a different era (when the Jews will return and conquer the Land of Israel). It would be especially difficult for a child to comprehend how the miracle of folding the Land under Yaakov would make it easier for Yaakov's descendants to conquer the Land hundreds of years later, particularly since the information arrived in a dream.

Therefore, Rashi does not explain that by lying down on the Land, Yaakov acquired it. Nor does he explain that this made it easier for Yaakov's descendants to conquer the Land (as implied by the Talmud). Instead, Rashi explains that the miracle of folding the Land under

Yaakov merely "hints" that it will be easy to conquer in the future. The purpose of God's statement was to inform Yaakov about the future, but not that folding the Land under him actively caused anything practical to occur in the future.

Another nuance in Rashi's comment will help clarify matters. When quoting this Torah verse, Rashi limits himself to only two words — "lying upon." He does not mention the most significant word of the verse, "Land." While very subtle, the absence of this word indicates that Rashi is not concerned about the place which Yaakov lay down upon; he is only concerned with the act of "lying upon." As well, when commenting on the Talmud, Rashi mentions that folding the Land will make it as easy to conquer as "four cubits" but he does not say so when commenting on this Torah verse.[2]

Generally, if it requires a certain number of words to explain a concept to the older and more mature student of the Talmud, it should require at least as many words to explain the same concept to a child. The fact that Rashi omits this reference to the "four cubits" means that Rashi is not concerned with the size of the piece of ground that Yaakov is lying upon. Rashi is only concerned with the act of "lying upon," but not with "what" or "how big."

Going back to God's instructions to Avraham — "Arise, traverse the length and breadth of the Land…" — there is no question about which Land God was referring to. It is obvious from the context that God is referring to the entire Land of Israel. Even though earlier (in Genesis 13:15), God told Avraham, "the Land that you see," it is clear that there was no intention to limit the amount of land that God intended to give to Avraham and his descendants. Even if Avraham had stood on a mountain, he could not have seen the entire land (especially since Israel is a land of mountains and valleys), so it is clear that the phrase "the Land that you see" encompasses the entire Land.[3] The same is true when the Torah says, "The land which you are lying upon." Here it is also clear that this refers to the entire Land of Israel — that it is the Land that God wants to give to Yaakov and his descendants.

What bothered the Talmudic sages (in *Chulin* 91a) when they asked the question, "Why is God promising only the piece of earth under Yaakov?" is not what bothered Rashi, for the simple meaning of the text was clear to him. However, what does require explanation is the words, "which you are lying upon," because that is a curious way of designating what Land God wants to give. When God indicated to Avraham, "the Land that you see," it is understood that God, out of love for Avraham wanted to show him His gift. This is always the case when we give someone a present — we want to see the person unwrap it so we can say, "Look, this is what I am giving you." However, "the Land which you are lying upon" is an unusual way of describing a gift. And therefore, Rashi informs us that this is not the purpose of the words. The purpose is not to designate the gift of a land, but something else...

Previously, we also cited the opinion of R' Elazar, who declared that, by walking around the Land, Avraham gained ownership. However, other sages disagreed with him. They said that, rather than indicating ownership, God told Avraham to traverse the Land in order to demonstrate His love for Avraham and thereby to give him a feeling of mastery over it. God wanted Avraham to experience himself as the owner of the Land, and therefore He told Avraham, "Arise, traverse the length and the breadth..."

This is also clear to Rashi, so much so that he does not even comment on it. As far as Rashi is concerned, the fact that God told Avraham, "Arise..." does not indicate ownership, but love and caring and a desire to impart a feeling of mastery.

Carrying this understanding over to our Torah verse, the words "which you are lying upon" convey the same message to Yaakov as "Arise, traverse the Land" conveyed to Avraham — God wanted to express His love for Yaakov and His desire to make him feel like the master of the Land. Just as "Arise..." conveyed God's love for Avraham, the words, "which you are lying upon" conveyed God's love for Yaakov. The only problem is that "Arise, traverse the Land" is a command to do something, while "which you are lying upon" is not a command at all. And if so, it seems that this verse has a different purpose.

Herein lies the secret of Rashi's comment that all this was "to hint that it would be easy for his descendants to conquer the Land." Unlike Avraham, who actually had to do something (walk the land), Yaakov did not have to do anything. All he had to do was lie down — just like King Hezkiyahu, who famously said, "I sleep on my bed and You [God] act" (Midrash Rabba on *Megilat Eicha* 4:15). It was not necessary for Yaakov to act, but merely to lie down, and the One Above brought the entire Land into Yaakov's possession so that it would be easy for his descendants to conquer.

Here, interestingly, we can see the power of understanding the *pshat* over the *drosh*. While on the *drosh* level, the Talmud (*Chulin* 91b) says that it would be easy for Yaakov's descendants to conquer the Land, it refers to some effort and labor that would be necessary — at least the same labor would be needed as was necessary to conquer the "four cubits" of personal space. But Rashi says that even this minimal effort would not be required. Yaakov need not do anything; he need not even lie down. But once he has done so, God brings the entire Land under him to let him know that he is the master of all of Israel.

In simple words, it would seem that it is enough for the Jews to simply "lie down" on the Land — that is, claim the Land as their own without apologies — and then all the nations of the world will concede that the entirety of Israel is the eternal inheritance of the Jewish nation, making war entirely unnecessary.[4] But there is a deeper explanation of this phenomenon.

In simple words, it would seem that it is enough for the Jews to simply "lie down" on the Land — that is, claim the Land as their own without apologies — and then all the nations of the world will concede that the entirety of Israel is the eternal inheritance of the Jewish nation, making war entirely unnecessary.

We know that the entire Torah includes four levels of explanation, ranging from *pshat* (the plain and simple meaning) to *sod* (the secret mystical meaning). Here, the secret meaning is that the collective Jewish ownership of the Land of Israel is associated with the highest levels of the Jewish soul. Three levels of the soul (the *nefesh*, *ruach* and *neshamah*) are enclothed within the body, and two (the *chayah* and *yechidah*) surround or transcend the body. The *chayah*, which includes our will, surrounds us while also being attached to us. However, the *yechidah*, which is the one level of the soul that is in constant connection with God, is said to exist in the "four cubits" that we occupy. That is, it is in our immediate vicinity. The *yechidah* is our essence, where we are united with God, even when we are unaware and unconscious of the connection.[5]

God "folded the Land of Israel under Yaakov" because his ownership of the Land was connected with his *yechidah*, the essence of his soul. And this connection takes place automatically and unconsciously, since the *yechidah* of the soul is the level on which a Jew is automatically united with God.

This is also the explanation of why it would be easy for the Jews to conquer the Land. The conquest would take place Above, automatically, since there is nothing that can oppose the *yechidah* of the soul and, therefore, it would be easy to take the Land of Israel without any war or opposition whatsoever.

One more amazing and very timely point emerges from Rashi's explanation. Rashi and the Talmud both state that it will be easy to conquer the Land of Israel, providing that the Jewish people want to do so.

The very first of Rashi's comments on the Torah (Genesis 1:1) states what we should answer non-Jews who accuse us of "stealing the Land of Israel." We are to tell them that the Land belongs to God and that He gave it to the Jews. However, Rashi in that commentary says nothing about how Jews should discuss the issue among themselves. And these days, there are more than a few Jews who need to be persuaded that the Land of Israel is important to the Jewish people, and in fact belongs to them. To such people, we find an answer in Rashi's commentary on our Torah portion — we need do nothing to take the Land; it is ours already, and all that is necessary is for us to "lie down" upon it and thereby take possession.[6]

From Likutei Sichot of the Lubavitcher Rebbe,
Vol 20, Pp 129–135

NOTES

1. Rashi comments on this: "Like conquering four cubits." According to Rashi, folding the entire Land under Yaakov made it as easy for Yaakov's descendants to conquer the entire Land as conquering the four cubits of Land upon which Yaakov laid his head.

2. In several editions of Rashi, the words "like about *dalet amot* [four cubits], the size of man" are added in parentheses (and sometimes without parentheses). However, in the first printing of Rashi, and all other printings in the Rebbe's vast library, the words do not appear.

3. Toward the end of *Sefer Breishit*, in *Parshat Vayechi* (Genesis 49:26), when Yaakov gives his blessings to Yoseph, Rashi says, "And they showed him only the Land of Israel," which seems at first glance to indicate that they showed him all of the Land of Israel. But this is not the case. For, nothing in Rashi's comment indicates that this occurred as a miracle, and therefore it had to be a natural occurrence. And, therefore, Rashi means only to explain that they showed him only the Land of Israel — and not *Chutz Laaretz*. (But see the Ohr HaChaim on *Parshat Lech Lecha*, who saw it as a miraculous event.)

4. See Rashi on Deuteronomy 1:8 — "No-one challenges you on this matter, and you do not need to make a war" (from which we understand that the future will occur in this manner). See also Rashbam on *Baba Batra*, and the *Maskil leDavid*.

5. This is explained in a discourse of the Mittler Rebbe, entitled, "You are One." See *Shaar HaTefila* of the Mittler Rebbe, *Padah beshalom*, Ch. 11–12.

6. All the more so that no Jews should create a situation in the Land of Israel, that instead of being "easy for the Jews to conquer," it becomes "easy for the non-Jews to conquer," by delivering cities close to the borders of Israel into their hands. This is the opposite of the halachic directive coming from *Eruvin* 45a and in *Hilchot Shabbat* 329, *seif* 6, in the Alter Rebbe's *Shulchan Aruch HaRav*, which states clearly that even if non-Jews request to enter the Land for a short period of time to acquire straw and grass on Shabbos, this is a prohibition involving Jewish lives in the entire Land, [and they must be turned away].

How Could Yaakov Marry Sisters?

Vayeitzei
29:23

After Rashi wrote his commentary on the Torah, most scholars no longer learned the *Chumash* without reference to Rashi's work. His commentary became indispensable, and virtually no one wrote another commentary that failed to take Rashi's into account. Later commentators either agreed or disagreed with Rashi, but they never ignored him. It is therefore interesting that in the two Torah portions where Yaakov appears most prominently (*Parshat Vayeitzei* and *Parshat Vayishlach*), Rashi says nothing about a matter that most other commentators find challenging — how Yaakov could marry two sisters, Leah and Rachel. Indeed, he married four sisters, because according to Rashi (Gen 31:50), the handmaidens Bilhah and Zilpah, who later gave birth to four of Yaakov's twelve sons, were the daughters of Lavan — just like Leah and Rachel — though they had different mothers.

If the forefathers (and their wives) kept the entire Torah even before it was given, how could Yaakov have married sisters, when that is an explicit Torah prohibition?

Since Rashi's task is to explain the simple level (*pshat*) of the Torah, it seems that his failure to comment on this means that there was nothing to explain, at least not from the perspective of a child learning the Torah for the first time. But that is strange because the question that arises is the kind of question that a child might well ask.

One answer is suggested by the Ramban. He states that the forefathers kept the Torah only when they were in Israel. But, when they were out of Israel, they did not. When Yaakov married the four sisters, he was in Charan, in the house of Lavan, outside of Israel.

However, this answer does not work for Rashi as is clear from his commentary on *Parshat Vayishlach* where Yaakov states, "I lived as a stranger with Lavan" (Genesis 32:5). There Rashi comments, "The numerical value of *garti* [meaning "I lived"] is 613 as if to say, 'I [Yaakov] have lived with the wicked Lavan and yet have kept the 613 mitzvoth...'"

Another possible answer[1] is that, even though there was a prohibition to marry sisters, nevertheless in a situation where there was a specific positive command from Above or from a prophet or one with divine inspiration (*ruach hakodesh*), that command overrode the Torah prohibition at that particular moment in time (not forever).[2] And in Yaakov's case, there was a command from his mother, Rivkah, who was a prophetess, to go to Lavan's house to find himself a wife. However, we do not find that she ordered him to take more than one wife.[3]

After Rashi wrote his commentary on the Torah, most scholars no longer learned the Chumash without reference to Rashi's work. His commentary became indispensable, and virtually no one wrote another commentary that failed to take Rashi's into account.

So, we are forced to continue the search for an answer to our question of how Yaakov could marry four sisters.[4]

There is a general question asked about the forefathers before the Torah was given. While it is known that they kept the principles of the entire Torah, the question arises: What status did that confer upon them? Were they considered to be a different people — the Jews, so to speak — even before the Torah was given at Mt. Sinai? Or did they remain *bnei Noach* ("the children of Noach") who were solely obligated to keep the Seven Noachide Laws? If the latter, then in essence they were no different from all the other peoples of the earth, except that they took upon themselves additional obligations by keeping the mitzvoth of the Torah as they understood them.[5]

But, if we say the former — that their observance of mitzvoth conferred upon the forefathers the status of "Jews" even before the Torah was given at Mt. Sinai — then we have an answer to our question. For, if the fulfillment of mitzvoth conferred upon Yaakov the status of a Jew, then the sisters must have "converted" to Judaism in order to marry him. And, if they converted, then they are considered by the Torah to be total strangers to one another. That is, the laws of conversion state that converts are no longer related to their biological family and, therefore, the four sisters were not sisters after they converted. And, of course, if they were no longer considered sisters in the eyes of Jewish law, they could all marry Yaakov!

But, there are several drawbacks to this answer, which render it insufficient:

1. First of all, nowhere do we find that the forefathers were considered fully Jewish.
2. Second, the entire concept of conversion originates with the giving of the Torah on Mt. Sinai. At that time, all of the Jews underwent circumcision, immersed in a *mikveh* (or the equivalent at the time) and accepted the mitzvoth, all of which are components of conversion to Judaism. Before the Torah was given, we do not find this concept anywhere.[6] So, it is difficult to say that Yaakov was permitted to marry the sisters because they were all converts (since they could not have been).
3. Third, the entire concept that "a convert is like a newborn baby" who no longer has any blood relatives is not a concept that fits into the realm of *pshat*. It is a halachic concept, not a textual concept. And, as such, it belongs in the realm of *drosh*. It certainly is not the kind of idea that a child, learning the Torah for the first time, can be expected to understand. Therefore, it cannot be the explanation according to Rashi (who deals only with the *pshat* in his commentary on the Torah).
4. Finally, on the *pshat* level of the text, blood relations are not the only reason that a man is forbidden to marry sisters. While it is true that certain relatives are forbidden to marry one another, in the case of the sisters whom Yaakov married, there is an additional factor to be taken in account, and that is the natural love that sisters generally have for one another. Sisters, who have grown up together in the same family, will naturally be close to each other. And this is a very good reason why they should not marry the same man; such a marriage is guaranteed to ruin the natural love that the they have for one another. Sisters competing for the attention of the same man are bound to become jealous. So, even if, as proper converts, the Torah no longer considers them to be blood relatives, nevertheless, according to *pshat*, the

Torah would frown upon such a marriage because it would only cause discord between them.[7]

So, we are back to our original quandary — how was Yaakov permitted to marry sisters?

As mentioned above, the concept of conversion did not exist before the Torah was given — conversion to Judaism became an option only afterwards. Therefore, we must operate on the assumption that the forefathers did not have the status of full Jews, even if their fulfillment of mitzvoth did earn them an additional share of appreciation from God. They were *bnei Noach* who took upon themselves additional obligations. However, there was one caveat regarding their fulfillment of mitzvoth — since the mitzvoth of the Torah were a stringency that they took upon themselves voluntarily, the forefathers could not fulfill such mitzvoth when they came into conflict with their obligations as *bnei Noach*.

At that point in history, all human beings were obligated in the Seven Noachide Laws. In addition, they all accepted upon themselves certain stringencies after the Flood (Rashi in Gen 34:7). For example, even though the original Seven Noachide Laws included a prohibition against incest, the *bnei Noach* went even further in order to avoid any kind of promiscuous relations (such as infidelity outside of marriage, for example). This meant that even relationships that were not technically defined as incest became forbidden. And, once all of the *bnei Noach* accepted such stringencies, even they became obligatory.

As a result, if a situation arose in which the forefathers wanted to fulfill a certain commandment of the Torah, but that fulfillment came into conflict with one of the Seven Noachide Laws (or with one of the added stringencies that the *bnei Noach* took upon themselves), then the Torah itself forbid them from fulfilling that mitzvah.

In other words, when the mitzvah conflicted with their Noachide obligations, the forefathers were obligated to forego the mitzvah and fulfill their Noachide obligation. This, for example, was the reason that Avraham did not circumcise himself before he was commanded by God. One of the Noachide commandments was not to murder and, as Rashi explains, that means not only to not shed the blood of others, but also their own blood.[8] This, of course, means that Noachides are commanded against suicide, but on the textual *pshat* level, it applies to any bloodletting whatsoever. And since circumcision requires that one cut off a piece of himself, resulting in the shedding of blood, it was forbidden to circumcise.[9] This is an example of a mitzvah from the Torah — circumcision — from which Avraham refrained, in order to avoid conflict with his Noachide command not to shed blood. Only when the command came directly from Above to circumcise himself did Avraham actually do so.[10]

A similar conflict faced our forefather Yaakov. Among the stringencies that the *bnei Noah* took upon themselves was not to lie and cheat one another. This is evident in Lavan's response when Yaakov complained that Lavan had promised him Rachel as a wife, "This isn't done in our place, marrying the younger sister before the older" (Genesis 29:26). And in his situation, after marrying Leah, Yaakov had no choice but to marry Rachel (and with them the maidservants as well).[11] He had to do this because he had already promised Rachel that he would marry her, and not doing so would have turned his promise into a lie and she would have felt cheated. In this regard, his obligation as a *ben Noach* overrode the Torah prohibition to marry sisters.

Before the Torah was given at Mt. Sinai, Yaakov's primary duty was to avoid lying and cheating another human being. And that is why, even though Yaakov kept all the mitzvoth of the Torah, he still married sisters.[12] Before the Torah was given, the prohibition did not stand up to the requirement to avoid cheating and lying to another human being. And this, of course, is a calculation that any straight-thinking child can grasp, which is why Rashi did not go out of his way to explain it.

We are permitted to take on stringencies in our performance of Torah and mitzvoth, but not at the expense of others.

What we can learn from this is the following:

We are permitted to take on stringencies in our performance of Torah and mitzvoth, but not at the expense of others. When our own adherence to a particular stringency interferes with another person's well-being (either physical or spiritual), then we must forgo it for the sake of the other person.

Stringencies are not a requirement of the Torah; they are a personal and individual embellishment, and thus they must not be allowed to conflict with the well-being of others.

From Likutei Sichot of the Lubavitcher Rebbe, vol. 5, pp.141–149

1. This answer comes from *Parshat Derachim* in the name of *Maharash Yafe.*

2. This would explain why Rashi offered no explanation regarding Avraham extending his hand in order to sacrifice Yitzchak during the *Akeidah* (Genesis 22:10), even though the *bnei Noach* were warned against shedding blood — because Avraham extended his hand as the result of a direct command from Above.

3. See Rashi on Genesis 29:34 — "The matriarchs were prophetesses and they knew that the Twelve Tribes of Israel would come from Yaakov and that he would marry four women..." However, even if they knew, Yaakov did not necessarily know. Moreover, from Rashi's comments (on Genesis 29:17), "She [Leah] thought she would have to marry Esav..." and (on Genesis 30:22), "She [Rachel] was worried [that Yaakov would divorce her and] she would end up with Esav..." — we know that, even if the matriarchs knew, they did not know ahead of time, or they did not know whom Yaakov would marry. In any case, their knowledge 1) did not constitute an instruction or command to Yaakov, 2) did not mean that Yaakov knew whom he would marry, and 3) quite the opposite — the verses prove that Yaakov had no intention of marrying Leah, or Bilhah, or Zilpah.

4. At first glance, it might have been possible to resolve the issue by noting that the four sisters were only sisters from their fathers and not their mothers, and therefore they were not sisters at all from a Torah point of view, since "among non-Jews, there is no fatherhood" (Rashi on Genesis 20:12). That being the case, marrying the four sisters did not present a problem for Yaakov, and he was still able to state that "I kept the six hundred thirteen mitzvoth..." (Rashi on Gen 32:5).

Although the forefathers kept the entire Torah before it was given, they did so only in regard to mitzvoth that would be given in the future (when the Torah would make it forbidden). But if the entire category of behavior would come into existence only after the Torah was given, then the forefathers did not take upon themselves this injunction. In our case, the category of "sisters from the same father" came into existence only after the Torah was given. From the Torah point of view, there was no such thing as "sisters from the same father" before the Torah was given, and therefore they were not considered sisters at all when Yaakov married them, and there was no need for Yaakov to adopt a stringent attitude and not marry all of them.

However, for a variety of reasons, we cannot resolve the issue in this way: 1) On the level of *pshat*, the reason a man may not marry two sisters is because it would destroy the natural love that the two sisters have for each other. This reason applies to sisters from the same father among non-Jews as well, and would therefore disqualify Yaakov from marrying the four sisters even before the Torah was given. 2) The forefathers were careful not to marry indirect relatives (see Rashi on Genesis 26:5 regarding *shniyot le'arayot*), such as relatives from the father's side (see *Yevamot* 21a). Therefore, we are forced to say that when the forefathers "kept the entire Torah before it was given," this included the category of *shniyot* (indirect relatives from the father's side), even though this category did not exist before the Torah was given.

Alternatively, we could suggest that the forefathers kept the entire Torah even when the category in question did not exist before the Torah was given, but only when another halachic category would later apply to the same person after the Torah was given. For example, even if marrying indirect relatives on the father's side (*shniyot*) was not an issue before the Torah was given, nevertheless since the *bnei Noach* would later be obligated by other mitzvoth after the Torah was given — such as "honoring one's father" (see Rashi end of parshat Noach), matters of inheritance (a *ben Noach* may inherit from his father), or matters that affect relatives (children from *bnei Noach* are related after their father — see Rashi on Numbers 25:45), we treat the sisters as if this category (*shniyot*) already applied even before the Torah was given.

3) The main reason — the fine distinction between a "category" that existed before the giving of the Torah or that came into existence only after the giving of the Torah — is not something that a child is likely to grasp on his own, without any assistance whatsoever from Rashi.

5. From Genesis 15:15 — "And you [Avraham] will [pass on and] return to your fathers…" it seems clear that the forefathers remained *bnei Noach*. For Avraham's father did not "convert" to Judaism since as Rashi mentions, "Terach was an idol worshipper" (a violation of one of the Seven Noachide Laws — see Rashi on Genesis 4:26 and 11:28). Terach merely did *teshuvah* for the sin of idolatry but nothing more.

6. This does not contradict what Rashi wrote (on Genesis 12:5): "Avram converted the men, and Sarai converted the women." First, this explanation is not fully according to *pshat*, as Rashi continues later in the same comment, "And according to *pshat*…" Rashi's intention here by using the word "convert" (*megayer, megayeret*) is not to the kind of transformation that changes the person's very existence [as real conversion would], since this kind of transformation (true conversion) was not available before the Torah was given. Note how Rashi uses the word *gerim* in Exodus 12:38 and 32:7 regarding the *erev rav* ("mixed multitude" of people who exited Egypt with the Jews) — "mixed nations of *gerim*." Rather, Rashi's intention was that Avraham (and later, Moshe) "brought them under the influence of the *Shechinah*" which also qualified them as *gerim* (but not the same category of formal *gerim* who converted after the giving of the Torah).

7. It would seem that, according to *pshat*, it is also forbidden for a *ben Noach* to marry sisters, since doing so would lead to strife between them. Therefore, since Yaakov was a *ben Noach*, it should have been forbidden for him to marry sisters because it would cause strife — but here, we find mitigating circumstances. Since Rachel gave the "signs" to her sister Leah before she married Yaakov (so that Yaakov would think that Leah is Rachel and Leah would not be embarrassed), we know that there was not strife between the sisters, so the reason of "natural love" does not apply, and Yaakov was permitted, as a *ben Noach*, to marry the sisters (according to *pshat*).

8. Ramban explains the injunction against drawing blood differently. He suggests that the injunction applies only to the interior blood of the heart and blood vessels, in which is found the *chayut*, or "vitality" of the person, but not to the more "external" blood of the limbs, which one may draw without fear of transgressing the injunction. However, Rashi does not explain in this manner: 1) Rashi mentions the "blood itself," without differentiating among different kinds of blood, and 2) on the word *naphshoteichem* ("your lives"), Rashi comments, "even one who strangles

himself," which is a situation in which no blood is involved. Also, according to Rashi, the injunction against drawing blood applies even to cases that do not lead to death, as derived perhaps from the word *damchem* ("your blood") which was unnecessary to state if the injunction applied only to cases of death, since the word *naphshoteichem* already suggested that.

9. Yet, Yosef commanded the Egyptians in Egypt to undergo circumcision. (At that point, Yoseph had "purchased" the Egyptians for Pharoah at their own request, and they became like his servants and "acquisitions" and therefore they were obligated to be circumcised.) See *Likutei Sichot*, vol. 10, p. 138 and onward.

10. The Riva (at the end of *Parshat Lech Lecha*) gives another reason why Avraham did not circumcise himself earlier in life. Since one can only circumcise himself once in life, Avraham waited until he received a direct command from Above, since "Greater is the one who performs a commanded mitzvah, than he who performs a mitzvah that is not commanded" (*Kiddushin* 31a). However, we cannot say that this is Rashi's reasoning, since 1) This is not a principle that falls in the category of *pshat*, nor is it mentioned in Rashi's commentary. And there is no room to declare the principle "so obvious that a child would figure it out for himself," since even Rav Yosef in the Talmud (*Kiddushin* 31a) initially thought the opposite — that "greater is the one who is not commanded..." 2) If this were the reason that Avraham waited to circumcise himself, it would contradict God's blessing to Yitzchak (Genesis 26:5), "since Avraham listened to My voice and fulfilled My ... commands and laws..." since Avraham would have been in compliance with God's commands only a minority of the years of his life, corresponding to the years that he lived after his circumcision.

11. Since the maidservants themselves were born from Lavan's maids, they did not have "family status," and therefore there was no natural love between them. They were considered the "property of the master," rather than as sisters.

12. There is no room to suggest that Rashi's comments at the beginning of *Parshat Vayishlach* (Gensis 32:5), "and I kept 613 mitzvoth," or in *Parshat Toldot* (Genesis 26:5) "Since Avraham kept my framework, commands..." do not stand up to scrutiny, because, in the last analysis, Avraham failed to circumcise himself [in a timely fashion] and Yaakov failed to observe the injunction against marrying sisters. There is no reason to suggest this, because 1) Rashi did not write *kiyamti* ("fulfilled" — as in *Yoma* 28b), or *asiti* ("I did" — as in *Kiddushin* 82a), but *shamarti* ("I kept"). And the opposite of "I kept" would be if Yaakov had transgressed a negative commandment or failed to fulfill a positive commandment, but not when he failed to follow the Torah because of an injunction of the Torah itself. Quite the opposite — to follow the Torah's command by marrying sisters before the Torah was given in order to prevent lying and deception — this itself is keeping the Torah. For example, when a positive mitzvah contradicts the requirements of a negative mitzvah, we follow the positive command. And the Torah tells us that situations of *pikuah nefesh* ("saving a life") take precedence over keeping the Torah when they come into apparent contradiction. To conclude, there are times when we fulfill (*mekayam*) the commands of the Torah precisely by not doing the mitzvah.

The Original Jewish Profession

Vayishlach
30:43

Throughout Jewish history, there were occupations which figured prominently at a given time — for example, that of shepherd. (Many of our illustrious ancestors were shepherds including Moshe and King David.) This was also the occupation of our forefather Yaakov, who spent a significant part of his life tending sheep. He was paid with sheep for the work he did by his father-in-law, Lavan. Indeed, sheep made him wealthy, as we learn from our Torah portion, *Parshat Vayeitzei*: "And the man became very, very wealthy, and he possessed many sheep and maid servants and servants and camels and donkeys" (Genesis 30:43). Rashi further explains that Yaakov would sell sheep in order to acquire all of his other possessions.

Despite the fact that sheep were the source of his wealth, we find in *Parshat Vayishlach* that Yaakov does not list them first when speaking with his brother Esav. As Esav approached Yaakov with intention to harm him, Yaakov sent a message to him, stating in part, "And I acquired oxen and donkeys, sheep and servants and maid-servants..." (Genesis 32:6). Although sheep are mentioned first in *Parshat Veyeitzei*, here in *Parshat Vayishlach* they take back seat to oxen and donkeys, even though they were Yaakov's main source of sustenance, the focus of his life and his occupation.

As we know, everything that happened to our forefathers contains a sign or directive for us, their descendants. Everything that happened to them, together with how they responded to the events in their lives, contains a core message of truth as well as a model for us in conducting our own affairs. Therefore, it is worthwhile to examine Yaakov's involvement with sheep. When we do, we find three significant details:

1. It was specifically sheep that earned Yaakov all of his massive wealth.
2. Even though sheep were his main concern, Yaakov exchanged some of them for other possessions, such as servants, camels and donkeys.
3. When he communicated with Esav, Yaakov mentioned his oxen and donkeys, before he mentioned sheep.

There is a spiritual message for every Jew in these details. To begin with, every Jew is called both a "sheep" and a "son" of God. We see this in the Midrashic commentary on the Song of Songs (*Shir HaShirim Rabba* 2:16), which states:

> He is for me like a father, and I to Him like a son …
> He is for me like a shepherd … and I to Him like a sheep.

But here the question arises: If we are like a "son" in relation to God, what can it possibly add to say we are like a "sheep" as well? What greater ingredient exists in the relationship between a shepherd and his sheep, than in the relationship between father and son?

A son, as close and as obedient as he might be to his father, is still an independent individual. He may be similar to his father, he may follow in his father's footsteps in many respects, but he is still another person, a separate entity from his father. A "son" possesses his own unique qualities. However, a "sheep" possesses only one significant quality: *Bitul*, or lack of ego. It has the ability to lose its own individuality in deference to the flock or in obedience to the will of the shepherd. Therefore, the quality that a sheep demonstrates more than any other is selflessness or self-sacrifice in the cause of the greater whole. Every sheep is an individual creature, but it expresses obedience to something beyond it.

The two descriptions, "son" and "sheep" also allude to two elements of divine service.[1] The "son" is one who studies Torah. He spends his time immersed in the tomes of the Talmud and the mystical dimensions of Kabbalah and Chassidut, increasing his knowledge and understanding of God. He is a "son" because he expands his intellect, as well as increases his love and awe of God. Even though he is subservient to God, the Giver of the Torah, he still maintains independent existence as one who thinks, understands, and therefore grows in intellectual comprehension. The very act of understanding, as well as feeling, implies a "self," which we call a "son."

But the "sheep" is involved in *avodat habirurim* ("service of refinement"). The one who embodies the qualities of a "sheep" goes out into the world and, by fulfilling Torah and its mitzvoth, brings to the fore the good and Godly potential that is hidden in the world. In Chassidic terminology, this is called *avodat habirurim*, or "returning the holy sparks to their source and reuniting them with the Creator." We see this in the very word for "sheep" in Hebrew — *tzon* — which is etymologically related to *la'tzeit*, meaning "to go out." Both imply leaving what is comfortable and what feels natural in order to deal with a world that yields its holy sparks only to those who are willing to be tested, and who manage to maintain a holy lifestyle against all odds. In so doing, the Jews create a "dwelling place for God in the lower realms," and imbue the physical world with Godliness.

The Jews are called "sheep" when they leave the study of Torah and apply themselves to uplifting and raising the spiritual level of the world around them. This manner of serving God demands selflessness and self-sacrifice because a Jew's natural habitat is within the "four cubits of Torah," studying, meditating and growing closer to God. To leave this habitat — in order to fulfill the Godly plan of uplifting the world and turning it into a dwelling place for Him — and to go out into an inhospitable world that is focused on physicality and materialism demands selflessness and self-sacrifice, and this is why the Jews are also called "sheep."

Now, we can understand the various details of Yaakov's involvement with sheep. In last week's Torah portion — *Parshat Toldot* — sheep are not mentioned. This is because Yaakov was not involved yet in *avodat habirurim* — he had not yet gone out to elevate and refine the world. He was involved only in learning Torah. Even when his mother, Rivkah, told him to leave the house to avoid the wrath of his brother Esav, he did not go immediately to his uncle's house in Paden Aram.[2]

It is only afterward, in *Parshat Vayeitzei*, that we find Yaakov involved with sheep. Only after intense preparation of learning and internalizing Torah was Yaakov able to face the outside world. But, when he did so, it was with the utmost selflessness. He worked with all his might (indeed, from Yaakov, we learn how a worker should devote himself to his work). He gave no thought to the negative atmosphere that surrounded him in the home of his uncle Lavan, who was an idol worshipper and a dishonest man. Instead, Yaakov focused on his work while building his family and fathering twelve sons who would become the Twelves Tribes of Israel.

His work ethic is what allowed him to become not only successful, but also "very, very wealthy" (Genesis 30:43). His ego-nullification to the will of God propelled him from the world of personal introspection and growth into success in the world of physicality and materialism. It was for this reason that his work involved sheep — since sheep embody the same principle of selflessness that Yaakov expressed. He was then able to retrieve the sparks of holiness within the sheep of his father-in-law and that made him "very, very wealthy."

However, Yaakov did not confine himself to sheep alone. He acquired oxen and donkeys — animals which symbolize inner strength and boldness in the way we serve God.

In order to face evil, we need inner strength and the ability to fend off those who mock us or want to deter us from the path of divine service. And for that, we need to exude confidence and strength. But both need to be built on a foundation of selflessness. Yaakov demonstrated this in the following two ways:

1. All of his possessions — the oxen and the donkeys — were acquired with sheep. Meaning that the other ways of Godly service worked only when rooted in selflessness.
2. Yaakov never sold all of his sheep, and they always remained the basis of his wealth. Meaning that when we go out into the world to do battle with the forces of deceit and concealment — which necessitate that we use weapons of strength and determination — selflessness is still paramount. Without the necessary ingredient of ego-nullification to a higher power, we are unable to access and elevate the holy sparks that are out there in the world, and we are not able to achieve victory over the "negative forces." That is why Yaakov never sold all of his sheep.

Because at the point of meeting Esav, Yaakov needed all the strength he could muster, he mentioned "oxen and donkeys" first followed by "sheep." But before that, when he was dealing with the outside world on his own terms, the "sheep" came first. (This is in keeping with our premise that selflessness is the basis of all divine service.)

In *Parshat Vayishlach*, Yaakov is faced with the task of taming Esav, who has come to kill him. When facing the forces that hide and conceal Godliness in the world, it is necessary first of all to broadcast confidence and power. If we begin with "sheep," we give the wrong message, because the enemy thinks that we are soft and passive. If, however, we broadcast boldness and power, the enemy knows that it must respect us. This boldness must be infused with selflessness because at no point should we give the impression — either to ourselves or to others — that our success is built on our abilities alone. Rather, our confidence should be based on faith and trust in the One Above. Nevertheless, our adversaries must sense our confidence, and thus Yaakov first mentioned "oxen and donkeys" as these possessions conveyed the message of might. Afterward, he could also mention "sheep," to let Esav know that all was subject to the One Above. However, by starting with mention of his oxen and donkeys, Yaakov let Esav know that, in the physical world, Yaakov was a man to be reckoned with as well.

The lesson of our Torah portion is that we have to go out and illuminate the world. We must first prepare for this mission by learning much Torah, but then we have to go out into the world and uplift it spiritually. The main work these days is not learning Torah, as it was in the days of our sages, but going out to elevate the world. In particular in our generation, the goal is not to turn an ignoramus into a Torah scholar, or to turn a minor scholar into an important scholar, but simply to save souls! The task is to seek out Jews who are blundering and lost in the darkness of exile and bring them to the light of Torah and its mitzvoth. In so doing, we save not only those particular Jews, but all of their descendants, so that they remain Jewish.

But, for our mission to be successful, it must be imbued with selflessness. When we remember that our mission comes from God, and we are His servants then, no matter the task before us, we are bound to succeed.

From Likutei Sichot of the Lubavitcher Rebbe, vol. 15, pp. 252–258

NOTES

1. Regarding the distinction between "son" and "sheep," see *Likutei Sichot*, vol. 20, p. 333 and onward, for an explanation of the saying, "Greater are the conversations of the servants of our forefathers, than the Torah of their offspring"

(*Breishit Rabba* 60:8, and Rashi on Genesis 24:42). See also *Ohr HaTorah, Parshat Re'eh* p. 801 (there, the Tzemach Tzedek writes that "sheep" represent the path of prayer — see *Likutei Sichot* there, vol. 20, p. 331, footnote 62).

2. Instead, he went to the yeshiva of Shem and Eber, where he learned Torah for fourteen years (*Bereishit Rabba* 68:13, mentioned in Rashi on verse 28:11).

Yaakov's Small Jars

Vayishlach 32:25

In our weekly Torah portion — *Parshat Vayishlach* — we find our forefather Yaakov at what might be described as the pivotal juncture of his entire life. Previously he succeeded in raising his large family and accumulating vast wealth in the strange environment of Charan and the household of his unscrupulous uncle, Lavan, and now he sought to "take it all home" — to return to Israel with his wives, children and possessions. But just at this point, he faced a major test. Yaakov was forced to wrestle with "a man" whom the Torah does not name (Genesis 32:25) but who is identified (*Bereishit Rabba* 77:3) as the spiritual archetype (angel) of his twin brother and nemesis, Esav.

For twenty odd years, Esav had been waiting for Yaakov's return to Israel. Now that the moment arrived, he wished to take revenge for what he considered to be Yaakov's theft of his natural birthright. Their wrestling match at a place called Peniel (meaning "where I met God face to face") determine the course of Jewish history.

After a prolonged struggle, Yaakov succeeded in vanquishing Esav and the Jewish people become established in the Promised Land. But if he hadn't, then the Jews would have suffered a serious setback.

The fact that all went well has a great deal to do with careful advance planning on Yaakov's part. Realizing that Esav was likely to receive him with animosity, Yaakov first sent messengers ahead to assess Esav's intentions to do him harm, as well as to inform his brother of his status. Then he divided his family group into two camps, so that at least one camp would be saved if the other was attacked. He sent gifts to appease his brother and he prayed. Finally, he prepared for a fight.

But, perhaps the most important aspect of his preparations was what may have seemed like an after-thought. Having sent his family on ahead, hopefully out of harm's way, Yaakov remained behind. Rashi says that he needed to collect some "small jars" that he had inadvertently left behind.

What were these mysterious "small jars"?

The Torah is not a novel, written for purposes of entertainment. Nor is it a blog, recording someone's daily activities so that others can observe and comment. It's a primary archetypal source, written down in order to give Jews living many generations later the ability to look into it and figure out how to act in similar situations. If Yaakov left some "small jars" behind, that means we are likely to do so also when faced with a major test in life like the one Yaakov faced. It makes sense, then to understand just what those "small jars" were. For that, we will have to delve into the secrets of the Torah — the Kabbalah.

If Yaakov left some "small jars" behind, that means we are likely to do so also when faced with a major test in life like the one Yaakov faced.

But first, we have to understand the messengers — in Hebrew, *malachim*, which also means "angels" — whom Yaakov sent ahead to assess his brother's intentions. Rashi states that they were real angels, spiritual beings who went right to the source — the soul of Esav — and ascertained his position. They also informed Esav of Yaakov's status, letting him know that Yaakov was no pushover — he was not afraid to deal with Esav on any plane that Esav chose. Then, they returned to Yaakov and informed him where Esav stood.

This is a level of intelligence that everyone needs when making a fateful decision. If you know what you are dealing with, then you can make informed judgments. For example, if one is thinking of undertaking a mission in life (*shlichut*), but not sure that it's for him, then he should test the waters first. He should send out "angels" — his "spiritual feelers." Their purpose is to collect information and bring it back to him. If, as he tries out the new environment, he is able to maintain his own psychological/spiritual equilibrium, then the mission may be a good fit for him. If, however, the new and strange environment causes him to lose his equilibrium and lower his spiritual level, then the task may not be for him, but for someone else who can maintain his or her level in this situation.

The "angels" are the sensitive "spiritual feelers" that we send out to allow us to size up the situation and decide. If they return with a report that leaves us with your spiritual world intact, then all is well and good. If not, it's time to look for a different mission.

But, what often happens in practice is that the answer is not so clear-cut. Often, the mission or proposed situation has elements that we can deal with, and elements that we find intimidating. That's as it should be. If the new situation is too easy and comfortable, then it's not a challenge, and there's no opportunity for growth. If we can detect no challenge and therefore no opportunity for growth, then it's unlikely that there are any new "sparks of holiness" awaiting our liberation and elevation to a whole new level. There must be something uncomfortable, something that makes us nervous in the new situation, if it's the right fit.

Such, for example, was the situation as the Children of Israel crossed the Reed Sea en route to receiving the Torah in the Sinai. No one knew quite what to do until one Jew jumped into the sea — and then the waters parted. But, before that, everyone was nervous and confused, because they sensed a situation that was beyond them. The goal is to reach the sparks of holiness on the other side — of the sea in the case of the Children of Israel, or the river in the case of Yaakov — that are waiting for liberation. In the process of their liberation, those sparks also empower their liberators to grow and ascend as well.

According to Kabbalah, the feeling of discomfort, the queasiness over a new situation, is associated with the "small jars" for which Yaakov returned. In the technical language of Kabbalah, they are the "shards of vessels of chaos (*tohu*) that fell below." *Tohu* — despite its name — is an unformed world of very high spiritual illumination, with no corresponding vessels to contain that illumination. Whatever vessels existed in *tohu* were unable to cope with the exalted light, and so they shattered. Their remnants fell to worlds of lesser illumination, including our own physical world, there to be known as "holy sparks."

These sparks are like our hidden aspirations, echoing in the chambers of our consciousness, waiting for actualization. When we succeed in uplifting these sparks, by meeting new challenges while fulfilling the mitzvoth of the Torah, we are presented with new sparks — new challenges and situations to elevate.

As we climb up the ladder of holiness, we are given higher and higher sparks to liberate and elevate. But, when we don't succeed, or succeed only partially, the sparks of the past remain behind to remind us. They are our territory, our challenge, and until we return them to their source, they remain with us in the form of one sort of challenge or another. When that happens, we have to return. We have to go back to the previous mission or task and make sure that we've done everything we can to meet previous challenges.

That's what Yaakov did — he went back to look inside himself and make sure he had not left any sparks behind. Before going on to the new challenge presented by his brother, he wanted to examine his own spiritual status, make an inner accounting and reinforce himself.

When Yaakov returned to collect the "small jars" that he had left behind, he returned to gather all his inner resources and prepare himself for the upcoming struggle. If he could send messengers (real "angels," as Rashi says) to gather intelligence on his brother, then he must have known that his own brother's "angel" may come to wrestle with him. That must have been a daunting prospect. If so, then returning for the "small jars" must have been Yaakov's way of dealing with it. He needed to prepare himself for this crucial moment of meeting his brother. He needed to collect the vessels for dealing with the challenge ahead. It was time to gain composure and to reach closure once and for all, and to elevate the sparks that were left over from Yaakov's previous encounters with Esav.

Another point:

The jars for which Yaakov returned may have been "small" because he had already finished his main job, the major task of uplifting the sparks in the house of his father-in-law. The "big" sparks had already been encountered and uplifted, during Yaakov's tenure as an employee of Lavan, and afterward, when he built his own flock. All that Yaakov was consciously aware of, he already dealt with and elevated. However, when Lavan ran after Yaakov in order to "look for his idols," (Genesis 31:30), that was a sign that the elevation/purification process was not yet complete. It was a sign that the refinement of the sparks that were stuck with Lavan had not yet been concluded. There still remained "small jars" — small matters that were not yet resolved.

Lavan ran after Yaakov for that purpose — to resolve the remaining small matters so that he would become completely uplifted and purified.[1] And those were matters that had to be resolved before Yaakov could move on to his next mission in life and confront his brother Esav to deal with him as well.

The "small jars," the remnants of the sparks from the world of *tohu*, challenge us. We always come back to them, until we succeed in fully elevating them. They make us nervous, but they are our potential. If actualized, they lead us on to the next task in life, elevating us to the highest holy heights.

By returning to gather the "small jars," Yaakov taught us a valuable lesson — we can't leave any sparks behind. Until we fully elevate one level, we can't move on to the next.

Adapted from Likutei Sichot of the Lubavitcher Rebbe,
vol. 10, pp. 100–108, and vol. 15, pp. 281–288

NOTES

1. See *Ohr HaTorah* of the Tzemach Tzedek, parshat Vayeitzei, volume 5, Page 869A.

What Turned Esav Around?

Vayishlach
33:4

At the end of *Parshat Vayeitzei*, the Torah relates how Yaakov prepared to return home to the Land of Israel. He did so with trepidation because his unscrupulous father-in-law, Lavan, didn't want to let him go, and because he had unfinished business with his twin brother Esav back in Israel. Esav had pledged to kill Yaakov, who had cleverly and rightfully obtained their father's birthright blessings. For this, Esav hated Yaakov and waited for an opportunity to settle the score. Yaakov feared the inevitable confrontation between them.

As we learn from this week's Torah portion, *Parshat Vayishlach*, before that confrontation could take place, Yaakov was accosted by an unidentified "man" who struggled with him in the night. (Genesis 32:25) Rashi tells us that this "man" was, in fact, Esav's angel.

Yaakov prevailed in this extraordinary spiritual struggle, and that guaranteed that he would prevail in the ordinary, physical realm, as well. However, he had no way of knowing that he would prevail, though he knew that Esav certainly had the power to do him grievous harm. For that reason, Yaakov was afraid. In advance of their actual meeting, he divided his household into two camps to protect at least one part if need be, he prayed, and he sent lavish presents to his brother. When Esav finally arrived on the scene, he was appeased. As the Torah tells us, "He [Esav] embraced him … and kissed him, and they both cried." (Genesis 33:4).

The question arises: What turned Esav around? Was it only Yaakov's gifts and entreaties? A lot of evidence suggests that this was not the case.

As mentioned, Yaakov also had a problem with his father-in-law,

Lavan, who wanted to do him harm after Yaakov left secretly for Israel, taking his wives (Lavan's daughters) with him. Incensed at Yaakov's subterfuge, Lavan pursued him, but when he caught up to him, he did nothing, explaining his change of intention: "It is within the power of my hand to harm you. But the God of your father spoke to me last night, saying 'Be careful not to say anything to Yaakov either good or bad.'" (Genesis 31:29)

So we see that Lavan had the power to harm Yaakov, but didn't because of the warning from God. But Lavan's anger at Yaakov could not compare with Esav's intense hatred. As the Torah tells us, "And Esav hated Yaakov … and said in his heart … 'I will kill my brother Yaakov'" (Genesis 27:41). That makes it difficult to believe that gifts and entreaties alone could have transformed this hatred into positive feelings.

Furthermore, we have Rashi's comments (on Genesis 33:4) calling attention to a difference of opinion among the Talmudic sages[1] whether Esav hugged and kissed Yaakov wholeheartedly. Some held that he did, but R' Shimon bar Yochai saw it another way: "It is a law (*halachah*) that … Esav hates Yaakov, but at that moment his pity was aroused and he kissed him wholeheartedly." The fact that R'Shimon equates Esav's state of mind with *halachah* means that Esav's hatred is an immutable, permanent condition (which extends to his descendants throughout time).[2]

All this makes it very difficult to understand why, in this instance, Esav changed his mind and failed to carry out his original intention to harm Yaakov.

Indeed, we can only conclude that Esav did not permanently change his attitude toward Yaakov and returned to his original state of hatred. Yaakov was worried about that very possibility, which is why he reminded Esav of the angel he had just subdued in their struggle the night before. As we will recall, after that wrestling match, Yaakov had named the place where it took place Peniel, meaning "God's face," and said, "for I have seen God face to face and my soul has survived." (Genesis 32:31). Now he said to Esav after their embrace, "I have seen your face like the face of God…" (Genesis 33:10)

According to Rashi, this was his way of hinting to Esav that he had met and prevailed over his angel, and can also prevail over him.

But that's not all. When Esav suggested to Yaakov that he would send some of his men to accompany him on the journey, Yaakov misled him about his final destination. This was in order to throw Esav off his trail in case he was thinking of luring Yaakov into a trap somewhere else. So, we see that Yaakov himself was suspicious of Esav's sudden transformation and sought to distance himself. Which leads us back to the same question: Why did Esav refrain from trying to harm him as he originally intended?

The answer comes from Rashi, who comments (on Genesis 33:16), "Esav was alone, since the four hundred men that came with him slipped away from him on by one." This is why Esav didn't harm Yaakov — he was alone. This is why he journeyed onward without hurting Yaakov. By himself, without the four hundred men who came with him, he could do Yaakov no harm, as there was a large group of men with Yaakov also.

That also explains why Rashi says that Esav's men left him "one by one." What does that add to the commentary? Why does it matter if the four hundred men ran away all at once or "one by one"? But, what Rashi wants to emphasize is that Esav's men, just like Esav himself, retained their hatred of Yaakov. If not, they would have run away openly, all at once. But, since they still hated Yaakov and wanted to do him in, they slipped away only reluctantly and slowly, out of fear.[3] Otherwise, they would have continued together with Esav. And if his men still hated Yaakov, all the more so is it true that Esav himself hated Yaakov.

Their anti-Semitism isn't a passing phenomenon — it's a permanent condition with which the Jews are faced, and something they would have to learn to live with until the End of Days.

We can now gain greater understanding of something else that Rashi mentions in his commentary. When the Torah relates that Yaakov misled Esav as to how far he intended to journey in order to throw him off the track (Genesis 33:14), Rashi comments, "When will Yaakov catch up with Esav? In Messianic times, as it is written 'and their saviors will ascend Mt. Zion in order to judge Mt. Esav' (Ovadiah 1:21)."

Clearly, Rashi is saying that until the Mashiach arrives, not only Esav himself but all of his descendants (who are today's Europeans) will hate the Jews. Their anti-Semitism isn't a passing phenomenon — it's a permanent condition with which the Jews are faced, and something they would have to learn to live with until the End of Days.

There is another element of Rashi's commentary which we need to examine. He states that, since the four hundred men who came with Esav slipped away and did no harm to Yaakov, they received a reward.

Asks Rashi, "How and where did God pay them back? In the days of King David, they escaped harm themselves, as it is written, 'Except for the four hundred young men who rode away on camels.' (1 Samuel 30:17)." This refers to an incident in which King David defeated a group of men who came to fight against him. He killed them all, except four hundred who managed to escape on camels. But, why would Rashi mention this story? Rashi's purpose is to explain the simple meaning of the text — that the men who came with Esav, as well as Esav himself, did not regret their original intention to harm Yaakov. They still hated him, but they were afraid and therefore ran away, as did the four hundred men on camels in the era of King David.

The four hundred men who escaped from David came initially to fight him. Like Esav's men, they came to fight against the leader of the generation. And also like Esav's men, they were afraid, and so they escaped. Since they were on camels, they were able to get away (unlike the rest of the troops who were on foot). This was their reward for not harming Yaakov. Just as the four hundred men who came to do harm to Yaakov bore him no good will, and the only good they did was to refrain from hurting him, so the four hundred who came to fight against David bore him no good will. And they got away with their lives only as a reward for Esav's four hundred men, who run away without hurting Yaakov.[4]

We have a precedent for this some generations earlier. According to Rashi (Gen 19:37, based on Bereishit Rabba 51:11), as a reward for her greater degree of modesty than her older sister, the younger daughter of Lot received a "prize." When? Much later, in the generation of Moses, when God commanded the Children of Israel not to offend the nation of Ammon (the descendants of the younger sister), even though they were permitted to act aggressively toward Moab (the descendants of the older sister).

From this, it is evident that, even on the simple level of understanding the text, reward for the deeds of one generation may take place many generations later. With his reference to the reward of the four hundred men, Rashi reinforces his main point, which is that neither Esav nor his men really changed their attitude. They still hated Yaakov and wished to do him harm, but were unable to do so. The men that were with him slipped away one by one, and Esav himself was left alone, unable to harm Yaakov.

Since the forefathers — Avraham, Yitzchak and Yaakov — were the first Jews, the events of their lives established a blueprint for the rest of Jewish history. In many historical instances (if not most), Jews have lived in an environment of anti-Semitism and hatred. This is certainly still true of Europe, though it may be less true of America. The steps that Yaakov took to deal with this condition are the steps that Jews have taken throughout history when dealing with enemies.

But it is important to realize that anti-Semitism is not something that Jews can control. It is a perpetual condition, not the result of a specific Jewish behavior or activity. Some Jews make the mistake of thinking that they are the cause, and if they change somehow, anti-Semitism will disappear. It won't for, as R'Shimon bar Yochai put it, "it is *halachah* that Esav hates Yaakov..."

Anti-Semitism is a condition that will not change because the Jews take one action or another. What the Jews can do is pray, attempt to appease the other side and, if necessary, fight. Attempts to appease alone, without praying or preparing to fight, will not be effective, just as showing weakness is never effective. The non-Jewish side needs to be aware that even though Jews are a modest people, we are prepared to stand strong for our principles and act, if need be. And then, when the Mashiach arrives, anti-Semitism will disappear and the world will live in peace, while the Jews will study Torah and Godliness permeates the creation, "like the waters cover the ocean bed." (Habakkuk 2:14)

From Likutei Sichot of the Lubavitcher Rebbe,
vol. 35, pp. 143–149

NOTES

1. The difference of opinion concerns the dots above the word *vayishakhu* ("and he kissed him") — Gen 33:4. See the *beraysa* of the Sifre 9:10 — "some say that the dots indicate that Esav did not kiss Yaakov whole-heartedly, R' Shimon bar Yohai said although it is a *halacha* that Esav hates the Jews, at that moment he felt mercy toward his brother and kissed him with all his heart."

2. Rashi prefaces his comment with the word *beyadua* ("it is known") to tell us that this *halachah* (that Esav hates Yaakov) is well known, which is why Yaakov suspected Esav's intentions, even though at the time, Esav kissed him with all his heart. Therefore, it was necessary for Rashi to add this word to explain why Yaakov distrusted Esav.

3. The reason for their fear was, as Rashi points out in a previous comment

(on Genesis 33:8), that they encountered a group of angels, who "hit them" and roughed them up until they admitted that Esav is "Yaakov's brother."

4. From these two events (Yaakov and King David), we also learn how even the slightest good deed, even in a negative context of hatred, does not go unrewarded.

YAAKOV SURVIVES "WHOLE"

Vayishlach 33:18

When Yaakov returned home to the Land of Israel (then called Canaan) after years of working hard for his father-in-law, Lavan, the Torah reports, "And Yaakov arrived whole in the city of Shechem" (Genesis 33:18), which means, according to Rashi, that Yaakov arrived, "whole in body, whole in wealth, whole in Torah."[1]

Rashi's explanation is based upon the Midrash, but there is an overall question that arises here: Why not explain simply that Yaakov successfully faced his adversaries (Esav and Lavan), and arrived "whole" in the city of Shechem? Why does Rashi find it necessary to go into these details?

In the narrative of our Torah portion — *Parshat Vayishlach* — we see how Yaakov escapes first from Lavan, and then from his brother Esav, without suffering any harm. So, we would think that's what the Torah is referring to when it says that Yaakov "arrived whole." Yet, Rashi tells us something else — that this is referring to his body, his wealth[2] and the Torah that he'd learned. So, obviously, Rashi seeks to explain the verse differently, to answer a question that had not occurred to us.

When Yaakov first set out on his path (after his mother sent him away to escape Esav's wrath at the end of *Parshat Toldot*), God spoke to him, saying: "Behold, I am with you and I will guard you wherever you go..." (Genesis 28:15). This promise of protection clearly referred to Lavan and Esav, so it is clear why Rashi did not consider them to be the focus of the verse above ("Yaakov arrived whole...). Since God had promised that Yaakov would come to no harm from Lavan and Esav, it wasn't necessary to report that, after his struggles with them, he was finally returning to the Land of Israel as a "whole" man. That was to be assumed.

Similarly, earlier in the Book of Genesis, it was not necessary to report that "Avraham arrived whole," since God promised that He would one day create a great people from Avraham, and the amount of traveling that he did would not detract from that in any way. This was clear from the divine promises, and therefore there was no need to write explicitly that he was whole.

Therefore, the verse is telling us something else — namely, that Yaakov remained "whole" despite other factors that were not included in the promise of divine protection. And Rashi goes on to tell us exactly what those factors were — namely his body, his wealth and his Torah learning.

As far as his body, it's true that Yaakov was limping as a result of his encounter with Esav's angel. But that angel was a messenger of God, and since the angel and the injury came from God, and not from Esav or Lavan, it was not included in the original promise of God to guard Yaakov from those who sought to do him harm. Therefore, says Rashi, the Torah seeks to tell us that even after the encounter with Esav's angel, Yaakov's body (despite the limp) was still "whole."

Yaakov's wealth also remained whole even after all the gifts that he gave to Esav in order to appease his brother. And although he was wealthy enough to give Esav gifts and remain rich himself, he could not have expected to replace whatever wealth he gave to Esav. The original promise from God to Yaakov was only that he would have enough "bread to eat and clothing to wear." (Genesis 28:20) So, Rashi explains, the verse tells us that Yaakov remained "whole" in his wealth, meaning that whatever he gave to Esav was also replaced.

And finally, Yaakov remained whole in his Torah, meaning that he did not forget the Torah that he learned, even while he worked for Lavan. This also was not something that could have been predicted from the promise that God gave Yaakov at the beginning of his journey. The promise was only that God would guard him from harm during his travels. It did not cover what could happen after he settled in Lavan's house. There, Yaakov worked very hard for twenty years, raising and tending his uncle's flocks, and he did not have time to learn or even to review the Torah that he learned in the yeshivah of Ever before he came to Charan. Yet despite that, Yaakov was whole in his Torah even in the house of Lavan — he did not forget what he had learned previously.

This explains another detail in Rashi's commentary on this verse which actually differs from his commentary on a passage in the Talmud (*Shabbos* 33b). Here, Rashi comments that Yaakov was "complete in his Torah learning because he did not forget his Torah while in the house of Lavan." However, in his commentary on the Talmud, Rashi explains that Yaakov "did not forget his Torah during the travails of his journey." At first glance, it would appear that Rashi's comment on the Talmud is closer to the simple (*pshat*) level of the text that Rashi ostensibly seeks to explain in words that a child would understand. The child is more likely to identify the events that happened during the journey immediately prior to Yaakov's arrival in Shechem as a reason he might forget his Torah, rather than the events that transpired in Lavan's house. So, why does Rashi say that Yaakov arrived "whole" because he "did not forget his Torah while in the house of Lavan"?

We can answer this question in the same way as above. Yaakov received a blessing at the very beginning of his journey that he would not be damaged wherever he went — now or later. Therefore, when explaining the *pshat* of the Torah, Rashi need not mention that Yaakov would not suffer damages while on the road. That was a given, because of the initial blessing from Above. However, that blessing did not cover what might occur in Lavan's home, which is why Rashi found it necessary to explain that, even in Lavan's house, where Yaakov worked very hard, he suffered no damage to his Torah learning.

Thus, the verse, according to Rashi, tells us three things that we could not have assumed from the original promise — that Yaakov would emerge "whole" from his struggle with the guardian angel of Esav, that all of his wealth would remain intact, and that he would remember all of the Torah he had learned before settling in the house of Lavan.

On a deeper level, perhaps the verse comes to tell us that Yaakov arrived "whole" in Shechem after the completion of his "spiritual journey" which included both his sojourn in the house of Lavan and the encounter with Esav's angel. According to Chassidic literature, both of these experiences had to do with Yaakov's personal spiritual task — elevating and refining the "sparks of holiness" that had fallen into the realm of Esav and the realm of Lavan.

Although most sparks which people encounter in life, and which they are meant to uplift are of the conscious variety, sometimes they are unconscious, or super-conscious. While in the house of Lavan, Yaakov knew that his spiritual task necessitated that he work with total devotion to increase Lavan's flocks, even while cleaving to the principles of the Torah that he had learned previously. Only in this manner would he be able to retrieve the fallen sparks associated with Lavan's sheep. This was a conscious task that enriched both him and Lavan. His physical wealth was only the residual reward of the process of spiritual refinement in which he was involved. When, after twenty years, Lavan no longer responded to him positively, and Yaakov himself had twelve sons to raise, Yaakov thought (and Hashem seemingly concurred — see Gen 31:3) that his job in Lavan's house was finished. He had done everything he could to retrieve the fallen sparks, and now it was time to leave.

However, the very fact that Lavan chased after him (as we saw in last week Torah portion, *Parshat Vayeitzei*) meant that the job was not yet complete. Yaakov considered it complete, but there were some sparks that were still left with Lavan. This is why Lavan ran after Yaakov in order to catch him, and perhaps to do him harm (but he was prevented by the dream in which God told him to leave Yaakov alone). That is what Lavan did consciously. But on the deeper spiritual level, Lavan had unfinished business, and this is why he pursued Yaakov without being consciously aware of why he was doing so. There were sparks that remained with Lavan, and they had to be transmitted to Yaakov. That's why Lavan chased after Yaakov, dueled with him verbally, and then kissed his daughters and grandchildren good-bye. In so doing, he transferred the final sparks of holiness hidden within him to Yaakov.[3]

But on the deeper spiritual level, Lavan had unfinished business, and this is why he pursued Yaakov without being consciously aware of why he was doing so. There were sparks that remained with Lavan, and they had to be transmitted to Yaakov.

In layman's terms, there are tasks which we take on consciously and do our very best to complete. We approach such tasks with all earnestness and undertake to see them through to the end. When we have finished, we assume that there is nothing more to do. But, in truth, sometimes there are forces beyond us at work. Since they are beyond us, we may not know what they have in store for us. If in truth there is more work for us to do, the task returns to us, just as it returned to Yaakov when Lavan caught up with him. We do the best we can, but if there is more than meets the eye, the One Above makes sure to find a way to enable us to finish our mission.

[There is a similar lesson regarding the "small jars" that Rashi says Yaakov returned to collect after dividing his family and sending the women on their way with his sons. (See Rashi on Genesis 32:25.) Sometimes, while dealing with the large picture, we neglect small details within ourselves that can be vital to our success. Sometimes, for all that we do to prepare for the physical task at hand, tending to all of the logistics required to put together a business deal (like Yaakov did when trying to appease his brother Esav), we forget that there is inner work to do. Then, we need to go back inside of ourselves and ask some basic questions: "Who am I? What am I trying to achieve? What is my goal in life?" Some introspection and perhaps some minor adjustments in the path may be necessary. Creating the necessary inner peace and equilibrium may be just as important as creating the external factors to ensure success. When the Torah says that "Yaakov remained alone" (Genesis 32:25), and Rashi says that Yaakov returned for the "small jars," perhaps what we are meant to understand is that he took time out for introspection and creating the proper climate inside to deal with his brother Esav. It's all about making an appropriate vessel (*kli*) to receive high spiritual illumination from Above. And sometimes the small details inside are what guarantee external success.][4]

From Likutei Sichot of the Lubavitcher Rebbe,
vol. 25, pp. 168–176, and vol. 15, pp. 259–264

NOTES

1. The source of Rashi's comment is the Talmud (*Shabbat* 33b) as well as *Breishit Rabba* (79:5, with variations). Other commentators (Rashbam, Chizkuni, Bahai, Akeida) explain that Shalem is the name of a city, but Rashi adopts the explanation of the Gemara.

2. Rashi does not mention (as the Midrash does) that Yaakov's gifts to Esav were worth nine years of work, because this does not fit with *pshuto shel mikra* — the simple meaning of the text.

3. See Ohr HaTorah of the Tzemach Tzedek, parshat Vayeitzei in vol 5 of Bereishit, page 869. There he quotes from the Magid of Mezritch that "Lavan ran after Yaakov to give him letters of the Torah that Yaakov had left behind with him."

4. The ideas contained in this paragraph are not from the *Likutei Sichot* above, but added by the translator.

The Outgoing Personality

Vayishlach
34:1

When it comes to the personalities of our patriarchs and matriarchs — as well as of the twelve sons of Yaakov, who were the progenitors of the Twelve Tribes of Israel — we don't have a lot of information to go by. Based on hints in the Torah, we can make certain assumptions, but it is difficult to accurately describe the personalities of our biblical ancestors. This is especially true of the women of the Torah. But in this week's Torah portion — *Parshat Vayishlach* — we get some hints about Leah and her daughter Dinah that are tantalizing and need more investigation…

As the Torah begins Dinah's story, she went strolling outside of the encampment of her father's household: "And Dinah, daughter of Leah, who was born to Yaakov, went out to meet the daughters of the land…" (Genesis 34:1).

Rashi comments, "Was Dinah the daughter of Leah, but not of Yaakov? Because of her outgoing nature, the Torah verse describes her as the 'daughter of Leah,' since Leah was also outgoing."[1]

Where do we see that Leah was outgoing? Where the Torah relates, "And when Yaakov came from the fields in the evening, Leah went out to meet him. She said, 'You will come to me …' And he was with her that night." (Genesis 30:16).

On the surface, Rashi's comment about Leah seems to be negative. Yet, why would Rashi, whose task is to clarify the simple meaning of the text (*pshat*) make a derogatory comment about Leah?

We cannot answer that Rashi's intention was to minimize the insult to Dinah and excuse her by suggesting that her behavior was not really her fault, since she was the daughter of Leah who was "outgoing." It simply would not be appropriate to excuse Dinah's behavior in such a way, at the expense of her mother.

And if Rashi's intention was to explain the extra words in the Torah — "daughter of Leah, who was born to Yaakov," whereas it would have been simpler to just say that she was the "daughter of Leah and Yaakov" — this discrepancy could be explained by his commentary elsewhere, specifically on Genesis 30:21. There, Rashi comments in a manner favorable to Leah, saying that she could have had another son, but she "pronounced a judgment on herself, 'If this pregnancy turns out to be a boy, then my sister Rachel [who was barren until then and who relied on her maidservant Bilhah to give birth on her behalf] will not even be equal to one of the maidservants. So, she prayed and the embryo transformed into a girl.'" That is, we could have easily explained that Dinah was the daughter of Leah because Leah actively prayed for a daughter, not because both Leah and Dinah were "outgoing."

However, most difficult of all to explain is Leah's act of going out to meet her husband in the fields to request that he spend the night with her. But as bad as it sounds, the results were good, for the Torah tells us, "God heard Leah. She conceived and bore a fifth son to Yaakov." (Genesis 30:17). And Rashi goes on to explain that Leah went out to meet Yaakov because she "desired to establish many tribes." So, how can we say that her going out to meet Yaakov was an act that warranted a negative character description?

Indeed, it appears that Rashi's intention was just the opposite! He wished to inform us that just as Leah's outgoing nature was positive, so Dinah's outgoing nature was also positive.[2]

Here is how we may explain this:

Earlier in our Torah portion, (Genesis 32:23), we read that when Yaakov prepared to meet his brother Esav, he divided up his camp, as the Torah relates, "And he got up that night and took … his eleven children…" At that point, Binyamin was not yet born, so there were only eleven sons. "But where was Dinah?" Rashi asks, and he answers, "Yaakov put her in a trunk and locked it, so that his brother Esav would not set eyes upon her. For this, Yaakov was punished for keeping her away from his brother, whom she may have transformed into a better person. Instead, she fell into the hands of Shechem."

At first glance, what was Yaakov supposed to do? Should he have endangered his daughter by exposing her to Esav's evil gaze, on the mere chance that Dinah might have had a positive influence on him? And even if so, why was the punishment for not doing this so severe that Dinah fell into the hands of Shechem?

We are forced to conclude that 1) Dinah's power was so strong, that she had the ability to cause Esav to do *teshuva* ("return") to the correct path of Godly service, or that 2) transforming a bad person into a good person is such a great matter that it would have been appropriate to place Dinah in danger, even if there was the mere possibility that she might have transformed Esav for the good.

[Based on the fact that Yaakov was punished for hiding Dinah, we can state with conviction that Dinah certainly would have transformed Esav into a better man. Although Rashi only writes that she "may" have had a positive effect on Esav, he is writing from the perspective of Yaakov, who could not have been sure that Dinah would have, in fact, transformed his brother since, after all, the choice lay with Esav and not with either Dinah or Yaakov.]

Assuming that Dinah would have had a positive influence upon Esav, we can conclude that Rashi's comment about her outgoing nature was a positive comment. Rashi meant to explain that since Dinah had the power to transform Esav into a good person, she certainly had the power, when she went out to "meet the daughters of the land," to have a powerful positive impact on them as well. Her outgoing nature was not immodest at all; in fact, she had the capability to transform and improve the lives of the "daughters of the land."

Rather, Rashi's intention was to explain that this positive character trait — the ability to positively transform the life of others — was something that Dinah received from her mother. With his question, "Was Dinah the daughter of Leah, but not of Yaakov?" Rashi intended to hint to us that Dinah's outgoing qualities were something she inherited from Leah, and not from Yaakov, who — quite the opposite — hid her in a trunk.

Nevertheless, this analysis requires more investigation. For, when we look closely, we see that Rashi's example of Leah's outgoing behavior is not really similar to Dinah's. Leah's guiding mission was to have more children [i.e. "she desired to establish many tribes"] and that's why she went out to meet her husband Yaakov as she did (Genesis 30:16).

However, Dinah's mission was to positively influence "the daughters of the land." What exactly was the connection between Leah's desire to "establish many tribes" and Dinah's ability to transform the lives of the "daughters" or that of Esav?

This question is particularly intriguing, since Rashi explains the Torah verse, "And Leah's eyes were soft" (Genesis 29:17) as "Leah was used to crying over her possible marriage to Esav, since everyone who knew Rivkah and Lavan (who were sister and brother), constantly said: "Rivkah has two sons, and Lavan has two daughters; the older son (Esav) will marry the older daughter (Leah) and the younger son (Yaakov) will marry the younger daughter (Rachel)." But Leah did not want to marry Esav, even though she may have had it within her power to transform him into a better man. And if so, what is the connection in all this with Dinah?

The best way to answer is with an explanation from the "inner dimensions" of the Torah — that is from the teachings of Kabbalah and Chassidut. As follows:

Even though all three — Avraham, Yitzchak and Yaakov — are called our forefathers, since they all bequeathed their spiritual genes to us, the Jewish people, nevertheless we have a stronger and more direct connection with Yaakov than with either Avraham or Yitzchak. This is because Yaakov sired the Twelve Tribes of Israel, all of whom passed on to us the traits found in the Jewish people.

Unlike Avraham and Yitzchak who each produced one good and one wicked son, Yaakov produced only the righteous descendants from whom we stem. This is why we are called by the same name as Yaakov, whom God renamed Israel — we are the Nation of Israel.

It follows then that the matriarchs — Sarah, Rivkah, Rachel and Leah, as well has Bilhah and Zilpah — functioned as intermediaries between Yaakov and his sons to develop the specific paths of divine service that were expressed by the tribes and passed on from them to us.

To illustrate, the relations between Yaakov and the matriarchs is similar to the relationship described in the *Tanya* (Ch. 2). There it says that the father contributes the raw matter (in the form of a "drop" from his mind), but that the mother is responsible for the development of the embryo into a human being. And that is why it was matriarchs alone who gave each and every son born to them (and therefore each and every tribe of Israel) its name. And that name was specific to that particular tribe's service of God (*avodat Hashem*).

Although the tribes all existed in potential "within Yaakov," nevertheless they were not distinguishable while still a part of Yaakov's physiognomy. He could not discern their individual paths of *avodat Hashem* before they were born, and that's why it fell to their mothers give them their names.

Even though the twelves sons — i.e. the Twelve Tribes of Israel — represented twelve distinct paths in *avodat Hashem*, in general they may be divided into two: 1) the path of *tzaddikim* (those who were born righteous and never sinned), and 2) the path of the *ba'alei teshuvah* (those who have strayed from the path and returned).

Now, it must be said that the path of *teshuvah* is not limited to *ba'alei teshuvah*, and it may be adopted by *tzaddikim* as well, since no matter how righteous we are, we can always experience distance from God and want to come closer to Him. And the path of the *tzaddikim* may also be used by *ba'alei teshuvah*, since sometimes the need to immerse ourselves in Torah and fulfill its mitzvoth is greater than the need to feel regret over our distance from God. In general, the distinction is not necessarily between people, but between different types of divine service. The path of *tzaddikim* is found within the world of holiness, while the path of *teshuvah* is found among those who must go out into the world, in order to transform "bad" into "good." And that is the difference between the *avodah* associated with those tribes of Israel who are the descendants of the sons of Leah and those who are the descendants of the sons of Rachel.

From the Zohar, we know that the most important part of the altar of the Temple was located in the portion of Israel associated with Binyamin (a son of Rachel). It was not found within portion of the tribe of Yehudah (a son of Leah), even though the tribe of Yehudah was the "pinnacle" of the tribes (the strongest and most modest of the tribes). The reason for this was that Binyamin was a *tzaddik*, while Yehudah was not. And even though Yehudah did *teshuvh* (over the sale of his brother Yosef into slavery), the altar had to be in a section that was associated with a *tzaddik* and not with a *baal teshuvah*.

From this it is understood that the ten brothers who participated in the sale of Yosef and later did *teshuvah* were *baalei teshuvah*, and not *tzaddikim*. But, Yosef and Binyamin, the two sons who did not participate in the sale, remained *tzaddikim* their entire lives.

We could take this one step further and suggest that these two categories of *avodah* were established by the two sisters, Rachel and Leah. It was Leah who founded the path of *teshuvah* (and therefore her sons were *baalei teshuvah*), and it was Rachel who established the path of *tzaddikim*, and passed it on to her sons, Yosef and Binyamin.

At this point, we can add a new interpretation to the phrase, "And Leah had soft eyes, while Rachel was well shaped and attractive" (Genesis 29:17). The reference to Rachel alludes to the *avodah* of *tzaddikim*, who are righteous from birth, and therefore she was "well shaped and attractive..." She was without blemish or fault.

[Note that "shape" has to do with the arrangement and placement of the limbs, each limb according to its appropriate form, while "attractive" refers to one's countenance, beauty/holiness radiating from the face.[3]]

It was Leah who founded the path of teshuvah (and therefore her sons were baalei teshuvah), and it was Rachel who established the path of tzaddikim, and passed it on to her sons, Yosef and Binyamin.

Leah, on the other hand, alludes to the *avodah* of *baalei teshuvah*, which is why Leah was known for crying — which is why she "had soft eyes" — since crying is associated with the *avodah* of *teshuvah* (the *ba'al teshuvah* feels far from God and cries over his perceived distance).

Now, it is known that "Yaakov loved Rachel" (Genesis 29:18), because Yaakov's approach was that of a *tzaddik*, one who has been righteous his entire life. Yaakov was among those who preferred to "sit in tents" (Genesis 25:27) studying God's law, which is an internal *avodah* within the realm of holiness, rather than to leave the "tents" and get involved with matters outside the realm of holiness.

This is also why — from the perspective of the *avodah* of *teshuvah* — Leah was deemed an appropriate wife for Esav (who needed transformation).

Applying our interpretation from the "inner dimensions" of Torah to Rashi's commentary, Dinah was described as "outgoing" because she was the daughter of Leah. Leah was the mother of the "outgoing" sons of Yaakov, whose task was "outside," in the external world, for the purpose of elevating that world. Through their *avodah* "outside," Leah's offspring were able to elevate even those aspects of the world that were not holy. And so Dinah, too, was "outgoing," because Dinah's ability to influence the "outside" was a trait that she inherited from her mother, Leah. That's why the verse refers to Dinah as the "daughter of Leah," since her form of *avodat Hashem* was to transform that which was "outside."

Inititally, Leah's "outgoing" trait was not obvious. Still, it was latent within her, and it came to full fruition in the children to whom she gave birth. And that is why Leah did not wish to marry Esav. However, she did go out to meet her husband, Yaakov, and as a result of this, she gave birth to more sons, whose *avodah* was to be "outgoing."

Ultimately, this trait fully emerged among Leah's offspring (both the sons and her daughter, Dinah) and became a full-fledged path of *avodat Hashem.*

To this we can add, that even though the "outside" brought trouble for Dinah (in the form of Shechem), the reason for that is explained simply by Rashi, who wrote that this was a punishment for Yaakov since he hid Dinah from his brother Esav. From this alone, we may deduce that Dinah's act of going out to "meet the daughters of the land," was not a negative deed, since her intentions were for the sake of heaven and she sought to transform others for the better. Perhaps we might even suggest that there was some good that emerged from Dinah's experience with Shechem. To a limited extent, the men of Shechem were transformed for the good, when her brothers succeeded in persuading them to circumcise themselves.

The process of "conversion" (*giyur*) — in order for the people of Shechem to join the family of Yaakov — required this, and this conversion applied not only to the males of Shechem, but also to females ("the daughters of the land"), as the Torah states quoting the sons of Yaakov, "We will consent, on this condition ... that you circumcise yourselves ... and then we will take your daughters for ourselves." (Genesis 34:15) That is, even though the men of Shechem deserved the death penalty because of their sins, which is why Shimon and Levi (Dinah's brothers) killed them, nevertheless, the desire of Dinah to transform and uplift the "daughters of the land" was fulfilled to a certain degree when the men circumcised themselves. By so doing, they made a covenant with the family of Avraham, Yitzchak and Yaakov.

That and more — "the daughters of the land," about whom Dinah was so concerned, were taken captive by the sons of Yaakov, and most likely served as maidservants in the households of her brothers.

Finally, there is here a lesson for all Jewish women. Even though the role of a Jewish woman is to be modest — since it is written "the entire honor of a woman is internal," (Psalms 45:14) and "she is the pillar of the house"[4] — her main purpose is to build a Jewish home and therefore she needs to remain "inside." Nevertheless, those women who have been blessed with abilities that allow them to have influence "outside" should make use of their abilities to bring the "daughters of the land," who are found "outside," into a better situation.

Although it is obvious that such efforts must be appropriately modest, so that even when the Jewish women go "outside," it is always recognizable that "the entire honor of the Jewish woman is internal," still, it is their responsibility to influence those Jewish women who are wandering "outside," and to bring them into the fold.

The natural softness and kindness of women will help them succeed in this work of "bringing hearts together" (*kiruv halevavot*). As we see clearly, when we work with others to draw them closer to God and His Torah in a pleasant and peaceful manner, we are much more successful. And the effect as well, is much more "internal" and lasts longer, than when we use argumentative and aggressive tactics as is the nature of men, since "it is the nature of man to conquer" (Rashi on Gen 1:28).

God created women this way, and it is understood that it's up to them utilize their strengths fully, not only in the house but also by having influence outside, in order to draw the Jewish daughters closer to their "Father in Heaven."

From Likutei Sichot of the Lubavitcher Rebbe,
vol. 35, pp. 150–155

NOTES

1. The Shach on the Torah suggests that Dinah was a male (perhaps a "male soul") and "it is the nature of a male be outgoing." The Lubavitcher Rebbe (in his *biur* to "Seven Torot of the Ba'al Shem Tov in Gan Eden") explains that a "male" or "female" soul is not an indication of gender, but rather whether the soul is "outgoing" or "introverted."

2. Nor does Rashi mention the Midrash (*Breishit Rabba* Ch. 80:1 at the end) that gives a negative interpretation.

3. These characteristics result from the perfect fulfillment of the 248 positive commands (called "limbs") and the 365 negative commands (called "sinews") which are associated with God's countenance.

4. Note that this is said regarding Rachel (Rashi on Gen 31:4, see also 46:19). Bereishit Rabba 71:2, Bamidbar Rabba 14:8)

THE STORY OF DINA

Vayishlach 34:7

Our Torah portion — *Parshat Vayishlach* — contains one of the more disturbing events that occur in the Torah. It relates that after our forefather, Yaakov returned to the Land of Israel (then called Canaan) with his entire family — including four wives and twelve sons and one daughter — he settled near the city of Shechem.

And this is where the very upsetting events occurred. Here is what happened:

Yaakov's daughter, Dinah, took it upon herself to get to know the "daughters of the land," and she went out to meet them. In the process, one of the "sons of the land" saw her, fell in love with her, violated her and then sought to marry her. But, as the Torah states, "he had committed an outrage against Israel to lie with a daughter of Yaakov; such a thing should not be done…" (Genesis 34:7)

This particular "son of the land" was named Shechem (like the city), and his father, described by the Torah as the "lord of the land," was named Chamor (which means "donkey," and implies *chumriyut,* or "physicality"). Shechem got his father involved, and they tried to cut a deal with Yaakov and his sons in order to enable both clans to live together in peace, do business together and marry each other's daughters. The sons of Yaakov seemingly agreed, but only on the condition that the men of Shechem circumcise themselves. Chamor had no trouble convincing the men, by telling them that, once this condition was met, all of Yaakov's family wealth would pass to them.[1] But once the men of the city of Shechem had circumcised themselves and were in a weakened state, two sons of Yaakov — Shimon and Levi — killed them, ransacked the place and freed their sister.

There are a lot of perspectives on this narrative that we can well imagine. One is the perspective of the other people who were living in the area at the time. They undoubtedly looked upon this as an act of aggression, which made them nervous and wary of Yaakov and his family. However, the contemporary dwellers of the land also had a tradition (Rashi on Gen 34:30, Bereishit Rabba 12) that the "children of Yaakov" would one day conquer the entire land of Canaan, so they maintained a healthy distance from Yaakov and his clan. In fact, the Torah records that as Yaakov and his family travelled away from Shechem following these events, "the fear of God" imbued the inhabitants and they refrained from attacking Yaakov. (Genesis 35:5)

Then, there is the perspective of Yaakov, who was disturbed by the events. He was afraid that his sons' action would disturb his relations with the surrounding people, with whom he preferred to live in peace. As he told his sons (Genesis 34:30), "You have churned the waters," meaning "clouded" his relations with the surrounding people.[2] Yaakov was also concerned about his sons' behavior from another perspective; he suspected that they were motivated not only by righteous reasons and zealousness to revenge their sister, but by a proclivity toward violence. Only when they said to him, "Should we allow our sister to be treated like a harlot?!" did Yaakov relax his suspicions and accept their explanation (Genesis 34:31).

Yet another perspective is that of Shimon and Levi, for what could have motivated them to commit such a rash and violent act? The clearest indication of their motivation is their own statement: "Should we allow our sister to be treated like a harlot?" In other words, Shimon and Levi were deeply angered by how their sister was treated. Indeed, they were so outraged at the inhabitants of the land and their immoral society, that they did not stop to think matters through, as their father Yaakov would have wanted them to. Instead, they acted out of a deep sense of commitment to the principles by which they lived, as well as to the principles of family loyalty. Those principles should have been shared, in theory, by the inhabitants of Shechem, since all of mankind had adopted mores of sexual propriety after the Flood. Indeed, all the descendants of Noach (*bnei Noach*) had promised not to engage in sexual immorality of any kind. Therefore, Shimon and Levi felt a high degree of righteous indignation, in addition to personal betrayal, over the way that their sister was treated. In their estimation, there was no room for any kind of deals. According to their reckoning, whoever acted against the rules of civilized society and mistreated their sister in this manner, had to be eliminated.

Looking at their actions "objectively," there is a basis to say that the brothers acted correctly (although there are also biblical commentators who suggest otherwise). There were several reasons why Shimon and Levi were justified in killing all of the adult males of Shechem.[3] In fact, we know that the two brothers did not transgress any sin, since the people of Shechem were already subject to a death sentence either because they failed to administer justice to Shechem for his misdeed,[4] or because of previous misdeeds of a similar nature by the entire population.[5]

As well, we see clearly that the brothers were carrying out God's divine will. A later passage in the Torah, when Yaakov is blessing his sons on his deathbed, makes this plain. Referring to Shimon and Levi, Yaakov says, "In their anger they killed a man..." (Genesis 49:6). While this may not sound positive at first glance, the Midrash[6] points out: "Did they kill only *one* man? The Torah says that they killed all the men of the city! But all of them together were no more than one man in the eyes of God." The use of the word "man" (according to the explanation of the Midrash) makes sense if the behavior of Shimon and Levi was acceptable in the eyes of God. Then, since all the males of Shechem were "like one man" in the eyes of God, we could say the same of Shimon and Levi — the males of Shechem carried the same "weight" in the eyes of the two brothers as they carried in God's perspective. The implication is that Shimon and Levi acted with divine assistance and carried out God's will.

Finally, the brothers acted out of righteous indignation (as noted previously), and not only out of a sense of personal outrage. As mentioned, the *bnei Noach* who encompassed all of mankind before the Torah was given, agreed to act with respect toward women. It was considered totally unacceptable to rape a woman, or even to engage in any kind of a relationship outside of marriage. Sexual impropriety was forbidden to *bnei Noach*, and a violation of the Seven Noachide Laws was punishable by death. Therefore, the brothers acted primarily out of a desire to execute justice and to "right the wrongs" that the people of Shechem had committed, in addition to giving vent to a sense of personal outrage.

On the other hand, there were several aspects of the brothers' action that were problematic.

First of all, they made life difficult for their father, as we known from his initial reaction. He told them, "You churned the waters." By this he meant that his sons caused a "desecration of God's name" (*chillul Hashem*) in clouding his relations with the people of the land. The last thing that Yaakov wanted at this stage of his life was a protracted struggle with his neighbors, and yet he suspected that is exactly what his sons' behavior would precipitate.

Given that Yaakov did not criticize his sons' behavior, but only its result ("You have clouded the waters...") and given that their act was in keeping with God's will (as explained earlier), then we must conclude that Yaakov also agreed with the killing of the men of Shechem. However, he was not happy with the way in which the brothers carried out the death sentence, since their behavior hurt his relations with the rest of the people of the land. This can be explained in one of two different ways: a) Either Yaakov regretted that Shimon and Levi killed all the residents of Shechem because the subterfuge caused a *chillul Hashem*, and he felt it would have been better to let them live,[7] or, b) Yaakov believed that the men of Shechem should have been killed, but not by subterfuge. Rather, the brothers should have killed them outright. Since in the eyes of God, they were all like "one man," there was no reason to fear them.

As well, Yaakov felt that their act, even if justified, smacked of professional murder. It was akin to the kind of behavior that was to be expected from his brother Esav, but not from Yaakov's sons. Yaakov suspected (and later events bore out his suspicions) that, underneath the brothers' righteous anger, there lurked a streak of violence, and that is why he was not happy with them.

Finally, there is room to suggest that even if their act was justified as a fulfillment of God's will, they disrespected their father by acting without consulting him. Assuming that *bnei Noach* are obligated to respect their parents (which is a subject for discussion), the very least they were obligated to do was inform their father before they impulsively carried out their plan, especially since their actions affected the entire family of which he was the head.

Their failure to do so raises questions about the obligation of *bnei Noach* to respect and honor their parents. Indeed, Rashi touches on this issue in his commentary on the Torah verse describing how "the two sons of Yaakov, Shimon and Levi, brothers of Dinah, each took his up sword" (Genesis 34:25). He points out that the description seems superfluous, since at this point it is well known that they were Yaakov's sons, but the wording means to convey the message that "even though they were sons of Yaakov, they acted like 'other people' who were not Yaakov's sons, since they did not seek his advice." From this we learn that they should have, despite their righteous justification, consulted their father. The implication is that simple respect demanded it. From Rashi's comment, it would appear that *bnei Noach* were obligated to honor their parents. But is that correct?

According to the Talmud (*Sanhedrin* 56b), a few weeks before the giving of the Torah at Mt. Sinai, God commanded the children of Israel to honor their parents. This happened at Marah, one of their stops in the desert. There God gave them three mitzvoth in addition to the original Seven Noachide Laws (*Sanhedrin* 56b) by which they had been obligated all along. These new three were: Honor your father and mother; keep Shabbat; and obey the civil laws concerning your fellow men. From the fact that the Jews were commanded to honor their parents as a unique and distinct mitzvah after they left Egypt, we can deduce that it was *not* required of the rest of mankind before the Torah was given. For if it were, it would have already been included in the Seven Noachide Laws and it would not have been necessary to spell it out at Marah. Therefore, it seems as if Shimon and Levi had no particular obligation to demonstrate respect for Yaakov by consulting with him before acting. And yet, it seems that we can find some traces of an obligation to honor parents among the *bnei Noah.*

Rashi, for example, tells us at the end of *Parshat Noach* that Avraham did not forfeit this mitzvah when he left his father in Charan though he was old and weak.[8] He also tells us that Yaakov was punished for not maintaining any connection with his father Yitzchak during the twenty-two years that he toiled for Lavan by being separated from his son Yosef for the same amount of time.[9] If so, then there was at least a rudimentary form of "honoring parents" among *bnei Noach.*

However, the Talmud (*Sanhedrin* 56b) clearly implies that the *bnei Noach* were not obligated in the mitzvah of honoring their parents. So how can we square this with the commentary of Rashi?

Earlier in the Book of Genesis, we read the story of Ham, one of the three sons of Noach, who intentionally disgraced his father and was cursed (Genesis 9:22–25). And then we read Rashi's commentary describing Lavan as "wicked" (*rasha*) because he pushed in front of his father to answer a question (Rashi on Genesis 24:50). In these cases, though, we can explain that even though *bnei Noach* were not commanded to "honor" their parents, they were expected not to disgrace or disrespect them.[10]

It is possible that this injunction can be learned from the behavior of ravens. We know that even if the Torah were not given, we would have been obligated to glean certain proper behaviors from animals in nature (Rashi on *Eruvin* 100b), and the *bnei Noach* would have been included in that obligation. And about ravens it is written, "The eye that mocks a father, that scorns an aged mother, will be pecked out by the ravens of the valley, will be eaten by the vultures." (Proverbs 30:17) So from ravens, the *bnei Noach* we would have learned not to mock, scorn or disgrace their elders.[11]

We know that even if the Torah were not given, we would have been obligated to glean certain proper behaviors from animals in nature (Rashi on Eruvin 100b), and the bnei Noach would have been included in that obligation.

However, the obligation of Avraham and also of Yaakov to honor their parents was qualitatively different. Here, the issue is not disgracing or scorning parents, but rather failure to honor their parents. And if so, the question remains: Were the sons of Yaakov — who were *bnei Noach* at the time — commanded to honor their parents?

In order to resolve the question of *bnei Noach* and their obligation (or lack thereof) to honor their parents, it is necessary to first understand the purpose of the Seven Noachide Laws. This, in turn, will help us to understand the purpose of existence of all kinds of people, Jews and non-Jews alike, and to grasp the importance of the respective missions of each in this world.

The sages tell us that the universe was created in order to enable the Jews to fulfill their mission of illuminating and uplifting the world by fulfilling the Torah's 613 mitzvoth.[12] However, in order to facilitate this, it is important to have a civilized society. If the basics of civilization — not to murder, not to steal, not to engage in sexual immorality etc., are not present, it becomes very difficult to have a foundation for creating a Torah environment.

Therefore, God gave the non-Jews these seven mitzvoth — the Seven Noachide Laws — in order to enable the establishment of a civilized world. These laws exist not only for the sake of the non-Jews, so that they live in a civilized world; they are also meant to establish a foundation for the Jews and enable them to fulfill their 613 mitzvoth. That's what is meant by the statement that the world was created for the sake of the Jews (Yirmiyahu 2:3, Bereishit Rabba 1:1). While the 613 mitzvoth possess intrinsic value and Jews fulfill them in order to turn this lowly world into a dwelling place for God, the non-Jews fulfill Seven Noachide Laws in order "to settle the world" (*lashevet yatzra*).[13] For the Jews to fulfill their own mission, it is important that the non-Jews do what they can to establish a world that is free of negative influences. For such a world to exist, and indeed become a refined and perfected world, it is necessary for the non-Jews to fulfill the Seven Noachide Laws. These include commandments that are between man and his neighbors (for example, establishing courts of justice) and those that are between man and the One Above (for example, rejecting idolatry). In this manner, non-Jews prepare and establish the world so that the Jews can perfect and elevate all creation to a state that is "beyond creation" — a dwelling place for the One Above.

Since honoring one's mother and father is certainly one of the cornerstones of "settling the world," it is included in the category of *dinim*, which according to the Ramban incorporates all of the civil laws that govern the non-Jewish world. This mitzvah — in its most complete form — was given to the Jews at Marah, but even before then, it was part of "settling the world" in its simple form, and as such was an obligation of the *bnei Noach*.[14] Nevertheless, since before the giving of the Torah, this mitzvah was included in the secondary purpose of "settling the world," Shimon and Levi did not sin by failing to consult with their father before carrying out the sentence on the men of Shechem.

In fact, the opposite is true. Since the men of Shechem violated the accepted norms of behavior of *bnei Noach* of that time by permitting the son of their ruler to rape Dinah, there was no room for consultations, not even with their father. The immediate task before the brothers was to re-instate the rule of law in accordance with the purpose of their existence. Only by killing the culprits could the brothers restore "the settling of the world" to its proper place. Therefore, their clear priority was to eliminate the men of Shechem. Their action was the correct response, as befit *bnei Noach*. And therefore, the brothers proceeded without consulting with their father.

In other words, if honoring one's parents were a commandment in its own right, they would been required to fulfill the will of God by consulting with their father even when circumstances dictated immediate action. But since, at the time, the reason to honor one's parents was for the sole purpose of "settling the world," then the proper conduct was just the opposite and the sons of Yaakov fulfilled their obligation of "settling the world" by acting decisively (even without consulting their father).[15]

At this point, we can finally appreciate what Shimon and Levi did when "each took up his sword." The abominable act inflicted on their sister, so touched the brothers in the very essence of their soul (in a negative way, obviously), that they conducted themselves as if they were "other people" — not the sons of Yaakov. They were so overtaken with zeal that there was no room for any other feeling, and so each one of them grabbed his weapon.

Yaakov's only concern was that his sons acted not only out of righteous indignation, but also because they possessed a negative trait of violence inside them that they should have uprooted. It was this blemish in their personalities that the Torah alludes to by calling them the "sons of Yaakov," even though that was clear (as indicated by Rashi). It was for that purpose (and not because of the act of killing) that they should have consulted with Yaakov.

After all of the biblical perspectives outlined above, there remains one more to explore. And that is, what do we — those of us living in this generation — derive from this story?

It turns out that from Shimon and Levi, we learn the age of Bar Mitzvah. Shimon and Levi were thirteen years old at the time of these events, yet the Torah calls them "men." From this, the rabbis deduce that thirteen is the age of maturity when a boy accepts upon himself the yoke of the 613 mitzvoth and becomes a man.

From Shimon and Levi we also derive an instruction for all Bar-Mitzvah-aged Jewish youth. When we are faced with a situation which demands that we act zealously and without compromise, we need to act without hesitation. Such situations occur every time we are faced with temptations. Since it is our eyes and our ears that lead us into temptation and from there, to transgression, a real "man" has to know how to fend off the temptations of his senses.

We are commanded "Do not follow after your heart or your eyes" (Numbers 15:39), because doing so separates us from the One Above just like a "harlot" separates a wife from her husband. Under such circumstances, there is no reason to even consider acting in a limited capacity. At that point we must act with total abandon — with total selfless devotion (*mesirat nefesh*) — in order to escape from the clutches of the temptation and protect our own spiritual health.

Once that message has sunk in — and we are capable of arousing our own reservoirs of *mesirat nefesh* in order to protect ourselves and the honor of the Jewish people — then we can begin to act according to logic and intellect, in a measured manner as defined by the Torah. But, in order to get there, each one of us must take up our "sword" which represents our reservoir of devotion that is beyond logic and intellect, and we must be prepared to act with selfless devotion when the situation demands it.

From Likutei Sichos of the Lubavitcher Rebbe, vol 5, Page 150–162

NOTES

1. "Their livestock, their possessions and all their cattle, won't it all be ours?" (Genesis 34:23)

2. Yaakov was not concerned solely with the safety of himself and his household. Rather, his concern was also over potential *chillul Hashem* ("desecration of the name of God") that his sons' behavior may have created. For if the action itself was proper, he would not have later said about the brothers, "In their *anger* they killed a man." And all the more so, he would not have said that that they used "violence," and that "violence is the province of Esav."

3. The Radak (Gen 34:27) says, "Many [of the inhabitants of Shechem] saw that he kidnapped Dinah, and they failed to protest." Here, some investigation is necessary to determine if there is such thing as a "death sentence" carried out by man, over failure to protest a wrongdoing. The Ohr Hachaim says that they were culpable because, "all the people of the city sought to prevent their king from being killed, or because some of them actually aided Shechem to capture Dinah." But if so, the Ohr Hachaim fails to explain why Yaakov was so angry with his sons, to the extent that he later said, "The instruments of violence are their wares."

4. Rambam, *Hilchot Melachim* end of Ch. 9.

5. Ramban in his commentary on the Torah (Genesis 32:13), and Ran on *Sanhedrin* 56b.

6. *Midrash Rabba* 99:7 and *Midrash Tanhuma, Vayechi* 10.

7. Possibly, Yaakov knew that the only way to kill the men of Shechem was by fooling them as Shimon and Levi did, but Yaakov was unhappy with the *chilul*

Hashem that this entailed. And therefore he held that it was better to leave them alive, similar to the case of the Gibonim described in the Talmud (*Gittin* 46a). The Gibonim turned out to be from the Canaanites who should have been killed by the Jews entering the Land under Yehoshua, but they fooled the Jews into thinking that they were not Canaanites. Since the Jews promised not to kill them, they were left alive even after their subterfuge was discovered.

8. It cannot be said that this is because Avraham fulfilled the entire Torah even before it was given (*Kiddushin* 82a, *Yoma* 22b), because (aside from the fact that according to the Ramban, Avraham only kept the entire Torah when he was in *Eretz Yisrael* but not when he was outside of the Land, and his father lived in Charan, outside of Israel), it is not appropriate to suggest that the nations of the world (*bnei Noach*) would come to him with such a claim: "You failed to honor your father even though it is a commandment of the Torah."

9. *Megillah* 17a, Rashi (*yashan*) end of *Parshat Toldot*, *Parshat Vayeishev* 37:34. It could be suggested that the fact that Yaakov did not receive any "honor" from Yosef during the twenty-two years that Yosef was in Egypt was not a "punishment," but rather a "result" of Yaakov's own failure to maintain a relationship of "honor" with his father Yitzchak while laboring for Lavan. Since in any case, as *bnei Noach* they were not "commanded" to fulfill the mitzvah of honoring their parents, all the more so they were not "guilty" when they failed to fulfill this mitzvah. Instead, this was a matter of "cause and effect" — since Yosef was not aware of any honor that his father Yaakov extended to Yitzchak, therefore, Yosef himself did not feel any obligation to go out of his way to honor Yaakov (see Rashi end of *Parshat Toldot*). But, from the language of the Talmud (Megillah 16b-17a) — "he wasn't punished" (for the period of fourteen years that he learned Torah with Shem v'Eber) — it implies that he was punished for the remaining twenty two years that he was out of contact with Yitzchak, and therefore there must have been a mitzvah to honor their parents.

10. From this we may derive a straightforward explanation of why it is forbidden for converts to Judaism to disgrace or strike their biological parents, so that they will not be able to say, "My origins were stricter..." — for *bnei Noach* were also commanded not to disgrace their parents. (Rambam, *Hilchot Mamrim* 5:11; Tur and *Shulchan Aruch*, *Yoreh Deah* 241, and see R' Akiva Eiger there).

11. Theoretically, it should be possible to derive this *halachah* from the narrative in the Torah itself, which records that Ham was punished for disgracing his father.

12. This is a *drasha* from the sages on the first verse of the Torah: *Midrash Tanhuma* 3 and 5, also *Breishit Rabba* beginning of Ch 1, and Rashi on the first verse of the Torah.

13. Isaiah 45:18. This directive applies to *bnei Noach* as well as to Jews.

14. Accordingly, the language the Rashi chooses to use in a number of places (*Megillah* 16b, and in commentary on the Torah, end of *Parshat Noach*), becomes understood: Rashi writes, "honoring his father," and not "the mitzvah of honoring his father" — which is the commonly used phraseology elsewhere, because at this time, there was no separate commandment to "honor one's parents." Instead, it was a detail within the category of *dinim*.

15. Though at first glance, the claim that Levi and Shimon did not consult with their father seems to be a fault in their behavior, nevertheless, Yaakov at the time accepted their reasoning, "Should we allow our sister be treated like a harlot?!" and relaxed his criticism. Nevertheless, he rebuked them later when their behavior proved that his initial suspicions were correct. When Yaakov became aware that the brothers had sold Yosef into slavery, he realized that there was an element of cruelty within their nature (because about the sale of Yosef, it was impossible explain their act away using the reason of zealousness as they had done with the incident of Dinah). The events with Yosef proved retroactively that within the motivation of Shimon and Levi to avenge their sister's mistreatment, was also mixed a streak of cruelty.

Life of a Tzaddik

Vayeishev 37:1

Parshat Vayeishev begins: "And Yaakov settled in the dwelling place of his father in the land of Canaan." (Genesis 37:1). Commenting on this verse, Rashi says that "Yaakov sought to settle in and relax, but was immediately beset by the problems of Yosef. The righteous seek to settle in quietly, but God says, 'The tranquility that awaits them in the next world should be sufficient, need they seek tranquility in this world as well?'"

The Torah narrative then proceeds to relate how Yaakov's son, Yosef, is sold into slavery by his brothers. Rashi's commentary implies that this happened because Yaakov sought "peace and quiet." In fact, that's exactly what the Midrash (*Breishit Raba* on the verse) says, "On account of Yaakov's request to relax in this world, he was accosted by the troubles of Yosef."[1]

That seems like an unusually harsh consequence. We know that even if *tzaddikim* occasionally make mistakes, their entire lives are devoted to doing good deeds. In this case, Yaakov simply wanted to be left alone in order to serve God in study and prayer. In reality, Yaakov's request was totally appropriate and fitting, since all he sought was to be left in peace to study, pray and meditate. So, how could it be that this resulted in all the bad things that happened to him and his son?

To answer that question, let's begin by understanding the nature of Yaakov's request. In general, *tzaddikim* want to be left alone in order to serve God, not for the sake of their physical health and wellbeing, but in order to fulfill God's will. They seek spiritual peace — but to this, God's reply is that true spiritual peace is a reward reserved for the next world, and does not exist in this world in which we live. In our world, the emphasis is upon labor — the labor of mastering and elevating the physical world. It's true that *tzaddikim* do not seek peace and rest for its own sake, but rather in order to serve God more fully in prayer and meditation. Nevertheless, God rebuffs them because such spiritual service is not the purpose of this world.

This we learn from what happened to Yaakov. He sought peace and tranquility in order to serve God undisturbed. Although in general, this world is a "place for labor," nevertheless God does provide *tzaddikim* with some time for their own personal *avodat Hashem*. He gives them a "taste" of the World to Come as a reward for their selfless divine service in this world. However, in Yaakov's case, he did not get this taste when he requested it. Instead, he was accosted by the "troubles of Yosef." So the question we must ask is: Why was Yaakov made to suffer like this? Had he not already suffered enough in his lifetime?

Apparently, he was accosted by "the troubles of Yosef" because he was not yet on the spiritual level that God wanted to grant him, and these additional travails were meant to uplift him to that higher level.[2]

Ultimately, God did grant a reward to Yaakov, which implies that his desire for some peace — not in the physical sense, but so that he could uplift his *avodat Hashem* — was not improper or out of place. It was an appropriate reward for his lifelong dedication. After the suffering that he endured from the apparent loss of his son, Yaakov did achieve the peace and tranquility that he sought. But, that was not until the final seventeen years of his life, when he moved with his family to Egypt.

But that leaves us even more puzzled.

We know that Yaakov was an honest man — he knew exactly what he deserved and what he could not yet expect. That being the case, why did he request a spiritual reward that was clearly beyond him at the time?

The answer: The tranquility that Yaakov requested was not the reward that he ultimately received. Yaakov only requested enough earthly quiet to enable him to fulfill his *avodat Hashem* without disturbance. He only wanted a break from life's ordeals in order to serve God in prayer and study, without disturbance. And in truth, God granted him this break for a short time. There were nine years during which Yaakov managed to serve God, while raising his family, relatively undisturbed. Those were the years he lived in Hebron — between the events in Shechem (where Dinah was violated) and the sale of Yosef (who, he believed, had been killed by wild animals). For the nine years between these sad events, Yaakov prayed and learned in Hebron without disturbance. Thus, for a short while, he achieved the tranquility and rest that he sought.[3]

But, God wanted to bestow upon Yaakov much more than just a "vacation" from his troubles. God wished to grant to Yaakov full "retirement." God wanted to raise Yaakov to an entirely new spiritual level while still in his lifetime. He wanted to grant him the reward of the World to Come, even as he remained in this world. But in order for that to happen, Yaakov first had to undergo the suffering associated with the loss of his son, Yosef.[4]

Yaakov's suffering was unique. In general, he was no stranger to hardship. He had previously endured the trials and tribulations foisted upon him by his uncle, Lavan, and his brother, Esav. But those hardships we can understand. Lavan and Esav were evil, and it was necessary for Yaakov to struggle against their nefarious aims and overcome them. He fought to maintain a Godly lifestyle while in the house of Lavan, and to redeem the birthright and defend himself against Esav. But, what was the purpose of his suffering over Yosef? In that case, there was no apparent need to stand firm against an adversary, nor was Yaakov aware of any reason that his son should have been taken from him. His suffering seemed to be a decree without reason. It seemed to be suffering merely for the sake of suffering.

But, in reality, it was a test meant to raise Yaakov to a higher spiritual level. His suffering was intended to refine and elevate him. If he could maintain his faith and divine service even while suffering the loss of his son for no apparent reason, then he was worthy of the reward of "retirement" — enjoyment of the World to Come even while living in this physical world.

How can we know that what Yaakov sought — a break from tribulations in order to serve God undisturbed — was not what he received?

The answer is that Yaakov merely wanted peace and quiet to serve God "in the land of his father," the Land of Israel. However, the end of his life was not spent in Israel, but in Egypt. It was there that God granted him the ultimate spiritual reward reserved for the World to Come. Clearly, the reward that God bestowed upon Yaakov was not the one that he sought but something far greater. But in order to receive that reward, Yaakov had to undergo further spiritual refinement through the suffering of Yosef.

This might seem strange since the Land of Israel is especially conducive to service and worship of God, while Egypt was then the lowest spiritual place on earth, where witchcraft and idol worship were practiced. Moreover, one is usually more "at home" in his own land and habitat. Yet, in Egypt, Yaakov found a physically beautiful area (Goshen) that was more tranquil than what he could have found in Israel. Under the protective watch of Yosef and Pharoah, Yaakov found a physical and spiritual tranquility allowed him to serve God with even more than the tranquility that he had requested some thirty years earlier, upon his return to the Holy Land. There, he received God's reward of infinite spirituality.

The answer contains a lesson for all of us. God wants to hear from us. He wants to hear our requests.

We could ask, if it were God's desire to grant Yaakov this reward, why did He wait until Yaakov requested peace and tranquility? If God wanted to grant him something far greater in any case, then why wait until Yaakov wanted something lesser?

The answer contains a lesson for all of us. God wants to hear from us. He wants to hear our requests. He "thirsts for the prayers of the righteous" (*Yevamot* 64a). So if we want the Final Redemption, then we must ask for it. It is up to us to ask, and then God responds with a reward that corresponds to the spiritual level that we deserve.

When all of us pray and plead with God for the Mashiach, He'll soon respond. Like Yaakov, the Jewish people have suffered more than enough in exile. Hopefully, without delay and without further suffering, God will respond by sending the Mashiach. And then the Final Redemption will be at hand.

From Likutei Sichot of the Lubavitcher Rebbe, vol. 30, pp. 176–183

NOTES

1. Even though the *brit bein habetarim* ("covenant between the pieces") required a form of "payment" (the Jews were required to go into exile, as Rashi says on Genesis 36:7), it was not required that the "payment" should come in the form of the "troubles of Yosef." Similarly, the punishment that Yaakov received when Yosef was out of contact with him for twenty-two years because he himself did not fulfill the obligation of honoring his father for twenty-two years (Megillah 17a, Rashi on Genesis 37:34 and end of *Parshat Toldot*) was only a "reason" for the separation itself. It does not explain the anguish and suffering associated with the separation,

to the extent that Yaakov did not even know that his son Yosef was still alive. See the commentators on Rashi, and see also *Likutei Sichot*, vol, 18, p. 130, 133 and on.

2. As the sages said (*Menachot* 53b, *Shemot Rabba* 36a), "When we squeeze the olive, the oil flows out." This saying is mentioned by the fifth Lubavitcher Rebbe, the Rebbe Rashab in regard to the imprisonment and liberation of the Alter Rebbe (see *Torat Shalom* p. 26) on *Yud-Tet Kislev*. See also *Likutei Diburim* of the Previous Rebbe, vol. 1, p. 94a and onward.

3. According to this explanation, the major questions that arise among the commentators regarding Rashi's statement, "Yaakov sought to settle in and relax, but was immediately beset by the problems of Yosef" is resolved. These commentators assume that God rebuffed Yaakov's request to settle in quietly, because "*tzaddikim* get no rest in this world." And therefore, Yaakov was "accosted by the troubles of Yosef." However, according to the current explanation, Yaakov's request was not rebuffed, but was accepted by God and Yaakov received nine years of "rest" while raising his family in Hebron before anything else happened. Moreover, the purpose of the subsequent "troubles of Yosef" was not to deny Yaakov the peace he sought in the "land of his fathers," but to lift him to a yet higher spiritual level. And in order to emphasize that was the purpose of the "troubles of Yosef," God first gave Yaakov nine years of quiet in Hebron before he brought on him the "troubles of Yosef." [Of course, it is understood that the two levels of quiet occurred in ascending order, from the lower level to the higher level. And we might say that the first level (in Hebron) was comparable to the "days of Mashiach" and the second level (in Egypt) was comparable to the "World to Come."]

4. There is an "old Rashi" (an early version of Rashi's commentary that was not clarified against the original) that implies that rather than requesting to "live in peace," Yaakov should have busied himself with conquering the "Kings of Esav." There it states: "Yaakov saw all of the leaders of Esav mentioned above and wondered, 'Who will be able to conquer them? …Yosef!' (See also Rashi's commentary on Genesis 30:25). During the period that Yosef was young, this wasn't possible, but as soon as Yosef became seventeen year old [when men are near their full strength] then began "the troubles of Yosef." Accordingly, the "troubles of Yosef" were "measure for measure" because Yaakov should have involved Yosef in conquering Esav, and when he did not do so, that's when the "troubles with Yosef" began.

Yosef's Dreams...

Vayeishev 37:10

The Ba'al Ha'Tanya made a famous declaration: "We have to live with the times." His Chassidim were puzzled by this until they clarified what the Alter Rebbe meant: "We must live with the weekly Torah portion."

Keeping that in mind, it is hard not to notice that our Torah portion — *Parshat Vayeishev* — is the third of four portions in which dreams play a major role. They begin rather simply in *Parshat Vayeitzei* with Yaakov's dream of a ladder to heaven, and later of his dreams about sheep. In *Parshat Vayishlach*, the dreams are also not complicated. Yaakov dreams of God telling him it's time to leave his father-in-law, Lavan, and Lavan dreams that he is not allowed to hurt Yaakov in any way. But now, in *Parshat Vayeishev*, the dreams get more cryptic. Yosef dreams of his family bowing down to him. This dream is clearly much more complex and requires some interpretation, as we shall see. Then, in next week's Torah portion — *Parshat Mikeitz* — we will read about Pharaoh's dreams, which nobody is able to interpret until Yosef does so with spectacular success.

Why are dreams so prominent this time of year? Perhaps it is because these four Torah portions coincide with the Hebrew month of Kislev. The month of Kislev is associated with sleep, according to the *Sefer Yetzirah*, the earliest extant text of Kabbalah. Kislev is also associated with a sense of "security" (*bitachon*). When we go to sleep with a sense of security, we are able to dream. In summary, Kislev is the month of *bitachon*, of sleep and of dreams, and that is reflected in the Torah portions that we read this month.

When we analyze Yosef's dreams, we will find that their true inner meaning was associated with a vision that occurred much earlier, in the life of Avraham. But first let us explore the simple meaning (*pshat*) of Yosef's dreams with the aid of Rashi…

After first dreaming that he was in the field with his brothers binding sheaves of wheat, and that the sheaves of his brothers bowed down to his sheaves, Yosef dreamt again. This time, he dreamt that the sun and the moon and eleven stars bowed down to him. "He told it to his father and his brothers, and his father rebuked him, saying, 'What is this dream that you have dreamt? Shall we — I, your mother and your brothers — bow to the ground before you?" (Genesis 37:10). Rashi comments on the "Shall we…" as follows:

> [Yaakov implied,] "Has not your mother [Rachel] already died?" But he did not know that the dream was referring to Rachel's maidservant, Bilhah, who raised Yosef as if he were her own son. And from this event, our sages learned that there is no dream devoid of meaningless events.
>
> Yaakov's intention was to "take the sting" out of the matter, so the brothers would not be jealous of Yosef. Therefore, he said, "Shall we…" to indicate to the brothers that just as it was impossible for Yosef's mother to bow down to him (because she was no longer alive), so the rest of the dream was also meaningless nonsense.

Several expositors of Rashi (Mizrahi, Gur Aryeh, and others), say that he is presenting us here with two different explanations:

1. Yaakov was unaware that Yosef's dream referred to Bilhah rather than to Rachel (as per the Midrash, *Breishis Rabba* 84:11).
2. There is no dream that is without some elements of meaningless nonsense (as per the Talmud, *Berachos* 55a).

If so, then according to the first explanation, Yaakov thought that the dream was meaningless nonsense because Rachel was no longer alive and therefore she could not bow down to Yosef.[2] He was mistaken in this understanding, because he did not realize that the dream referred to Bilhah and not to Rachel.[3] But, according to the second explanation, Yaakov knew that the dream was real, and he also knew that the detail about Rachel was a false detail. This is because there is no dream without elements of meaningless nonsense in it, even when the dream itself portrays reality.

Rashi's conclusion applies to the second explanation: He informs us that Yaakov knew that the dream was real.[4] He knew that every true dream has elements of untruth in it, but the brothers did not know this. By pointing out and emphasizing the untrue detail of the dream, Yaakov successfully persuaded the brothers that the entire dream was false, and thus mitigated the effects of the dream in their eyes.

However, when we look at the next verse in the Torah, the "two-explanation" theory of Rashi's expositors becomes questionable. There (in Genesis 37:11), we read that Yaakov "guarded the matter." Rashi explains: "He watched and waited for it to occur." Since Yaakov was "watching and waiting," it was clear that he believed that Yosef's dream was real and would certainly come to fruition, and his only question was *when* it would occur.

To simplify and clarify Rashi's comment, perhaps we could suggest that he sought to give only one explanation, rather than two. Perhaps his explanation is the following: "Yaakov did not know that the dream referred to Bilhah, but he did believe the dream to be real (this we know from the statement that he "guarded the matter"). And then Rashi adds a side point (not intended as a proof for another explanation, but as a derivation from this one): Because Yaakov didn't know that the "moon" alluded to Bilhah and therefore considered that detail to be incorrect, and yet he believed the dream to be true overall, our sages learned from this that "there is no dream that is devoid of meaningless things."

This approach to explaining Rashi is well-grounded because, in general, when Rashi seeks to bring two different explanations, he inserts a phrase between them such as "Another interpretation…" or "Our sages opined…" However, here Rashi uses another transitional phrase: "And from this event, our sages learned that…" From this, we can infer that what follows is not a new comment or explanation, but an addition to the previous comment. Yaakov's opinion was that even though the dream in general was real and was to be taken seriously because it would certainly come to fruition, nevertheless, this particular detail (that his mother would bow before him), was one of the unacceptable elements of the dream, since Rachel was no longer alive. In fact, the "moon bowing down" contained a true element because it referred to Bilhah, but since Yaakov understood the moon was referring to Rachel, he considered this to be a false detail of the dream. Rashi continues, "And from this event, our sages learned that…" Since Yaakov accepted the dream even though he understood that it contained a false element, our sages learned from here learned from here that "there is no dream that is devoid of meaningless/false events."

Finally, Rashi concludes that even though Yaakov knew that the dream would come to fruition, nevertheless he challenged Yosef ("Shall we...") in order to "take the sting out" of the message it contained which was surely going to arouse further anger in the brothers. They did not know that there is such a thing as a dream that is real even though it contains meaningless/false details, and therefore it was possible for Yaakov to persuade them to reject the entire dream ("Just as the detail about Rachel is nonsense, so the entire dream is nonsense"). But Yaakov himself believed Yosef's dream to be real.

But, if we accept this explanation, we have a problem. If, according to Rashi, Yaakov held the entire dream to be true, but he understood that it contained a false detail, then in truth the entire dream is true, and it was just he who got it wrong! And if so, how could the sages "learn from here" that there is no dream that is devoid of meaningless/false events?[5]

In order to answer this question, we need to take a step back and look at the bigger picture in this narrative.

After hearing his son's dreams, the Torah tells us that Yaakov "guarded the matter," which Rashi explains that he "watched and waited" for it to happen. But this is strange. The implication is that Yaakov waited with great anticipation to see Yosef's prediction become reality with Yaakov and his family bowing down to Yosef. Although there is a general rule — that "one is jealous of everyone aside from his son and his student" (*Sanhedrin* 105b), meaning we don't experience jealousy over a child or student who rises to a higher position that we did — nevertheless, it is not reasonable to expect a father to await with great anticipation for the opportunity become a servant to his son. That is just not reasonable.

Some commentators (e.g. *Melechet Hakodesh* on Rashi) claim (basing themselves on the Midrash, *Breishit Rabba* 84:11) that what Yaakov was waiting for was the resurrection of the dead.[6] That is, Yaakov's great anticipation was not over Yosef's impending reign as a king (for bowing down to his son would have been unacceptable to Yaakov), but over the resurrection of the dead that he thought would occur in his lifetime, during which time Yosef's mother Rachel would return to life. However, aside from the obvious difficulty of fitting this explanation into Rashi's commentary, which does not even hint at it, it is also clear that Yaakov "guarded the matter" refers to the content of Yosef's dream.

What Yaakov "watched and waited" for was not the resurrection of the dead, but for the contents of the dream to come true.

However, according to the commentaries that we mentioned above, his intention was quite the opposite — Yaakov considered this detail of the dream (that Yosef's mother would bow down to him) to be one of the nonsensical elements of the dream. That is, Yaakov did not think that Rachel would bow down to Yosef. So clearly, Yaakov was not waiting for Rachel's resurrection, and if so, for what did Yaakov "watch and wait" with such great anticipation?

By being very precise in citing Rashi's words, we may be able to answer this question. Rashi writes, "from here, the sages learned that there is no dream without meaningless events." The clue is that Rashi writes "events" (*devarim*) in the plural. Every dream contains more than one meaningless/false detail. We pointed out one such detail in our initial analysis — that, according to Yaakov the dream referred to Rachel, when in reality, it referred to Bilhah. But Yaakov actually found more than one false detail — he also could not imagine that he would ever bow down to Yosef. According to his understanding of Yosef's dream, that was also a false detail. However, Yaakov agreed to the overall content of the dream because it indicated that Yosef would ascend to greatness, perhaps even become a king. But Yaakov considered some of the other details, including that he and Rachel would bow down to the ground to Yosef, to be nonsense. And indeed, Yaakov never did bow down to the ground to his son; the Torah only records that, while on his sickbed, Yaakov bowed "at the head of his bed" (Genesis 47:31), where, as Rashi indicates, "the *Shechinah* dwells."[7]

We can now say that Yaakov disagreed with more than one detail of Yosef's dream — Yaakov did not think that either he or Rachel (the "sun" and the "moon") would bow down to Yosef. Yaakov did not say, "all of the dream" is false, but "the rest is false…" The "rest" does not mean "the rest of the dream," but "the rest of what I know to be false." Thus, Yaakov avoided misrepresenting his view of Yosef's dream, which he held to be essentially correct. He only disagreed with some of the details, but he expressed himself in such a way that the brothers would think that he was referring to the entire dream. In this manner, he made sure to "take the sting out" out of the dream for the other brothers, hoping to mitigate their anger at Yosef.

At the same time, we now know the important matter that Yaakov looked forward to. Yaakov waited for the brothers' bow down to Yosef (giving recognition to his superior form of *avodat Hashem*) to take place. Since in Yaakov's estimation, neither he nor Rachel would bow to Yosef, all that was left of Yosef's dream was for the brothers to bow down.

Nevertheless, our explanation still fails to answer a basic question. Even after we understand the nature of Yosef's dreams, and the angst of his brothers and his father's concerns, there is something strange in this "big picture." And that is — Yosef was the son of Yaakov's old age, and his favorite son, and it was natural for Yaakov to want him to succeed and even to become a ruler. Even so, why should Yaakov, the father, want to see his son rule over his brothers? And why was this hope so great that Yaakov awaited it with great anticipation?

The answer comes from understanding Yaakov's perspective of Jewish history. Yaakov remembered the vision of Avraham, his grandfather, at the "covenant between the pieces."

In fact, that's exactly what Rashi refers to few verses after Yosef's narration of his dreams. Commenting on the Torah verse (in Genesis 37:14), "And [Yaakov] sent him [Yosef] from the depths of Hebron..." Rashi does not seem intent on explaining the simple meaning (*pshat*) of the text as is his usual style. Here on the words, "from the depths of Hebron," Rashi writes, "from the deep wisdom of the *tzaddik* [Avraham] who is buried in Hebron." And then Rashi tells us what that advice was: "in order to fulfill what was said to Avraham at the covenant between the pieces: 'Your offspring will be sojourners in a land not theirs...' (Genesis 15:13)."

In other words, way back in the days of Avraham, there was already a prophecy that the Jews would have to go into exile. And since that prophetic tradition had been passed down to Yaakov, the scion of the family, he wondered how that exile would come about. Therefore, upon hearing Yosef's dreams, he anticipated the completion of Avraham's vision, "your offspring will be sojourners in a land not theirs." Realizing from Yosef's dreams that Yosef was to become a ruler, Yaakov looked forward to the path that would take him and his family to the "land not theirs," where Yosef would be the king.

According to Rashi's comment, then, the entire narrative of *Parshat Vayeishev* — in which Yosef was first sent north to observe his brothers, and then ended up sold by them into slavery in Egypt — took place in order to put into motion the "deep wisdom" that Avraham received at the "covenant between the pieces." If so, then the event for which

Yaakov was waiting with such great expectation was Avraham's prediction: "your offspring will be sojourners in a land not theirs."

There were any number of ways in which this prediction could occur. One possibility was exactly what happened in the end — that one of Yaakov's offspring would become a ruler in a foreign country, and thereby pave the path for the rest of the Jews to come to that country and live there in safety and prosperity. According to this scenario, Yaakov was not interested in Yosef being a king for the sake of ruling and raising himself above the rest of the family so that he and his sons would have to bow down to him. He was interested in the "big picture" of Jewish history, and he waited with great anticipation to see how the prophecy received by his grandfather Avraham would play out. For, as the sages said, Yaakov could have been led down to Egypt in chains, against his will, since the prediction did not say how his offspring would end up in a foreign land. But, when he heard Yosef's dreams, he realized that if Yosef were indeed to become a ruler, he (Yaakov) could be led into exile in a very safe and respectable manner, and his offspring could be very well taken care and well treated even while in a land "not their own." It was this that he looked forward to with great anticipation.

Still, this explanation does not fit well with the simple meaning of the text of the Torah. The text in which Yosef narrates his dreams, does not relate to Yosef's rule over the world in general. Rather, it tells of eleven stars and the sun and moon — apparently his family — all bowing down to him. Moreover, Rashi's comment — that Yaakov, upon hearing the dream, "watched and waited" for it to take place — is not well understood. There was no reason for Yaakov to hope for the imminent beginning of exile outside of Israel. Although it was appropriate for Yaakov to await the concretization of Yosef's dream, it did not make sense for Yaakov to anticipate when it would occur.

Therefore, it would seem that the real meaning of Yosef's dreams and Yaakov's anticipation had to do not with Yosef's reign, but with the effect that Yosef would have on his immediate family as well as on all Jews for all generations. The Jews are often called "Yosef," as the verse in Psalms (80:2) states, "You, who leads Yosef like a flock." They are called "Yosef" not only because Yosef aided his family and fed them during the years of famine, but because Yosef passed on his spiritual traits and qualities to all Jews for all generations.[8]

It is known that the brothers (aside from Yosef) who gave rise to the twelve tribes could serve God in prayer and study only by leaving the cities and population centers with all of their distractions, and tending their sheep in the fields, meadows and pastures away from people.[9] The only way that these tribes could serve God properly was by escaping the hubbub and distractions of urban life and focusing on the One Above while they were in nature, away from people.

Yosef, however was capable of serving God on another level entirely. While very much in the midst of worldly matters, he could still manage to maintain his focus on *avodat Hashem* and cultivate love and awe of God. Such was the spiritual level of Yosef.

Even as the viceroy of Egypt, when he was under tremendous pressure, Yosef never lost sight of the fact that his main purpose in life was not tending to the Egyptian population and Pharaoh, but tending and cultivating his lifetime connection with God. Throughout the three phases of his life in Egypt — first as a servant in the house of Potiphar, then as a prisoner, and finally as the viceroy of Egypt, Yosef never became detached from God. In fact, even during these extremely hectic times of his life, Yosef remained a vehicle for the expression of Godliness in the world, because of his humility and readiness to fulfill God's will. Not only did Yosef maintain his own focus, but he also managed to influence and uplift his own surroundings in Egypt. It was this power and ability to not only persist in *galut,* but even to influence and change the world for the better, that Yosef passed on to the Jews for all generations. That is why the Jews are often called "Yosef."

But, still, what was Yakaav waiting for with such great anticipation?

From Avraham's vision at the "covenant between the pieces," Yaakov knew that the Jews would have to go into exile in a foreign land. Yaakov also knew that the only way the Jews would survive in exile was if they were united behind one leader, one king, who could guide and direct them. The only way to receive the necessary positive direction and influence in life while in exile was by being nullified to a Jewish leader such as Yosef, who, with his superior spiritual traits, could meet the spiritual and physical needs of the Jews. That was what Yaakov saw in Yosef's dreams — the tribes all bowing down to Yosef represented their subservience to him as the king and unifying force, who could meet all the physical and spiritual needs of the Jews in exile.

That was why Yaakov "watched and waited" — he wanted to see the concretization of tribal unity under Yosef as the king who could help them through the exile. Among the brothers, only Yosef had the power to ensure that the Jews would stay focused on God and serve Him throughout the trials and tribulations of exile that could lead them astray.

However, the question remains: Why would Yaakov be focused on what was, after all, the Godly service and approach of the Jews in exile? Why would this "*galut* mentality" be something that Yaakov would want to see occur soon in the near future?

That was why Yaakov "watched and waited" — he wanted to see the concretization of tribal unity under Yosef as the king who could help them through the exile.

In the final analysis, we are forced to say that what Yaakov was "watching and waiting" for was not exile in a land "not theirs," but actually the imminent arrival of *geula* — "redemption" — with the Mashiach at the helm.

We already know that all that we read in the Torah alludes to the lifetimes and events of all Jews for all times. *Parshat Vayeishev* is not merely about Yosef, his father and his brothers. It is also an instruction for each and every Jew throughout the generations, about how Jewish history will unfold in the future. As the Midrash (*Breishis Rabba*, Chapter 85) says, "The brothers were busy with the sale of Yosef, Yosef was busy fasting and mourning, Reuven was busy fasting and mourning, Yaakov was busy fasting and mourning, Yehudah was busy looking for a wife, and God was busy creating the light of the Mashiach."

The explanation of this Midrash is not that each of the brothers — Yosef, Reuven and Yehudah — was involved in their own private matters while God was busy with another matter (bringing the Mashiach). Rather, the meaning is that each and every one of them, in his own way, was really involved in bringing the Mashiach. By the end of the Torah portion, we understand that Yehuda's union with Tamar, for example, was for the purpose of bringing the Mashiach. Indeed, the entire Torah portion is about bringing the Mashiach.

It was Yosef's dreams, and his narration of his dreams to his family, that set about the chain of events related in *Parshat Vayeishev*, and thus it is clear from the beginning that Yosef's dreams, as everything else in this portion, is associated with bringing the Mashiach. It was for this reason that Yaakov "watched and waited" with great anticipation for the rule of Yosef, which refers to the Mashiach ben Yosef, his descendant, who will arrive before the ultimate Mashiach, the Mashiach ben David.

To "watch and wait," as Yaakov did in great anticipation, implies that one is expecting something to occur in the very near future, if not immediately. The fact that Yaakov was waiting for the imminent arrival of the Mashiach meant that we can and should do the same, especially since we are now in the era known as the "heels of the Mashiach," and we expect him to arrive not only any day now, but any hour.

We pray for the immediate arrival of the "light of the Mashiach" in a manner that will be obvious to everyone, and then he will bring all of the Jews — men, women and children — to our Holy Land, immediately if not sooner!

From Likutei Sichot of the Lubavitcher Rebbe, vol. 35, pp. 156–162

NOTES

1. Every month has its own "letter," according to the *Sefer Yetzirah.*

2. It could be argued that even according to the first explanation, Yaakov understood the dream to be true but he did not know the interpretation of the dream (since he did not know that the dream alluded to Bilhah). And Yaakov "guarded the matter" means that he waited and anticipated even though he did not know how the dream would come to fruition. (Mizrahi and Gur Aryeh)

3. Ramban argues that Bilhah already passed away by the time that Yaakov descended to Egypt [making it impossible for her to bow down to Yosef]. However, the Midrash on our verse states unequivocally as Rashi wrote in his comment. See also the *Targum Yonatan* on Genesis 50:16 , "And they commanded to Yosef…" There *Targum Yonatan* translates "and they told Bilhah" from which we understand that Bilhah must have been alive even after Yaakov's passing. And so is stated in *Yalkut Shimoni* and *Midrash Lekach Tov* and other Midrashim. See also the *Bereishit Rabati* of Rabbi Moshe Hadarshan on Genesis 50:18 — "Bilhah went first and bowed before Yosef and afterward the brothers came and vowed before him. At that time, the verse, "the sun and moon…will bow down" was fulfilled. (The Ramban's opinion is also discussed among the commentators on Rashi.)

4. There are several commentators who claim that Rashi's conclusion (that Yaakov sought to "take the sting out" of Yosef's dream for the brothers) applies to the first explanation as well — (see the Maharik here, Maskil l'David and others). They hold that Rashi brings two explanations, and Rashi's conclusion applies to both of them. The Maskil l'David bases his opinion on the *Breishit Rabba* cited in Rashi, that Yaakov was waiting for the resurrection of the dead to occur in his days.

5. As for why Rashi did not learn that Yosef's dream did not refer to Bilhah, and that was the "false detail" that was contained in the dream — perhaps that is because Bilhah did indeed take Yosef under wing immediately after Rachel passed away and raised him like her own son, as we see clearly in Genesis 30:3–6 and in Rashi. But since it would have been very awkward to suggest that Yaakov was aware of this but nevertheless suggested that the dream was referring to Rachel, and that "Rachel already passed away," whereupon it would have seemed like Yaakov was not completely honest, Rashi was forced to conclude that Yaakov did not realize that the dream alluded to Bilhah. And the fact that Yaakov nevertheless thought (wrongly according to the first explanation) that the dream alluded to Rachel was because even though it was very acceptable to call the woman who raised Yosef his "mother" (and the son or daughter also feels that such a woman is her/her "mother"), nevertheless, it was not appropriate to include her (Bilhah) with equal status in the same sentence and same expression as the father (Yaakov), as occurred in the dream. This also makes it easier to explain Rashi's expression: "... he didn't know that the matter applied to Bilhah." For the dream itself ("sun and moon...') did not apply directly to Bilhah in the same manner that "sun" applied to Yaakov. Rather, since "his mother already passed away," therefore the dream "applied" to Bilhah since she raised Yosef "like her son" — and therefore Yaakov considered this among the false details of the dream.

6. In the *Melechet Hakodesh*, "Therefore Yaakov waited and anticipated the arrival of Rachel, the *akeret habayit* ("pillar of the house"), and then also his grandfather Avraham and Shem and Eber would arise and he would learn Torah from them. Even though the dream was negative ... since he and his sons would have to bow down to Yosef — the benefit from the dream was greater than the negative ramifications."

7. Rashi comments, "To the fox in his season, take a bow..." [In vernacular English, "Every dog has his day"]. However, the commentaries there explain that according to Rashi "this was not a bow of subjugation to Yosef (as a normal bow would have been), for it would have been a terrible humiliation for Yosef if his father had bowed down to him. This is obvious from the fact that Yaakov did not bow immediately upon meeting Yosef, but only a week later (see the Gur Aryeh and the Nahalat Yaakov). Rashi continues and explains that Yaakov "turned to the side of the *Shechinah*," which was the direction to which he bowed. In particular according to Rashi's "other explanation," that Yaakov "bowed toward the head of the bed" means "because his 'bed' was complete" (all of his children were *tzaddikim*) — see R' Ovadia Bartenura and Maharik. See also Chassidus in *Torah Ohr* of the Alter Rebbe (28:3) and *Torat Chaim* of the Mittler Rebbe (69:4), that Yaakov's "bow" was from above to below.

8. See *Likutei Sichot* vol. 25, p. 253. There, on p. 255, it is explained that the power to persist during the *galut* is a trait that no one else possessed, not even Yaakov.

9. See *Torah Ohr* of the Alter Rebbe, Page 28A, *Yomtov shel Rosh Hashana 5666* of the Rebbe Rashab, Page 418 (315 in the old print).

Yaakov "Guards" Yosef's Dreams

Vayeishev **37:11**

When we have an idea in mind, and we want to actually make it happen, there are generally three stages from potential to its realization. At first, the project exists only as a seminal idea in our head. Then, it begins to take form as we plan it out and put it into effect. And, ultimately, it emerges into full-fledged reality with all of its details expressed in time and space.

That's what happened with the forefathers and their offspring as they gave rise to the Jewish nation.

When Avraham fell into a trance during the "covenant between the pieces" and received the prophecy that his descendants would go down to Egypt, the process of exile and redemption became a foregone conclusion. This is because the Jewish people needed to emerge from an archetypal state, existing in the minds of their forefathers, to a nation of individuals, each serving the One Above in his or her unique fashion. They could only do that by going through the crucible of slavery in Egypt.

According to Kabbalah, the souls of the Jewish people were all included in the soul of Adam, and afterward in the soul of Yaakov as well. When his son, Yosef, dreamt of his entire family bowing down to him, it was a sign to Yaakov that it was time for the individual souls of the Jewish people to emerge. The dreams were unique in four respects:

1. They were a form of prophecy
2. They demonstrated that the time for the archetypal souls to become born had arrived
3. They were the first event in the long intermediate stage that we

call the "the era of the tribes," when the characteristics of the Twelve Tribes of Israel were developed

4. They demonstrated that within this intermediate stage of development, Yosef's role would stand out

When the time arrived for the content of Avraham's prophecy to begin to become come true, the Midrash[1] tells us that "Yaakov took out a pen and wrote down the day, the hour[2] and the location of Yosef's dream."[3] However, strangely, Yaakov did not write down what seemed to be the most important element of Yosef's dreams — their content.

This can be explained in the following way:

As we know, all the events that transpired during the lifetimes of our forefathers serve as signs and directives to us, their descendants. Often, the sign or directive can be interpreted almost literally. Before he is even conceived, a child exists (in a primordial way) in the minds and genetic material of his parents. After he is born, he is independent, existent in his own body, contributed to him by his parents. However, there is an intermediate stage, in which he exists as an embryo, developing into what he will later become — an independent soul in a physical body. The intermediate state is the stage of pregnancy, when the child in the womb takes on his own individual form, but has not yet emerged into the air of the world.

In the context of our Torah portion, *Parshat Vayeishev*, the dreams of Yosef represent the intermediate stage of pregnancy — when the child is no longer in the mind of his parents but does not yet exist as an individual in an independent body. When Yosef dreamt, Yaakov knew that it was time to "guard" the matter (Genesis 37:11) — somewhat like a woman who guards her pregnancy.

How did Yaakov know that? One thing about dreams is that they follow the interpretation given to them.[4] It is possible that this is why Yosef told his brothers of his dreams, even though the dreams were bound to anger them. Nevertheless, he wanted to give the brothers the opportunity to interpret the dreams as they saw fit.[5] Thus, if they didn't like the message of bowing down to Yosef, they could interpret the dream in such a way as to correct it. In any case, the brothers left the second dream (of the sun, moon and stars bowing down to Yosef) un-interpreted. They did not respond to it, aside from, as the Torah tells us, disliking Yosef even more intensely.[6] But, when Yaakov heard the second dream,[7] he scolded Yosef: "Do you really think that I, your mother and your brothers will bow down to you?" (Genesis 37:10)

Rashi says that this was a way of taking the sting out of the dream for the brothers, who were resentful. However, at the same time, his statement shows Yaakov using the opportunity to interpret Yosef's dreams in the manner most agreeable to his own outlook — a prophecy of things to come.

According to this explanation, Yaakov did not challenge Yosef. Outwardly, he only sought to take the sting out of the dreams for Yosef's brothers. But as for himself, Yaakov used the opportunity of interpreting the dream to verify and confirm that it would, in the future, occur.

If that's the case, it becomes evident why Yaakov did not find it necessary to record the content of the dream — but only to "guard" it by noting the date, hour and place of the dream. That was because it was he, Yaakov, who determined the contents by lending it his own interpretation. Since his reaction to the dream was to give it meaning, it wasn't necessary for him to also record the contents. He determined the contents by virtue of his interpretation.

Simultaneously, Yaakov determined the future course of the Jewish people. He realized that Yosef's dream was about each individual's path of divine service, and that each brother would soon pioneer a new path in serving the One Above. Each brother — and subsequently each tribe — would soon feel the advantage and benefit of its own style of *avodat Hashem*,[8] and Yaakov realized that they would need a unifying factor, a *tzaddik* whom they could all look up, in order to keep them together as the Jewish people.

The dream indicated to Yaakov that the time had come to create a bridge between himself (as the archetypal forefather) and his descendants (the Jews who were to serve God each in his individual manner).

From Yaakov's interpretation of Yosef's dreams we know that he accepted that Yosef would be that *tzaddik*. Yaakov recognized that Yosef would play a dominant role in the unification of the tribes after their upcoming individuation. This, Yaakov could foresee, and he wanted to leave his imprint on each of his sons' individual paths and to ensure that there would be a unifying factor. In order to do so, he recorded the date, hour and place of the dream.

The dream indicated to Yaakov that the time had come to create a bridge between himself (as the archetypal forefather) and his descendants (the Jews who were to serve God each in his individual manner).

That bridge would be formed by the twelve brothers, the progenitors of the Twelve Tribes of Israel.[9]

Yaakov knew (from Avraham's dream) that they were headed for Egypt and that they would emerge from there as the Jewish nation.[10] How could Yaakov bridge the gap between himself and them, while transferring the seminal message of Judaism and preserving it? By recording the time and place of the dream. That's why the Torah (in Genesis 37:11) says, "and his father guarded the matter."

The message of Yosef's dream was that even as a Jew finds his own path in serving God, he must maintain the unity of Judaism since we are all serving one God. Yosef represented that unity, elevating all of the other tribes and their individual spiritual paths. He could unite all of the brothers, but only if they would recognize his spiritual path as the unifying force. But, instead of recognizing him as "Yosef the *Tzaddik*," they resented his role. At that time, his father "guarded the matter." He wanted it to occur, and he could make it happen.[11]

Yaakov, as the forefather, could not predict the exact path of each of his sons. He could not know who would serve God with love, who with fear, and who with mercy. What he could do was preserve their essential unity. He could ensure that they all acted through Yosef the *Tzaddik*, who was the unifying force behind all the different paths of divine service. And that was why the Midrash says that Yaakov wrote down the date and time and place. By establishing the precise hour and the location, the dream took on a specific place and time, establishing its unique identity and physical reality. It wasn't necessary to record the content — that Yaakov had already established by interpreting the dream. But by recording the date and place, he could create a vehicle of preservation. By so doing, Yaakov united the path of service of each of the tribes with its purpose and goal. Thus he achieved two things:

1. the tribes would place emphasis not upon themselves as individuals, but upon their respective paths of divine service
2. they would realize that they were not only individuals, but that each of them was part of an overall plan in which all of them were united

That's what was achieved by writing down the time and location. The message of the forefathers, in Yaakov's head, was faithfully transmitted to the Jews for all time by writing down the time and place of

Yosef's dream. That's why the Torah says, "and his father guarded the matter." The Torah doesn't say that he guarded "Yosef's dream," but that he guarded the "matter" — the essential unity of the Jewish people.

Something similar happened within the Chassidic Movement, which had its own forefathers. The Ba'al Shem Tov gave birth to the idea of Chassidism, the Maggid of Mezeritch developed a plan for the *tzaddikim* (his students) to take the message to the people, and the Alter Rebbe (founder of Chabad) put it in intellectual form that could be communicated and taught (via the *Tanya*).

Just before he passed away on the 19th day of the Hebrew month of Kislev (*yud-tes Kislev*), the Maggid said to the Alter Rebbe, "*Yud-tes Kislev* is our holiday." (Later on, the Alter Rebbe was also freed from prison on this date). With this statement, the Maggid passed on to the Alter Rebbe the secret of uniting all of his students, each with his individual Chassidic path. By mentioning "our holiday," the Maggid united all of his students into one Chassidic group. Similar to Yaakov and his sons many generations earlier, the Maggid realized that his students would all go their own ways and would need a leader to unite them in order to preserve the overriding message of Chassidism. By saying to the Alter Rebbe that *Yud-tes Kislev* was "our holiday," the Maggid gave him the power to transmit and preserve the message. Then even after all of them went their separate ways, the students of the Maggid could remember two things:

1. that what was important was not themselves, but their divine service
2. that all of them were not only individuals but also integral members of a group whose goal was to spread Torah and bring the Mashiach

That's why we celebrate *yud-tes Kislev* this week, during the reading of *Parshat Vayeishev*.

Adapted from Likutei Sichot of the Lubavitcher Rebbe, vol. 25, pp. 204–212

NOTES

1. *Bereishit Rabba* 84:12 on Genesis 37:11.
2. Investigation is needed as to which hour — the hour of the first dream, the hour of the second dream, or the hour at which Yosef told his dreams to Yaakov?

3. A second explanation also appears in the commentary on the Midrash: "Since the events prophesied in the dreams would come to fruition only twenty-two years later, therefore Yaakov 'wrote down the day and hour to know for how long he would have hope.'" (*Berachot* 55b) However, to be aware of such a limit on hope that would occur twenty-two years in the future, it would be more important to write the month and year, rather than the day and hour — yet the statement does not mention the month or year at all!

4. *Berachot 55b*, end of page.

5. Abarvanel, Ohr Hachaim, Gur Aryeh, and Shach on the Torah — but Rashi mentions nothing of the sort.

6. The Zohar (*Vayeishev* 183b) says, "If the brothers would have [interpreted the dream] in a transformative [i.e. positive] manner, it would have taken place in that manner."

7. The Zohar (*Vayeishev* 183a, end of page) in regard to Yosef's first dream, says that since Yaakov' responded with apparent surprise and suspicion ("Do you really think that me, your mother and your brothers will bow down to you?"), the dream did not come to fruition for twenty-two years.

8. Here it is appropriate to draw attention to *Likutei Sichot*, vol. 7, p. 342, as well as vol. 22, p. 139, regarding the saying of the sages (*Yevamot* 62b), that the students of R'Akiva "failed to regard each other with respect." See also *Likutei Sichot*, vol. 19, p. 88 in explanation of the saying of the sages (*Baba Batra* 75a) that "everyone is 'burnt' by the *chupah* of his neighbor."

9. The division of the Jews among the tribes and the names of the tribes (in which is expressed the approach and style of their individual *avodat Hashem*) came from the matriarchs. See *Likutei Sichot* vol. 10, p. 97 and footnotes there. Thus, the comparison of the tribes at this stage to an embryo in the mother's womb becomes more comprehensible.

10. Which is why the Jews crossed the Reed Sea in twelve different paths, and why when they entered the Land of Israel, it was divided among the twelve tribes.

11. We have to say that [the results of] Yaakov's actions, such as sending Yosef from "the depths of Hebron," were not matters of which he was clearly aware and conscious. That is why the sages comment on "the depths of Hebron" — "from the deep advice of Avraham" — because [the real reason for his action related to back to Avraham] and not to Yaakov [who was not consciously aware that sending Yosef to see his brothers would result in his sale and descent to Egypt]. (See *Likutei Sichot* vol. 5, p. 184.) Similarly, we cannot say that Yaakov's extra love for Yosef was because he consciously foresaw that Yosef would be the instrument for keeping the Jews together in Egypt. However, Yosef's dreams were prophecy from Above, not matters that contradicted man's free choice and behavior, and the dreams could be transformed by way of verbal interpretation.

What Happens in Shechem...

Vayeishev
37:14

There are four "holy cities" in the Land of Israel, and some people add a fifth. The four are Safed, Tiberias, Jerusalem and Hebron. Of course, all of Israel is holy — it is the Holy Land — but these cities take on additional holiness because of their unique history.

There is a fifth "holy city" that for some reason never seems to quite make the list with those cited above, and that is the city of Shechem (today known as Nablus). It is traditionally considered the city to which the Jews first arrived as they entered the Land of Israel, although they never remained there, and perhaps that is the reason why it never made the "A-list."

Still, it was where Abraham first arrived when he migrated from Charan, where Yaakov came on his way from Paddan Aram, and ultimately was the place to where Yehoshua led the Jews forty years after the Exodus from Egypt. Additionally, Yaakov bought a piece of land in Shechem, and that is where Yosef was buried when the Children of Israel brought his body with them from Egypt (Rashi, Gen 48:22).

Shechem figures prominently in this week's Torah portion — *Parshat Vayeishev* — which deals with Yosef and what happened to him near Shechem.

At that time, Yaakov was living in Hebron, while most of his sons were up north near Shechem, grazing the family sheep. (Genesis 37:12) Therefore, Yaakov sent Yosef, who was then seventeen years old, to check how they were faring. (Genesis 37:13–14)

Rashi states (in his commentary on Genesis 37:14) that Shechem is "a place that is primed for punishment."[1] He then goes on to list some of the events that occurred in Shechem: "There, the brothers misbehaved, there Dinah was humiliated, and there the kingdom of Israel split away from the kingdom of David."

Among the questions we could ask here are:

1. Why did Rashi list the events out of order? Chronologically, Dinah's humiliation occurred prior to the brothers' misbehavior, yet Rashi mentions their "misbehavior" first. In fact, the Midrash from which Rashi draws his information, as well as the Talmud, both mention Dinah before the other events, so why did Rashi change the order?[2]
2. Why does Rashi say only that the brothers "misbehaved?" In truth, they committed serious crimes — certainly, the sale of Yosef into slavery was a serious crime. Rashi should have used another terminology that emphasized the serious nature of the events, rather than just "misbehavior."
3. Throughout Jewish history, other events occurred in Shechem, both positive and negative. For example, on the negative side, Shechem is where Avimelech ben Yerubaal killed his seventy brothers (Judges 9) and where ten of the tribes rebelled against the Kingdom of Yehudah, eventually creating their own Kingdom of Israel (1 Kings 12). But on the positive side, Shechem is where Avraham received the divine announcement that his descendants would inherit the land of Israel (Gen 12:7). And it is where Yehoshua established the "covenant of Torah" with the Jews, ensuring that all are guarantors for each other in ensuring mitzvah fulfillment (Yehoshua 24:1). Taking all that into consideration, why did Rashi say that Shechem is "a place that is primed for punishment," when positive events also emanated from the city? Why does Rashi not mention these events in his commentary?

Before answering that question, let's first try to answer another question that arises regarding Rashi's commentary. And that is, why does Rashi find it necessary to say anything whatsoever about this particular verse?

Rashi's self-declared task is to explain any questions that arise regarding the simple meaning of the text. He seeks to answer whatever questions a child, learning Torah for the first time, might come up with. In this case, the child might ask why it is necessary for the Torah to mention the name of the city of Shechem three times (in Genesis 37:12, 13 and 14):

"His brothers went off to pasture their father's sheep in Shechem. Israel said to Yosef, 'Your brothers are shepherding in Shechem. I will send you to them' … And he [Yosef] came to Shechem. " Why all the repetition? Indeed, this is what Rashi seeks to explain — and he concludes that the Torah is trying to tell us not just "where" Yosef was sent but to "what kind of place" he was sent. And, so Rashi says, "to the place primed for punishment."

Rashi's self-declared task is to explain any questions that arise regarding the simple meaning of the text. He seeks to answer whatever questions a child, learning Torah for the first time, might come up with.

However, as it turns out, there are many times that the Torah mentions a place repeatedly, when it is perfectly clear from the context to which place it is referring. For example, we see the following sequence in our Torah portion: "And Yosef's master took him and placed him in prison … and he remained in prison … and he gave Yosef control over all the prisoners in the prison…" (Genesis 39:20–22). It is perfectly clear where Yosef is, and yet the Torah goes out of its way to mention "prison" several times. So, the repetition of Shechem as the name of the place does not present a problem in understanding the simple meaning of the text. It is the way of the Torah to repeat the name of a location even when it is clear. So, this is not what is bothering Rashi.

What is bothering Rashi is the ending of the verse, "he arrived to Shechem." The events that occurred there which imply that Yosef's arrival in Shechem was an important occurrence in its own right. It was in Shechem that Yosef met the "man" (according to Rashi, this was actually the angel Gavriel) who informed him that his brothers had "travelled on from here." So, Yosef's brothers were no longer in Shechem; indeed, they were in Dotan. That is where he found them and that is where all the dreadful events befell him. It seems, therefore, that the sojourn in Shechem was only a stop on the way to Dotan (where the sale of Yosef took place).

That being the case, Rashi is bothered by the fact that the Torah emphasizes Yosef's arrival in Shechem as an event that is worthy of attention in its own right. If the goal was to get to his brothers in Dotan, why does the Torah focus so much on Shechem?[3] And Rashi answers, "this is a place that is primed for punishment."

All that happened to Yosef subsequently — in Dotan, in Egypt and elsewhere, began in Shechem. Yosef's brothers were in Shechem before they proceeded to Dotan and, while in Shechem, they plotted what to do with Yosef. As they pondered, they prepared his "punishment" even before they journeyed on to Dotan. Therefore, according to Rashi, Shechem took on an importance of its own. It was the place where Yosef's punishment was predetermined, even if it ultimately took place elsewhere.

And that is why Rashi lists only negative events that were associated with Yosef. He does not mention the event from Judges in which one brother kills his seventy brothers (since they were not related to Yosef), nor does he mention the positive events regarding Avraham and Yehoshua. He wishes to point out the importance of Shechem to Yosef, as the place where the beginning of Yosef's punishment took place.

However, looking at the expression, "a place primed for punishment," we might get the impression that Shechem is a place from which punishment emanates in general — not just specifically in relation to Yosef. From this perspective, we might think that Yosef was sold into slavery as a result of his arrival in Shechem, which is a place known to deliver punishment. That is, Yosef did nothing to deserve this punishment, but since he wandered into Shechem, it fell upon him. This is why Rashi goes on to forewarn us that this is not the correct understanding. He makes it clear that Yosef was the target of punishment, and that Shechem, because of events that occurred there, was the place from which the punishment began.[4] Accordingly, Shechem is not a place from which punishment emanates in general, since we see that positive events also occurred there. According to Rashi, it was from Shechem that a specific punishment was meted out to Yosef. With his arrival in Shechem, Rashi tells us, Yosef became the target of that punishment.

As part of his explanation, Rashi reverses the order of the first two events — Dinah's humiliation and the brothers' misbehavior. Even though the humiliation/rape of Dinah in Shechem took place earlier, Rashi first mentions the misbehavior/plot of the brothers. Then Rashi lists three transgressions that Yosef attributed to his brothers and reported to his father, which turned him into the target of his brothers' wrath. According to Rashi, Yosef's accusations were the following: the brothers were eating *aiver min hachai* ("flesh from a living animal"), were engaging in *arayot* ("sexual improprieties") and in *lashon hara* ("demeaning speech") — the latter concerned the sons of the concubines whom, Yosef said, they described as "slaves." For each of these accusations — which Rashi calls "slander" — Yosef received a punishment, and in each case, the punishment originated from Shechem. (Rashi on Genesis 37:2)

Rashi continues his explanation:

The brothers responded to Yosef's accusation of eating *aiver min hachai* by planning to slaughter an animal, whose blood would be used to fool his father. The blood was to be put on Yosef's colorful garment to convince Yaakov that Yosef had been killed by a wild animal. Since Yosef accused them of eating from a live animal, they responded with blood from a live animal. In this manner, Yosef was to be paid "measure for measure" for his negative speech against the brothers. This was how the brothers planned Yosef's punishment from Shechem, even though it later occurred in Dotan. Since it provides the clearest indication of the intention of the verse (that Yosef's punishment began from Shechem), Rashi listed it first, even before mentioning the humiliation of Dinah (though it occurred first, chronologically). In addition, this is the reason that Rashi refers to the "misbehavior" of the brothers toward Yosef, and not something more serious, such as "murder" or "kidnapping." The plan was only hatched in Shechem, but did not take place there. Therefore, their plotting was only a "misbehavior," and not something worse.

As for the other punishments, they were also associated with Shechem. In each case, the events that befell Yosef show that his punishment began in Shechem with the original plot of his brothers against him. And in each case, there were events occurring in Shechem that either "set the stage for" or "echoed" what was to occur to Yosef:

Since Yosef accused his brothers of sexual impropriety, he was later punished when he was accosted by the wife of his Egyptian master, Potiphar. When he resisted her sexual advances, he was ultimately thrown into prison. However, the precedent for this punishment already existed. It began in Shechem, when Dinah was seized and raped in Shechem. This made Shechem the origin from which Yosef's punishment at the hands of the wife of Potiphar would ultimately emerge.

Finally, Yosef was punished for accusing his brothers of insulting the sons of the concubines by calling them "slaves." The punishment was that he himself was sold into slavery by his brothers. For this as well, there were events in Shechem that corresponded to his false accusation. Several generations later, a descendent of Yosef was responsible for the split between the northern Kingdom of Israel and the southern

Kingdom of Yehudah. In creating the rebellion, this descendent (who came from the tribe of Ephraim, son of Yosef) showed disrespect for the line of Yehudah. (1 Kings 11–13). This echoed Yosef's accusation, that his brothers disrespected the sons of the concubines. Thus, Rashi establishes that Shechem is a place from which punishment was meted out to Yosef for his three false accusations. All of those events are associated with Yosef's sins, and prove that the negative events that emanated from there were associated with Yosef and not with anyone else.

Thus we see that when Rashi said that Shechem is "a place primed for punishment," he wasn't referring to punishment of all Jews. Rather, he was referring specifically to Yosef. To all other Jews, Shechem is a city that portends blessings and unity, as we see from God's promises to Avraham, and by the covenant that Yehoshuah made with all the Jews together.

From Likutei Sichot of the Lubavitcher Rebbe, vol. 15, pp. 318–323

NOTES

1. Rav Ovadia Bartenura comments in Genesis 37:14 the Torah does not say "Shechem," but *Shechemah* meaning "to Shechem." This word is similar to the one used in Hoshea (6:9), "Like gangs awaiting a man [to rob] a band of priests murders on the road with one will (*shechma*), for they devised a plan." There the word *shechmah* also indicates "punishment." (See the *Midrash Sechel Tov* here). In the *Biurei Maharai* (also cited in the *Tzeida Laderech...*), the word *shechem* means "portion" or "part" as Rashi explains in *Parshat Vayechi* ... and every "portion" (fraction) is "devoted to punishment." But in the realm of *pshat*, 1) there must be a necessity within the text in order to "interpret" a name, [as proven byRashi himself who does not comment on Genesis 37:12–13 [where the name Shechem also appears] that Shechem is "a place devoted to punishment"] and 2) the verses from Hoshea and from *Parshat Vayechi* are not hinted to at all in Rashi's commentary.

2. In addition to the fact that Rashi lists the events out of chronological order, it would have made more sense to first mention Dinah's capture and rape that occurred there, because her capture and rape makes it very clear that Shechem was already a place that is "primed for punishment." And it does not make sense to claim that the sale of Yosef occurred in Shechem because it is a place that is "primed for punishment," while simultaneously claiming that the first proof of that is the sale of Yosef that took place there.

3. In *Sefer Yehoshua* (24:32), Rashi explains that the brothers "captured Yosef" in Shechem (citing *Sotah* 13b), but as mentioned in several places, Rashi's commentary on the Prophets and Writings does not necessarily follow *pshat*, as does his commentary on the Chumash. As Rashi says in *Parshat Vayechi* (Genesis 48:22),

"And I also gave you a portion in which to be buried, and that is Shechem" — and accordingly there is no necessity to explain that Yosef was "captured" in Shechem, because according to this answer, there is no room for the question of the Gemara ("Why Shechem?") to begin with, since Yaakov had bought a piece of land there [which is likely why that was the place that he sent Yosef].

4. When describing the events surrounding Yosef and his eventual sale and arrival to Egypt in our Torah portion, even Rashi seems to forsake his usual approach of explaining the text according to *pshat.* Here on Genesis 37:14, "And he sent him from the depths of Hebron..." Rashi comments, "from the deep advice of the *tzaddik* who is buried in Hebron..." which is not an explanation on the level of *pshat.*

Yosef's Personal Development

Vayeishev 39:2

Yosef's sojourn in Egypt — detailed in this week's Torah portion, *Parshat Vayeishev* — involved three levels of servitude as he grew up and matured:

First, he began as a servant in the house of an Egyptian minister — Potiphar — where he was given free rein to run the household. Second, after being implicated in an affair with Potiphar's wife, Yosef, who was innocent, was incarcerated. This time, he was no longer a servant, but a prisoner. But here as well, he was given free rein to administer the prison.

And, finally, Yosef became viceroy to Pharaoh, a position in which he was the most important person in Egypt, next to Pharaoh himself. That meant that it was Yosef who, in effect, governed the land. It must be noted that for a Jew, this is still a form of captivity, since a Jew's natural state is to be free to serve God through Torah study, meditation and fulfillment of mitzvoth in the Land of Israel. And yet, Yosef was stuck in Egypt. Even though during his many duties as viceroy of Egypt, Yosef clung to God, he was unable to serve God in the same way that he would have as a free man in the Land of Israel. Nonetheless, Yosef set an example for the generations of Jews that followed him, who practiced Torah and mitzvoth while in exile. They, like Yosef, clung to God even while practicing their professions and making a living. Yet, nobody disputes that the true profession of a Jew is to serve God in our own Land.

Yosef's sojourn in Egypt also involved two levels of success. The Torah relates that while he served in the house of Potiphar, "all that he put his hand to, God made successful" (Genesis 39:3). But, when he was incarcerated, "All that he did, God made successful" (Genesis 39:23). In the telling of the story of his imprisonment and his success even then, the Torah omits the phrase "put his hand to."

We can understand the difference between these two levels of success by studying the commentary of the Tzemach Tzedek (third Lubavitcher Rebbe) on another verse (Genesis 39:2): "And God was with Yosef and he became a man of success." There (in *Ohr HaTorah* on *Parshat Vayeishev*, p. 278), the Tzemach Tzedek says that "success is a matter of *mazal* ("fortune"), since we call a successful man a *bar mazal* (a "man of fortune").

Now, *mazal* is not something that man can achieve by his labor. It is a gift from Above, a phenomenon that is above nature, and it imparts a level of success that man cannot attain on his own.[1] However, within this success, there are two levels. At one level, success comes in combination with some effort and participation of man, even if it is still out of range of what the man himself could have achieved. The fact that this man is always successful, or that whatever he gets involved in succeeds, proves that he is a *bar mazal*.[2] His success is not a one-time event that fails to repeat itself. The One Above blessed him with good fortune in all that he does.[3]

But, there is a yet higher level, and that is when the success is totally supernatural, completely beyond human capabilities. This success occurs in a way that cannot be attributed to human accomplishment. It is immediately apparent that the success is from Above, and it is the result of intervention by Divine Providence.

These two levels of success are what Yosef experienced while a servant in the house of Potiphar, and while a prisoner. In the former situation, while a servant, he succeeded as a *bar mazal* (a "man of fortune").[4] This is why the Torah says, "All that he put his hand to, God made him successful." The success was bestowed upon him in everything he put his hand to (in other words, his actions became the vehicle for his God-given success).

[And this is also the reason that the Torah emphasizes, "All that he did was successful." The only way that Potiphar recognized Yosef as a successful man was because "all" that he touched turned out well. He was always successful, and this is what identified him as a "man of fortune."]

But, while he was a prisoner and placed in charge of the prison, the second level of success became manifest: "And all that he did, God made successful." Whatever he did, it was immediately evident that it was not his doing — not the effort of his hand, so to speak — but work of the hand of God. His level of success was so great, that it could only be the result of intervention from Above. As a prisoner, he did not have the means to create a vessel for success. Therefore, it was not appropriate to mention any accomplishments of "his hand" — the success due to God alone, but it occurred because of the presence of Yosef. In prison, Yosef had so completely nullified his ego that there was no "self" on which to pin the success — it could only be the result of intervention by the Divine Providence.

[And for that reason, it was not necessary for the Torah to emphasize that "All that he did was successful," because the main emphasis here was upon the quality of the success, and how it was beyond his power — "God made him successful."]

We can explain the different levels of success that Yosef attained in his respective positions as (first) a servant, and then (second) a prisoner, as follows:

It is known that man's success is a function of the "vessel" that he creates in order to receive the blessing that God sends from Above. Ego-nullification (*bitul*) is this vessel for blessings and success from Above. The more subservient he is to God, the more divine light flows into his vessel (like a cup of water — the more empty it is, the more liquid can be poured into it). Similarly, the less ego is present in man, the more potential there is for divine light to illuminate him from Above and make him successful in ways that are completely beyond nature. And that is the key difference between Yosef as a servant, and Yosef as a prisoner...

Similarly, the less ego is present in man, the more potential there is for divine light to illuminate him from Above and make him successful in ways that are completely beyond nature.

Although Jewish law tells us that, "All that a servant acquires belongs to his master," (*Kiddushin Perek* 1 Mishna 3) this does not mean that the servant has no identity of his own. He exists and he works, and he may even generate products of major importance for his master. Still, all that he produces is for his master. Yet, even so, he lives and maintains his own identity. His efforts, and the results of his efforts are for his master, but he is his own man.

However, a prisoner is not meant to produce anything. Quite the opposite; his hands are tied (sometimes literally), and he has no possibility to work or do anything, as talented and capable as he might be.[5] At no time can he move at will and, consequently, he has no potential to grow spiritually from one level to the next. And, therefore, any work that he might do is only because he has been forced to do it, and the result is that nothing belongs to him whatsoever; all that he does is as if he did nothing.[6]

And so it was regarding Yosef. Living as a servant in the house of Potiphar had the effect of turning him into a servant of God as well. And this is why we do not become aware of Yosef's status as a *bar mazal* until after Yosef was sold into slavery. Only in his state of servitude did he begin to create the "vessel" that could contain the divine blessing for success. Only as a servant, whose every action was for his master, could Yosef be subservient to God in such a way as to call down the blessing for success "in all that he put his hand to." Nevertheless, since in this manner of serving God, Yosef maintained his own identity (even while his service was for the sake of God), the blessing that descended was associated with his "hand" — that is, his own efforts.[7]

However, when Yosef found himself a prisoner, he uprooted his own identity completely. His level of ego-nullification was so great that it was as if he did not exist.[8] And that was why he reached an even higher level of success. Now, his success was no longer in the human category; it was completely disassociated from any efforts of "his hand," as now it came about strictly by "the hand of God."

Even though the verse reads, "all that he did, God made successful," implying that Yosef engaged in some kind of labor or activity, nevertheless he was so nullified to the One Above that the resulting success was not considered his own. It was as if he did not exist. And, therefore, the level of success that he enjoyed was no longer limited by the laws of nature, but rather it was from beyond — it was Godly success.

With this explanation in mind, we can examine Rashi's commentary on the first part our verse, "And his master saw that God was with him [Yosef] and all that he put his hand to, God made successful." (Genesis 39:3) How did Potiphar conclude this? Rashi says of Yosef that "the name of heaven was constantly on his lips." But why is Rashi moved to offer this explanation? Surely, there is nothing to explain here — Potiphar saw that Yosef was successful; that's it. What forces Rashi to say that Yosef was constantly calling upon the name of God? When it comes to other verses mentioning Yosef's success (Genesis 39:2 and Genesis 39:23), Rashi says nothing, thus implying that we should understand them on the surface level; why then does he choose this verse (Genesis 39:3) to explain that "the name of heaven was constantly on his lips"?

The reason is as follows:

True, Potiphar saw that Yosef was successful. But, as an idol worshipper and one who did not even know of God's existence, how was Potiphar going to attribute Yosef's success to God?[9] This is why Rashi explains how Potiphar knew — because Yosef was constantly referring to God.[10] This is how Potiphar understood that all of his success was attributable to the One Above. However, later, when Yosef was in prison, and "all that he did, God made successful," it was not necessary for Rashi to explain anything since the verse does not refer to anyone specific observing Yosef's success. Since there is no reason to explain the verse, Rashi leaves it as is without making any comment.

Still, we may ask: Considering just how successful Yosef was in the prison, was there not room for the Torah to mention that the "minister of prisons" observed this, just as Potiphar observed it previously? If the earlier verse mentioned Yosef's success in the eyes of Potiphar, shouldn't the latter verse also do so, since Yosef was even more successful in prison?[11]

The answer is that the Torah is not merely trying to tell us what Potiphar or the minister of prisons observed. It is coming to inform us of the nature of Yosef's success. In the first instance, Yosef was successful partly through his own efforts, so the verse mentions that Potiphar observed his success in running the house.

However, in the second instance, when his success in prison was not related to his own efforts, and he was so subservient to God that success simply followed him about, there was no reason for anyone to relate the success to Yosef's actions — i.e. "his hand." The success that Potiphar noticed, because Yosef constantly mentioned God in Potiphar's house, bore a relation to Yosef. It was Yosef's success. But the success in prison was not expressed by anything that Yosef said or did. It was totally divine. It was the success that "God made" and it was simply not attributable to a human being.

From Likutei Sichot of the Lubavitcher Rebbe,
vol. 25, pp. 213–219

NOTES

1. See the Gemara in *Moed Katan* 28a, Zohar on *Parshat Vayeishev* 181a (mentioned in *Ohr HaTorah* p. 278), *Sefer Hashoreshim* of the Radak, p. 128 ("success is not dependent on the person"). In the language of Kabbalah and Chassidut, *mazal* is associated with *keter* (above *seder hishtalshelut*, the spiritual "chain of creation").

2. Similar to a "miracle enclothed in creation," in which we see clearly that all the "reasons" for the miracle were supernatural" (*Torah Ohr* on *Megillat Esther*, p. 93 end of 3rd column, as well as p. 100a).

3. As the sages (*Shabbat* 156a) said, "For the Jews, there is no *mazal*" (especially after the giving of the Torah). As for what God said to Avraham, "Leave your astrology ... because for the Jews there is no *mazal*," even though this occurred before the Torah was given, is because Avraham took on halachic status of a Jew. (There is much Torah discussion on this subject, but this is not the place...)

4. See *Sha'arei Teshuva* of the Mittler Rebbe, sec. 1, p. 66a, regarding two kinds of wealth: "successful wealth" that results from effort and activity, and "essential wealth." There, the Mittler Rebbe regards Yosef's wealth as "successful wealth" arising from his efforts and activity.

5. We have already mentioned on several occasions (*sichot* of Purim and Shabbat *Parshat* Tzav 5736/1976, and *Parshat Naso* and *Parshat Korach* 5745/1985) that very likely this is the reason that "jail" and "prison" are not mentioned in the Torah as a punishment. Since man is "born to work," it is not appropriate for the Torah to punish him by forcing him to sit in jail in a manner that he cannot fulfill his God-given task, to "labor in the world."

6. In the series of Chasidic discourses, *YomTov shel R"H 5666*/1906 of the Rebbe Rashab on the subject of "servants" vs. "sons" (see the discourse entitled *Mikneh Rav* and onward), a "simple servant" does his work because he is forced to do so and he accepts the yoke of his master, and therefore he possesses no identity of his own whatsoever (see page 325 and onward, regarding the pleasure of the "simple servant" — it is the pleasure of his master, not his own, and his work is considered the work of the master). Nevertheless, upon deeper analysis, there is a difference between a "simple servant" whose task is to serve his master, and a prisoner, whose task is the opposite — he is imprisoned and as if non-existent at all.

7. In particular in light of what is written in the discourse above (*YomTov shel R"H* 5666, pp. 310, 312, 322), that Yosef was considered not a "simple servant," but a "trusted servant" in the house of Potiphar (and "also afterward when he functioned as Grand Vizier of Egypt" omitting any reference to Yosef's success while in prison — see p. 322 there).

8. See the letter of the Previous Rebbe, (*Likutei Diburim*, vol. 4, p. 610b and onward, as well as his *Igrot Kodesh* vol. 4, p. 84) regarding the "great spiritual benefit" that accrues in prison.

9. As Pharaoh said to Moshe (Exodus 5:2), "I know nothing of God (*Havaya*)." And here (regarding Potiphar), it is before Yosef was introduced to Pharaoh in order to interpret his dreams, when Yosef explained, "God — *Elokim* — will answer ..." (Genesis 41:16).

10. One could ask regarding Avimelech who said, "We saw and we see that God is with you," (Genesis 26:28) and yet Rashi does not explain there that this was because Yitzchak constantly called upon the name of God. However, it could be answered that Avimelech had already been made aware of God in a dream regarding Avraham (Genesis 20:6), so he was aware of God (*Elokim*). About that awareness,

Avimelech later said to Yitzchak, utilizing a double verb, *rao rainu* — "we saw and we see" — and Rashi explains that *rao* applies to Avraham while *rainu* applies to Yitzchak. Avimelech saw the supernatural success that Yitzchak experienced when he harvested *meah shearim* — one hundred times the crop that he sowed — even though it was a difficult land in a difficult year (Rashi on Genesis 26:12).

11. Here, it could be answered simply that the "minister of the prison" (who put Yosef in charge of all that happened there) was not usually in the same environs as Yosef, and therefore did not hear Yosef speak and constantly call upon the name of God (especially since the prison was a dungeon i.e. a pit dug into the ground (Genesis 40:15, 41:14 and Rashi there). This was not true of Potiphar since Yosef was in Potiphar's house.

Why Yosef Did Not Inform His Father

Mikeitz
37:33

Reading the Torah narrative concerning Yosef's sale into slavery — in our Torah portion (*Parshat Mikeitz*) and in the previous portion (*Parshat Vayeishev*) — we could easily fall into despair over the lack of brotherly love and infighting among siblings.

What happened not only caused Yosef distress, but possibly caused his father, Yaakov, even more distress. Yaakov had already suffered through a twenty-two-year-long exile in the house of Lavan. All he asked for upon his return to the Land of Israel, was to live a quiet, uneventful life, free of the troubles that had plagued him earlier — with Lavan, with Esav and with Dinah.

Indeed, he received a reprieve when he returned and went to live with his father, Yitzchak, in Hebron; there, no serious disturbances took place for a good nine years. But then, his sons reported that one of them, his beloved Yosef, was killed by a wild animal (even though they actually sold him into slavery) and he spent the next twenty-two years mourning the loss of his son. Of course, Yosef was alive and well in Egypt, but Yaakov didn't know that.

And here's the big question: Why didn't Yosef himself inform his father that he was alive and well? Why did Yosef allow his father to wallow in grief over what he thought was the loss of his favorite son, for twenty-two long years?

Rashi says nothing about this subject. And, as we know already, if Rashi says nothing, then either the answer is so simple that a child learning Torah for the first time can figure it out, or it means that the answer is found elsewhere in Rashi's comments on another verse. Whichever explanation applies here, Rashi says nothing on this verse, so we are left to our own devices…

Now, obviously, many of those twenty-two years which Yosef spent in Egypt, he couldn't contact his father. First, he was a slave, and then a prisoner. We can assume that during these periods of time, Yosef was not a free man and, therefore, he was unable to transmit a message and have it delivered to his father, who lived some five days travel away from Egypt.[1] But, after he was made the viceroy of Egypt, Yosef certainly had the ability to contact and inform his father, either by way of one of the frequent caravans traveling to Canaan, or via an oral message sent with a courier. Why did he fail to do so for nearly ten years?[2]

At first glance, it might appear that we could answer this question by referring to Rashi's commentary[3] on a verse (Genesis 37:34) in the previous Torah portion, where it states: "The twenty-two years from the time that Yosef separated from [his father] until Yaakov descended to Egypt … correspond to the twenty-two years that Yaakov failed to fulfill the mitzvah of respecting his own father." (For twenty-two years while in the house of Lavan, Yaakov also failed to contact his father, Yitzchak.) From Rashi's comment, we might infer that this was the reason for Yosef's silence and failure to be in contact with his father. Yosef did not attempt to notify his father because Yaakov's punishment was required to last for twenty-two years, corresponding to the time that he failed to fulfill the mitzvah of honoring his own father. However, we cannot accept this answer because:

- First of all, how could Yosef know that Yaakov was to be punished for twenty-two years for failing to honor his own father?
- Even if we want to say that Yosef knew, why didn't he merely inform his father that he was alive, without letting him know where he was? In that manner, Yaakov's punishment would have been more "fair," since his own father at least knew that Yaakov was alive and well during the twenty-two years that he was not in contact with him.
- Such behavior — hiding information in order to punish his father — would have been totally inappropriate. Even if Yosef knew that a twenty-two-year punishment had been decreed from Above, that would in no way allow him to further punish his father by failing to inform him that he is alive![4]

- Similarly, even if the brothers knew that Yosef was destined to go down to Egypt and become a ruler there and that their father was to be punished for twenty-two years in his absence, would that have given them permission to sell Yosef? Obviously, not. The same answer applies here: it would not have been appropriate to suggest that Yosef could deliberately punish his father by failing to notify him.

Rashi clarifies this matter in his commentary (on Genesis 37:33) regarding why God Himself did not reveal to Yaakov that Yosef was still alive: "The brothers created a pact among themselves and cursed anyone who would reveal this to Yaakov, and they brought God into the pact with them ... Yitzchak knew that Yosef was still alive, but he said to himself, 'How can I reveal it, if God Himself does not want to reveal it?'"

In order to understand this statement from Rashi, we need to analyze it carefully by asking and answering a number of questions:

- Who is included in this "pact," and on whom did the obligations of the pact devolve?

  We cannot say that the pact refers to "anyone who would reveal [the sale] to Yaakov," for if so, Rashi's statement that "Yitzchak knew ... but he said to himself, 'How can I reveal it..." makes no sense. If the pact applied to everyone, then also Yitzchak would not have been able to reveal the secret even if he wanted to.

- Why was there a need to include God in the pact, if in any case, the pact applied to "everyone" [including, so to speak, to God]?[5]

  Therefore, we have to say that the pact did not include "everyone," but only those who made the pact among themselves — the brothers. And by "cursed everyone who would reveal this..." the brothers meant only those were present and who participated in the pact when it was made. And that, of course, included God (except for the curse) as well (since He is everywhere, including among the brothers).[6]

  But if so, Rashi's language indicates that Yitzchak did not want to reveal the secret to Yaakov, since "God Himself does not want..." However, it should not matter whether God "wanted" or not; God was sworn into the pact with the brothers and, therefore, even God "could not" reveal the secret even if He wanted!

- If God "could not" reveal the secret because of the pact, why did Yitzchak refrain from revealing the secret to Yaakov?

God was "sworn" to secrecy and could not reveal the secret, but Yitzchak, was not part of the pact and was not sworn to secrecy, so there was no reason for him to refrain from revealing the secret to Yaakov![7]

- What was the point of this pact? It should have been perfectly possible for the brothers to make a simple agreement among themselves not to reveal the secret to Yaakov. As for God, they could have prayed to Him and requested that He not reveal the secret. Why was there a need for a formal contract among them?[8]
- We find nowhere in the simple text of the Torah (nor in Rashi) that the brothers cancelled the pact before they revealed to Yaakov that Yosef was still alive! If their pact was that none of them should reveal this secret to Yaakov, how could they do so without first cancelling the pact?[9]

There are commentators (the Gur Aryeh) who suggest that, according to Rashi, God was not part of the "pact" that the brothers created, but only served as a sort of "witness" or "guarantor." They base themselves on the Midrash Tanhuma (*Vayeishev* 2), from where Rashi takes his information about the pact.

The Gur Aryeh explains that the brothers "brought God into the pact" since it could not be made without a *minyan* of ten — and Reuven was gone from the group at that time. But, according to his explanation, God's participation in the creation of the pact had nothing whatsoever to do with His ability to reveal the secret to Yaakov. Nevertheless, God did not reveal the secret that Yosef was still alive, because He did not want to make light of the pact between the brothers.

According to this explanation, we can understand why the brothers "brought God into the pact," as well as Rashi's concluding words, that "God Himself did not want to reveal it," but not that God was sworn not to reveal the secret. Since God was not one of the sworn members of the pact, He was not required to withhold the information from Yaakov. Nonetheless, He did not inform Yaakov, simply because He did not want to do so. And, for that reason as well, Yitzchak also decided not to tell Yaakov. However, it turns out to be impossible to explain Rashi in this manner, because:

1. Aside from the fact that nowhere in Rashi is the timing of the pact discussed, it makes sense that the brothers waited until Reuven

returned so that the pact would also apply to Reuven since, otherwise, Rashi would find it necessary to explain why Reuven (as the oldest son) wouldn't reveal the secret to Yaakov.

2. In the text of the verses and in Rashi, there is no indication that ten were needed in order to make the pact. If ten were required, then Rashi would have said so in his commentary. Therefore, it seems that, according to Rashi, God was sworn to secrecy and was also unable to reveal the secret to Yaakov.

This means that all of our previous questions remain in place.

Now, there are also commentators on Rashi who ask another hard question: "How did the brothers know that God agreed to be part of their pact?" For it is impossible to include anyone in a pact in which all the members agree not to reveal a piece of information without receiving that person's agreement! So how was it possible for the brothers to bring God into the pact without first obtaining His permission? (The brothers had no way of knowing at that time whether God agreed with them or not. Only later when they saw that God did not reveal this detail to Yaakov, did they have a clue that, indeed, God did agree with them.)

These commentators proceed to outline several reasons why God would not have wanted to reveal the secret to Yaakov, and therefore the brothers could be certain that God agreed to join their pact:

1. God would have wanted to see the fulfillment of the "covenant between the pieces" during which He had revealed to Avraham that his offspring would descend to Egypt.
2. God wanted to punish Yaakov for the twenty-two years that he did not fulfill the mitzvah of honoring his father.
3. God did not want Yaakov to curse his sons for selling Yosef, which would have resulted in Yaakov's descendants becoming cut off from their family roots.

However, in addition to whatever difficulties are associated with each of the above reasons, it is impossible to fit this attempted explanation into Rashi's comment, and here is why:

Each of these three reasons justifies the withholding of the truth from Yaakov as to the sale of Yosef into Egyptian slavery. But none of the reasons is sufficient to justify withholding from Yaakov the fact that Yosef was still alive. In order to ensure that the divine plan outlined in

Avraham's vision unfolded, or that Yaakov be punished by not seeing his son, or that Yaakov be prevented from cursing the brothers, it was sufficient to withhold the overall story about Yosef from Yaakov. But it was not necessary to withhold the detail that Yosef was still alive. It would have been possible to indicate that Yosef was alive, without explaining what happened to him. That would have been sufficient to fulfill the prophecies of the "covenant between the pieces" and the twenty-two-year "punishment" and also to ensure that Yaakov would not curse his sons (since he would not know that they sold Yosef into slavery).

However, that is not what concerns Rashi in his commentary. Rashi explains, "But Yitzchak knew that Yosef was alive…" This indicates that Rashi is not concerned with the overall narrative, but with the simple fact that Yosef was alive.[10] As far as Rashi sees it, that is what God did not want to reveal to Yaakov and, consequently, Yitzchak as well did not want to reveal that detail. And, therefore, the reasoning of these commentators does not mesh with Rashi's commentary on the Torah.

And so, we must return to our original question: Why did Yosef fail to inform his father that he was alive?

But in order to answer, we need to first ask another, very poignant question: How could it be that in the entire course of the twenty-two years when Yosef was in Egypt, that not one of the brothers broke down and told their father the truth? How is it that not one of these *tzaddikim* could bring himself to do *teshuvah* and relieve their father's suffering by informing Yaakov that his beloved son was still alive?

How could it be that in the entire course of the twenty-two years when Yosef was in Egypt, that not one of the brothers broke down and told their father the truth?

This question stands out especially in light of the fact that the brothers were determined, upon entering Egypt twenty-two years later, to find Yosef and ransom him in order to bring him back to their father. Among themselves, they were heard regretting their deed, "And they said to one another, 'We are guilty concerning our brother for we saw his suffering and torment as he pleaded to us…" (Genesis 42:21). So how is it that none of them broke down and revealed what happened to their father?

This is where the pact between them came into play. This was precisely their motivation for making the pact — the brothers suspected that, after their anger abated, at least one of them would regret his action and damage the others in the process. So, therefore, they "cursed" anyone who would reveal the secret to Yaakov. Henceforth, not a single one of them (or a splinter group) had permission to reveal this secret. But there is no reason to suggest that if all of them decided to reveal the secret, they would still be bound by the pact. If each brother on his own reached the conclusion that the time to reveal Yosef's existence had arrived, then there was nothing holding them back. With unanimous consent among them, there was no need to formally sever the pact, which referred only to individuals. That is why we don't find anywhere in the narrative that they formally cancelled the pact before revealing the secret to Yaakov.

Nevertheless, a certain possibility still lingered even after the pact between the brothers was made preventing any one of them (or a splinter group) from revealing the secret to Yosef. And that is that perhaps one or a few of the brothers might persuade the rest to reveal the secret. Indeed, something similar was related earlier by the Midrash soon after the sale of Yosef, when the brothers said to Yehudah: "If you had advised us to return the boy [Yosef], we would have listened to you." (Rashi on 38:1) Therefore, in order to prevent the possibility of this happening, the brothers "brought God into the pact."

In practice, this meant that the decision if or when to reveal the secret depended strictly on God — He was the one to determine when Yaakov would find out. None of the brothers, or even all of them together, could make this decision without the agreement of the One Above. (Their intention to include God in the pact was not in order to prevent Him from revealing the secret to Yaakov. For, as stated earlier, they had no way of knowing whether or not He agreed to participate. Rather, their intention was to make all of them dependent upon His consent. Only with a sign from God would they reveal the secret to Yaakov. Since they had taken it upon themselves to keep it secret, God would certainly make sure to let them know when He saw fit to reveal it.)

That God did not reveal the secret, as Rashi writes, "was because they made a pact … and made God a 'partner.'" Since they brought God into the pact, promising that they would not reveal the secret without His consent and agreement, therefore He also participated in their pact. That being the case, nullifying the pact and revealing the secret to Yaakov could only occur if all of them, including God, agreed to do so.

Now, Rashi's words can finally be understood. The reason that God did not reveal the secret to Yaakov was not because He was obligated to stick to the pact made by the brothers, but because He did not want to reveal the secret. And from the fact that God "did not want," Yitzchak also inferred that he (Yitzchak) could not.

From this we can also glean the answer to our original question: Why did Yosef not inform his father that he was still alive? The answer is that Yosef, like Yitzchak, assumed that God did not want him to reveal the secret. He thought that if his father does not know that he is alive, it means that God does not want him to know. And, therefore, he should not be the one to inform him. If God did not inform him, this meant that Yaakov did not yet need to know and, therefore, Yosef also said to himself, "How can I reveal to my father the secret which God Himself does not want to reveal to him?"

[Consequently, we can also understand why Rashi did not explain why Yosef did not at least inform his father that he was still alive. Rashi relied on his earlier comment regarding Yitzchak, who did not want to reveal the secret, because how could he reveal it, "if God Himself does not want to reveal it?" From this, it should be clear to a child that Yosef also made the same calculation: "If my father is supposed to know, then God will inform him."]

However, one matter still remains unresolved: Since the pact between the brothers prevented them from revealing to Yaakov that Yosef was still alive, how could Yosef have instructed them to tell their father that he was still alive, especially since God had not revealed this secret?

Rashi explains this detail as well in his commentary on the Torah verse: "And Yaakov saw that there was grain in Egypt" (Genesis 42:1). There, Rashi states that Yaakov saw in an unclear vision that there is "sustenance" in Egypt. This was not a real prophecy informing him about Yosef, although the brothers knew that this is what it meant. From this, they deduced that the time had come to begin to search for Yosef and then get back and inform Yaakov. This was the sign from God they had been waiting for, letting them know that it was time to inform Yaakov.

At that point, "the brothers of Yosef descended to Egypt" (Genesis 42:3), and as Rashi explains there, "they regretted selling Yosef and dedicated themselves to acting with brotherly love in order to redeem him at whatever cost was necessary."[11]

And from Yosef's side, once he understood that they were searching for him and came to redeem him, he also realized the potential significance of the moment. However, since he did not know with certainty that the moment had arrived, and even more so, since he knew that if he would inform his father before his brothers had a chance to do so, this would damage the relations between his father and the brothers, he refrained from revealing the secret. He himself did not inform his father by way of a messenger. Instead, he revealed himself to his brothers, "I am Yosef your brother," (Genesis 45:4) and then they, who made the pact, knew with certainty that now God wanted to reveal to Yaakov that "Yosef still lives" (Genesis 45:26).

From Likutei Sichot of the Lubavitcher Rebbe, vol. 10, pp. 129–135

NOTES

1. *Raboteinu Ba'alei Hatosfot*, write that when Yosef was a slave in the house of Potiphar, he preferred not to inform his father because the information would cause him more distress, and the same applied to when Yosef was imprisoned. But this explanation does not explain the *pshat* level of the text, for if he had informed his father, at least his father would no longer mourn for him. (See Rashi on Genesis 37:35 where he cites the Midrash that Yaakov said, "I have a sign that as long as none of my children die during my lifetime, I am promised from Above that I will not see *gehinom*.") On the simple level then, we have to say that Yosef was unable to contact his father as either slave or prisoner. And if he were able to notify his father, this would have set in motion a demand to free Yosef, as Yosef himself said, "For I was actually stolen from the land of the Hebrews." (Genesis 40:15)

2. *Raboteinu Ba'alei Hatosfot* add that, "even after Yosef became viceroy of Egypt, his father would not have believed him, just as the brothers did not believe Yosef when he informed them that he is the ruler." But obviously on the simple level of the text, this is not a sufficient reason to justify Yosef not informing his father, for in the end when Yosef sent the brothers back to Canaan with the wagons of supplies as a sign, his father ultimately did believe that Yosef was alive (see Rashi on Genesis 45:27). Similarly, Yosef could have sent a sign of life via a messenger or caravan traveling there…

The Ramban states, "Yosef did not want to tell his brothers, 'I am Yosef your brother, hurry and go to our father' … as he did the second time when all the brothers were present … because then his father surely would have come … Instead, Yosef did everything properly at the right time in order to fulfill the predictions of his dreams, since he knew that they would truly come to fruition. And also, the other thing that he did with the goblet was not because he wished to torment them, but because he suspected that they harbored resentment against Binyamin…"

The reason that Rashi did not resolve the question in the same manner as the Ramban (in addition to the fact that Ramban's answer only resolves why Yosef did not reveal his identity immediately to his brothers, but not why he did not inform his father for at least seven years before the brothers arrived) is that according to the simple level of the text, it is not logical that Yosef would leave his father in sorrow and grief over this period of time only in order to see his dreams fulfilled down to the last letter (as asked in the *Akeidah, Sha'ar* 29 and by the *Chatam Sofer* on the Torah). Similarly, it is difficult to accept the words of the Ramban in his conclusion…

3. See also Rashi's commentary on *Megillah* 17a.

4. None of these questions bear any connection to the issue of whether the *bnei Noach* are obligated to respect their parents (see Rashi end of *Parshat Noach*, as well as *Likutei Sichot* vol. 5, pp. 147, 153) and whether the need to inform his father is included in the category of "respecting one's parents." (See the letter from the Alter Rebbe in *Meah Shearim* 4a.) It is obvious the Yosef would not trouble or torment anyone over a period of years, and certainly not over such a sensitive issue and not his own father!

5. *Raboteinu Baalei Hatosfot* (on Genesis 37:35): "From here it may be proven that when the members of a congregation all agree to make a pact, and one person opposes them … and says, "I will not join you in this pact," nevertheless he is included in the pact against his will [by virtue of the will of the majority]. For Yosef was not a part of the pact among the brothers yet, nevertheless, he did not want to reveal and inform his father that he was alive." See also Rabbeinu Bahaye there (Ch. 33 at the end): "Binyamin did not reveal the secret, since the other nine brothers and Hashem agreed not to reveal the matter to Yaakov."

Raboteinu Ba'alei Hatosfot, commenting on Parshat *Mikeitz*: "They created a pact and included God in it, and they also made Yosef take an oath that he won't reveal the secret. The Scripture proves this, because it says (in Genesis 45:1), "Remove everyone from me," because he [Yosef] did not want any strangers to know, because of the oath." So it is also written in *Paneach Raza* (on *Parshat Vayigash* there), "Also Yosef was included in the pact and oath not to reveal that he was sold." But according to *pshat*, it is very difficult to accept that at the same time that the brothers saw "his sorrow as he pleaded" (Genesis 42:21) they also extracted an oath from Yosef and included him in the pact against his will (even though if the secret were revealed to Yaakov, the result would have been to free Yosef from Egypt). In addition, to suggest that all this is "simple and obvious" in the *pshat,* to the extent that Rashi need not even hint at it, even to child [stretches the imagination]…

6. Of course, this did not mean that the brothers "cursed Him" (God forbid) if He were to reveal the secret, for as we will see, quite the opposite - the brothers left it up to God to determine when the secret will be revealed. Obviously, the "curse" applied only to the brothers themselves.

7. From the *Maskil l'David*: "Since God agreed to the pact, no man could violate it. This is similar to the declaration (*Moed Katan* 17a) that 'Whomever is not permitted to associate with a [certain] teacher, is not permitted to associate with his student.' And that is why Yitzchak said, 'How can I reveal this secret to Yaakov,

that even God does not reveal…' But according to the *pshat*, there is no necessity to claim that, because God agreed to their request to join them, it became forbidden for any person to reveal the secret. In addition, from Rashi's language, 'How can I reveal?' it is understood that Yitzchak was not forbidden to reveal the secret [but rather chose not to do so]."

8. There is no room to claim that by praying they could find out what was the divine desire of God and whether He agreed with the brothers or not. It was not certain that their prayers would be answered and that God would not reveal the secret and, therefore, it was necessary to bring Him into the pact, because even when they did bring Him into the pact, it was not certain that they did so with His agreement.

9. But in the Midrash Tanhuma (*Parshat Vayeishev* 2) it states: "And they cancelled the pact." We find the same in Raboteinu Baalei Hatosfot (beginning of Ch. 42), and in the *Baal Haturim* 45:26. [The reference in *Likutei Sichot* to 25–26, is a printing error.]

10. There is room to suggest that the brothers made a pact not only to stop each other from revealing that Yosef had been sold, but from revealing that Yosef was still alive. And that is why Rashi states that "Yitzchak knew that Yosef was alive, but he said 'How can I reveal it, if God Himself does not reveal it?'" That is, since the pact in which they brought in God as a partner was only to silence those who would reveal that the brothers had sold Yosef, and, nevertheless, it was apparent the God did not reveal that Yosef was alive (even though the pact did not preclude this possibility), implies that God simply did not want to reveal the secret, which is why Yitzchak said, "How can I reveal…" However, it is not at all logical that the brothers would make a pact only about the sale, and not about revealing that Yosef is alive. It was the brothers who brought Yosef's coat of many colors to Yaakov full of blood and claimed that a wild animal attacked Yosef. What forced the brothers to bring the coat — thereby turning the pact into an agreement not only to conceal the sale of Yosef but also to conceal that he was alive — was the fact that Yaakov sent Yosef to them, and now that Yosef was no longer among them. This meant that there was much room for suspicion that the brothers had acted against Yosef, and they sought to allay that suspicion by claiming that it was a wild animal that killed Yosef.

11. From Rashi on Genesis 42:3: The brothers did not immediately reveal to Yaakov that Yosef was alive (when Yaakov dreamt about "sustenance" in Egypt) because Yaakov would not have believed them, as we can deduce from the verses. Thus, it becomes clear why they wanted to find him and bring him to Yaakov.

Beginning or the End?

Mikeitz 41:1

Our Torah portion — *Parshat Mikeitz* — begins with the words, "*Vayehi mikeitz sh'natayim yamim…*" which is usually translated as, "It was at the end of two years."

That's the way Rashi explains it. But, why does Rashi have to explain anything here? The word *mikeitz* has previously appeared a few times in the Torah (Genesis 4:3, 8:6, and 16:3), and Rashi didn't say anything there, so why does he find it necessary to say something here — that *mikeitz* means "at the end"?

Moreover, Rashi doesn't suffice with explaining; he brings proofs. He cites the understanding of the Targum Onkelos,[1] then adds that everywhere the word appears, it means the same thing — "at the end."[2] If Rashi didn't need to explain the word previously, why does he go to such lengths to prove his point at this juncture?[3]

It must be that, although the word *mikeitz* usually means "at the end," there is something unusual about the way it is used in *Parshat Mikeitz*. And that makes it necessary for Rashi to explain that, even here, *mikeitz* means "at the end."

In all the previous occasions the word *mikeitz* appeared in the Torah, it was always at the end of an event that lead up to and caused the next event. For example, in the story of Kayin and Hevel, we read that Kayin was a farmer who worked the land, and "at the end (*mikeitz*) of a number of days Kayin brought an offering from the produce of the land" (Genesis 4:3). Then in the story of Noach, we read that after the waters of the Flood receded enough for the mountains to appear, which was "at the end (*mikeitz*) of forty days, Noach opened the ark..." (Genesis 8:6). Finally, we read that "at the end (*mikeitz*) of ten years in Canaan" during which Avram and Sarai were without offspring, Avram took Hagar, his wife's handmaiden, as a concubine (Genesis 16:3). In all cases, *mikeitz* — "at the end" — followed a situation that was causally related to the event that followed.

However, in our Torah portion, the situation is different. When Pharaoh dreamt, it was already two years after Yosef interpreted the dreams of Pharaoh's ministers — the butler and baker — in the prison. The butler was freed, but immediately forgot about Yosef. Indeed, that is how the previous Torah portion — *Parshat Vayeishev* — ends: "The butler did not remember Yosef, but forgot him" (Genesis 40:23). This strongly suggests that what happened was in the past, and there is no causal relation to the dreams of Pharaoh which begin our *parsha*, *Parshat Mikeitz.*

Precisely because there is no apparent causal apparent relationship between the end of one Torah portion and the beginning of the next is why Rashi found it necessary to explain that, even here, *mikeitz* means "at the end" of the previous events. It was Pharaoh's desperate search for a dream interpreter that triggered the butler's recollection of Yosef, but there was no causal connection between Yosef's earlier interpretation and Pharaoh's dreams, especially since the butler forgot about Yosef in the intervening two years. Even so, *Parshat Mikeitz* still refers back to those events and means the same thing as it does elsewhere — "at the end."

Despite Rashi telling us that, wherever we find the word *mikeitz*, it means "the end," there is actually another way of understanding the word. The Ibn Ezra (who, like Rashi, explains the simple meaning of the Scripture), says that *mikeitz* can mean either "at the end" or "at the beginning" (Numbers 13:25). This is because Ibn Ezra understands the word *mikeitz* to mean "edge" (Psalms 119:96) rather than "end." An "edge" may be either a beginning or an end.

If we understand *mikeitz* to mean "at the beginning," then we would read the verse: "At the beginning of the two years, Pharaoh dreamt...." Thereafter, he brought Yosef out of prison to hear his dreams interpreted, and then at the end of those two years, the seven years of plenty began. However, this understanding presents a major difficulty, since Yosef states that the repetition of the same themes in Pharaoh's dreams means that they were about to be fulfilled, immediately after the dreams. That made it exceedingly unlikely that two years would pass between when

Pharaoh dreamt and when the actual events (abundance followed by famine) would occur. It's therefore difficult to agree with Ibn Ezra and say that *mikeitz* means "at the beginning." Nevertheless, Ibn Ezra's understanding is preferable to explaining that *mikeitz* means "the end" of something that is not clearly not connected to what came before.

To grasp the actual meaning of this verse, it's helpful to go to another level of interpretation that gives us deeper insight. On one hand, "at the end" (as in Rashi's commentary) alludes to the days Yosef spent in prison, forgotten and alone. It was undoubtedly the darkest period of Yosef's life. But, as the Previous Rebbe of Lubavitch, Rabbi Yosef Yitzchak Schneersohn, said of our last days in exile, "the darkness is greatest just before dawn." And so, the very same period was the beginning (as in Ibn Ezra's commentary) of the redemption of Yosef and his elevation to the second highest position in the land.

These two perspectives correspond to the Kabbalistic commentaries on our verse:

The Zohar describes *mikeitz* as the "end of the left side (*din*, or judgment)," and the Ari describes *mikeitz* as the "beginning of the right side (kindness)." The Zohar, then, is emphasizing (like Rashi) the end of the previous two bad years which Yosef spent in prison. And the Ari is emphasizing (like Ibn Ezra) the two good years which saw Yosef freed from prison and achieving respect and honor in Egypt.[4]

In truth, these two perspectives are connected, and the commentary of Rashi leads up to the commentary of the Ibn Ezra. For it is the *keitz desmola:* "end of the left side (negativity)" that leads to the *keitz hayamin:* the "beginning of the right side (positivity)."

Yosef's years in prison were necessary in order for him to grow spiritually and refine himself and his surroundings, elevating the sparks of holiness that were trapped there. When he had done so, while strengthening his faith and attachment to G-d, he prepared his own redemption from prison. Then, once out, he was able to begin the start of a long period of redemption.

[The end of the previous "negative period" is what is necessary in order to prepare us for the beginning of the final "positive period." And we see the same in our own segment of Jewish history, during which we have risen from the ashes of the concentration camps — the lowest point yet of the Jewish people in exile — to ascend once again to our home in the Land of Israel.

Although it's far from perfect, and it's still in the process of creation, the Jewish state has already attracted nearly half of the Jews of the world in the space of sixty short years. There is much work still to be done in order to create a true Jewish haven of Torah and mitzvoth in *Eretz Yisrael*, but we can see the hand of G-d in bringing us from the gehenna of Europe to the Holy Land.

As the Previous Rebbe said, the darkest period occurs just before dawn, but as the number of Jews in the Holy Land increases, and their observance of Torah and mitzvoth also increases, we draw yet closer to the final day that we've been hoping and praying for — when the Mashiach finally arrives and we dwell securely in our homeland and built the third and final Temple!][5]

From Likutei Sichot of the Lubavitcher Rebbe, vol. 5, pp. 196–201

NOTES

1. The Targum Onkelos (the translation of Onkelos from Hebrew to Aramaic) is close to the *pshat*, which is one reason why Rashi cites it to support his own commentary.

2. The "proof" from Targum Onkelos is not enough for Rashi, since there are many occasions in which Rashi does not agree with the Targum Onkelos, starting with the very first verse of the Torah. Moreover, even in the places where Rashi does write *k'targumo*, meaning that he agrees with the translation of Onkelos, it is because Rashi in any case holds that his explanation is correct, but since there may be a specific difficulty with his comment (or for similar reasons), he brings additional proof.

3. The Gur Aryeh (Maharal on Rashi) says here that, "Rashi seeks to explain that the word *keitz* means "end," and not "edge." And the Maharal wants to "prove" this from Rashi's statement that "everywhere the Torah uses the word *keitz*, it means "end." According to the Maharal, if it meant "edge," then it would be sometimes necessary to explain the word *keitz* as "beginning," and not "end," since sometimes an "edge" can be a "beginning." This is why Rashi does not explain the word *keitz* on any of the previous occasions that it appeared in the Torah — because on those occasions, it did not matter if the word was explained as either "edge" or "end." But on our verse, if the word means "edge," it means that the edge is an integral part of the object itself, which is incomplete without its "edge" (as in the verse, "And he made one *cherub* on this edge..." meaning "on the *kaporet* (top of the ark) itself, at its edge). And if so, the explanation of, "And Pharaoh dreamt..." occurred before the two years were completed, which according to the Gur Aryeh, "is not plausible." And therefore, Rashi writes, "As the Targum states, 'at the end,'

meaning 'at the end of the two years.'" However, there are several difficulties with this explanation of the Gur Aryeh on Rashi:

1) In several instances, Rashi explains the meaning of a word even though it makes no difference in the *pshat* if the explanation is as Rashi claims or otherwise. Among them: Genesis 2:5 in which the word *terem* can mean either "until" or "prior to," Rashi explains that it means "until" (*ad lo*) even though the *pshat* of the verse is the same either way. And Genesis 30:8 where Rashi interprets *naftuli* from the word meaning "wrestling," unlike Menachem ben Saruk who interprets the word meaning "joined together," even though the *pshat* in the verse is the same with either interpretation. Since this is so, Rashi could have given his explanation of *keitz* the very first time that it appears in the Torah in Genesis 4:3.

2) In one of the prior instances (Genesis 16:3) — "at the end of ten years" — there is a halachic difference that is dependent upon our explanation of the word *keitz.* A man may be required to marry another woman after ten years of marriage to a wife who bears him no children (see Rashi there).

3) In Yirmiyahu 34:14 — "At the end (*mikeitz*) seven years, every Jewish man should set his Jewish servants free..." According to *pshat,* we must explain that the verse refers to the "beginning" of the seventh year, since the relevant verse in the Torah is: "...he will serve you for six years." So, when Rashi wrote that, "everywhere the Torah uses the word *ketiz,* it means "end," he must have been referring even to units or objects that are incomplete [because here, if "seventh" means the beginning of the seventh year, and the servant is set free at the beginning of the seventh year, his seventh year is "incomplete"; see Ramban's commentary on the verse, "at the end of seven years" (Deuteronomy 15:1) — "every seventh year" includes its beginning as the end of the number"]. Thus, it emerges that Rashi's statement, "everywhere the Torah uses the word *keitz...*" cannot be a proof that that the word means "after two years have completed."

4. The Zohar 193b explains that *mikeitz* [the first significant word of the verse] is "the place of no memory" [Pharaoh's butler "did not remember Yosef and forgot him"]. And the second two words *shenatatyim yamim* (literally, "two years' worth of days") is a "return of one level to the next, where there is memory." Accordingly, the explanation of the Zohar that *mikeitz* is the "end of the left side" does not connect with the following words, "two years" [*mikeitz* is a "stand-alone" word referring to the end of hiddenness and concealment]. But, the explanation of the Ari that *mikeitz* refers to the "beginning of the two years" [does connect to the following words, and therefore does allude to the next "two years" of light and revelation]. This explanation according to *sod* fits well with the two opinions of Rashi and Ibn Ezra on the *pshat* of the verse: According to the explanation that *mikeitz* means the "beginning," so it is the beginning of two years. But according to the explanation that *mikeitz* means the "end," then it is not the conclusion or result of the following two years.

4. This section is not from the Rebbe's *sicha.* It was added by the translator.

Unique Dream Interpretations of Yosef

Mikeitz 41:33

When the Torah — in *Parshat Mikeitz* — reports Pharaoh's dreams along with Yosef's interpretations, it all seems to make sense. Pharaoh dreamt of seven cows who emerged from the Nile River, fat and healthy. They were followed by seven thin and emaciated cows, who emerged from the same river, stood next to the healthy cows, and then proceeded to consume them. Pharaoh woke up, only to fall asleep once more and dream of seven healthy sheaves of wheat, followed by seven thin sheaves which consumed the healthy sheaves. He woke up again, and the Torah records that "he was distraught" (Genesis 41:8).[1] He called on his advisors, who interpreted the dream, "but none could interpret them for Pharaoh" — in other words, their interpretations failed to satisfy him. At that juncture, Pharaoh's butler recalled that, two years earlier, his own dream had been successfully interpreted by Yosef. So Yosef was removed from prison and brought before Pharaoh.

Yosef's interpretation was that the seven healthy sheaves and the seven fat cows represented seven years of plenty — an abundance of grain and produce to feed the Egyptians — while the seven wilted sheaves and emaciated cows represented seven years of famine and deprivation. After reporting his interpretations, Yosef proceeded to advise Pharaoh how to run his kingdom: "Pharaoh should appoint a man who is understanding and wise to administer the land of Egypt … Gather all the food of the upcoming good years and put it under Pharaoh's surveillance in the cities" (Genesis 41:33–35). In other words, save the food from the good years in order to feed the Egyptians during the bad years.

Pharaoh was very impressed with Yosef's advice and made him viceroy of Egypt in order to carry out this plan.

Here are the questions:

1. What is so remarkable about Yosef's interpretation? It is fairly clear that the fat cows and the healthy wheat represent times of plenty. And it is obvious that such things occur in cycles, so why couldn't Pharaoh himself, together with his advisors, come up with this interpretation?
2. How could Yosef, fresh out of an Egyptian prison, presume to mix in the government of Egypt and offer advice to Pharaoh on what to do about the upcoming predicament? Yosef had been called upon only to offer his interpretations of the dreams, not to offer advice to Pharaoh![2]
3. After Yosef gave his advice, the Torah states that "the thing was good in Pharaoh's eyes" (Genesis 41:37). Why did Pharaoh not praise Yosef's dream interpretations first, before going on to assess his advice as "good"?

In order to answer the above questions,[3] we need to understand why Rashi, in his commentary, cites the erroneous dream interpretation offered by Pharaoh's advisors — which was that Pharaoh would sire seven daughters and also bury seven daughters. Since this explanation was rejected by Pharaoh, why does Rashi find it necessary to mention it at all?

The fact that he does mention it leads us to conclude that Rashi considers the interpretation to be reasonable on the simple level of the text, even if incorrect. And by analyzing the difference between the advisors' interpretation and Yosef's interpretation, we can better understand what motivated the advisors in their thinking as well as the great novelty of Yosef's interpretation.

The Abarbanel suggests that the distinction between Yosef and Pharaoh's advisors was the following: The advisors were knowledgeable regarding dream interpretation, as well as how the human imagination works to generate parables and symbols in dreams. That is why they interpreted Pharaoh's dreams in symbolic terms, rather than trying to understand them in a straightforward manner. However, Yosef worked not only with knowledge and understanding of dreams, but also with divine inspiration (*ruach hakodesh*). In this case, his divine inspiration told him that these were no ordinary dreams to be interpreted symbolically, but rather that these were dreams that meant exactly what they said, and they needed to be interpreted simply.

However, the Abarbanel's commentary does not fit with the simple meaning of the previous Torah narratives related to dreams. In fact, all previous dreams in the Torah were meant to be understood simply, not symbolically. There was the dream of Yaakov and the ladder, and there was Yaakov's dream of the sheep as they were mating. These were dreams that occurred naturally and meant exactly what they showed — angels ascending and descending, sheep breeding. The same is true of Yosef's dreams regarding his brothers — they applied to his family situation and it was not necessary to find any symbolic meaning behind them.[4] Therefore, according to Rashi, it would be difficult to say, as the Abarbanel does, that the difference between Pharaoh's advisors and Yosef was the level of interpretation, since no dreams in the Torah up to this point were interpreted symbolically. And, in any case, it is always more elegant to find a simple interpretation rather than a symbolic one that may or may not be accurate.

And, in any case, it is always more elegant to find a simple interpretation rather than a symbolic one that may or may not be accurate.

The more apt explanation is as follows:

Both Yosef and the advisors experienced a difficulty with one specific detail of Pharaoh's dreams. When the thin and emaciated cows emerged from the Nile, they first stood next to the fat cows before devouring them (Genesis 41:3). If the accurate interpretation is, as Yosef said, that the cows represented good and bad years, then the thin cows should have followed the fat cows and eaten them, but not stood with them. Just as one year follows another, and a set of seven years follows a previous set of seven without overlap, so the thin cows should have followed the fat cows, without standing together with them before devouring them.[5] It was incumbent upon Yosef as well as upon Pharaoh's advisors to explain this inconvenient detail.

The advisors found a way out by going with a symbolic interpretation. By saying that the dreams symbolized "seven daughters born and seven daughters buried," they got around the detail of the fat cows standing next to the thin cows in Pharaoh's dream. In those days, a ruler could take several wives and concubines, and it was entirely possible that daughters from seven different wives or concubines would be born and live while daughters from others would die. Since it may also occur that some daughters would die while others would be born, it was possible for the two to be simultaneous. This is why Rashi mentions the interpretation of the advisors, rather than just stating simply that it wasn't acceptable to Pharaoh. Rashi sought to draw our attention to the detail that was problematic, and for which Yosef ultimately found a solution that satisfied Pharaoh, who knew that his own dreams had to do with his governance of Egypt and not with his personal situation.[6]

Rather than giving a symbolic interpretation of Pharaoh's dreams, Yosef found a way to explain them elegantly, on a simple level. He said that the thin cows stood next to the fat cows because the thin years would have to overlap with the fat years at the same time. During the fat years, produce would have to be stored in order to prepare for the bad years — this meant that the bad years would (in a sense) be existing at the same time as the good years. That is, if Pharaoh followed the advice implied in his dreams, the thin years would accompany the fat years because, as Yosef told him, it was necessary to gather and store the produce during the fat years in order to prepare for the thin years.

Since Pharaoh now had knowledge of the upcoming years of famine and could prepare for them by storing food during the preceding years of plenty, it would be as if both sets of years existed together, just as the thin cows stood next to the fat cows.

And now we may understand why Yosef had the chutzpah to offer advice to Pharaoh, even though he was only a slave just taken out of prison. Indeed, Yosef did not offer advice. Rather, he revealed to Pharaoh the counsel that was contained in his dreams — to prepare now for the upcoming years of famine. To do so, it was necessary to establish an administrator over all of Egypt, who could ensure that produce was stored and not consumed. This advice was contained in Pharaoh's dreams; it was not injected by Yosef. Rather than simply predicting seven good years and the seven bad years, the dreams informed Pharaoh how to prepare for the lean years. This is what Yosef told Pharaoh. The detail that was difficult for the advisors to interpret — that the thin cows stood next to the fat cows — was what Yosef was able to interpret to Pharaoh's satisfaction.

And that is why the Torah says that "the thing was good in the eyes of Pharaoh." Pharaoh was more impressed with the advice contained in the dreams than he was with Yosef's interpretation, but in truth the advice emerged from within the interpretation. The advice was one with the interpretation; it was not Yosef's invention.

As well, there were deeper dimensions to all this. Pharaoh's dreams and Yosef's interpretations were both the reason for, and the beginning of, the exile of the Jews to Egypt. This is obvious on the simple level, since it was soon after Yosef's appointment as viceroy in Egypt that Yaakov and his sons arrived there. It is written, "When the Lord brings back the captives of Zion, we will be like dreamers..." (Psalms 126:1) So, it is understood that within dreams and their interpretations are to be found the riddles of exile. Just as in dreams, we find impossible opposites existing together, so in exile we find opposites co-existing. The opposites within Pharaoh's dreams — the famished cows standing next to the healthy cows — are reflected in the reality of our lives in the Diaspora. On the one hand, we strive for a life of spirituality, so that during prayer we can ascend to great heights. On the other hand, we are faced with the worrisome demands of making a daily living and putting food on the table. The two exist together — the thin cows correspond to the need to make a living, while the fat cows correspond to spiritual ascendancy.

It is Yosef who taught us how to live with these two opposites. His interpretation of Pharaoh's dreams showed that a life of spirituality may co-exist with a life of physical demands. We learn this from the juxtaposition of opposites in dreams.

Because, at his soul-source, Yosef was from a world that joined opposites together, he was able to put this world-view into action in this physical world. His perception of Godliness, even while in Egypt was pure and unadulterated. We, however, may feel overwhelmed with the demands of exile — the need to make a living as well as to help others — and, therefore, our perception of Godliness may be contaminated with worldliness. It is Yosef who taught us how to overcome the worldliness and resist the darkness, while simultaneously growing spiritually.

From Likutei Sichot of the Lubavitcher Rebbe, vol. 15, pp. 339–347

NOTES

1. Rashi says that he was like someone who had forgotten something important and needed to be reminded.

2. Furthermore, what was the great wisdom demonstrated by Yosef when he offered his advice to Pharaoh to prepare the land of Egypt during the seven years of plenty for the seven years of famine? It is obviously understood that the proper approach is to save produce from the plentiful years for use during the famine years.

3. All of these questions are concerned with the simple level of the text. So why doesn't Rashi raise these questions? The fact that Rashi says nothing to answer the above questions means that their answers are patently obvious, even to a child learning Torah for the first time, and therefore there is no need for Rashi to offer explanation.

4. Although it could be argued that the sheaves of Yosef's first dream and the planetary bodies of his second dream were also symbols, because they weren't literally dreams of Yosef and his family, nevertheless since the intention of the dreams was to prophesy events to take place in the future, therefore the dreams had to be enclothed in some form of symbolism, even if the symbols were very close to the literal meaning. In the case of Yosef's dreams, the first dream of sheaves of wheat indicated that the brothers would have to approach Yosef for a financial reason (as did occur ultimately, since the brothers went down to Egypt in order to secure grain for the family, and needed Yosef for that purpose). And the sun, moon and stars of the second dream indicated that the protagonists of the dream — Yaakov and his family — were important, just as the sun, moon and stars are important. (From *Likutei Sichot*, vol. 10, p. 116, footnote 10.)

5. This is not a mere technicality. The detail of the sets of cows standing next to each other stands in direct contradiction to the concept of a chronological narrative suggested by the numbers (seven cows of each type). Therefore, it cannot be argued that this is one of the "false details" that must be present in any dream, including dreams that are true overall. Since in the dream, the thin years followed the plentiful years in a way that "consumed" the plentiful years, meaning that the good years were "nullified" by the bad years, it is not possible to suggest that they existed "together." And yet, that is what is implied by the thin cows standing next to the fat cows. Since this detail stands in diametric contradiction to the apparent message of the dreams, it cannot be dismissed as one of the "false details" that all dreams contain. Moreover, when the sages said there is no such thing as a "dream without false details," they were referring to details that would not take place, but not to details that did not seem to fit a particular interpretation. (*Likutei Sichot,* vol. 10, p. 116, footnote 11)

6. According to the Abarbanel, this is one of the details about which Yosef differed with Pharaoh's advisors: whether the dreams were about Pharaoh himself (the advisors) or about his nation in general (Yosef).

Chanukah Candles and Shabbat

Rambam
Hilchot Chanukah 4:14

If you have only one candle, and the Shabbat of Chanukah is approaching — during which you are supposed to light both Shabbat and Chanukah candles — what do you do?

You light the Shabbat candle, because "it brings peace into the home." So says the Rambam (at the end of the *Laws of Chanukah*).[1] He goes on to add that the entire purpose of the Torah is to bring peace to the world.

Now you might think that Rambam would discuss this law in the section on the *Laws of Shabbat*, wherein we learn all of the laws regarding Shabbat candle lighting. But for some reason he chooses to discuss it at the end of the *Laws of Chanukah*.

The mitzvoth of the Torah are divided into two categories: positive and negative. The purpose of the positive mitzvoth is to bring spiritual light and illumination to the world through positive action. The purpose of the negative commandments is to deflect and vanquish negativity, by refraining from activities that amplify spiritual darkness. Chanukah, together with the other mitzvoth from our sages, is unique in that it involves a positive action (lighting the Chanukah menorah, or *Chanukiah*), which achieves the same thing (or more, since Chanukah achieves more than repelling darkness — it transforms it) as a Torah-based negative commandment — driving away spiritual darkness.

Here's where it gets interesting:

If, as the Rambam says, the entire purpose of the Torah is to bring peace to the world, then two mitzvoth — such as lighting the Shabbat candles and lighting the Chanukah candles — cannot come into conflict with each other. After all, the two mitzvoth have similar though different purposes. The Shabbat candles bring light and warmth to the home so that "no one will stumble over wood or stone." (*Shulchan Aruch HaRav* 263:1) And the purpose of the Chanukah candles is to light up the public arena, thus driving away darkness.

True peace does not mean that one party is victorious and righteous while the other is a vanquished loser. In our case, it must mean that each mitzva — Shabbat candles and Chanuka candles — contributes to "peace" it its own particular way. Taking matters one step further, it must be that true peace means that one side persuades and includes the other. It must be then that the Shabbat candles do not take precedence over the Chanukah candles, but rather that they somehow include the content of the Chanukah candles. It must be that lighting the Shabbat candles (when one has only one candle) somehow includes the effect of lighting the Chanukah candles as well.

Shabbat is, in essence, a positive mitzvah. While it's true that most of the laws of Shabbat involve avoiding various labors, nevertheless the underlying principle of Shabbat is rest, study and prayer. That is, the negative mitzvoth of Shabbat (the 39 forbidden labors and the various decrees of the rabbis) are the mechanism that enables the positive experience of keeping Shabbat. In essence, Shabbat is positive, and the Shabbat candles come to lend honor and enjoyment to the holy day. As a further consequence, they also provide light and peace in the home (*shalom bayit*).

Chanukah, however, is a holiday that we celebrate as a result of our success in repelling negative forces from the holy Land. It took a war and tremendous self-sacrifice to rid Israel of the Hellenistic influences that were sprouting in the Land. The celebration of Chanukah, then, comes as the result of victory over negativity. The Chanukah candles celebrate the happiness of victory, but it was a victory of light over spiritual darkness. The purpose of the Chanukah candles is to proclaim and publicize that victory (and accompanying miracle), and to impart power to drive away adversaries.

Thus, when one has only one candle, the Shabbat candle (symbolizing the positive experience of peace in the home) clearly trumps the Chanukah candle (symbolizing victory over darkness). Moreover, the Shabbat candles provide real, physical light in the house that prevents "stumbling over wood and stone," while Chanukah candles only symbolize the victory of light over darkness, but do not necessarily provide *physical* light to illuminate the public arena. We light the Chanukah candles in the doorway or in a window to symbolize the principle of illumination of the public arena, but the light is not sufficient to illuminate such a large area. Moreover, it is forbidden to benefit from the light of the Chanukah candles, so they do not carry the same positive message as the candles of Shabbat.

The simple peace without any resistance (that is Shabbat) overrides the peace via victory over opponents (that is Chanukah). However, this is not a nullification or dismissal of that victory. Rather, the Shabbat candles include the power of the Chanukah candles. Simple, pure peace without opposition presumes and includes the power to vanquish enemies. That's why if you have only one candle, you light it as a Shabbat candle. And that's also why the Rambam assigns this *halachah* to the laws of Chanukah, and not to the laws of Shabbat. It is the laws of Chanukah themselves that dictate lighting the Shabbat candle in this situation, because the Shabbat candles bring simple peace that includes the power of light over darkness, and as the Rambam said, the Torah is all about peace.

The simple peace without any resistance (that is Shabbat) overrides the peace via victory over opponents (that is Chanukah).

There is something else unique about lighting the Chanukah candles. Not only do we place the Chanukah candles on the left side of the door, but we perform the lighting from the left to the right, whereas almost all other mitzvoth are done on/with the right side or the right hand. In fact, some of the commandments concerning the Temple are invalid if performed with the left hand; only the right is appropriate.[2] Yet, the Chanukah candles are to be lit on the left side of the door (as one enters the house) and are lit from left to right.

All of the rabbinic mitzvoth, including Chanukah lights, have their origin and root in one or more of the 613 mitzvoth of the Torah.[3] Of those 613, only one mitzvah from the Torah gives precedence to the left side over the right, and that is the mitzvah of *tefillin*. *Tefillin* are put on the "weaker" hand, which usually is the person's left hand. This suggests that not only do Chanukah lights and *tefillin* have something in common, but that Chanukah lights have a source in the mitzvah of *tefillin*.

Like so many things that demand elucidation in the Torah, the explanations here come from the inner dimension (*sod*) of the Torah. According to Kabbalah and Chassidut, the right side draws goodness and light down into the world. It is associated with *chessed*, or "kindness," that comes to us from above to below. In contrast, the left side deflects and repels negativity. It is associated with *gevurah*, or "judgment and stringency," and gives us the power to elevate from below to above.

Since *gevurah* is the tool exercising judgment, it may have a side-effect: it leaves room for negativity to attach itself and get "nourishment," as it were. This can be understood psychologically; when a person disciplines himself and works hard to improve himself, he may develop a tendency to judge others as well. He may tend to look at others with a jaundiced eye as if they are not up to his standards. This is not the way it should be; one should judge only himself, while accepting others as they are. Yet sometimes it's "only human" to direct criticism at others. When this is done lovingly and constructively, there is room for it, but when undertaken out of an overflow of self-discipline, it can have negative consequences. The same is true on a metaphysical level: where there is a *gevurah*, or judgment, negative forces can push their way in. Thus, spiritual forces of negativity are associated with the left side in Kabbalah and Chassidut.

Now here is the reason that the Chanukah candles are lit on the left side of the door, or in an area that overlooks the public arena. Both the left side (as noted previously) and the public arena are places where negative forces tend to congregate. Wherever there is either an excess of judgment (the left side), or none at all (the public arena, especially as it becomes dark), is where negative forces tend to attach themselves. The Chanukah candles symbolically illuminate and tame the public arena, while the Shabbat candles illuminate and bring peace into the home. Therefore, the Shabbat candles are for inside, and the Chanukah candles are for outside.

The other mitzvah of the Torah that is done with the left side is *tefillin*. And like Chanukah candles, we find that there is a significant element of "driving away and repelling" of negative forces associated with this practice.

The Zohar states that we bind *tefillin* upon our left arm in order to tie up the *yetzer harah*, or "evil inclination," which resides in the left side of the heart. And the Torah itself tells us that the purpose of the head *tefillin* is to instill fear of God in those who see them. So, not only Chanukah candles but also *tefillin* are for the purpose of illuminating and fixing that which is "outside" of ourselves, on the "left side." (This is one more reason to establish *tefillin* booths outside, in the public arena, for those who have not yet put them on that day.)

All this is encapsulated in the Talmudic story of the would-be convert, who approached the great sage Hillel with the request that he teach him the whole Torah while standing on one foot (*Shabbat* 31a). The Chassidic Rebbe, R' Yehoshua Hurvitz explains (in his book *Ateret Yehoshua*) that the would-be convert was not making fun of Hillel. He came to the great sage on Chanukah and stood on his left foot. He knew that Chanukah is the time when the holy sparks of the public arena "come in from the cold." He knew that he was "outside" of the realm of holiness and he wanted in. He was coming from the "left side," and he wanted to join the side of holiness.[4]

Hillel recognized the sincerity of his request. He said, "what is hateful to you, do not do unto others," couching it in negative terms. He could have expressed it positively, by saying for example, "do only good unto others." However, he wanted to meet the man where he was, on the "left [negative] side," and bring him over to the side of holiness.

And then Hillel concluded, "Now go and learn." For, this is how he could bring him under the wings of the *Shechinah*.

Based on sichot of the Lubavitcher Rebbe,
vol. 5 (pp. 223–227) and vol. 15 (pp. 372–381)

NOTES

1. Based on *Shabbat* 23b.

2. Mitzvoth related to the *korbanot*, when performed with the left hand, are invalid even retroactively. (See the Rambam, *Hilchot Beit Mikdash* 5:18.)

3. Tanya, *Igrot Kodesh* 29, p. 150a.

4. This story is not from the *sicha* of the Rebbe, but added by the translator to illustrate the point of the *sicha*.

Understanding the Chanukah Miracle

RAMBAM
Hilchot Chanukah 3:2–3

It might seem strange to analyze miracles since, by definition, they defy human understanding. However, we can use our intellect to "classify" miracles, and when we do so, we find that they come in different shapes and sizes, so to speak — such as quantitative, qualitative and a combination of each.

Let us take the miracle of Chanukah. The outnumbered Maccabees managed to kick the Hellenists out of Israel for a good two hundred years. But that wasn't what got the sages excited enough to declare a holiday. The physical survival of the Jews is an "ordinary" miracle that we've gotten used to already.[1] What drew the sages' attention was what happened afterward, when the Maccabees recaptured the Temple. They found a little jar of pure oil, ostensibly good for one day of light. But, when they used it to light the Menorah, it ended up lasting eight days.

Now, that was a miracle the sages could sink their teeth into as it encapsulated what the whole war was about. The Hellenists weren't threatening the physical well-being of the Jews; they were attempting to annihilate the Jewish faith — they sought to "make us forget the Torah, and to oppose the will of God."[2] That little jar of pure oil represented the pure faith that motivates a Jew, and when it lasted for a full eight days — enough time to provide more pure oil — that was something to get excited about and establish a holiday.

But what exactly was the miracle of the oil? Did the amount of oil increase, so that when they lit the Menorah, all of a sudden there was enough fuel for eight days? If so, it was a quantitative miracle that occurred daily, as the menorah was lit each day. But that raises a question in Jewish law which requires that the Menorah be lit with pure but *natural* olive oil. That means, of course, that the oil had to come from natural sources. If the oil came from a supernatural source, even if it possessed all of the physical qualities of olive oil, then it wasn't appropriate for the Menorah (at least according to some authorities). That makes the quantitative hypothesis questionable, and we'll have to try another angle…

Possibly, the miracle was qualitative. That is, perhaps it wasn't that the amount of oil increased suddenly, but that the nature of the oil changed. The amount of oil that was good for one day, suddenly became good for eight days. You might say that it became more concentrated and burned at a slower pace, using only one eighth of the original jar of oil each night. But here, too, we have a problem. Jewish law dictates that the Menorah's lamps be filled with a certain amount of oil every day — enough to last from the evening until the morning. If the amount of oil used was only one-eighth of that amount, then the priests were not following the precepts of the law. Moreover, the Menorah's lamps were supposed to be full — so how could the priests put into the lamps only one-eighth of the required amount?

We're forced to search for a new approach to the Chanukah miracle, one that not only avoids the problems encountered above, but that also gives us an entirely new way of understanding the miracle. This new approach is based upon the 16th century writings of Rabbi Yosef Karo, author of the *Shulchan Aruch*, in his commentary to the *Tur* (*Orech Chayim siman* 670). There, R' Karo writes: "They put all the oil in the Menorah … and in the morning found it full with oil." Perhaps what he meant here is not that the oil was used up every night and miraculously re-appeared every morning (that would be equivalent to the "quantitative miracle" already discussed, wherein the amount of oil miraculously increased). Perhaps what he meant here is that the oil burned, and yet none of it was consumed. If so, the Chanukah miracle was a combination of two opposite, but simultaneous events: a fire that burned oil — naturally and in accordance with Jewish law — but the oil was not consumed. [Note that a similar event is related in the Torah when God spoke to Moshe through the burning bush, which was not consumed by the fire even as it continued to burn (Exodus 3:2).]

RAMBAM
Hilchot Chanukah 3:2–3

This new category of miracle is neither quantitative or qualitative. It is the incursion of supernatural forces into natural events, in such a way that leaves the natural order intact. The fire was fire, and the oil was oil. The fire burnt, but did not consume the oil. This is the supernatural co-existing with the natural in order to express Godliness in the physical world.

Another example of this phenomenon was the Ark of the Covenant, which fit into the space of the Holy of Holies, even though there was no apparent room for it. If one measured from wall to wall of the Holy of Holies, it was twenty cubits wide. And, when the Ark was in place, if one measured from either side of the Ark to the wall, it was also twenty cubits — ten cubits on each side — even though the ark itself occupied one-and-one half cubits. The rabbis of the Talmud (Rebi Levy) describes this as "outside the realm of measurement" (Megila 10B). The ark existed in its appointed place, apparently without occupying physical space. It was a case of natural limitations meeting supernatural forces; the miracle was that both existed simultaneously. One could measure the Holy of Holies and find no room for the Ark, and simultaneously see and feel the presence of the Ark.

Similarly, according to this understanding, the lights burned, and yet consumed no oil. Such was the nature of the miracle, which expressed the essence of Godliness in the physical world.

Similarly, according to this understanding, the lights burned, and yet consumed no oil. Such was the nature of the miracle, which expressed the essence of Godliness in the physical world.

Looking at the various ways of describing the Chanukah miracle, we also find different time frames for when the miracle took place. According to the quantitative description (that the amount of oil miraculously increased), the miracle was a nightly event that occurred as soon as the Menorah was lit. Thereafter, the oil burned naturally.

According to the qualitative description (that the nature of the oil miraculously changed, becoming more concentrated), the Chanukah miracle took place when the Menorah was lit and continued as the oil burned. That is, we know that the oil changed qualitatively, allowing it to burn slower and longer. So, although the miracle took place immediately when the Menorah was lit, it appeared to continue as the oil burned. Since one eighth of the oil turned out to be enough for a full night, the results of the miracle were evident as the oil burned. But the miracle itself only took place in the beginning, when the nature of the oil changed and became more concentrated.[3]

According to our third way of understanding, the miracle took place at every instant. It was ongoing and continuous — even while the oil burned, it was not consumed. The Menorah was lit, but no oil was used up. This is exactly the type of miracle that could be expected from the One Above, who knows no limitations. He is not limited to the physical, nor is He limited to the supernatural — He created both and can cause them to occur simultaneously.

The Menorah in the Temple provided inspiration for all Jews for all time. Although the Temple is no more, every day we figuratively light a menorah inside of ourselves, and hope to remain inspired for the entire day. The time for lighting is during the morning (*Shacharit*) prayers, during which we take time to meditate on the One Above and then pray. Afterward, we go about our business, and the level of inspiration that remains with us depends upon how we prayed in the morning. There are three possibilities, each representing a different way of serving God, and each corresponding to the three categories of miracles:

1. There are those who pray, but then launch their day without feeling the effects of their prayers. They may recite the *Shema* with total devotion, but go about their daily routine as if detached from spirituality. In truth, their prayers do influence their day in a hidden manner — it cannot be otherwise — but they don't feel their influence. There is no apparent connection between their prayers and what they do the rest of the day. Of course, they follow the path of Torah and do not stray, but there is no inspiration permeating their behavior as they go through the day. This corresponds to the "quantitative miracle" of Chanukah that occurred only in the beginning, when the Menorah was first lit.
2. Then, there are those who pray with a higher level of inspiration that leaves an impression on their entire day. The inspiration from such prayer comes through from time to time as they go through their daily routine. Sporadically, they are reminded of God and how He oversees all of their activities. This corresponds to the "qualitative miracle" which took place when the Menorah was lit, but which appeared to extend for the duration of the burning of oil.

3. Finally, there are those who pray with such devotion that it stays with them for the entire day; they are thinking of God and Torah all the time. Nothing interrupts their connection with Him. As a result, they are ready at a moment's notice to drop whatever they are doing and throw themselves into any mitzvah or opportunity to learn Torah or help another Jew. Their path of divine service corresponds to the third category of miracles — the ongoing miracle of melding opposites. Just as the Menorah stayed lit without any oil being consumed, so these Jews are motivated by self-sacrifice (*mesiras nefesh*) that energizes them constantly. They are not consumed; quite the opposite — their constant connection to God is what motivates them to help other Jews and fulfill the mitzvoth according to His will.

These three forms of Godly connection and service (corresponding to the three categories of the Chanukah miracle) are associated with distinct periods in Jewish history. When the connection between God and the world was as it should be, it was enough to pray in the morning and the connection between the person and God remained in place during the rest of the day. Such was the situation during the time when the Temple stood in Jerusalem, where God revealed Himself to the Jews when they came to offer sacrifices there. Prayer was generally optional. An occasional appearance in the Temple was sufficient to inspire every Jew throughout the rest of the year.

However, when God is hidden — as He is today when the Jews are still in exile — the relationship between Him and us can no longer be based upon prayers in the morning alone. When God is hidden and we have no place to go to find His presence, we need to be constantly reminded that we are His people, and that He expresses Himself in every aspect of our daily lives. To that end, we need to surround ourselves with Torah learning and opportunities to do mitzvoth, in order to remain connected.

And finally, as we approach the imminent arrival of the Mashiach, even normal fulfillment of Torah and its mitzvoth is not sufficient. At this time, the forces that are opposed to anything holy gather their strength for a final fight. When the winds of negativity blow and threaten the very foundations of Judaism, *mesirat nefesh* is the antidote.

It is no longer enough to rely upon the existing structures and institutions of Judaism that have spiritually nourished the Jews throughout exile. It is necessary to build new institutions, to actively reach out to more Jews, and to be ready at a moment's notice to do whatever is demanded in support of Torah. This strengthens and reinforces our own connection with God, to say nothing of helping others connect. Only by throwing ourselves into the task of influencing all Jews to do mitzvoth are we able to stand against these negative forces, both within and without, which seek to uproot anything holy in the world.

That is the deepest message of the Chanukah lights which have the ability to light up the public arena and shine light into darkness — it is ongoing dedication and self-sacrifice that will bring the Mashiach now!

From Likutei Sichot of the Lubavitcher Rebbe, vol. 15, pp. 183–190

NOTES

1. According to Rambam (beginning of *Hilchot Chanukah*), Chanukah was declared a holiday not only because of the miracle of finding the oil, but also because of the victory in war. However, that Chanukah lasts eight days today is only a result of the oil that lasted eight days. And, obviously, the fact that we light the Chanukah candles and dedicate the holiday to the praise of God is a result of the miracle of the oil. Moreover, it is the oil that caused the holiday to be called "Chanukah," for it was with the oil that the sages rededicated the Temple — *Chanukat* Habayit.

2. Nusach of the Chanukah insert that we recite during the *Shemoneh Esreh*

3. The oil becoming more concentrated is not "opposed" to the essential nature of oil, nor was the oil transformed by this miracle. There was merely an addition to the quality and concentration of this particular oil that was in use. Among oils in general, and among olive oils themselves, there are different levels of quality. Even in a single olive, there are different levels of oil. The Mishna and Talmud (*Menachot* 86a) records that there are three categories of olives, each of which further sub-divides into three categories according to the refinement of the oil that they provide. They are not equal in speed at which they burn upon lighting, as can be clearly observed.

Status of the Jews at the End of Exile

Vayigash 44:18

It's important to be able to see an event from all possible angles. Every angle contributes its own facet of the truth, and no single angle reveals all of the truth. With that in mind, we can discern at least three angles in the story of the two brothers, Yosef and Yehudah in this week's Torah portion — *Parshat Vayigash*. From these two protagonists will emerge two prominent figures in prominent Jewish history: Mashiach ben Yosef and Mashiach ben David. It makes sense, then, that we can learn something about them from the behavior of Yosef and Yehudah themselves.

First of all, the angle of Yehudah: He saw in front of him the all-powerful viceroy of Egypt, who put into effect all of the policies of Pharaoh and even determined many of them. When he was facing the viceroy, Yehudah had no idea that this powerful politician was his own brother, Yosef. Nonetheless, Yehudah played the role that every Jew in exile plays with respect to the rulers and ministers of the host nation. That is, Yehudah was not afraid. He was polite, but firm. He had an agenda, and he didn't hesitate to lay it out in front of the superpower of his time. He did not hesitate to approach the viceroy of Egypt with claims and demands. He described the series of events that had befallen his brothers, asked for an explanation, and told Yosef what he wanted.

The same should be true of all of us Jews in whatever continent we live, among whatever people. Only by standing up for the principles that constitute Jewish life and worship can we expect to receive full rights of life and worship.

When Yehudah did so, it was suddenly revealed to him that the viceroy of Egypt was none other than his brother Yosef. Yosef heard Yehudah's words and revealed his true identity — that he was the very same brother they sold into slavery years before, and that he had arisen to prominence in Egypt.

This was a second angle to the story, but it followed upon the first angle, demonstrating that when a Jew makes firm but just demands from those in power, the world reveals itself as his supporter and promoter. All of a sudden, the veil is torn asunder and the world is revealed as a Jewish brother. Not only that — when a Jew presents his just demands to the world, it becomes evident that we Jews are in charge of our own destiny.[1] The purpose of creation is to enable the fulfillment of the Torah and its mitzvoth. When the world seems to prevent the Jew from doing what he should, it is because it presents a test to the Jew, to see if he will truly stand up for his faith and religion. If he withstands the test, the curtain is pushed aside and the world becomes revealed as what it really is — a means to allow the Jew to fulfill his mission.

And then there's the third angle — the mystical angle, the "true" angle that transcends both Yehudah and Yosef.

According to the Zohar and to Chassidut, Yehudah alludes to *tefillah* ("prayer") while Yosef represents *geulah* ("redemption"). Just as Yehudah approached Yosef with a request, so the Jews approach the One Above in prayer. And just as Yosef had it within his power to redeem the brothers and help them, so the One Above can redeem the Jews from all of their travails. When they come together, it's called (by the Zohar), "joining prayer and redemption."[2]

In Kabbalistic terms, Yosef and Yehudah represent the two *sephirot*, or Godly attributes, of *yesod* ("foundation/connection") and *malchut* ("kingship/lowliness"). *Yesod* is the "masculine" attribute personified by Yosef, while *malchut* is the "feminine" attribute personified by Yehudah. More specifically, Yehudah alludes to the ability to acknowledge/thank God (*modeh*), which is the basis and foundation of prayer as well as fulfillment of the mitzvoth. Yosef is the ability to add (*moseph*) light to the world by learning Torah.

While in Egypt, Yosef embodied the role of redeemer, bringing light and sustenance to his father and brothers. He did so by learning Torah.

For us, the lesson of Yosef is that, even in exile, even while overwhelmed with the details of making a living and struggling to keep our head above water, we should look to the Torah for spiritual refuge. Yosef was able to simultaneously function in the world and also to rise above the fray and stay connected to God. When the power of his Torah connected with the simple acknowledgement of his brother Yehudah, it brought redemption to the all the children of Yaakov and through them to all Jews for all time.

We can connect all of these angles together by offering a deeper interpretation of the first verse of *Parshat Vayigash*, "And Yehudah approached him." The word "him" in that verse refers to Yosef, but can also be interpreted as "Him" — the One Above.[3] When a simple Jew approaches God in prayer, he is able to carry on an intimate conversation with the One Above.

Now, if we combine with this new interpretation the first perspective of how a Jew should approach the rulers of his day, we realize that Jews have the power to influence kings and rulers. For, when a Jew in exile prays to God, he has the ability to influence the mind of kings and rulers, since "their heart is in the hands of God" (Proverbs 21:1). It then becomes clear that the true kingship is in the hands of the Jews themselves.

Today, in our personal divine service (*avodat Hashem*), this means that those of us whose main activity is fulfillment of the mitzvoth (like Yehudah), are dependent upon those whose emphasis is on Torah learning (for example, one may forego a mitzvah in order to learn Torah, as long as there is someone else who can fulfill that mitzvah). Therefore, Yehudah (whose emphasis was on mitzvoth and prayer) had to approach Yosef (whose emphasis was on Torah learning). However, in the future, the tables will be turned.

Chassidic literature[4] also tells us that Yehudah represents the "power of deed" — the power of simple actions that connect the heavens with the earth. When we fulfill the mitzvoth using physical objects, we achieve a connection with the ultimate, with the very essence of God. While intellect and understanding connect us with specific spiritual levels and revelation of Godliness, simple deeds connect us with God Himself. For that very reason, it will be the Mashiach ben David, from the line of Yehudah (representing deeds/action) who will bring redemption to the entire world. The ultimate redeemer will not come from the line of Yosef (representing study/learning Torah), but from Yehudah.

When the Mashiach arrives, it won't be necessary to withstand the "tests" of a world that hides Godliness. The world itself will proclaim that God is the one and only reality. That is why in the future the tables, will be turned, and Yosef (Mashiach ben Yosef) will come to announce the arrival of the scion of the House of Yehudah and of King David, the Mashiach ben David.

Immediately before that takes place however, we will find ourselves in a unique situation that is analogous to the status held by the Jews in Egypt during the final seventeen years of Yaakov's life in Goshen (seventeen being the gematria or numerical value of *tov*, meaning "good"). The Torah records that the Jews in Goshen, "...sunk roots and were fruitful and multiplied greatly" (Exodus 1:7). That occurred not long before they were redeemed by God and their exodus from Egypt took place. But the redemption had already started when Yaakov moved with his family to Goshen. And similarly, we are also very close to the Final Redemption, and some "rays" of that "new dawn" already illuminate our lives.

The difficulties associated with the Egyptian exile served to emphasize the tight connection that the Jews developed with the One Above. Despite their enslavement, the Jews maintained their Hebrew names, language and style of dress, and they married only among themselves. The transformation of that darkness into light (which is the ultimate purpose of the exile) is a major component of the narrative of *Parshat Vayigash*. *Vayigash* teaches that, even during the exile, God is in charge, the rulers of the world are in His hands, and He listens to the Jews who approach Him in prayer. Pharaoh was so positively influenced by the Jews that he gave them the "best of the land" to live on — the area known as Goshen (Genesis 47:6). Even in exile, even while no longer "at their father's table" (*Berachot* 3A), the Jews lacked nothing. And this, in itself, is an example of transforming the darkness of exile into light.

The same phenomenon is recurring in our generation. We, too, are in exile, and we too, are now experiencing a "taste" of redemption. As we prepare for the final transformation that will coincide with the arrival of the Mashiach (when we will become aware that all the travails of exile were in order to further "sweeten" the redemption), we are already beginning to feel some of the light of the transformation. That may be one of the reasons that this concept — that even during the exile, the hearts of rulers are in the hands of God, and that He listens to our prayers to influence them with the result that we receive greater support and aid from the nations of the world — is especially obvious in our generation, just as it was apparent to the Jews whom Pharaoh settled in the "best of the land — in Goshen."

Since our generation is the last generation of exile and the first generation of redemption, the preparation for transformation is already in full swing. In fact, we can already "taste" it, and during these last days of exile, we are experiencing something akin to Yaakov's seventeen final years in Egypt. This "rays" of a "new dawn" becomes stronger and stronger as we progress toward the ultimate transformation of darkness into light.

This trend has been especially in evidence since the arrival of the "Yosef" of our generation — R' Yosef Yitzchak Schneerson (the Previous Rebbe of Lubavitch) — to the Western hemisphere, also known as the "lower half of the globe." Since the Previous Rebbe moved to the "kingdom of kindness" (the United States), the treatment of the Jews here has been the opposite of what they experienced in their previous countries of residence (in Europe). And even after the Previous Rebbe passed on, the illumination from his holy soul remains with us. This illumination persists, since after a *tzaddik* passes on, his soul is no longer limited to a body and continues to illuminate those who were associated with him. Moreover, forty years have transpired since his passing, which has brought us to a situation analogous to the juncture in time when the Jews completed forty years in the desert — we now have "a heart to know and eyes to see and ears to hear" (Deuteronomy 29:3). In the meantime, even the previous kingdom of our persecution has been transformed into a nation that aids and assists Jews to live well … and all of this is because we are very close to the true and complete redemption, which means that the arrival of the Mashiach is imminent!

Since the Previous Rebbe moved to the "kingdom of kindness" (the United States), the treatment of the Jews here has been the opposite of what they experienced in their previous countries of residence (in Europe).

Based upon sichot of the Lubavitcher Rebbe, Parshat Vayigash, 5751 (1991)

NOTES

1. Just as Yosef ruled Egypt (and the Jewish people in general are co-named "Yosef," as in Psalms 80:2).

2. For more on Yehudah's approach to Yosef from the Chassidic angle, see *Torat Shmuel* 5629 (1869) of the Rebbe Maharash, p. 13, *Sefer Maamorim* 5643 (1883) of the Rebbe Rashab, p. 209, the series of *Maamorim Yomtov shel Rosh Hashanah* 5666 (1906) from the Rebbe Rashab, pp. 119, 487. *Hemshech Beaha'ah Shehikdimu* 5672 (1912), vol. 2, p. 794. *Maamorim melukatim* of the Rebbe, vol. 5, p. 127.

3. *Sefer Likutim* of the Ari (beginning of *Shemot*): "Yosef — this is *Hakadosh Baruch Hu* (Hashem)." Perhaps Yaakov statement to Yosef, "Swear to me...Take me out of Egypt" (Gen 47:30–31) alludes to all Jews ("Yaakov," from who all Jews are descended) requesting the One Above, so to speak, to take an oath to lift the Jews out of exile in a manner of "lifting and elevation." (*Likutei Sichot*, vol. 25, p. 274, footnote 37.

4. *Ohr HaTorah* of the *Tzemach Tzedek*, beginning of parshat Vayeishev, *Torat Shmuel 5634* (1874) of the Rebbe Maharash, page 86, *Sefer Maamorim 5678* (1918) of the Rebbe Rashab, page 119

Yosef Seeks to Relieve Yaakov's Suffering

Vayigash
45:1

The climactic showdown between Joseph and his brothers occurs in this week's Torah portion — *Parshat Vayigash*. Until now, the brothers, who came to Egypt to buy food during a period of famine, had no idea that the man who was running the Egyptian Empire was the brother they had sold into slavery some twenty-two years earlier. They thought he was merely a tough administrator, watching zealously over Pharaoh's domain. But, after Yosef found ways to bring all eleven brothers to him and prostrate themselves to him (thus actualizing the dream that he had many years earlier), Yosef could no longer contain himself, as the Torah relates:

"And Yosef could no longer hold himself back in front of all those who were present, and he cried, 'Everyone out!' whereupon Yosef stood alone with his brothers. And he allowed himself to cry, and the Egyptians heard, as did the entire house of Pharaoh. And Yosef said to his brothers, 'I am Yosef, is my father still alive?' And his brothers were unable to answer because they were so astonished at him." (Genesis 45:1–3).

We already know that Rashi's task is to explain the simple level of the Torah text, so that a child reading it for the first time will understand it.[1] And yet here, regarding some puzzling details of these verses, Rashi says nothing whatsoever. For example, immediately after revealing his identity, Yosef asks, "Is my father still alive?" But Yosef already knew the answer to this question! From the context of his conversation with Yehudah regarding his brother Binyamin, Yosef already knew how precious the youngest son was to his father, and how it would ruin his father if any harm came to the boy. So, what logic was there behind Yosef's question, "Is my father still alive?"

Furthermore, we do not find that Yosef waited for an answer to his question.[2] As soon as he saw that his brothers were so astonished that they could not speak, he immediately switched the conversation to other topics, in an attempt to persuade them that he was indeed their brother who had become the viceroy of Egypt. He then concluded by saying, "Hurry and go up to my father..."[3] So, not only is his question, "Is my father still alive?" strange, but Yosef does not even wait for an answer to it. All of this suggests that, in truth, Yosef was aware that his father was still alive, and he meant something else when he asked that question.

The Abarbanel suggests that Yosef's question was only an introduction, meant to draw his brothers into conversation with him. Seeing that his brothers were not only surprised, but also ashamed when they found out who he was, he sought a way to find common ground with them, and therefore asked about his father. And Rashi says nothing by way of explanation, because a child would have recognized such a possibility after reading Rashi's explanations of previous verses.

Commenting on Genesis 3:9, when God asks Adam (after he ate from the Tree of Knowledge), "Where are you?" Rashi explained that, "Of course, God knew where Adam was, but He wanted to draw him into conversation so that he would not be too confused to answer Him." Similarly, regarding Kayin after he killed his brother Hevel, Rashi explains Genesis 4:9, which reads, "Where is Hevel, your brother?" as "[This question was posed by God] in order to draw him gently into conversation..." We can assume, therefore, that Rashi relies on this explanation for our Torah portion, and does not say anything more.

Here, however, this explanation does not fit well. For, if Yosef's purpose was to draw his brothers into conversation, he should not have asked about his father, but about their respective families. In this way, he would have gained their confidence. But, by asking suddenly about his father, he may have only added to their confusion.

Another possible way to understand Yosef's question was that perhaps it was an exclamation and statement of confirmation, rather than a question. For example, when God announced to Avraham and Sarah that they would have a son, Avraham exclaimed, "Can one who is a hundred years old be fruitful?!" (Genesis 17:17). Here, Rashi explains that rather than challenge God by asking a question, Abraham exclaimed in surprise. Here also, perhaps Yosef's question expressed something similar — he was both surprised and gratified that his father was still alive.

But, if this is the explanation, then three things do not make sense:

1. At that time, Yaakov was 130 years old, much younger than his father and grandfather who passed away at the ages of 180 and 175, respectively. And if so, why would Yosef be surprised that his father is still alive?
2. What is the connection between Yosef's question and the statement that preceded it — "I am Yosef"?
3. Why did Yosef ask this question of his brothers right after revealing his identity to them? If Yosef was indeed asking a question, perhaps we could say it was so important to him to know the answer immediately. But if, in truth, he knew the answer and this was not a question but an exclamation, then why make it precisely at this juncture?

There is a simple answer to all this — and it explains why Yosef was surprised, and yet had no doubt that his father was still alive:

We know from a previous verse (Genesis 37:35) that Yaakov was inconsolable after the loss of Yosef. He refused to be comforted, and our sages say that it was because Yosef was still alive. From Above, it is decreed that the deceased slowly ease themselves out of our mind and consciousness, but when a loved one is still alive, the loss is ever present. That is why Yaakov "mourned for his son for many days" (Genesis 37:34). Thus, it emerges that Yaakov had been mourning for Yosef for twenty-two years without interruption. Yosef understood that his father's mourning had been very deep because of the unique and special relationship between them — indeed, Yaakov loved Yosef even more than his other sons. And that is the reason for Yosef's concern; it was as if he was asking, "How could my father still be alive after so many years of mourning?"

That explains, as well, why Yosef's question was addressed to his brothers immediately after the revelation of his identity; it was an introduction to the next item on Yosef's agenda, which was to tell them to bring their father immediately down to the land of Egypt. The reason for the urgency with which Yosef directed his brothers, "Hurry and go to my father..." (Genesis 45:9), and "Come down to me, do not delay..." (Genesis 45:13) was because it was a matter of *sacanat nefashot* — "life threatening danger." Even if the brothers did not inform Yaakov that his son was still alive, nevertheless such a long period of mourning could even now have a negative effect on Yaakov's health. So, it was imperative that the brothers bring Yaakov immediately to Egypt to see Yosef in person.

Now, we may also understand why, after identifying himself and asking if his father is still alive, Yosef reiterated no less than three times that his very presence in Egypt was an act of God. He said, "For purposes of sustenance God sent me before you," and "And God sent me before you," and "It was not you who sent me here, but God" (Genesis 45:5–8) — all in order to emphasize that he was not in Egypt of his own will. Rather, he was there in order to carry out a task and, therefore, he could not do the obvious thing and go to his father himself. Simple respect for his father would have required Yosef not to ask his brothers to bring Yaakov to him, but to go see his father himself. But, since he was under the command of Pharaoh, and that itself was at the behest of God, therefore Yosef could not leave Egypt, and so it was incumbent upon the brothers to bring Yaakov to him.

There is another element in Yosef's instructions to his brothers to hurry to their father and bring him down to Egypt. Rashi already mentioned (in his commentary on Genesis 37:3) that the twenty-two years that Yaakov mourned for Yosef corresponded to the twenty-two years that Yaakov himself was not in touch with his parents, while in the house of Lavan and returning to Canaan. And this is another reason why Yosef seemed to be in a hurry; he knew that the period of twenty-two years of mourning was now up — Yaakov no longer had to mourn. And if so, there was no reason to delay whatsoever. Yaakov had to be brought immediately to Egypt. This also explains why Yosef instructed his brothers to "bring my father," and not "our father." Since it was because of Yosef that Yaakov was mourning, and the period of mourning had now come to an end, Yosef in a sense bore more responsibility for his father's state of mind. Now that the full twenty-two years had passed, Yosef was eager to honor his father. Because of this, he requested that the brothers bring "my father," and not "our father."

Even though it is necessary from time to time to act with strictness and judgment (gevurah), this option should be exercised with a maximum of care and sensitivity.

There is something for us to learn here for our own *avodat Hashem*. And that is, even though it is necessary from time to time to act with strictness and judgment (*gevurah*), this option should be exercised with a maximum of care and sensitivity. Only when the situation clearly calls for it should we apply stringency in dealing with others. And, when the situation turns around, and *gevurah* is no longer called for, we should not wait even one moment. As soon as possible, we should return to the path of kindness and mercy (*chessed*) rather than continue to apply *gevurah* when it is no longer necessary.

From Likutei Sichot of the Lubavitcher Rebbe, vol. 15, pp. 387–390

NOTES

1. When Rashi cannot find any explanation according to the *pshat*, even though there may be an explanation according to *drosh*, Rashi writes, "I do not know" or something similar. See *Likutei Sichot*, vol. 5, p. 1, footnote 2 for a lengthy explication.

2. We cannot say that the brothers did answer Yosef, but that the Torah does not record their answer (as occurred in *Parshat Mikeitz*, Genesis 43:7, when Yosef asked, "Is my father still alive?" or in our Torah portion, Genesis 44:19 when Yosef asks, "Do you have a father or brother?") because in our case, the Torah states clearly, "And the brothers were unable to answer."

3. The Kli Yakar and the Ralbag and others suggest that Yosef asked, "Is my father still alive?" even though Yehudah had already told him that Yaakov was living, because he suspected that Yehudah told him so only for the purpose of achieving his own goal of retrieving their brother Benyamin (see Rashi on Genesis 44:20). But the fact that Yosef did not wait for an answer, and ultimately instructed them to "hurry and bring my father" indicates that he harbored no such suspicions. Moreover, Yosef had previously asked the brothers (not only Yehudah), "Is your father well, is he still alive?" (Genesis 43:27–28), and they had answered in the affirmative and, in this situation, there was no reason for them to lie.

Distress over Leaving Israel

Vayigash 46:3

In this week's Torah portion — *Parshat Vayigash* — a familiar theme arises. As Yaakov prepares to leave the Land of Israel to join his long-lost son, Yosef, he gets nervous. He doesn't want to leave. But then the One Above responds to him, saying, "I am the Lord, God of your father; do not be afraid to go down to the Land of Egypt, as I will make you into a great nation there." (Genesis 46:3)

Commenting on this verse, Rashi puts a different twist on it — so much so that he appears to actually change the meaning. Although the verse states that Yaakov was fearful of going down to Egypt (and God had to reassure him, "do not be afraid..."), Rashi writes that Yaakov was "troubled."

Although there is a small difference between "fearful" and "troubled," it is significant:

1. "Do not be afraid" is *al tira* in Hebrew, but Rashi uses the term *mitzar*.[1]
2. The verse speaks specifically about Yaakov's fears about going down to Egypt, but Rashi implies that Yaakov was upset about leaving Israel in general, not specifically about going to Egypt.

Possibly, the two descriptions are really one. The descent to a new and foreign country, and in particular to Egypt, aroused fear and worry in Yaakov regarding the future. At the same time, the prospect of leaving Israel aroused distress and sorrow. Nevertheless, we need to understand why Rashi explains the verse in a way that seems to change the simple meaning of the text.

Moreover, according to Rashi's commentary, the verse lacks continuity. The point of God's message was to reassure Yaakov that he and his family would thrive in Egypt: "I will make you into a great nation there." This reassurance makes sense if Yaakov was afraid of going down to Egypt. But, if Yaakov was merely troubled over the prospect of leaving Israel (as Rashi states), then how did the reassurance that he will be made "into a great nation there" alleviate his discomfort over leaving Israel?

Perhaps the reason Rashi did not explain that Yaakov was afraid of descending to Egypt was because the Jews would have their own conclave once they arrived there. That is, since the Jews would live by themselves in an area called Goshen and be independent of the Egyptians, there was no reason for Yaakov to be afraid of their negative influence upon the Jews. However, this is not enough of a reason to justify changing what seems to be the simple meaning of the verse. Certainly, leaving one's home and going to a foreign country is a cause for concern. This would be especially true regarding Egypt, which was known to have the lowest moral standards in the world at the time. In fact, the atmosphere in Egypt was the total opposite of what Yaakov had become accustomed to in his own homeland, Israel.

Therefore, it is difficult to understand why Rashi would comment that Yaakov was not afraid of Egypt, but merely troubled over leaving Israel.

There are those (the Ramban and Targum Yonatan ben Uziel) who say that Yaakov realized the time had come for the exile predicted by God during Avraham's "covenant between the pieces" (*brit bein habetarim*). At that time, God told Avraham that his descendants would descend to a "foreign land" and remain there for four generations before returning to the Land of Israel. When Yaakov saw that he was being led to Egypt (in order to see his son), he realized that this time had come. And that's what made him afraid.

At first glance, this explanation actually makes more sense than Rashi's commentary. For, while Rashi refers to the private experiences of Yaakov, this interpretation speaks of the collective experience leading to the formation of the Jewish people. It also fits well with the ending of the verse: "I will make you into a great nation there." If that's the case, why does Rashi not use this explanation, rather than giving one that seems to alter the meaning of the verse?

Possibly, the explanation of Rashi is based on the order of the verses in the Torah. That is, God's reassuring statement to Yaakov occurred only after Yaakov had already departed on his journey, but before he actually left the Land of Israel. First, the Torah tells us that "Israel journeyed with all that he possessed..." (Genesis 46:1), and only after God says to him, "Do not be afraid..." (Genesis 46:3). Since this raises a question — Why did God not reassure Yaakov even before he left on his journey?[2] — Rashi seeks to explain that it was not necessary, because Yaakov was not afraid of the journey. He had no fear of the future. In fact, he was happy about going to see his son, Yosef. But, the happiness gave way to distress as Yaakov journeyed. He was upset over leaving Israel, which is why Rashi explains that Yaakov was "troubled," but not that he was "afraid." And the feeling of sorrow became stronger as he journeyed, which made it necessary for the One Above to reassure him.

Nevertheless, we could ask: If so, why didn't God reassure him earlier? Why did God wait until Yaakov reached the city of Beer-Sheva before uttering those reassuring words? Something must have happened in Beer-Sheva to make it the right time and place to comfort Yaakov and relieve him of his distress.

Beer-Sheva is the southernmost city from which it is possible to exit the biblical boundaries of Israel (most opinions put that boundary about halfway between Beer-Sheva and Eilat, but there was no city south of Beer-Sheva at that time). So, it was natural that, in Beer-Sheva, Yaakov felt the impending exit from the Land of Israel, and it troubled him. Until now he had been traveling in relative tranquility, with the expectation of seeing his son Yosef. But, as the moment of truth approached and he realized that he was about to leave Israel with all of his family and possessions, he became upset. Even though he knew from the onset of his journey that he would have to leave Israel, the pain that he felt was most intense as the moment of crossing the border approached. That was why God waited until Yaakov was in Beer-Sheva before reassuring him that all would be well.

However, God's words to Yaakov need more explanation. If the purpose was to reassure him, why tell him "...because I will make you into a great nation there"?[3] Why not just tell Yaakov that all will be well, and that he had no cause for concern? Moreover, Yaakov had once before left the boundaries of Israel, and we don't find the he was in need of reassurance at that time. When he left Israel for the first time, traveling to

Charan, to the house of his uncle Lavan, he wasn't nervous, so why was he nervous when he left Israel to see his son in Egypt?[4]

The answer lies in the difference between Yaakov's situation in Charan and his situation now. In Charan, Yaakov was a single lad, without possessions, and without a family to call his own. But, in the ensuing years, he married Leah and Rachel, sired twelve sons, and built a large clan of family members who formed the nucleus of the future Jewish people. His distress in Be'er Sheva was not a matter of apprehension over his own personal safety nor a sentimental sadness over leaving Israel. His apprehension was over the future growth and welfare of his family. If, as promised by God, his descendants were to multiply and inhabit the Land of Israel, then Israel was the most appropriate location for them to live and prosper. A long side trip outside the Land of Israel could derail the long-term plan for the Jewish people indefinitely, and over this Yaakov felt apprehension. That is why God sought to assure him now, as he was about to leave Israel from Be'er Sheva, that not only all would be well with him, but that his entire family would become a great people as a result of their sojourn in Egypt.

Generally, we don't find that the forefathers were concerned about leaving the Land of Israel. When necessary, for reasons of famine or family to leave Israel, they did so. The *halachic* restrictions about leaving Israel (regarding marriage, learning Torah or making a living) did not apply, since the Torah was not yet given. And although the forefathers strove to keep the principles of the Torah even before it was given, the Land of Israel did not yet possess the necessary holiness since the Jews had not yet conquered it and begun to fulfill the mitzvoth of the Torah in the Land. Therefore, the forefathers were free to come and go as they pleased.

However, that does not mean that they took the matter lightly. Indeed, God told Yitzchak, "Don't go to Egypt..." (Genesis 26:2). And Rashi explains regarding Avraham that, in the Land of Israel, people knew God as the God of both the heavens and the earth. In Israel, Avraham accustomed people to thinking that God had a profound effect upon the physical world as well as upon the spiritual realms. However, outside of Israel, people only knew of God as the God of the heavens. For that reason, it was natural for Yaakov to feel apprehensive about taking his family out of Israel, even though it was entirely permissible for him to do so.

That is why Rashi says that Yaakov was "troubled" and not that he was "afraid." If Rashi had written that Yaakov was "afraid," it might have implied that he was nervous over the immediate future of his family in Egypt. Therefore, Rashi chose the word "troubled" to inform us that Yaakov real concern was not over the future in Egypt but over the necessity of leaving Israel, which was the natural "incubator" for the Jewish nation.

If God had reassured Yaakov at the beginning of his trip and even so his apprehension had grown, then it would have been clear that he was "afraid" of entering Egypt. But, since God only reassured him toward the end of his trip, we can understand that Yaakov's real distress was over leaving Israel. Israel was the appropriate place to develop the tribes into a nation of Jews that serves God, and that's why Yaakov was "troubled" over his departure.[5] He knew that he was allowed to leave, but he also knew that his natural habitat — and the natural habitat of the Jews for all ages — was in the Holy Land that he was about to leave behind.

From Yaakov, it is possible to learn how a Jew should relate to life in exile among foreign peoples. On the one hand, we have to realize that our real home is on Jewish soil, in the Land that was promised to us by God, because that is where our mitzvoth have the most effect in bringing holiness down to earth. On the other hand, we must not be afraid of living in exile, if that is what is necessary. We weren't exiled of our own volition, and the Final Redemption will not emerge from our efforts alone, but only when God decides the time is right.

On the one hand, we have to realize that our real home is on Jewish soil, in the Land that was promised to us by God, because that is where our mitzvoth have the most effect in bringing holiness down to earth.

In fact, it's possible that the two possibilities ("trouble" over leaving Israel, versus "fear" of the future in Egypt) coincide and explain Yaakov's behavior in depth. God said to Yaakov "Don't be afraid…" but Rashi explains that Yaakov was only troubled, not afraid. It's possible that Yaakov didn't have to be afraid, because he was troubled. When a Jew knows that his proper place is in the Holy Land, he has nothing to fear from life in exile. He may be troubled, being outside of his natural habitat, but he need not live in fear. He knows that all the mitzvoth that he fulfills in exile are ultimately for the purpose of the Final Redemption, and thus he has nothing to fear.

From Likutei Sichot of the Lubavitcher Rebbe, vol. 30, pp. 229–235

NOTES

1. Elsewhere Rashi usually uses the word *doeg*, or *da'aga* ("troubled" or "distressed") in explanation of the word *tira* ("afraid") in the Scripture. See, for example, Genesis 15:1, Rashi end of *Parshat Eikev*. See also *Sefer Hashoreshim* of the Radak, under *d'ag* (*dalet-aleph-gimmel*).

2. The Radal on *Pirkei d'Rebi Eliezer* writes that when Yaakov agreed earlier to descend to Egypt, saying, "I will descend and see..." he originally intended to descend to Egypt for a visit and to return to Israel immediately. Only when Hashem said to him, "Do not be afraid..." did Yaakov decide to "load all of his belongings on wagons and take his cattle..." etc. But if so, it is difficult to understand the previous verse in which the Torah tells us that, "And Israel travelled with all of his belongings and arrived to Beer-Sheva..." It makes little sense to suggest that "all of his belongings" referred only to his personal belongings and not to the rest of his family's personal effects.

3. The Ramban suggests that Hashem's communication with Yaakov ("Do not be afraid...") took place after Yaakov "offered up sacrifices to the God of his father, Yitzchak" (Genesis 46:1). However, if we say that Yaakov's offerings were in order to induce God to communicate with him, then Yaakov should have brought the offerings before his trip to Beer-Sheva. And it does not fit with the *pshat* of the verses to suggest that Yaakov offered the sacrifices because of the importance of Beer-Sheva in Yaakov's eyes on account since his father was blessed there (Genesis 26:23)because, if so, Rashi should have said so.

4. From the perspective of *pshat*, when Yaakov left for Charan (Lavan's house), it was not with the intention of remaining there, but with only being there for a while (and for this period of time, Yaakov requested a blessing from God; see Genesis 28:20). The same is true of Avraham's journey to Egypt when there was famine in the Land of Israel (Genesis 12:10), and the same regarding Yitzchak's intention to descend to Egypt (before God told him not to go to Egypt; see Rashi on Genesis 26:2). Here, however, Yaakov prepared to descend to Egypt for the purpose of remaining there for some time, and that was what distressed him.

However, this needs more investigation. For if we say that also during the days of the forefathers it was forbidden to leave the Land of Israel, and even though during a famine it is permitted to leave, but preferable not to do so (see the Rambam's *Hilchot Melachim* 5:9 and in the *Keseph Mishneh* there), so then it makes sense to experience distress over leaving the Land, even though it is permitted. Note that, according to Rashi, Avraham left the Land even before the famine (and after the "covenant between the pieces"; see *Likutei Sichot* vol. 15, p. 202, footnotes 17 and 23).

5. Similar words ("I will make you into a great nation...") were also spoken by God to Avraham, and in his case they applied to the Land of Israel. However, there, God's intention was not about the Jewish nation in general. Rather, God's intention was to tell Avraham that "here, in the exile," you will not merit to have children, as Rashi explains at the beginning of *Parshat Lech Lecha*.

Jews Named After Yosef

Vayigash
47:12

The Jews (*Yehudim*) are called by several different names in the Torah and the Hebrew Bible (*Tanach*). They are called Hebrews (*Ivrim*), Israelites or Children of Israel (*Bnei Israel*), and also Yaakov, Ephraim and Yosef.

The latter we see in the Book of Psalms — "He who leads Yosef like a flock" (Psalms 80:2). As Rashi explains, this is so because Yosef took care of the Jews while they were starving. He cites a verse in this week's Torah portion — *Parshat Vayigash* — "And Yosef supplied his father and his brothers and all of his father's household with bread in proportion to the [needs of] the children" (Genesis 47:12). Interpreted simply, this means that the Jews were co-named Yosef because they were dependent upon him before Yaakov arrived in Egypt and after he passed away. (Once Yaakov arrived, the famine ceased and didn't return until after his passing.)

However, this raises a couple of questions:

1. Why should the Jews take on Yosef's name permanently on account of something he did for a relatively short time?
2. Rashi's explanation is based on a verse in Psalms that requests God to listen to the prayers of the Jews and lead them "like the flocks of Yosef." Why should the fact that Yosef fed and supplied the Jews cause God to listen to their prayers?

Stepping back and analyzing the lives of Yaakov and his son Yosef, we see many similarities. In fact, the events of Yosef's life seem to correspond to Yaakov's life, but with a subtle difference. Yaakov was independent, even as an employee of his uncle Lavan. As an independent employee of Lavan, his divine service went uninterrupted. He was a shepherd and that enabled him to remain apart. He could work and, at the same time, meditate, study and pray.

While Yaakov was on such a high level that he transcended the world, his sons — who were also shepherds — needed to escape from the world in order to serve God. Yaakov was successful because he was essentially above his work. Indeed, his success in the spiritual realm (through his *avodat Hashem*) was the catalyst for his success in the physical world as well. Because Yaakov's spiritual service of the One Above was so powerful, he automatically succeeded physically as well. But his sons were not on such a high level. If they had been forced into any other profession, their divine service would have suffered disturbances and interruptions. They needed to be shepherds precisely in order to escape the world. They couldn't be intimately involved in world matters and also meditate, pray and study. Therefore, they minimized their involvement in the physical world in order to succeed in *avodat Hashem*. They could do this because it was their father, Yaakov, who created the wealth, and all the sons had to do was to manage it properly.

But Yosef was a different story. His *avodat Hashem* was on such a level that he could be intimately involved in the physical world and simultaneously wrapped up in meditation, prayer and study. His was a new level of cleaving to God that had never been brought into the world before.

Furthermore, Yosef was not just an employee, as his father Yaakov had been in the house of Lavan — Yosef was a slave. From the time he was sold to the caravans and brought down to Egypt, he was not independent. First, he was a slave to Potiphar, though he advanced to become the overseer of his master's entire household. Then, as a prisoner, he rose to take charge of the prison. Finally, once released, he was appointed the viceroy of Egypt. But even in this position, he was not his own man and was still subservient to whatever Pharaoh might decree. Throughout all this, Yosef never abandoned his *avodat Hashem* — his study, prayer and meditation — nor his quest to get closer to God. In other words, Yosef wasn't only "above the fray," as was his father Yaakov; he was above the fray even while he was in the fray and very much a part of it. Unlike his brothers, Yosef didn't find it necessary to run away from the world. Even while totally immersed and involved in the accounts of the Egyptian empires, he was able to serve the One Above and cleave to Him. And that explains why the Jews were co-named Yosef.

Like Yosef, we are living in an exile that requires us to be intimately involved with the physical world that demands we immerse our minds and bodies in physical matters as businessmen, scientists and professionals in all walks of life. The power to continue to serve God despite our total immersion and involvement in physical matters comes from Yosef.

All that we find here in the physical world comes from its spiritual counterpart in the worlds above. As the Torah states, Yosef supplied the Jews with all that they needed in the time of famine (Genesis 47:12). This means that if there was a physical famine down here, it meant that there was a spiritual famine as well. That is, the Jews weren't getting what they needed in order to serve God properly on the spiritual level. They didn't have the ability to meditate, pray and study as they should. But Yosef changed that.

The power to continue to serve God despite our total immersion and involvement in physical matters comes from Yosef.

The ability to do both — to serve God even as we remain involved in the physical world — comes from Yosef. Just as Yosef kept the Jews fed with physical sustenance (grain and bread), so he looked after their spiritual needs. And because Yosef was able to supply the Jews with their spiritual needs, he succeeded in meeting their physical needs as well. Yosef was the first to bring down to the world the ability to serve God even while immersed in matters of business, and that is why the Jews, in this exile, are called Yosef.

That also explains why we ask God to listen to our prayers because we are like the "flock" of Yosef. When we say a prayer to get out of exile, first we mention the name Israel because Yaakov (renamed Israel) was completely above the fray, and we all have a piece of him inside of us, and so, first of all, we call upon that aspect of ourselves to arouse the connection with the One Above: "Listen, shepherd of Israel..." (Psalms 80:1). And then we ascend to the higher level and mention Yosef, because he is within all of us as well: "He who leads Yosef like a flock" (Psalms 80:2). Yosef gave us the power to serve the One Above even while involved below. In the path of Yosef, we are able not only nullify the darkness of exile but also to turn it into light and redemption.

From Likutei Sichot of the Lubavitcher Rebbe,
vol. 25, pp. 252–257

Yaakov Finds Out Yosef Is Alive

Vayigash 47:28

The drama of Yosef and his brothers reaches a climax in this week's Torah portion — *Parshat Vayigash*. After Yosef orchestrated the arrival of all his eleven brothers in Egypt (thereby actualizing his dreams that he told them about much earlier), he revealed who he was — the same brother whom they sold into slavery twenty-two years earlier. He was very young at that time and did not yet have a beard, so seeing him now with a beard, his brothers didn't recognize him. Consequently, he shocked them by revealing who he was, and what had transpired during the intervening years. Once they were reunited, what remained was to pass the message on to his father — that Yosef was alive — and convince Yaakov to come down to Egypt.

Toward that end, Yosef sent his brothers back to the land of Canaan laden with all kinds of goods on *agalot* ("wagons"). The Midrash explains that this was meant to be a sign to his father that Yosef still remembered what they were learning together when he was so tragically torn away — the subject of *eglah arufa* (the calf that was slaughtered if a dead body was found in the field and it was not known who had killed that person). If Yaakov failed to believe the brothers, then by seeing the *agalot*, he would be reminded of the *eglah arufa*, whereby he would know that Yosef was fine and that he remembered the Torah they learned together.

And that is what happened. The brothers returned to Canaan, explained that Yosef was alive, and presented their father with the wagons laden with presents. The Torah relates that, when he saw the wagons, Yaakov proclaimed, "Great! My son Yosef still lives..." (Genesis 47:28)

The Midrash (*Bereishit Rabba* 94:3) explains what he meant by that: "The power of my son is great; since he underwent so much suffering and yet he still stands in his righteousness — he is greater than me." The simple understanding of this Midrash is that in addition to the satisfaction that Yaakov received from knowing that his son was still physically alive, he received additional pleasure from knowing that Yosef was still very much spiritually alive and connected to God, as well. The sign that Yosef sent with his brothers was effective; it conveyed to Yaakov that Yosef was not only alive physically but also spiritually.

Still, the Torah is very precise and communicates on all levels, so it stands to reason that Yosef's message to his father went beyond external symbolism. Since everything that occurred to the forefathers carries a message for us, we may assume that the *eglah arufa* is not only a symbol with which Yosef communicated with his father, but that its content carries an important message for all of us. While the symbolism of the *eglah arufa* informed Yaakov that Yosef was alive and well, the content of this mitzvah told Yaakov about the nature of Yosef's spiritual state.

When a dead body is found in a field, and it is not known who murdered him, the rabbis are called out to measure from the field where the body lay, in order to determine which is the nearest town. They then take a young calf (the *eglah arufa*) and break its neck, while the people of the nearest town declare, "Our hands did not spill this blood." This publicizes the murder, and makes it easier to find the perpetrator. Moreover, it has a deterrent value — communicating to the population that a murder in an out-of-the-way place will not remain hidden.

Applying this mitzvah to our own divine service (*avodat Hashem*), we can say that the corpse represents one who has lost his connection with God; he no longer cleaves to the One Above (or perhaps he never did). This could only happen because he was "in the field" — in the place of Esav, as the evil inclination (*yetzer hara*) is sometimes called — in a place that is far from the synagogue and study hall. When studying Torah and praying, we remain connected to God, but when we leave the synagogue and the study hall, we find ourselves out "in the field," and that is where Esav (the "man of the field" — Genesis 25:27) can prey on us. Ultimately, if we are not sufficiently strong, the "field" can disconnect us completely from the One Above.

The reason that the rabbis go out to the field and perform this rite of absolution is because they are ultimately responsible for taking care of Jews who stray out to the "field." It is the teachers and sages of the day who are responsible for providing the "food and clothes" that protect the Jews when they make a foray out to the "field," away from the synagogue and study hall. In this context, the "food" is the Torah that we learn, and the "clothes/garments" are the mitzvoth that we fulfill. With Torah and mitzvoth, the Jew is protected in the field, even when he is far from the synagogue and study hall. Without Torah and mitzvoth, he is vulnerable to the elements.

And that is the deeper reason that Yosef studied about the *eglah arufa* with his father before he was sold into slavery in Egypt. Since, ultimately, Yosef was to end up in Egypt, far away from his sources of inspiration, he needed special protection. The protection came from learning with his father about the responsibility of the leaders and sages to protect the Jews who were out "in the field" — in exile.[1] So, when Yosef sent the wagons (*agalot*) to his father, it was a sign that he had maintained his connection with God, even after all that he had been through. The *agalot* were a reminder of the *eglah arufa*, and Yosef used this sign to inform his father that he was not only physically alive, but spiritually healthy as well. By maintaining his vision of what he had learned with his father (*eglah arufa*), Yosef was able to withstand the negative influences of Egypt. Rather than be "slaughtered" by his surroundings, Yosef maintained his spiritual level and grew in Torah and righteousness. Yaakov got the message and his spirit was revived (Genesis 45:27). The news about Yosef was enough to provide Yaakov with a new and unexpected boost of divine energy.

It is the teachers and sages of the day who are responsible for providing the "food and clothes" that protect the Jews when they make a foray out to the "field," away from the synagogue and study hall.

Nonetheless, Yaakov's verbal response (according to the Midrash) was curious. He said that since his son Yosef underwent so much suffering and yet maintained his spiritual level, he was "greater than me" in righteousness and connection with God. And this is not so easily understood, since Yaakov himself underwent similar tests in the house of his uncle Lavan, and yet emerged unscathed. Similar to Yosef, Yaakov labored hard for many years in a house and a land that was not his own. Yet, when he returned to his homeland, he was able to declare, according to Rashi, "With Lavan I lived and still managed to keep 613 mitzvoth" (Rashi on Genesis 32:5). That is, he maintained his spiritual level even though he endured much hardship. If so, why did he say that his son Yosef was on a higher spiritual level?

The answer lies in the special level of Yosef. We know already that the rest of the forefathers were shepherds. They chose that occupation because it allowed them to pray and commune with God without disturbance. To remain in "the city" among people, doing business, while trying to maintain a connection with God would have been much harder. So they preferred to become shepherds. Yosef, however, was not disturbed by being among people. He was able to maintain his connection with God even while in Potiphar's house, even while in the prison, and even while running Pharaoh's affairs. He was on such a high level of cleaving to God that he was not knocked off course even while being intimately involved in the finances and court intrigues of his day. And that is the reason that the exile in Egypt began with Yosef — he was the one who could inspire the Jews of later generations to remain connected to God even when in the worst forms of exile.

But, even this analysis is not sufficient, for it only explains the "negative" aspect of Yosef's *avodat Hashem.* It only explains how Yosef — and, after him, other Jews as well — could resist negative influences even when they were "in the field" in exile, separated from their sources of spiritual inspiration. It does not explain the second facet of Yosef's divine service, the aspect that emerges from his name.[2]

When he was born, his mother Rachel named him Yosef — from the Hebrew word *le'hosif*, meaning "to add." As the Torah relates, she said, "May God add to me another son." (Genesis 30:24) This means that Yosef had the ability to "add" to the holiness of the world. He could find "another" (one who is not yet connected to holiness) in a foreign environment and transform him into a "son" (one who is connected).

Yosef himself moved the Egyptians population all over the land from one corner to another, buying their land for Pharaoh, and persuading them to keep the Seven Laws of Noach.[3] Similarly, a Jew must enter the public arena and do whatever he can to transform it, elevate it and bring it into the realm of holiness. This is what is meant by "add to me another son" — to bring more of the world into the realm of holiness and unity with the One Above.

These two facets of Yosef's divine service — his ability to maintain his spiritual level in the face of adversity, and his ability to transform the spiritual environment — were passed on to the Jews after him in two different ways. The first, the ability to cope with exile and maintain our spiritual level, was passed down to *all* Jews. This became an intrinsic Jewish trait enabling all of us to maintain our spiritual level in the face of foreign influences. But, the second facet, the ability to transform the environment, was part of Yosef's private makeup, and it was not passed on automatically to all Jews. Rather, this ability was passed only to those Jews who are the "emissaries of Yosef." Most Jews do not have the automatic ability to transform their environment, but if they try to do so as the emissaries and representatives of "Yosef" (and there is a "Yosef" in every generation), then they can succeed.[4]

Most Jews do not have the automatic ability to transform their environment, but if they try to do so as the emissaries and representatives of "Yosef" (and there is a "Yosef" in every generation), then they can succeed.

This explains why the episode in which Yosef speaks to his brothers is divided into separate *aliyot* (the second and third of the seven opportunities to read from the Torah scroll on Shabbat), even though it is all one speech. At the end of the second *aliyah*, Yosef tells them, "For sustenance God sent me before you … to provide for you in the land and to sustain you…" (Genesis 45:7). This refers to maintaining his brothers and protecting their families. But the beginning of the third *aliyah* he says, "And now, it was not yourselves who sent me here, but God, and He has established me as a patron to Pharaoh and the lord over his house, and governor over all of Egypt" (Genesis 45:8). Here, we see that Yosef actually rules over and transforms Egypt. Since this is a distinct facet of Yosef's divine service, it appears in a separate *aliyah*.

This may also be the reason that the speech of Yaakov, in response to seeing the *agalot* that were sent by Yosef, is divided into separate *aliyot* as well. It would have made sense for the entire response to have been contained in one *aliyah*, since all of it is Yaakov's response to the news about Yosef. But, since there are two facets here, they are distributed among two *aliyot*. The first facet emerges at the end of the third *aliyah*: "And he saw the *agalot* that Yosef sent," indicating that Yaakov grasped that Yosef was still alive and had maintained his spiritual level, and therefore "Yaakov's spirit was revived" (Genesis 45:27). But, this is not so much of a surprise to Yaakov since he himself had maintained his spiritual level in the house of Lavan.

But, the second facet, that Yosef actually ruled over Egypt and transformed his spiritual milieu, was something new to Yaakov. That Yosef could not only maintain but also add to his spiritual level, by transforming his environment, was new and surprising. Thus, the beginning of the fourth *aliyah* reads, "Great! My son Yosef still lives," (Genesis 45:28) and the Midrash comments that according to Yaakov, Yosef's spiritual accomplishments were greater than his own. This was because Yosef had the ability to not only maintain but add to the realm of holiness by transforming and uplifting the world. Since this was a second facet of Yosef's *avodat Hashem*, it appears in a separate *aliyah*, distinct from the previous *aliyah*.

There was a "Yosef" in our generation as well. He was the Previous Rebbe of Lubavitch, Rabbi Yosef Yitzchak Schneerson, father-in-law of the Rebbe (Rabbi Menachem Mendel Schneerson). His life work provided the example that even in the most extreme situations (such as spreading Torah in Soviet Russia in the 1920's), it is possible and necessary to influence and transform our environment. The Previous Rebbe "opened the channels," so to speak, of such influence, and now a Jew who so wishes, may proceed with the blessing of the "Yosef" of our generation, as his emissary, and successfully spread Torah in the world. Such emissaries are already at work all around the world, and with their help the Mashiach will soon arrive, God willing, and speedily!

From Likutei Sichot of the Lubavitcher Rebbe,
vol. 30, pp. 222–228

NOTES

1. From the Godly perspective, it was known that Yosef's departure from his father was the beginning of his descent to Egypt. Even though Yaakov was not consciously aware of this, nevertheless his *mazal* was aware. See Rashi on Genesis 37:14 — ("from the depths of Hebron" — "from the deep advice of the *tzaddik*, Avraham who is buried in Hebron").

Note that some commentators (Rabbeinu Baal Hatosfot, Riva, Bartenura on the Torah, Kli Yakar) write on the same verse ("And he sent him [Yosef] from the depths of Hebron…") that Yaakov accompanied his son as he left Hebron, which is why they were involved in the subject of *eglah arufa*, whose inner content is "we did not see him off … without accompaniment…"

2. The two facets of Yosef's *avodat Hashem* are also reflected in the names of his two sons, Menashe and Efraim. "Menashe" expresses the opposite of "forgetting my father's house [in Israel]" while Efraim expresses, "God made me fruitful in

the land of affliction [Egypt]" (Genesis 41:52). Thus Efraim reflected the *avoda* of *ithafcha* — "transforming darkness into light." See *Likutei Sichot*, vol. 15, p. 433.

3. Yosef's activities vis-à-vis the Egyptians paralleled the instructions of the Rambam (*Hilchot Melachim* end of Ch.8), "Moshe our teacher commanded [all the Jews] to persuade all the peoples of the world…" and this command to persuade the non-Jews to keep the Seven Laws of Noach occurred at the giving of the Torah. Perhaps it is included in the category of *dinim* ("laws" of civil society), as well as the category of *lashevet yatzrah* ("to settle the earth") in which all non-Jews are obligated as well. (See Tosefot *lo latohu* in *Gittin* 41b, second solution regarding servants. See also *Likutei Sichot* vol. 5, p. 159, footnote 63).

Yosef also persuaded the Egyptians to circumcise themselves, and it is possible that he was obligated to do so because they were like a "financial acquisition." See *Likutei Sichot*, vol. 10 p. 139 and footnotes there.

4. Expressed differently: The first matter — the ability of the Jew to cope with *galut* while maintaining our spiritual level — can be described as "revealing that which was hidden." This is the aspect of Yosef that reveals the strength of the soul within us, which is otherwise hidden. The second matter — the ability to transform our environment — is "new." It is a novel element that Yosef introduced into the Jewish psyche that is not present otherwise within us.

Yosef Swears to Bury His Father in Israel

Vayechi 47:29

At the beginning of our Torah portion — *Parshat Vayechi* — as our forefather Yaakov realizes that his time in the world is drawing to a close, he requests the presence of his son, Yosef, who was then the viceroy of Egypt. And he asks Yosef to commit to burying him in the Land of Israel after he passes away: "Please do not bury me in Egypt. Let me lie with my fathers [Avraham and Yitzchak]. Lift me out of Egypt and bury me in their grave." Yosef agrees, "I will do as you say." But the conversation does not end there. Yaakov insists that Yosef take an oath: "Swear to me …" (Genesis 47:29–31).

An obvious question arises: Why was Yaakov not satisfied with Yosef's promise to fulfill his request. Why did Yaakov demand that Yosef actually swear that he would carry it out his wish?

There are those (Ramban, Sforno, Kli Yakar, Ohr Hachaim and others) who answer that the oath was not so much meant for Yosef, but was intended to put pressure on Pharaoh. In order that Pharaoh shouldn't be able to demand that Yosef leave Yaakov's body in Egypt, Yaakov had Yosef take an oath. That way Yosef would have an excuse — he would be able to tell Pharaoh that his father made him take an oath to bury him in Israel.

However, we find that Rashi says nothing about this here, which implies that this is not a question according to the straightforward meaning of the text (*pshat*) that Rashi seeks to explain. And yet, Rashi does mention this explanation later regarding another verse (Genesis 50:6). Over there, after Yaakov has passed away, Pharaoh tells Yosef, "Go up, and bury your father, as he made you swear." Rashi comments that if it weren't for the oath, Pharaoh would not have allowed Yaakov's body to leave Egypt. The very fact that Rashi does not make this comment at the original verse but a later one indicates that this is not the real reason that Yaakov forced Yosef to take an oath. In this respect, Rashi differs from other commentators, who hold that the oath was intended to apply pressure on Pharaoh. According to Rashi, the reason for the oath was not to pressure Pharaoh into allowing Yaakov's body out of Egypt, but in order to strengthen Yosef's resolve (as will be explained). And if so, our question is back in place: What was lacking in Yosef's original response that caused Yaakov to demand an oath as well?

When a person takes an oath to do something, the oath binds him in ways that go beyond a simple commitment; even if difficulties and obstacles arise, the person who took an oath will not rest until he has accomplished what he swore to do. And similarly, there is a difference in the ways that a person prepares for the task that he agreed to undertake. When he simply agrees to do something sometime in the future, he generally won't worry about it until the time comes. And then, he might start to consider how exactly to fulfill whatever it is they agreed upon. However, if he takes an oath, it stays ever-present in his mind; he is always thinking about his commitment, lest he fail to keep his oath.

And that is the simple reason why Yaakov made Yosef swear. Since they were in Egypt, in a land that was not their own, it was possible that, with the vicissitudes of time and fortune, Yosef might have other priorities demanding his attention and fail to attend to his father's burial in a timely fashion. A major disruption in schedule, such as Yosef leaving Egypt for several days, demanded preparation. It was important that Yosef pave the way with Pharaoh so that there would not be obstacles when the time came. Therefore, Yaakov deemed it necessary that Yosef not only make a verbal agreement, but actually take an oath. Only in that way could Yaakov guarantee that, under all circumstances, Yosef would make sure that Yaakov was buried in Israel and not in Egypt.

However, this explanation is not completely satisfying. For, even if Yosef was required to take an oath, his conversation with his father did not have to undergo two stages — first a verbal commitment followed by an oath. It was not necessary for Yaakov to first extract a verbal commitment, and then insist upon an oath. Yaakov certainly foresaw the difficulties that could arise if Yosef left his post, even temporarily, to bury him in Israel. He could have told him immediately, "Take an oath that you will not bury me in Egypt ... that you will take me to Israel." Why is it that he first requested a commitment, and only afterward demanded an oath?

The real answer is that the oath was meant for Yosef himself, and not for anybody else. For, removing Yaakov's body from Egypt was not in the interests of the Jews. Since God told Yaakov that He Himself would descend to Egypt together with him, it was counter-intuitive for Yosef to remove his father's body from Egypt, while Yosef and the rest of the Jews were still there. It was for this reason that Yaakov required Yosef to take an oath. This becomes more clear when we compare what happened to the bodies of Yaakov and Yosef upon their respective passings.

Yaakov, as mentioned above, told Yosef, "Please do not bury me in Egypt. Let me lie with my fathers [Avraham and Yitzchak]. Lift me out of Egypt and bury me in their grave." This instruction left no room for doubt; Yaakov's body was not to be interred in Egypt even temporarily. He had to be immediately buried in Israel. Regarding himself, however, Yosef made the Children of Israel swear that when they were finally redeemed from Egypt, they would take his body with them: "God will remember and redeem you, and then you shall lift my bones from here..." (Genesis 50:25–26). And this is what happened. Josef was embalmed and his body remained interred in Egypt for the remainder of the time that the Jews were there, some two hundred years more. Only at the time of the Exodus did it become feasible to remove Yosef's body in order to take it on what proved to be a long trek to Israel.

The explanation behind this distinction — according to Kabbalah, the "inner dimensions" of the Torah — is the following: Yaakov was a soul from the World of Atzilut ("Emanation"). The World of Atzilut is removed from the our physical world, which is called the World of Asyiah ("Action"). Therefore Yaakov — even when he descended to live in Egypt for the final seventeen years of his life — was above and beyond the life of Egypt.[1] Yosef, even though also a soul of Atzilut, was on such a level that he could live very much among the Egyptians. Unlike his father, Yosef's task was to bring down the spirituality of Atzilut so that it could imbue the lower realms with higher Godliness. And in order to do that, he had to live among the Egyptians.

Consequently, after his passing, Yaakov could not remain even for a moment in Egypt, and his body was brought immediately for burial in Israel. However, Yosef's body remained in Egypt, so that in his merit, the Jews who were there could enjoy his protection and inspiration until they themselves left Egypt with Moshe during the Exodus. That is why Yosef instructed his brothers take an oath to take him out with them. The Jews had descended to Egypt for one reason alone — for the ascent that they would achieve afterward. They descended to Egypt in order to raise all of the sparks of holiness that were trapped there, and when they left carrying Yosef's body, the remaining sparks of holiness exited with them, leaving Egypt "like a pond without any fish" (Ex 12:36, tractate Berachot 9B).

This is the reason that Yaakov insisted that Yosef take an oath. He knew that Yosef's own *avodat Hashem* required him to stay in Egypt, and he knew that from Yosef's perspective, it would be preferable to have his father with him in Egypt as well, so that "his merit would protect his son" (Zohar on *Parshat Vayechi*, 222a). That is, it would have made perfect sense for Yaakov to stay in Egypt and, with his presence, aid Yosef in his own tasks in Egypt. And that is why Yaakov insisted that Yosef take an oath, forego what was seemingly best for him, and follow his father's instructions to the letter.

However, it remains to be explained why Yaakov considered it out of the question for his body to remain in Egypt after he passed away. If, indeed, his presence would aid Yosef in raising the holy sparks out of Egypt, why should his body not remain with Yosef there?

Perhaps the answer lies in the adage, "a prisoner cannot free himself from jail" (*Berachot* 5b). In order to free and elevate the concealed holy sparks, a higher power is necessary that transcends the sparks themselves. It was Yaakov, projecting his spiritual status and illumination from Israel, who provided that power. From Israel, Yaakov could project the holiness that was necessary to attract the sparks to their real home in the Holy Land and aid Yosef and the Jews to leave Egypt. In fact, by forcing Yosef to take an oath, Yaakov created the bond that lifted the Jews and the sparks out of Egypt. The oath bound Yosef to Yaakov in a way that allowed Yaakov to project his holiness throughout Egypt. Precisely because he was in Israel, Yaakov's illumination shone to aid the Yosef and all the Jews in their divine service, reminding them of the holiness of their own land, the Land of Israel. Yaakov's holy presence was projected through his son Yosef, enabling him to lift the sparks that were trapped in Egypt. And the oath that Yosef took, at the insistence of his father, is what produced that bond.

All of the above is a special instruction for how we should live in the final days of exile (*galut*). As good as things might be — and they can be good in exile even spiritually[2] — nevertheless, we must know and remember that the goal is to ascend to our Land. Exile is not the appropriate place for a Jew; rather, our goal is to "lift" ourselves out of there.

All of the above is a special instruction for how we should live in the final days of exile (galut). As good as things might be — and they can be good in exile even spiritually — nevertheless, we must know and remember that the goal is to ascend to our Land.

Furthermore, the commitment to leave *galut* must express itself as an "oath." In addition to being one of Rambam's Thirteen Principles of Faith ("to wait and hope for the Mashiach even though he may tarry…"), the hope for the Final Redemption must be seared into our soul, so that in essence we are hoping and working for one thing — to be "lifted" out.

If we do so, *galut* will have no negative effects on our spiritual descent, but rather the opposite. The commitment to "lift" ourselves out of *galut* transforms the very reality of the *galut* into an "uplifting" experience. From exile emerges elevation, to such an extent that all Jews then "raise even their heads" (Ex 30:11 — parshat *Ki Tissa*) and raise themselves to the higher possible level.

From Likutei Sichot of the Lubavitcher Rebbe,
vol. 25, pp. 270–274

NOTES

1. In Egypt, the Jews lived in their own separate area called Goshen, leading a life of mitzvoth (at least during Yaakov's lifetime). They did not mix in or assimilate with the Egyptians, and Yaakov, more than anyone else, symbolized the distance that the Jews maintained from Egyptian society. They created their own enclave and lived disconnected from the rest of Egypt.

2. This is described by the Alter Rebbe who states that "since Yaakov established a place of learning in Egypt, he 'lived' fully in Egypt, both spiritually and physically." (from *Hayom Yom* 18 Tevet).

The Influence of Ephraim and Menashe

Vayechi 48:17

Previously, we discussed the contributions of the forefathers (Avraham, Yitzchak and Yaakov) to the Jewish people and compared them with the contribution of Yaakov's son, Yosef. The forefathers (and mothers) gave us our "Jewish genes" — our inner qualities of kindness, modesty and mercy. Yosef, however, gave us something more outwardly directed — the ability to light up our environment and elevate it.

That ability lies in the hands of Yosef's successors. It is called *shlichut* — or sense of "mission" — and we can also tap into it by being connected to the people or person who possesses that characteristic. If we cleave to a *tzaddik* ("righteous person") — the Yosef of our generation — then we, too, can gain the ability to uplift and elevate our surroundings.

If that is the case, what specifically did we, the Jewish people, receive from the sons of Yosef — Ephraim and Menasheh?

Both Ephraim and Menasheh were born in Egypt, nearly a decade prior to the arrival of Yaakov, their grandfather. Yaakov spent seventeen peaceful years in Egypt, and then, feeling that his time to depart this world was near, he sought to bless the boys. Yosef brought them before his father, placing Menasheh on Yaakov's right, in order so that he could receive the traditional blessing of the *bechor* ("first born," who receives a double portion in any inheritance). His younger son Ephraim Yosef placed on Yaakov's left in order that he receive the expected blessing of the second child. Yaakov, however, reversed the blessings. He placed his right hand upon the younger child and his left hand upon the older child, implying that Ephraim, and not Menasheh would receive the more important blessing. Even though Yosef pointed out to his father that he was inverting the birth order, Yaakov persisted, saying that Menasheh's offspring would indeed do well, but that his younger brother's descendants would fare even better.

Regarding blessings and spiritual influx brought down from above, it is inconceivable that a *tzaddik* could make a "mistake." To Avraham was given the ability to bless whomever he chose (as well as to curse whomever he chose), and that ability was passed on to his son Yitzchak and his grandson Yaakov. Since the paths of spiritual well-being and progress are evident and obvious to the *tzaddik*, it is literally impossible for him to make the wrong choices and direct the influx from above to the wrong places below.

Regarding blessings and spiritual influx brought down from above, it is inconceivable that a tzaddik could make a "mistake."

Therefore, we have to say that both Yaakov and Yosef were correct, each from his own point of view. From Yosef's point of view, Menasheh was his firstborn and therefore deserved Yaakov's primary blessing, while from Yaakov's point of view it was Ephraim who took precedence, and to him he sought to convey this blessing.

Why did Yaakov consider Ephraim to be the more important son while Yosef considered Menasheh to be the dominant one? The answer becomes apparent by looking at their names. Menasheh was so named because, "God caused me to forget (*nashani*) all my hardships and all that was in my father's house" (Genesis 41:51). Thus, Menasheh (the older of the two) reminded Yosef that God brought him to a place that could cause him to forget his past (even if Yosef was determined not to forget it). And Ephraim was so named because, "God has made me fruitful (*hefrani*) in the land of my travails" (Genesis 41:52). Ephraim did not remind Yosef of his past, but rather of his rich and constructive life in the present, in the land of Egypt. Overall, then, Yosef saw Menasheh as the son deserving of the blessings since he represented the transmission of the past into the future. And Yaakov preferred to give his most important blessings to Ephraim because he saw in Ephraim the true extension of his mission in a faraway land.

When Yaakov looked at his two grandsons, he did not place as much emphasis on Menasheh's biological and emotional connection with his father (and hence with the past), but on the current style of divine service of each grandson. He saw that Ephraim's emphasis on his current spiritual status in Egypt (even though he was clearly aware of his past) was a more fruitful and productive *avodat Hashem*, so Yaakov sought to bless Ephraim. Even though Menasheh was the biological first-born, his connection with his father's past meant that he emphasized the spiritual path of *sur marah* ("turn away from bad"), which is not as high as the path of *aseh tov* ("focus on good") that characterized Ephraim.

Going back two generations, we see that Yaakov was a paragon of virtue while in the house of his uncle Lavan. Despite all of Lavan's attempts to fool and rob him, Yaakov maintained his faith in God and kept all the principles of the Torah. He emerged from the house of Lavan with all of his spiritual achievements intact. However, he did not succeed in transforming the house of Lavan; he managed only to protect his own spiritual level. Lavan remained an idol-worshipper even after Yaakov left his house. But, Yaakov's son, Yosef, not only maintained his holiness while in the house of Potiphar and in prison, but even elevated the spiritual level of the entire Egyptian Empire. He made sure that the Egyptians were circumcised and he (together with Yaakov) converted many of them to monotheism. It was Yosef's connection with his father Yaakov that enabled him to raise the spiritual level of his environment.

Of the two sons of Yosef, it was Ephraim who carried on the path of transforming his environment (as implied in Ephraim's name — "fruitful in the land..."). Even without the direct intervention of his grandfather Yaakov (since he was born before Yaakov arrived), Ephraim acted to elevate and transform the spiritual level of Egypt. The older son, Menasheh, managed to protect and maintain his own piety, as Yaakov himself did when in the house of Lavan. But, when Yaakov arrived in Egypt, he saw in Yosef and in his grandson Ephraim the natural extension of his own spiritual attainments. While Yaakov did not manage to change the spiritual level of Lavan, Yosef did manage to influence the spiritual level of Egypt, and it was his son Ephraim who continued on this spiritual path. That why it was natural for Yaakov to feel that Ephraim — and not Menasheh — deserved the greater blessing. Menasheh's task as the first-born was to guard and maintain what Yaakov had already achieved, but it was Ephraim who carried the work forward together with his father Yosef in Egypt.

Analyzing this idea more deeply, we see there are three ways in which a Jew today may interact with his environment while in exile (*galut*):

1. He may respond by simply shutting out the environment and focusing on his own spiritual wellbeing. In this way, he fends off whatever influences knock him off balance and maintains his own spiritual equilibrium but fails to have any effect on his surroundings.
2. Sometimes the difficulties of living in *galut* bring out even deeper qualities in a person. With the help of these deeper soul-qualities, he not only maintains his level, but grows and thrives spiritually in ways that he would not have if he were not faced by these challenges. In such a case, the challenges of exile also bring out of him latent and unlimited powers that allow him to influence and uplift his environment.
3. Sometimes a person's spiritual level is so well established within that he elicits spirituality in his environment as well. That is, one who is secure in his own spiritual level need not get overly involved in actively influencing his environment, for simply by acting as a Jew, he is able to bring out the holiness in his environment and to uplift it, turning darkness into light.

Basing ourselves on the above, we could ask: Wouldn't it have been more logical for Yosef to see Ephraim as the deserving son, and for Yaakov to see Menasheh as the son to bless? If Ephraim was the son who would carry on the path of elevating the environment, as did Yosef, why didn't Yosef see him as the son more deserving of the blessing? And if Menasheh was the son who placed emphasis on the past, why didn't Yaakov see him as the grandson who could best carry on the tradition and therefore to whom the blessings should go?

To answer this, we must delve deeper into the respective spiritual paths of these three giants; Yaakov, Yosef and Ephraim.[1]

As stated above, Yaakov was a *tzaddik* whose path consisted of maintaining his own very high spiritual level in the face of adversity. And his son Yosef not only maintained his high spiritual level in the face of adversity, but even turned the tables and managed to raise the level of his environment. However, he was able to do so only because he was attached to his father. When Yosef was faced with temptation in the house of Potiphar, he resisted it by calling to mind his father's face. By so doing, he managed to escape the trap that awaited him. But his son Ephraim symbolized a new level of this *avodah.*

Ephraim initially had no connection with Yaakov, since he was born before Yaakov came to Egypt. We can assume that Ephraim heard about his grandfather from Yosef, but he never met him personally. Therefore, Ephraim knew little about his grandfather or about the Land of Israel. He only knew about life in Egypt, in exile, far away from the sources of Jewish inspiration. And yet, even under these circumstances, he managed to blossom, exerting an elevating influence on the Egyptians. That is, he absorbed his father's spirituality and teachings while in a foreign land, detached from the spiritual sources that nourished his father, and yet he managed to not only develop his own connection with God but to have an influence on others as well.

In summary, then, we see that there are three levels of Jewish experience:

1. The Jew who maintains his own spiritual level, without affecting others.
2. The Jew who not only maintains his own spiritual level, but succeeds in affecting others as well, raising their spiritual level. But, he only succeeds in doing so because of his attachment to his own mentor. Because others sense within him the spirituality of his mentor, they themselves become elevated.
3. The Jew who successfully affects his own environment, even without any apparent inspiration and connection from anyone else. Such a Jew may be exceptionally inspirational because people sense that his inspiration is his own, and that helps elicit inspiration from within themselves as well.

Our forefather Yaakov represented the first level. He received his inspiration and knowledge by clinging to the One Above, but his spiritual level was so high that it was not feasible to bring it down to bear upon the physical world below. Yaakov's son, Yosef, represented the second level. He was capable of influencing his environment, but only because of his intense connection to his father. And Yosef's son, Ephraim, represented the third level.

After Yosef had paved the way, elevating Egypt via his father's connection to God, Ephraim continued on his path, even without any obvious inspiration from his grandfather, Yaakov. Unlike his father Yosef, Ephraim did not rely on the illuminating influence of Yaakov to guide him. Since he did not meet Yaakov until his grandfather descended to Egypt, Ephraim lacked the inspiration from the past that could have connected him with his current environment. Nevertheless, the hidden core of Yaakov's message affected Ephraim indirectly, and he managed to achieve something much higher.

Ephraim so internalized and actualized the message of Yaakov and Yosef from within himself, that he did not need revealed inspiration from without. His environment and the people around him responded to his illumination precisely because it came from within him. Ephraim was able to rely on his own efforts with which he transformed darkness into light even in places where Yaakov's light did not shine.

By the time of Ephraim's generation, the concept of one God had begun to permeate Egypt, so that the mere presence of the Jews there began to uplift the entire spiritual environment. There were Egyptians who, of their own volition, sought out a connection with the One God. But they needed someone like Ephraim to show them the way. And that was why, in Yaakov's eyes, it was Ephraim who deserved his blessing. Menasheh may have been Yosef's biological first-born, but it was Ephraim who extended Yaakov's and Yosef's spiritual path to its natural conclusion — wherein the environment becomes uplifted of its own volition. And that is why Yaakov saw fit to bless Ephraim more than Menasheh.

We are *tzon Yosef* — the "sheep of Yosef" — and therefore, we inherit his approach and spiritual path of *avodat Hashem*. That means that we must not only maintain our own spiritual level but reach out to others and show them the way as well. When they respond to the light of Torah spirituality, we know that we are doing our job. And when a critical mass of such people accepts the obligations of Torah, it will transform the darkness of exile into light — it will bring about the arrival of the Mashiach and the building of the third and permanent Temple as well.

From Likutei Sichot of the Lubavitcher, vol. 15, pp. 432–438

NOTES

1. The Jewish people have been called by many names, including Hebrews, Jews (after Yehudah), Yaakov/Israel, Yosef and Ephraim (but not Menasheh).

Yaakov Seeks to Reveal Date of Mashiach

Vayechi 49:1

When a man has lived a full and satisfactory life and feels that his time is drawing near, he focuses his thoughts on what will be after he is gone. He considers who will continue in his footsteps and how well he has prepared his children and his grandchildren to follow the path he set out for them. Indeed, these were Yaakov's concerns as he lay on his deathbed, according to this week's Torah portion — *Parshat Vayechi* — which recounts Yaakov's last words to his sons and grandsons.

In fact, Rashi (on Genesis 49:2) explains that Yaakov thought so far into the future that he was actually aware of and sought to reveal to his sons the date of arrival of the Mashiach. It's literally impossible to think further ahead than that since, with the arrival of the Mashiach, the whole nature of time will change. But, Yaakov found that once he sought to communicate this secret, it disappeared from his awareness. The question is, how did Rashi know this, and what does it have to do with us now?

First of all, *Parshat Vayechi* tells us that Yaakov requested all of his sons to come to him: "And Yaakov called all of his sons and said, 'Gather around and I will speak to you about what is destined to happen to you in the end of days." (Genesis 49:1) They did so, and then Yaakov repeated, "Gather around and listen..."

But we don't find that anything happened between the first time he said "gather around" and the second time. Yet, something must have happened, or the repetition would not have been necessary.

After the second call to his sons to gather around, Yaakov went on to bless each one, and he mentioned Shiloh in his blessing to his son Yehudah (Genesis 49:10). Rashi (basing himself on *Midrash Rabba* 99:8) tells us that Shiloh is a reference to the Mashiach, who will come from the line of Yehudah.

From this, we may deduce that whatever Yaakov originally intended to reveal had something to do with events surrounding the arrival of the Mashiach. If his second, "lesser" revelation to his sons included a veiled reference to the Mashiach, then his first intended, "greater" revelation must have had to do with the Mashiach also, but on an even higher level. However, how do the sages know that what Yaakov wanted to reveal was when the Mashiach would arrive?[1]

To answer that question, we must carefully analyze the terms that the Torah uses regarding verbal communication. There are three: to "talk" (*le'daber*), to "say" (*l'omar*), and to "speak" (*le'hagid*).[2] The Zohar and later Chassidic literature explain that these terms apply to three different levels of expression. "Talk" (*le'daber*) comes from the mouth. It doesn't have to be either sincere or deep. But when we "say" something (*l'omar*), it's from the heart. Usually, such utterances from the heart express something that we feel, but not necessarily everything that we feel or the true depth of our feelings. However, when we "speak" (*le'hagid*) the words come from the depths of our heart. In the hierarchy of the Zohar, speech is the highest and most essential verbal expression. We don't "speak" words that are superficial or insincere. On this level of verbal communication, we communicate only what we sincerely mean and deeply feel. (This is one reason that the secrets of the Torah are embedded in the *aggadah*, or the "stories" of the Talmud).

When we look at Yaakov's first call to his sons, we see that he said, "Gather around and I will speak (*ve'agida*) to you…" This is a clue that he intended to transmit the deepest secrets of his heart but could not for some reason. From this, our sages deduced that, with his first call to gather his sons, Yaakov intended to reveal the deepest secret of all — the date of the coming of Mashiach — but found himself unable to do so.

Rashi explains that this was because the *Shechinah*, God's indwelling presence, abandoned him. Why doesn't Rashi explain this more simply, by saying that the secret was hidden from Yaakov? And if it had to do with a lack of spiritual revelation from Above, why do we see that immediately after this, Yaakov blessed his sons with prophetic blessings that did require revelation from Above? If the problem was that the *ruach hakodesh* ("divine inspiration") departed from Yaakov at that point, then how was he able to bless his sons with such prophetic utterances?

The answer is that Yaakov himself was not the obstacle — to him, the date of the arrival of the Mashiach was a known fact. The problem lay with his grandsons, the sons of Yosef, Ephraim and Menashe (Rashi on 48:8). In their presence, it was not proper to reveal this information. Yaakov wanted to share the secret, but the *Shechinah* did not find his audience appropriate, so the *Shechinah* abandoned Yaakov when he wanted to reveal it. He knew it but he was unable to pass it on.

That being the case, one could ask, why does the Torah tell the story at all? If one of our forefathers — Yaakov — knew when the Mashiach would arrive but couldn't tell us, why should the Torah (according to Rashi) make a point of letting us know this fact?

Here also, the Zohar and Chassidic literature provide an explanation. The Zohar tells us that all of Moshe's spiritual attainments were previously attained by Yaakov (albeit in a less tangible, more transcendent fashion). Before Moshe passed away, he wished to impart the power of spiritual "sight" — the ability to directly comprehend Godliness — to the Jewish people. Since Moshe himself was on the spiritual level of "seeing," his entry into the physical Land of Israel would have empowered the Jewish people to achieve the same level. However, God did not permit Moshe to enter Israel, but only to look upon it from afar. By so doing, Moshe imparted to the Jewish people the ability to "see in the mind's eye" — that is, to meditate and understand a Godly concept so deeply that it is as if one sees.[3] Nevertheless, because this kind of "seeing" is intellectual ("in the mind's eye," but not seen with the naked eye), it remains in the category of "hearing," and that is why Moshe proceeded to gather the Children of Israel before his passing and tell them "And now listen, Israel, to all the laws..." (Deuteronomy 4:1)

Something similar happened to Yaakov before he passed away. He wanted to impart knowledge to his sons, the progenitors of the Twelve Tribes of Israel, but was prevented by reasons that were beyond his control. Realizing this, he said to them for a second time, "Gather together..." He wanted to enable them to see the end of days and the coming of the Mashiach, but instead could only impart to them (and through them to us) the ability to know of such things from afar. That's why he said "Gather together and *hear* ..."

Nevertheless, even this vague knowledge is enough to influence our relationship and connection to the One Above. With the knowledge that the Mashiach is on the way, it is possible to learn Torah and fulfill its mitzvoth in such a way that nothing has any influence over us. The knowledge that the Jewish soul transcends nature was transmitted to all of us by our forefathers, especially by Yaakov.

From Likutei Sichot of the Lubavitcher Rebbe, vol. 10, p. 167

NOTES

1. We cannot say that the sages deduced this from the introduction to his blessings (Genesis 49:1) when Yaakov said, "I will speak to you about what will happen to you at the end of days," because the phrase "end of days" (*acharit hayamim*) is used elsewhere in the Torah to refer to events that will occur before the arrival of the Mashiach. For example, Bilam used the phrase when describing to Balak what King David will do to the Moabites (Numbers 24:14; see Rashi there).

2. There is also to "recount" — *le'saper* — but that seems to be similar to *l'omar.*

3. See *Likutei Torah* of the Alter Rebbe, *Parshat Ve'etchanan* near the beginning. See also *Sha'arei Teshuva* of the Mitteler Rebbe, sec. 2, *Lehavin hefresh bein Torah leTefila*. Also see *Ohr HaTorah* of the Tzemach Tzedek, *Parshat Ve'etchanan.*

The Tribes and the Animals in Yaakov's Blessings

Vayechi 49:9

As we read the final Torah portion of Genesis — *Parshat Vayechi* — we find ourselves leaving the period of the forefathers and entering the period of the Twelve Tribes of Israel.

In *Parshat Vayechi*, Yaakov, the last of the forefathers blesses his sons — the progenitors of the tribes — on his deathbed. And one of the most curious things about his blessings is that they compare some of the tribes to wild animals. Binyamin is compared to a wolf, Naftali to a gazelle, Yehudah to a lion, and so forth. There's room to wonder why the blessings equate some of the tribes with wild animals, since the job of a Jew is to overcome his animal nature.

There's room to wonder why the blessings equate some of the tribes with wild animals, since the job of a Jew is to overcome his animal nature.

Obviously, the given tribe demonstrated one or more of the traits associated with the animal in Yaakov's blessing, but moreover, there must have been something of the entire animal kingdom associated with the tribes that found expression in Yaakov's blessings. Otherwise, there was no reason to compare them to animals, and Yaakov could have merely mentioned their positive/negative traits without mentioning the animals themselves.[1]

The Babylonian Talmud (end of *Kiddushin*) states,

> R' Shimon ben Elazar said, "I never saw a deer who worked as a guard (over a field of drying figs), or a lion as a porter, or a fox as a shopkeeper,

yet they all make a living without any trouble. And they were created to serve me, and I was created to serve my Maker, so shouldn't I also make a living easily? However, since my deeds were inappropriate, I lost my livelihood..."

Some commentators say that R' Shimon ben Elazar mentioned tasks that fit the qualities of the animals — since a deer is constantly alert, and even sleeps with one eye open, it could be a good guard; since a lion is strong it can carry heavy objects like a porter; and since the fox is clever it could be a smart shopkeeper. However, why are only these qualities mentioned, and not others? For example, a deer is very fast on its feet, and therefore it would do well as a messenger. Yet, R' Shimon ben Elazar does not mention that trait. Why not?

Every category of creation was created in order to serve and benefit humanity. As the Rambam says (in his introduction to *Pirush Hamishnayot*):

> "All creations exist for man alone. Among the animals are those that we eat, such as the sheep, cattle and others, and there are animals that are there for other uses, such as the donkey to carry whatever man cannot carry by hand, and horses to arrive to a far-off destination [and so likewise among trees and plants]." And so it is among human kind as well. In order for the perfected human being to be able to involve himself in Godly wisdom and good deeds, an entire world was created for him including people, who supply him with all of his needs in life in order to enable him to have the time and ability to learn and acquire wisdom.

Moreover, every category of creation is meant to become elevated and included in the level above it, until ultimately the entire physical world rises to spiritual status. For example, the vegetable world consumes and transforms the mineral world, the animal world consumes and transforms the vegetable, and ultimately the Jew, by fulfilling the mitzvoth of the Torah, elevates the entire physical world and transforms it into a fitting dwelling-place for God. This is why R' Shimon ben Elazar compared the Jews to animals since both the Jews and the animals transform the world. Jews, of course, operate on a higher level in the hierarchy, since they eat and (when the Temple is standing) offer animals as sacrifices in order to elevate all of the creation to a higher, spiritual level.

However, R' Shimon ben Elazar did more than draw a general connection between those lower and those higher in the hierarchy. He wished to emphasize that "the world was created to serve me" *because* "I was created to serve God." The whole hierarchy was created in order to enable man to serve God and, therefore, there is a causal relationship between the animals lower on the totem pole, and the Jew at the top. In fact, from R' Shimon ben Elazar we understand that when we fail to utilize the lower categories of creation for divine purposes, the lower categories also fail to serve our other purposes. However, before the Jew can transform the world and make a physical object into an object of holiness (*kedushah*) by fulfilling a mitzvah with it, three things are required — a "guard," a "porter" and a "shopkeeper." These are the three tasks that prime creation for spiritual elevation.

In order for an object to be made ready for use in the fulfillment of a mitzvah, it must undergo three stages: 1) a change in its status, 2) a change in its location, and 3) a change of its ownership. These are the three stages alluded to by the "guard" (deer), the "porter" (lion) and the "shopkeeper" (fox). The guard, ever alert, must be able to bring the object into the open and guard it until it reaches a state of perfection. That's why the role of "guard" is played by a deer. R' Shimon ben Elazar compares the deer to a *kaitz* — one who guards figs in the field until they are dry and ready for eating. But after the figs are dry, it is necessary to move them to another location. This is the job of the "porter" (lion), who is able to carry heavy burdens and move them from one place to another. Ultimately, the figs must be "sold" — brought under the jurisdiction of the one who can elevate them to their ultimate level. This is the task of the "shopkeeper," or fox, who is clever enough to know to whom to sell the produce.

On the spiritual plane, this means the following:

Often, we are in the dark about a mitzvah; we don't know how to fulfill it because we don't know enough about its status. For example, certain activities may be permissible on Shabbat under the category of *pikuach nefesh*, or life-threatening situations. However, until we consult with a doctor or other health care professional, we don't know if a situation is indeed life-threatening.[2] Or, we may not know if a certain food is kosher because we don't know where it came from. The one who can clarify the status for us fulfills the role of the "guard," who can watch over the object until we clarify its status. Moreover, the "guard" must be able to watch the object as it becomes prepared for its ultimate task — a mitzvah. "Illumination" is required to clarify the status of the object (as the sun illuminates the field), and therefore a "guard" (deer) is necessary.

For example, when an *etrog* ("citron") grows on a tree, or an animal skin is tanned in preparation for the making of *tefillin*, it is necessary for the guard to watch it.

Thereafter, the object must be brought to a place where it can be used to fulfill the mitzvah. If the object is in a place of idol worship (for example, India), or it is in a place where there is a bad smell (from open sewage or the like), it is impossible to use it to fulfill a mitzvah there. It must be brought into another area that is appropriate. This is the job of the "porter" (lion) who can carry a heavy load from one place to another.

Even after the object has been brought into an appropriate location, it must come into the possession of a Jew. For example, most *etrog* orchards outside of Israel (in such places as Italy) are in the possession of non-Jews. But there are usually Jews found there, watching over the orchards and ensuring that the *etrogim* are grown on the right kind of plant under the correct circumstances but, ultimately, these *etrogim* must be bought by a Jew in order that he use them to fulfill the mitzvah. The same is true of most mitzvoth — in order to elevate the physical world by performing a mitzvah with it, the Jew must have the object in his personal possession. This is the task of the "shopkeeper" (fox) who transfers the object into the proper hands, i.e. into the possession of a Jew.

Now we can understand why Yaakov blessed his sons, the Twelve Tribes of Israel, by comparing them to wild animals. Just as the ideal task of the animals (deer, lion, fox, etc.) is to prepare objects in the physical world for use as mitzvoth, so it was the task of the tribes to prepare the world for accepting the Torah and its mitzvoth. The forefathers (Avraham, Yitzchak and Yaakov) brought Godliness into the world, making the inhabitants of Canaan aware of the one God, king of heaven and earth. But now it was almost time to prepare for the giving of the Torah, an event which would allow the Jews to elevate the physical world deed by deed and make it a fitting dwelling-place for God.

One of the reasons for the sojourn and slavery of the Jews in Egypt was that they were not yet ready to use the physical world to draw down Godliness so that it permeated creation. What transformed them into the Nation of Israel and made them ready to accept the Torah with its physical mitzvoth was their experience in the "iron furnace" of Egypt. That experience seared into their souls the connection between God above and the Jews below.

The Egyptian exile began when Yaakov and his sons descended from the land of Canaan to dwell in Goshen and receive sustenance from Yosef. However, this transformational experience reached its zenith only after both Yaakov and Yosef died. That is why Yaakov blessed his sons by comparing some of them to animals. This was Yaakov's way of describing the tasks/abilities of each tribe to change the status of the world and uplift it spiritually. Prior to the giving of the Torah, the world was a physical creation that opposed revelation of Godliness and spirituality. The spiritual world was "above," so to speak, and the physical world below, and they "did not meet." It was only with the giving of the Torah that spirituality began to permeate the physical world. The agent for this transformation was and is the Jews and their fulfillment of mitzvoth. But in order to be prepared for the job of using the physical world to serve God, the Jews had to undergo the slavery in Egypt.

Then began the privations of slavery that culminated in their redemption, cementing the quality of faith in the souls of the Jews. Just as animals manage to survive under difficult circumstances, the Jews coped and survived. In fact, they went beyond survival and managed to learn how to use the world for Godly purposes. And the blessings of Yaakov, comparing the tribes to animals in the field, gave the Jews strength to endure the "iron furnace" of Egypt and prepare the world for the next stage in Jewish history — accepting the Torah and fulfilling its mitzvoth in order to permeate the world with Godliness.

*From Likutei Sichot of the Lubavitcher Rebbe,
vol. 15, pp. 447–458*

NOTES

1. The idea developed in this translation, deep as it is, is only one of the themes of this *sicha* from the Rebbe. The other themes have to do with whether one should fulfill a mitzvah at first opportunity, or wait until it is possible to fulfill it in a manner that is more *mehudar*, as well as whether the present takes precedence over the future in relation to fulfillment of mitzvoth. These themes were deemed to be too complicated for the current presentation, but are part of the Rebbe's *sicha* on this topic.

2. It is important to act upon our doubts immediately, if they are regarding health issues, and consult with a doctor. This holds true even if, for example it is just before Shabbat.

Blessings for All the Tribes

Vayechi 49:28

Sefer Bereishit (Genesis) concludes with the blessings that our forefather, Yaakov, gave to his sons, the progenitors of the Twelve Tribes of Israel. It is from them that we learn about our divine service (*avodat Hashem*) via prayer, study and meditation.

For example, Yaakov's first-born son, Reuven, served God through spiritual sight, achieved by understanding spirituality so well that it was as if he could see Godliness in his mind's eye. This corresponds to his name, which could be translated as "the son who sees." His younger brother, Shimon served God by incisive analysis based on received information. This is reflected in his name, which means "the son who hears."[1] And so forth. Every son had his own style, which he passed on to the members of his tribe, and they passed it on down to us many generations later.

If so, we could ask, why are we required to serve the One Above in many different ways — such as by praying, by studying, and by doing good deeds? If each tribe was blessed with one particular quality and talent for serving God in the best way possible, why wasn't it enough for each tribe to focus on its own talents and blessings and pass that on to its descendants? It is true that all Jews must fulfill the 613 commandments of the Torah in thought, speech and in action. Yet, Yaakov's blessings to each individual son emphasized that son's — and subsequently, that tribe's — talent, so why should all Jews living now be required to adopt the styles of divine service of all the tribes?

The reason for that is embedded in the language of the blessings themselves. When Yaakov concluded speaking to his sons, the Torah states: "*All* these are the tribes of Israel, twelve of them, and this is how their father spoke to *them* and blessed *them*. Each according to his own blessing, so were *they* blessed." (Genesis 49:28). Note that the language of the verse is in the plural indicating that all the tribes were included in all of the blessings. Also, the Midrash and Rashi both say that not only did each tribe receive its own individual blessing, but it also received the blessings of the other tribes as well.

1. The *Midrash Rabba* (99:4) states, "Since Yehudah was blessed with the qualities of a lion, and Dan with the qualities of a snake, and Naftali with the qualities of a deer, and Binyamin with those of a wolf, the finale of [Yaakov's] blessing included all of them together, making all of them similar to lions and snakes, etc..."
2. The *Midrash Tahuma* (*Vayechi* ch. 16) states, "Lest you declare that one tribe is greater than another, [Yaakov] included all of them in the final blessing."
3. And finally, Rashi states, "Lest you think that they all received only their own blessing, the verse concludes by including all of them in all of the blessings of the tribes."

The message of the three statements above is the same — all the tribes received not only their own blessing but also those of the other tribes. However, the subtle variations in the language suggest that the two Midrashim and Rashi have different ways of looking at how the inclusive final blessing came down to the tribes, and from them to us.

Basically, the blessings could have come from each tribe to all the others, or each blessing could have come directly from Yaakov to all the tribes. That is, either the twelve tribes were one united group that exchanged blessings among themselves as a community, or each received all of the twelve blessings directly from their father Yaakov. If the former, then there are also two possibilities: 1) either each tribe received only the benefit of the blessing of the other tribes, or 2) each tribe received the full blessing itself.

For example, it is well known that there was a special relationship between the two tribes, Yissachar and Zevulun. Yissachar sat in the study hall and learned Torah, while Zevulun engaged in business and supported Yissachar. And yet, according to the above, each tribe also received the blessing of the other, meaning that Yissachar not only learned Torah but also received the blessing to engage in business. And Zevulun not only engaged in business, but also received the blessing of Torah study. That could be understood as follows:

1. Yissachar received the benefit of Zevulun's largesse, but did not get involved in making money. And conversely, Zevulun received the reward of Yissachar's studies, but did not study

Or:

2. Yissachar not only learned Torah (as the main activity), but also whenever possible participated in deeds of kindness, similar to the *tzedakah* of Zevulun. And Zevulun not only gave of their hard-earned money to support Yissachar in Torah study, but also took some time to learn Torah themselves.

However, there is a third way to understand these blessings:

3. It's possible that each tribe possessed not only a major trait and several minor traits with which they served God, but every tribe possessed all of the other traits completely. That is, each tribe received not only a "major" blessing directly from Yaakov, specific for that tribe, but also "minor" blessings from the other tribes (which those tribes developed in a major way).

For example, when Yissachar practiced acts of kindness, it wasn't a deviation from the tribe's regular schedule of Torah study. Yissachar performed the kindness with full power and concentration in accordance with God's will. And when Zevulun learned Torah, it wasn't only in order to fulfill the commandment incumbent upon every Jew to learn Torah in addition to fulfilling the other mitzvoth. Rather, Zevulun's learning, even if part-time, was done with full attention and focus, as if it were not only Yissachar's blessing, but Zevulun's as well.

These three, it turns out, correspond to the nuances and detailed language of the explanations by the Midrash and Rashi. The *Midrash Tanhuma*, which states "lest you conclude that one tribe was greater than the other, the blessing concludes with all of them together..." refers to the first approach. Since the *Tanhuma* makes no mention of specific sharing by the tribes with each other, we can assume that all of the tribes shared all of their benefits with each other, equally. Each tribe was involved in its own main function, while sharing in the results (but not the traits themselves). As the *Tanhuma* continues: "After they came to the Land of Israel, Yehudah was granted a parcel of land for growing barley while

Binyamin received a parcel of land for growing wheat; nevertheless they all shared [what they grew] and, therefore, each tribe was included in the blessing that was received from every other tribe.

The *Midrash Rabba* tells us that all of the tribes were like "lions, snakes, etc." That is, every tribe possessed the traits of the others. The twelve tribes shared not only the results and benefits of each other's major strengths, but the strong points themselves. In actual practice, each of them exercised its own particular strength, but inside, they all had the other qualities as well and would express them as necessary.

But, Rashi was not satisfied with the theory that the tribes received their blessings from one another, as secondary traits/results. He understood that the blessings for each tribe and for all of the tribes, came directly from the source — Yaakov our forefather. As Rashi saw it, Yaakov blessed each tribe not only with its own major characteristic, but also with all of the qualities of the other tribes as well. That's why Rashi writes, "the verse concludes by including all of them in all of the blessings." Rashi implies that, not only the unique blessing of every tribe, but all the blessings of all the tribes came to them directly from Yaakov. The greater directness of this blessing expressed itself in the following manner — not only did each tribe practice its own approach to God, but it was completely versant with all the other paths of the other tribes and would use those paths when appropriate. Each tribe had its own approach, but it also received and practiced (at times) the traditions of all the other tribes.

It makes a vast difference in our approach to God when we know that it is not only appropriate to choose one path, but to be versant in other paths as well.

All of the above may seem like subtle sophistry, but it's not. It makes a vast difference in our approach to God when we know that it is not only appropriate to choose one path, but to be versant in other paths as well. In order to travel as far as possible, we have to choose a path. Some people wish to live their whole lives jumping from one spiritual path to another; they wish to create a spiritual "smorgasbord," choosing whatever pleases them from one path, then jumping to another path and then tasting a third approach. This works for a short time, before each Jew finally has to choose a singular path. But once it has been chosen, that path becomes one's path for life.

However, that does not preclude learning from and even using elements of other approaches as well. In fact, every Jew should cultivate a level of ego-nullification (*bitul*) that allows him or her to learn from every other Jew. Every Jew comes from one of the twelve tribes and has received the blessings of all the twelve tribes from Yaakov, our common forefather.

In order to properly operate, God created various paths of behavior and worship for us. As Rashi implies, this means that, even after having chosen one path of spiritual pursuit within Judaism, we should not hesitate to become aware of and incorporate other paths as well.[2] When we all perfect our individual paths of divine service, together with the paths of the others, we achieve the greatest "unity of the tribes of Israel," and become one unit, described as the "tribes of Hashem" (*shivtei yud-hei*). That itself elicits a blessing from the One above, "Bless us our Father, all of us together," which is necessary in order to bring the Mashiach, speedily in our days!"

From Likutei Sichot of the Lubavitcher Rebbe, vol. 25, pp. 285–292

NOTES

1. One who "hears" Godliness does not experience it directly. Instead, he infers it from what he sees around himself and hears from others, and then analyzes the information to draw intellectual conclusions.

2. Obviously, this refers to the paths of the Twelve Tribes of Israel — as described in the *Tanach*, from which we learn that all of the tribes were God-fearing people and followed the principles of the Torah. When the tribes deviated from the Torah, disaster and exile followed.

OTHER BOOKS BY THE AUTHOR

Love Like Fire and Water — an essay on Jewish Meditation (translation and commentary of *Kuntres Ha'avoda* of the Rebbe Rashab) — published by Moznaim Press 2005

Inner Lights from Jerusalem — excerpts from the *Shem Mishmuel* — Moznaim Press 2007.

Meditation like Fire and Water — the Siddur with Chassidut (also known as Daven Chabad and Mind over Heart) — translated excerpts from Chabad Chassidus on prayer, including translations of virtually all that was written on the subject by the Rebbe Rashab) — 2012

Praying Like Fire and Water — a companion siddur to Love like Fire and Water, with a commentary designed to help the student apply the principles of Love like Fire and Water (*Kuntres Haavoda*) to prayer — 2017.

Jerusalem Connection

is a non-profit organization dedicated to Jewish outreach and education. It was created with the blessing of the Lubavitcher Rebbe in 1991 and has since flourished in the old city of Jerusalem. It is frequented by Jewish university students, tourists and new immigrants to Israel who seek spiritual guidance and connection with the One above and also instruction in the inner dimensions of Torah (Chassidic and Kaballistic literature).

For more information, visit us at www.jerusalemconnection.org or email jerconn1@ gmail.com

www.ingramcontent.com/pod-product-compliance
Lightning Source LLC
Chambersburg PA
CBHW050400110426
42812CB00006BA/1754
* 9 7 8 1 7 3 2 1 0 7 9 7 7 *